Hidden Patrons

Women and Architectural Patronage in Georgian Britain

Amy Boyington

BLOOMSBURY VISUAL ARTS
LONDON • NEW YORK • OXFORD • NEW DELHI • SYDNEY

BLOOMSBURY VISUAL ARTS
Bloomsbury Publishing Plc
50 Bedford Square, London, WC1B 3DP, UK
1385 Broadway, New York, NY 10018, USA
29 Earlsfort Terrace, Dublin 2, Ireland

BLOOMSBURY, BLOOMSBURY VISUAL ARTS and the Diana logo are
trademarks of Bloomsbury Publishing Plc

First published in Great Britain 2024
Reprinted 2024

Cover design by Eleanor Rose
Cover image: Portrait of Mrs Sarah Clayton c. 1769
by Joseph Wright of Derby (1734–1797). © Artefact/Alamy

A catalogue record for this book is available from the British Library.

Library of Congress Cataloging-in-Publication Data
Names: Boyington, Amy, author.
Title: Hidden patrons : women and architectural patronage in Georgian
Britain / Amy Boyington.
Description: London ; New York : Bloomsbury Visual Arts, 2023. | Outgrowth
of the author's thesis (doctoral)–University of Cambridge, 2018, under
the title: Maids, wives and widows : female architectural patronage in
eighteenth century Britain. | Includes bibliographical references and index.
Identifiers: LCCN 2023011340 (print) | LCCN 2023011341 (ebook) |
ISBN 9781350358614 (hardback) | ISBN 9781350358607 (paperback) |
ISBN 9781350358645 (pdf) | ISBN 9781350358638 (epub) | ISBN 9781350358621
Subjects: LCSH: Architects and patrons–Great Britain–History–18th
century. | Women art patrons–Great Britain–History–18th century. |
Architecture and society–Great Britain–History–18th century. | Architecture, Georgian.
Classification: LCC NA2543.P38 B69 2023 (print) | LCC NA2543.P38 (ebook)
| DDC 720.82094109/033–dc23/eng/20230602
LC record available at https://lccn.loc.gov/2023011340
LC ebook record available at https://lccn.loc.gov/2023011341

ISBN:	HB:	978-1-3503-5861-4
	PB:	978-1-3503-5860-7
	ePDF:	978-1-3503-5864-5
	eBook:	978-1-3503-5863-8

Typeset by Integra Software Services Pvt. Ltd.
Printed and bound in India

Hidden Patrons

CONTENTS

ILLUSTRATIONS

ACKNOWLEDGEMENTS

This book has been a roller-coaster of a ride. It originated as a PhD thesis, which I completed after three blissful years at Corpus Christi College, Cambridge. This amazing opportunity was made possible by the Full Doctoral Award granted by the School of Arts and Humanities, for which I will be forever grateful. My PhD experience was enhanced by the many teas, biscuits and the odd glass of Champagne, enjoyed with James Campbell, Wendy Andrews and Karey Draper. All three, together with Adam Menuge and Alexander Lumley, have been unfailingly supportive over the years. Following the PhD, I was fortunate to have been given further financial support from the Paul Mellon Centre for Studies in British Art which allowed me to expand my research.

This book has been pulled apart, shaped and reworked through the many conversations I have had with the most fascinating people. Sometimes these conversations were painful, but necessary, while others were delightfully exciting. All, however, were invaluable and I am truly grateful to the following for their words of wisdom and constant support: Emily Burns, Oliver Cox, Emily Lees, Amy Lim, Emily Knight and Martin Postle.

Thanks are also due to the archival staff at the various archives and libraries at which I conducted research, including the British Library, the National Archives, Bedford and Luton Archive and Record Services, Gloucester Archives, Plymouth and West Devon Record Office, Shakespeare Birthplace Trust, Surrey History Centre, Lincolnshire Archives, the Lambeth Archives and the Sir John Soane Museum.

My greatest debt of thanks, of course, must go to Joris de Vries, whose unwavering enthusiasm for my research has ensured that this book is here today. He has been the greatest champion, editor, wine-bringer and support a girl could wish for. This book is dedicated to him.

NOTE ON THE TEXT

All dates, as far as it has been possible to ascertain, are given according to the modern Gregorian calendar, which ran eleven days ahead of the old Julian calendar, with the year changing on 1 January, rather than 25 March. Where events took place on the Continent, or where ambiguity may arise, both dates are given, with the Julian ('Old Style') preceding the Gregorian (or 'New Style'). England officially adopted the Gregorian calendar in 1752, following the passing of The Calendar (New Style) Act 1750.

All archival material has been transcribed retaining, as far as possible, the original spelling, punctuation, capitalization, underlining and paragraphing. As a result, the use of *sic* has been omitted.

ABBREVIATIONS

Add. MS	Additional Manuscripts collection
BHO	British History Online
BL	British Library, London
BLARS	Bedford and Luton Archives and Record Service, Bedford
BM	British Museum, London
BRO	Berkshire Record Office, Reading
GA	Gloucester Archives, Gloucester
HHA	Holkham Hall Archives, Holkham Hall
LA	Lambeth Archives, London
ODNB	Oxford Dictionary of National Biography (online version)
PWDRO	Plymouth and West Devon Record Office, Plymouth
RIBA	Royal Institute of British Architects
SHC	Surrey History Centre, Woking
SM	Sir John Soane's Museum, London
SoL	Survey of London
TNA	The National Archives, Kew
V&A	Victoria and Albert Museum, London
WYAS	West Yorkshire Archive Services, Leeds

1

Introduction

In 1963, according to the historian G. E. Mingay, most 'eighteenth-century ladies stayed in the background' busying themselves with 'their family, in entertaining, in household cares, clothes, and all minutiae of family life'.[1] He continued:

> When not bearing children they enjoyed an active social life, they visited, attended balls, played cards, read novels, rode to hounds and wrote letters – but none of this made any discernible impression on the character of the times. Indispensable yet insignificant, they played out unobtrusively their vital role in the life of the ruling class.[2]

Mingay's mistaken assumption that women had no discernible impact on their surroundings or society typifies the misguided views that historians maintained well into the twentieth century. Thankfully this opinion is now completely outdated, but it, and others like it, contributed to the misconception that women's role in eighteenth-century architecture was non-existent. Traditionally, historians have advocated that eighteenth-century architecture was purely the pursuit of privileged male patrons and their talented male architects. As such, history has recorded that it was men who owned grand estates and houses, who commissioned famous architects, who embarked upon elaborate architectural schemes, who collected great art collections and who had the financial and legal independence to do so. The role of women has generally been reduced to that of a daughter, wife and mother, forever dependent and lacking agency.

Women were of course not absent during this period, neither in society as a whole, nor in the sphere of architecture. In 1747 Mary (Molly) Hervey, Baroness Hervey (1700–68), wrote energetically to her friend, the Reverend Roger Morris: 'I have a dozen plans, a compass, ruler, &c. lying before me, and expect Mr. Flitcroft every instant … Here comes the executor, so the architect must give her directions'.[3] Her obvious enthusiasm plainly demonstrates that women engaged with architecture and could be patrons in their own right. Lady Hervey evidently felt no restrictions, whether societal, financial or legal, in pursuing her architectural ambition and even declares herself to be the architect. As will be illustrated throughout this book, Lady Hervey was certainly not the exception in her architectural pursuits. Her architectural patronage, drawings, knowledge and discourse were interests shared by many women in the eighteenth century. Far from being the preserve of elite men, architecture was a passion shared by both sexes, intellectually and practically, as long as they possessed sufficient wealth and autonomy.

Women's involvement in eighteenth-century architecture and design has remained an under-researched area of history. The patronage of royal women has received the most attention and their influence over architectural trends and design is now widely recognized.[4] Conversely, the architectural patronage of their elite and wealthy subjects, ranging from courtiers to courtesans, is far less known. The difficulty in identifying surviving archival sources relating to women, as well as the transient nature of buildings, has rendered their involvement in architecture less easy to recognize.[5]

In recent decades, however, a stream of new scholarship has sought to recover women's involvement in eighteenth-century architectural patronage and display, particularly within the country house.[6] Such scholarship has gone a long way in highlighting the crucial role that women played in the creation, management, survival and longevity of country houses across Britain and Ireland. Similarly, recent research has also emphasized women's contributions to the establishment and design of London town houses.[7] Scholarship on town house architecture has traditionally focussed on the 'genius' of the male architect,[8] whereas more modern investigation has been more nuanced, reasserting the involvement that women had in the design and building of their houses.

Despite such progress, the true scope of women's patronage is still largely underemphasized. This book, for the first time, places women at the centre of eighteenth-century architectural discourse, and instead of focussing on one building type in isolation, such as country houses or town houses, it will demonstrate that women enjoyed commissioning and improving buildings of every shape and size. In doing so, it will lift female patrons out of historical obscurity.

Due to the expensive nature of building, most of the women explored within this book were wealthy by eighteenth-century standards, and some were immensely so. Consequently, the majority belonged to the aristocracy and formed part of the social and political elite. They were privileged, educated, accomplished and sometimes well-travelled individuals who sought to shape their surroundings. The enlightening stories of these women will come to life through newly discovered personal letters, diaries, journals, account books, architectural drawings, newspaper articles and inventories.

Although this book concentrates on elite women, that does not mean that women from other social classes, such as merchants and the gentry, were not also involved in architectural patronage. In fact, it is highly likely that they were, but due to the scarcity of surviving archival material, their lives and their building projects have, thus far, been largely lost to us.

The legal, social and financial status of women in the eighteenth century

Why has the misconception persisted that elite women were unable to commission and engage with architectural works? The reasons for this can be traced back to the legal landscape of the eighteenth century itself, where the legal standing of a woman was determined by her marital status. Once married, a woman's legal standing in common law became that of *feme covert,* meaning that her legal identity was eclipsed by that of her husband, resulting in her inability to contract, sue or be sued independently.[9] The consequence of this was that, once married, a woman relinquished control over her finances, land and property, which therefore meant that she was no longer free to commission architectural projects without her husband's agreement. This, together with the patriarchal right of primogeniture, which only allowed the eldest male child to inherit the family estates, further limited women's opportunity to own property or enjoy financial independence. This was in direct contrast to a *feme sole,* which referred to an unmarried or widowed woman.

Marriage was a serious affair for the upper classes and was seen as a union between two families rather than the private union of two individuals, and thus arranged marriages were the norm. Marriage was, quite literally, a business contract and from a very young age elite girls were raised with the sole purpose of securing a 'good match'. Prior to the wedding ceremony, lengthy negotiations on behalf of the bride and bridegroom occurred, culminating in the signing of the marriage settlement. This settlement or contract principally stipulated the financial arrangements agreed between the parties; namely the bride's portion (dowry), the wife's 'pin-money' (annuity), the widow's dower or jointure and the provisions made for any children that should arise from the union.[10] The most common form of settlement was the 'strict settlement', which was primarily designed to protect the groom's estate by entailing it upon the eldest son produced by the marriage.[11] The objective was to defend primogeniture and to keep the estate intact for future generations.

William Hogarth colourfully depicted the phenomenon of the marriage settlement in the first of his satirical *Marriage A-la-Mode* series (Figure 1.1). The scene, entitled *The Marriage Settlement*, shows the fat, gouty Earl Squander and a rich, self-advancing City of London Alderman concluding their negotiations for the marriage of their miserable children. The pompous earl hopes to use his daughter-in-law's large dowry to complete the building of his new Palladian house, which can be glimpsed through the sash

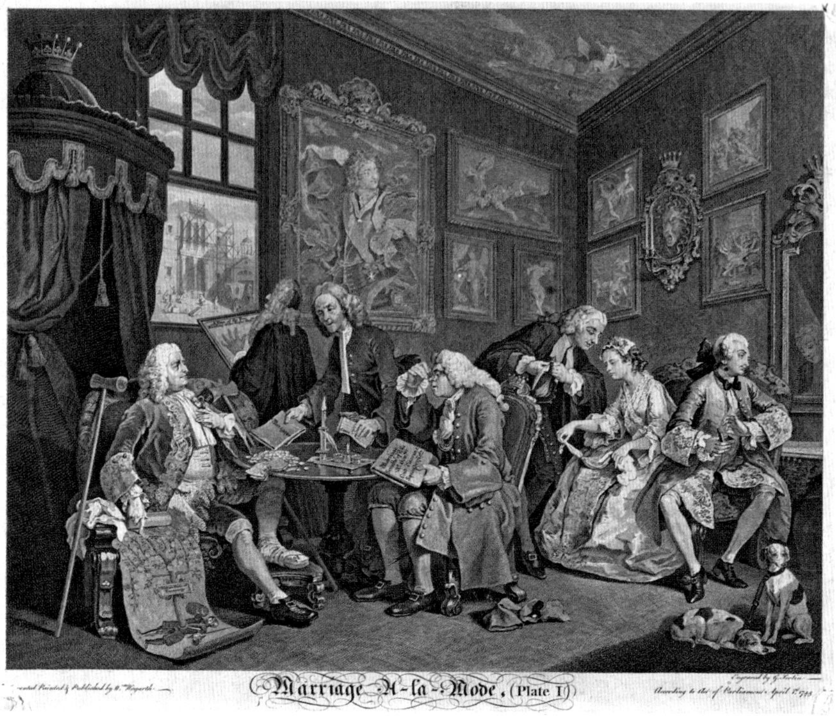

FIGURE 1.1 Gerard Jean Baptiste Scotin, after William Hogarth, *Marriage A-La-Mode, Plate I: The Contract*, 1745, engraving. Yale Center for British Art, Paul Mellon Collection, B1981.25.1431. Courtesy of the Yale Center for British Art, Yale University.

window, whilst the calculating Alderman seeks to advance his social status by connecting his family to the nobility.

The merchant's daughter sits desolately next to her husband, sobbing, while being comforted by the family lawyer Silvertongue, who whispers predatorily in her ear. She sits inconsolably without any power to change her fate. The young Viscount Squanderfield ignores his distressed bride while he admires his face in a mirror. He is dressed in the latest Parisian fashions and sports a black spot on his neck, indicating that he has syphilis. The ill-matched couple are destined for an unhappy, loveless marriage, a fact symbolized by the two dogs that are gloomily shackled together in the corner. The girl's father has married her off without care or consideration for her well-being, and now she is legally and financially beholden to her vain, foppish, uninterested husband.

Although satirical, Hogarth's work highlights the lack of autonomy experienced by many eighteenth-century daughters in Britain. Unmarried women, whilst legally independent as *feme soles*, were in reality utterly dependent, both financially and socially, upon their fathers (or other male relatives) until they married. This almost childlike dependency then transferred to their husbands via the marriage settlement. Given this constrictive environment, it is perhaps unsurprising that historians have largely assumed that women's lack of agency resulted in their exclusion from the architectural sphere. Although it is certainly true that women's opportunities to engage in architecture were more limited than those of their male peers, this by no means meant that they were passive bystanders. In many cases, women, when possessed of the necessary funds and autonomy, were able to successfully navigate the limiting social and legal landscape of the eighteenth century to shape their architectural surroundings.

To truly appreciate the significance of female architectural patronage within the legal landscape of the eighteenth century, we must first delve a little deeper into the implications of differing marital statuses. This book will classify women as belonging to one of three types of marital status: unmarried, married or widowed. Women within these three marital categories differed significantly in their freedoms. Whereas unmarried women generally lead a second-rate existence and married women were completely beholden to their husbands, widowed women enjoyed a large degree of autonomy, often for the first time in their lives.

Indeed, due to the complete dependency of unmarried daughters on their fathers, their interaction with architecture has usually only been considered in relation to how they used and managed the buildings in which they lived. This is a naïve interpretation and neglects to consider the rare circumstances in which single women did shape their surroundings if they were given the opportunity to do so. Heiresses, for example, were that exceptional category of single women who were freely able to spend how they pleased, and thus many commissioned great building works as a result. Wealthy courtesans and mistresses form another fascinating group whose architectural patronage has, hitherto, remained in the shadows.[12] Just as these women spent fortunes on luxurious clothes, diamonds and carriages, so too did they spend heavily on the buildings they inhabited.

The predominant marital category is, of course, that of married women. On the whole it has been supposed that wives were simply relegated to the 'woman's domain', allowed only to run the household, rather than to create the house itself. This supposition has been compounded by the surviving architectural plans and drawings dedicated only to the husband, by the building accounts compiled purely for the husband's inspection and by the bills settled only by the husband. However, even within the most traditional of circumstances, wives often influenced building schemes because the creation of the marital home was, more often than not, the equal endeavour of both the husband and the wife. Married women not only assisted their husbands with the design process of new buildings, but also managed entire building projects from conception to completion, and autonomously commissioned buildings of their own.

Widowed women were perhaps the most likely category of women to commission architectural schemes because they possessed the greatest social, financial and legal autonomy. Following the deaths of their husbands, widows were free to forge their own way in society, and thus were also free to pursue their own architectural ambitions. Many widows, as was stipulated in the marriage settlement, were bequeathed a life interest in either a dower house or a London house, thus providing a smooth transition (in theory) from marital life to widowhood. When a family did not possess a dower house, a widow was free to rent, buy or build a house of her choice using the money provided by her jointure. This usually took the form of a town house or villa and, as such, many widows flocked to London and surrounding environs to establish themselves at the heart of fashionable society.

Architecture as an intellectual pursuit

Women's engagement in architecture was often fuelled by their intellectual interest and understanding of architectural drawing, styles and history. During the Age of Enlightenment, wealthy girls were tutored in drawing and painting, which frequently extended to their tutoring on the subjects of architectural drawing, draughtsmanship and surveying.[13] Drawing was seen as a sophisticated accomplishment for girls, and thus many were depicted in portraits holding their drawing equipment. For example, John Hoppner's elegant painting of *The Frankland Sisters* (1795) depicts Marianne and Amelia Frankland seated in a landscape, with Amelia holding a portfolio of sketches and a porte-crayon (Figure 1.2).[14] Another, by Thomas Gainsborough of his two daughters, shows them at their drawing lesson, with Margaret seated holding her sketches and a porte-crayon, while Mary stands observing a classical sculpture.[15]

Although women were encouraged to take lessons and engage with art and drawing, it was virtually impossible for them to practise these skills professionally. A few notable exceptions exist to this rule, such as Angelica Kauffman and Mary Moser, both of whom were successful professional painters during the eighteenth century. So much so that they were both founding members of the Royal Academy of Arts in London in 1768.[16] However, their position as Academicians always remained ambivalent due to their gender, a fact strikingly epitomized in Johan Zoffany's *The Academicians of the Royal Academy* (1771–2), in which they are the only founding members to be excluded. Instead, the only indication of their existence is given by their somewhat lacklustre portraits on the back wall.[17]

Throughout the eighteenth century, while painting and drawing were certainly accomplishments encouraged by society as suitable female pursuits, it is apparent that forging a career as a professional artist was a step too far. Although there were no codified rules that prevented women from painting professionally, the hegemony of men was so deeply ingrained into society that they could never hope to gain the professional recognition bestowed upon their male peers. Indeed, despite the successes of Kauffman's and

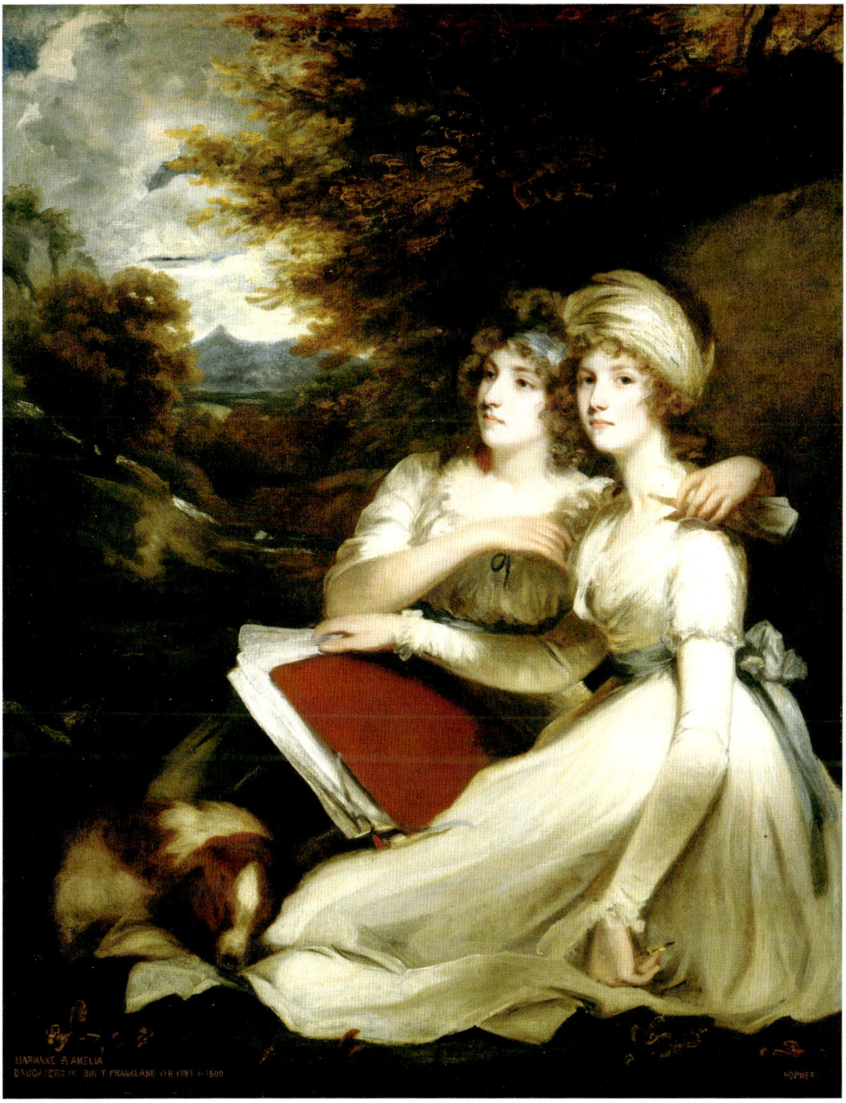

FIGURE 1.2 John Hoppner, *The Frankland Sisters*, 1795, oil on canvas. National Gallery of Art, Washington, DC, 1937.1.111. Courtesy of the National Gallery of Art, Washington.

Moser's careers, they were still prohibited from the Council (the committee which oversaw the running of the Royal Academy), life drawing classes and the Academy's annual dinner.[18] In fact, women were not allowed to join the annual dinner until 1968, and no further women were admitted to the Academy until Dame Laura Knight was elected in 1936.[19]

Despite this prohibitive and male-dominated professional context, some women nevertheless displayed a keen talent and predilection for architectural sketching and expression. For instance, Lady Amabel Yorke (1751–1833) (later Lady Polwarth, then Baroness Lucas and then 1st Countess de Grey) received lessons in drawing and painting from Alexander Cozens, a renowned landscape painter in watercolours.[20] Lady Amabel was the eldest daughter of Philip Yorke, 2nd Earl of Hardwicke, and his wife, Lady Jemima Campbell, 2nd Marchioness Grey, sole heiress of her maternal grandfather Henry Grey, 1st Duke of Kent. In 1780 she married Alexander Hume-Campbell, Lord Polwarth, and thus became Lady Polwarth.

Lady Amabel became particularly skilful under Cozens' tutelage, to the point that her topographical drawings of her family homes of Wimpole Hall, Cambridgeshire, and Wrest Park, Bedfordshire, were included on the Wedgwood Green Frog Service for Catherine the Great in 1774.[21] Four were chosen of the Wrest Park gardens, and of the Wimpole landscape, two were chosen, including one of the Wimpole Folly, a rusticated Gothic ruin built between 1768 and 1772 (Figure 1.3).[22]

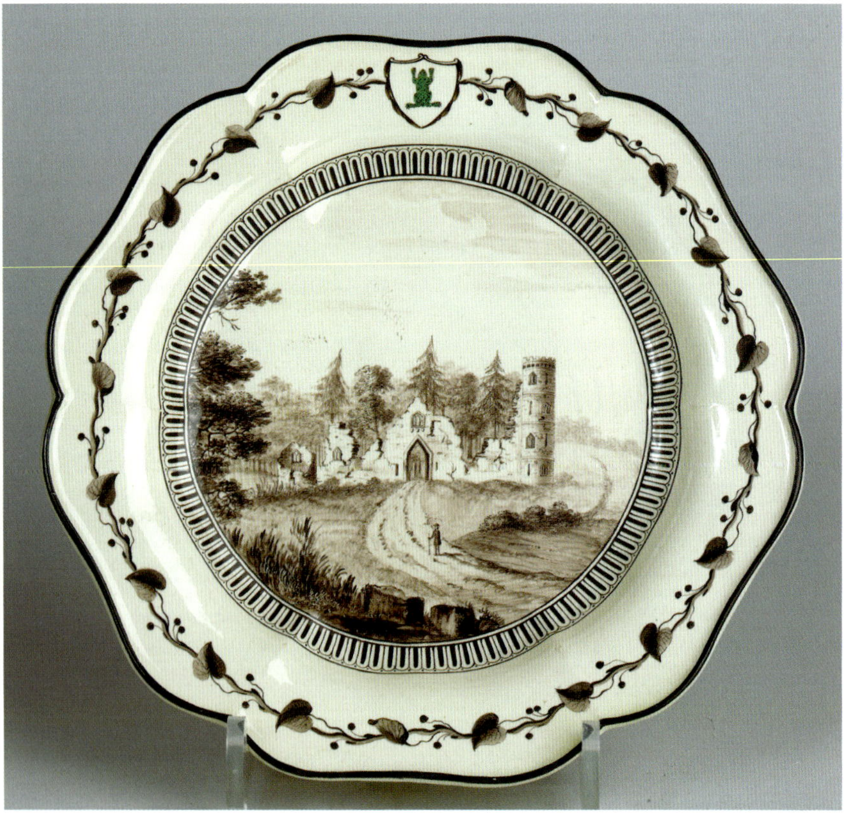

FIGURE 1.3 Dessert Plate ornamented with a view of a ruin at Wimpole, painted by Amabel, Lady Polwarth, 1773–4. The Hermitage Museum, St Petersburg. ГЧ-9152. © The Hermitage Museum.

The skill of architectural drawing was also transferable to embroidery as demonstrated by a surviving Scottish sampler by Margaret Eiston (1797–1875) which depicts an elevation of Dalquharran Castle in Ayrshire; designed in 1785 by Robert Adam for Thomas Kennedy (Figure 1.4).[23] The elevation stitched by the thirteen-year-old Margaret is based upon Adam's original

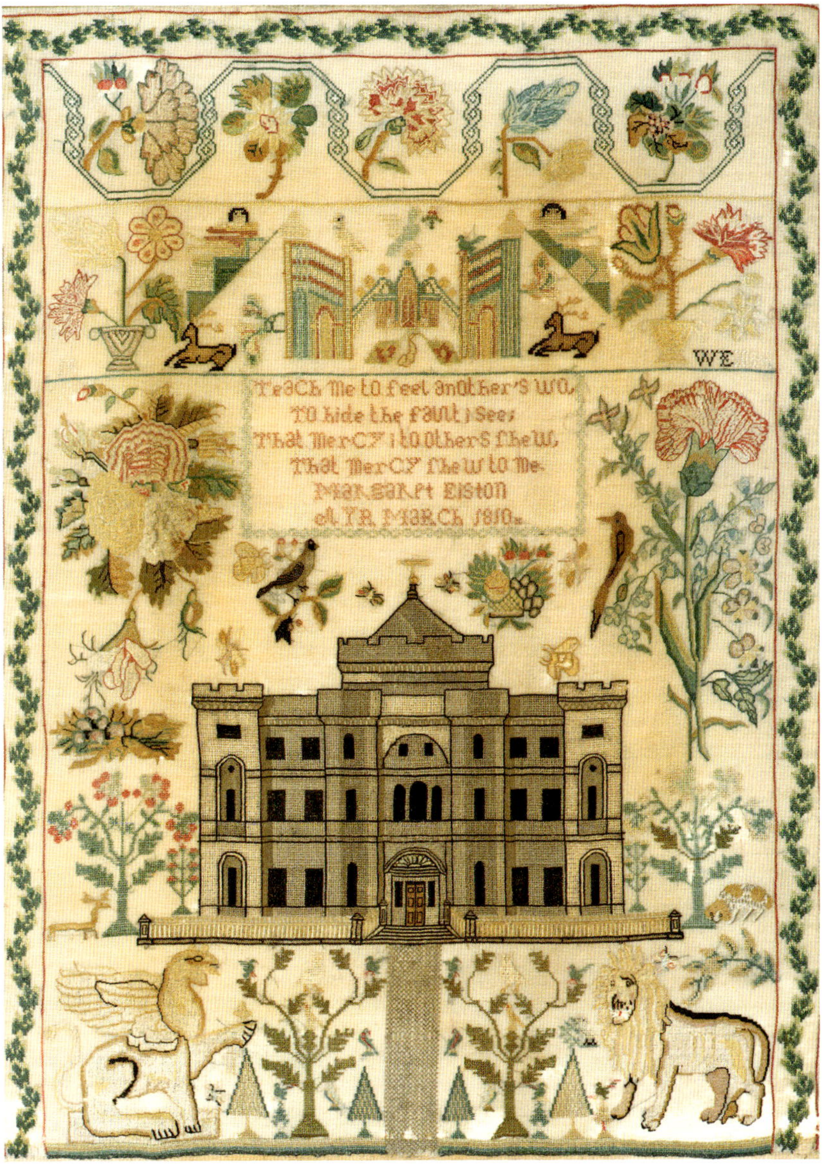

FIGURE 1.4 Scottish sampler by Margaret Eiston, Ayrshire, 1806, silk on linen. Private collection of Leslie B. Durst. Photo: Rebekah Johnson.

architectural designs, which were never published, signifying that she had access to the drawings and studied them carefully in order to recreate them in embroidered form.[24]

Some women were determined to truly master the art of architectural drawing and hired tutors accordingly. Queen Charlotte of Mecklenburg-Strelitz (1744–1818) was one such woman; she took architectural drawing lessons with her husband from Sir William Chambers and lessons in perspective drawing from Joshua Kirby, later Clerk of Works at Kew.[25] By 1768, Kirby was describing himself as 'Designer in Perspective to their Majesties', indicating that Queen Charlotte had a long-standing intellectual interest in architecture.[26] Kirby also designed a silver architect's protractor for her in 1765, which survives in its original fitted wooden case, covered in green ray skin and lined with dark green velvet.[27] The Queen no doubt engaged in architectural drawing and may have even designed some buildings, but unfortunately none of her drawings have survived.

This predicament is likely true for a number of eighteenth-century women, whose skill in architectural drawing and draughtsmanship has been lost to time. Even if they did not seek to gain the proficiency of professional architects, many women engaged in the practice of drawing plans and sketches simply to relay architectural information to their architects, contractors, family and friends. For example, in 1779 when Mary Yorke (*c.* 1741–1824), daughter of Isaac Maddocks, Bishop of Worcester, was managing the remodelling of the Bishop's Palace in Gloucester, she sent a rough plan of the building to her sister-in-law, Jemima, Marchioness Grey (1723–97), so that she could ask for architectural advice:

> As your ladyship always so kindly interests yourself in the comforts of our habitation I take the liberty of inclosing a plan I took of our House at Gloster with all its bendings & turnings, perhaps you will kindly consider in what manner we can connect the two ends of the House together without passing thro' the Hall.[28]

The plan referred to still survives, and although a coarse sketch, the layout, proportions and names of the rooms are adequately represented, with the windows, doors, passages and staircases all indicated (Figure 1.5). Such a sketch would have allowed Lady Grey to provide architectural solutions without ever having laid eyes upon the building.

To further their architectural education and remain abreast of the latest styles and designs, women subscribed to and owned the most fashionable treatises of the day. In volumes one and two of *Vitruvius Britannicus*, published in 1715, there were eight female subscribers, accounting for fourteen copies, of which Sarah Churchill, Duchess of Marlborough (1660–1744), a prolific architectural patroness, was one, and in the third volume, published a decade later, this had increased to fourteen women, accounting for eighteen copies.[29] Although a small percentage of the subscribers as a whole, it is clear that these women were publicly declaring their independent

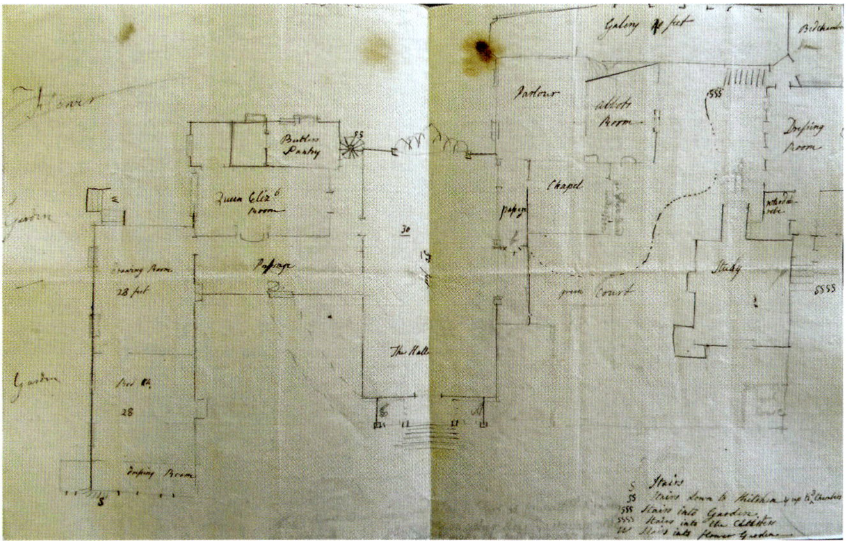

FIGURE 1.5 Mary Yorke, plan of the Bishops Palace, Gloucester, 1779. Bedford and Luton Archive and Record Service, L30/9/111/22. Courtesy of the Bedford and Luton Archive and Record Service.

interest in architecture and facilitating their inclusion into architectural discourse and debate.

For William Kent's *The Designs of Inigo Jones* (1727), eighteen women subscribed, including Caroline of Ansbach, when Princess of Wales (1683–1737), and her husband's mistress, Henrietta Howard, later Countess of Suffolk (1689–1767). Caroline, when Queen consort, went on to build a series of follies in the gardens of Richmond Lodge and commissioned William Kent to build a beautiful library at St James's Palace.[30] And Henrietta Howard, as will be discussed later in this book, went on to build a fashionable Palladian villa on the bank of the River Thames in Twickenham. Similarly, during the 1760s a flurry of architectural publications relating to the latest archaeological discoveries and excavations proved to be popular. For instance, there were twenty-nine female subscribers listed for James Stuart and Nicholas Revett's *Antiquities of Athens* (1762).[31] Of these subscribers, many had already commissioned architectural works of their own, or soon went on to do so.

Women as architects?

While some women possessed a keen intellectual interest in architecture and attained great proficiency in draughtsmanship and design, it was virtually impossible for them to practise as professional architects, as was true for any other form of artistic expression. In fact, there are no known professional female architects of the eighteenth century, and, for those who did engage in the practice of architectural design, their role has been categorized as that of an amateur. This, however, is not necessarily derogative, because in Abraham Rees's *Cyclopaedia* of 1803, he described the word amateur as follows:

> a foreign term introduced and now ... current amongst us, to denote a person understanding and loving or practising the polite arts of painting, sculpture, or architecture, without any regard to pecuniary advantage.[32]

This definition, then, could be applied to some of the women within this book, because they designed and drew because they enjoyed the art, rather than in expectation of remuneration. Elizabeth, Lady Wilbraham (1632–1705), for example, is a patron often credited with the designing and rebuilding of both her own and her husband's country seats and is therefore sometimes touted as Britain's first female architect.[33] Born Elizabeth Mytton in 1632, Lady Wilbraham was the daughter of Edward Mytton and Cecily Skeffington. At the age of six she inherited her father's estates, which included Weston Park in Staffordshire, and in 1651 she married Sir Thomas Wilbraham, 3rd Baronet, of Woodhey, near Nantwich in Cheshire. Lady Wilbraham's architectural endeavours are poorly documented, but in her copy of Godfrey Richard's 1663 English translation of Andrea Palladio's *First Book of Architecture*, there are fourteen pages of her architecture-related notes on the flyleaves (Figure 1.6).[34] They

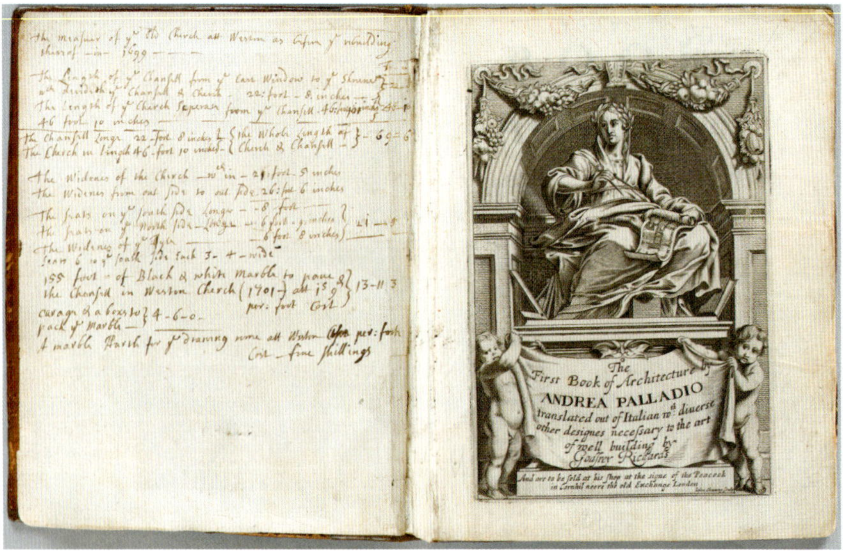

FIGURE 1.6 End papers of Lady Wilbraham's copy of Godfrey Richard's first English translation of *The First Book of Architecture* (1663), annotated in her hand. Weston Park, Library, acc. no. 118.0539. Copyright Trustees of the Weston Park Foundation.

mostly refer to the building work of Woodhey Hall (her husband's seat), the construction of a chapel at Woodhey and the building of a church at Weston Park.[35] Weston Park itself is referred to in the past tense or as a model for the builders at Woodhey.[36]

Lady Wilbraham's practical and technical knowledge of architecture and of the building process has resulted in her being described as an amateur architect.[37] Nonetheless, without any surviving drawings it is impossible to ascertain the extent to which Lady Wilbraham was involved in the designing process. This, in turn, has led historians to conclude that she was simply a responsible, knowledgeable and highly engaged patron, who worked alongside executant architects and master builders to enact her vision.[38]

At Charleville Castle in Co. Offaly, built between 1800 and 1812, the extent to which Catherine Bury, Countess of Charleville (1762–1851), daughter of Thomas Townley Dawson, designed the building is much clearer.[39] Contemporaries were aware of her collaboration with the architect Francis Johnson, leading Judge Robert Day to write in 1812 that the castle 'Does great credit to the taste and munificence of the noble owner, or rather her ladyship, who I understand projected the whole under the auspices of Johnson'.[40] And yet, notwithstanding this contemporary account, and despite it being clear that Lady Charleville had enjoyed architectural drawing from a young age, the surviving drawings of the castle's proposed

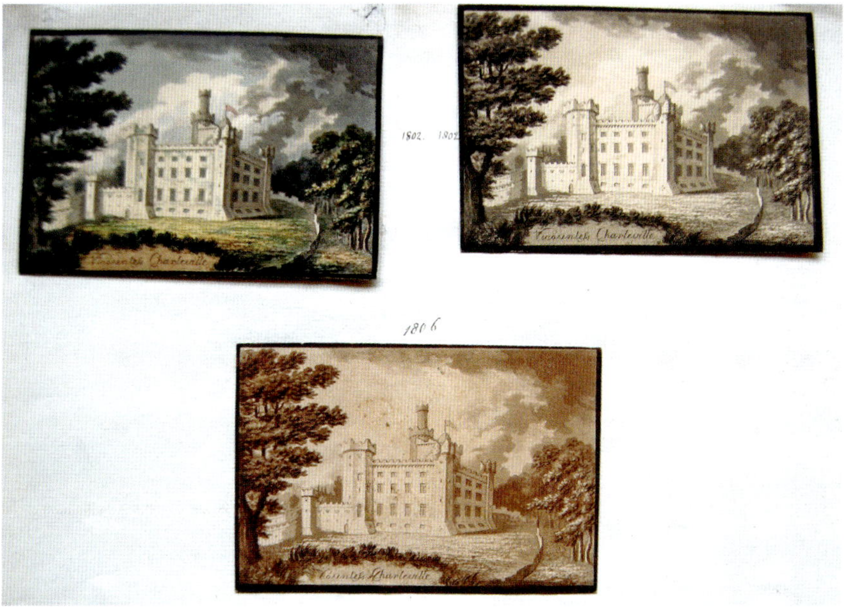

FIGURE 1.7 Three visiting cards belonging to the Countess Charleville, with views of Charleville Castle, *c.* 1802–6, etching. British Museum, C,1.631–3. © The Trustees of the British Museum.

design were automatically attributed to her husband, Charles William Bury, 1st Earl of Charleville, who she had married in 1798.[41] Many drawings have since been reattributed to Lady Charleville, thereby reasserting her 'active role in formulating the initial concept of the castle [and in] developing the design of the structure'.[42] Such was Lady Charleville's evident pride in the designing and building of Charleville Castle, that she even used her designs to decorate her visiting cards (Figure 1.7).[43]

Another recognized amateur architect is Anna Maria Dawson (1770–1820), daughter of Blayney Townley Balfour and Letitia Leigh, who also worked with Francis Johnson in designing her brother's new Neo-Classical country seat, Townley Hall, in Co. Louth.[44] A set of rough plans for each floor dating to *c.* 1797 have recently been reattributed to Anna (Figure 1.8).[45] Anna's sketches reveal her to be a competent draughtswoman

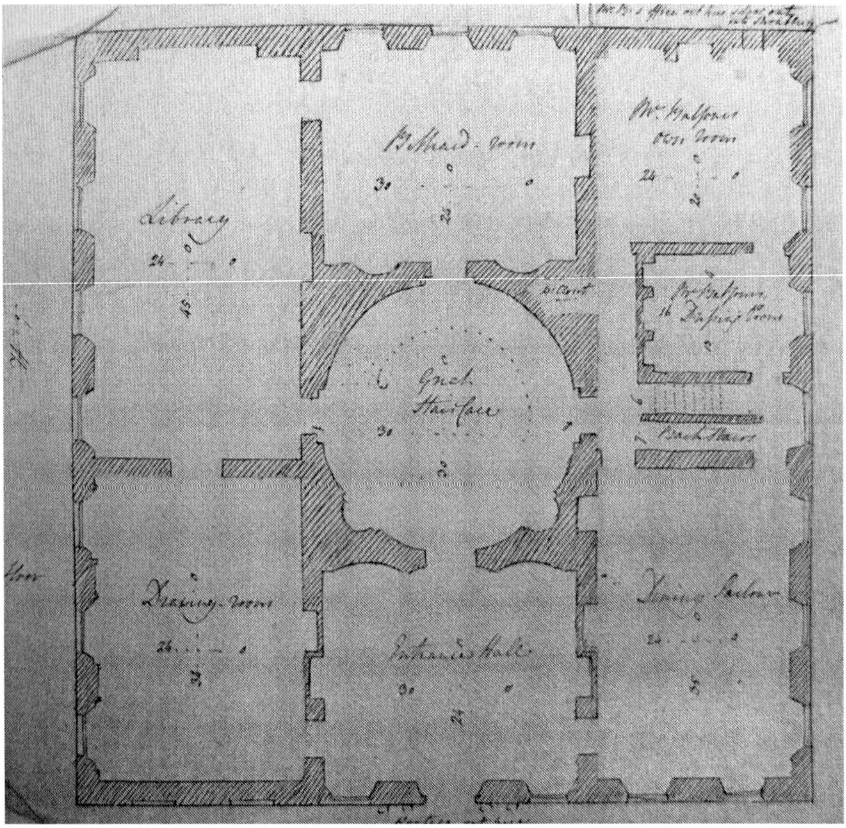

FIGURE 1.8 Anna Maria Dawson (att.), plan of the principal floor of Townley Hall, *c.* 1797. National Library of Ireland, AD 2496–2499. Courtesy of the National Library of Ireland.

and her annotations, which include room names and measurements, also incorporate other important practical details, such as the location of water supplies.[46] Following her marriage to the Rev. Thomas Vesey Dawson in 1793, Anna was also the driving force behind the design of her modest marital country seat, Fort Weston (later called Galtrim House), in Co. Meath. Her sketch books contain drawings of her architectural vision, with her most accomplished sketches depicting her proposals for the entrance and garden elevations.[47] In these she depicts a refined Neo-Classical house complete with fashionable features, such as balconies, windows set into recessed arches and a semi-circular bow window.

Of these three women, none would claim to be a professional architect. Although they controlled the designs of their buildings, they relied on their paid architects to help develop ideas and enact their visions. An exception to this rule is Mary Townley (1753–1839), a woman who is perhaps the closest we have to a professional eighteenth-century female architect. She is credited with designing a number of buildings in Ramsgate for her property-developer husband, James Townley – notably without the assistance of a professional architect. Surviving sketches by Mary provide the necessary proof that she was a skilled draughtswoman.[48] She was an accomplished and imaginative designer, comfortable with both the Classical and Gothic styles.[49]

Mary's most well-known building is Townley House (Figure 1.9), a town house that she designed and built in the Neo-Classical style for her family in 1792.[50] By 1809 she had also designed Townley Castle (demolished in the 1920s), a guests' annex built in the Gothic Revival style (Figure 1.10). She also designed 35–42 Spencer Square, 1–3 Royal Road, Pier Castle, Royal Crescent, Devonshire Place and Albion Place.[51] Given Mary's integral role in the family property business, it is almost certain that she directed the building works to ensure that her designs were properly executed, as any architect would. Her practical understanding of building construction is evidenced by the patent she took out on the 8 June 1810 for 'a method applicable to the prevention or cure of smokey chimnies'.[52] Nevertheless, despite Mary's talent, significant output and local prominence, her architectural achievements are now all but forgotten.

In short, women's intellectual interest in architecture during this period cannot be denied. Their subscriptions to the latest architectural treatises and their proficiency in architectural design and draughtsmanship are testament to their passion for the discipline and their desire to shape the world around them. Fuelled by their learning, women often channelled their knowledge of the latest architectural and aesthetic trends into building commissions of their own.

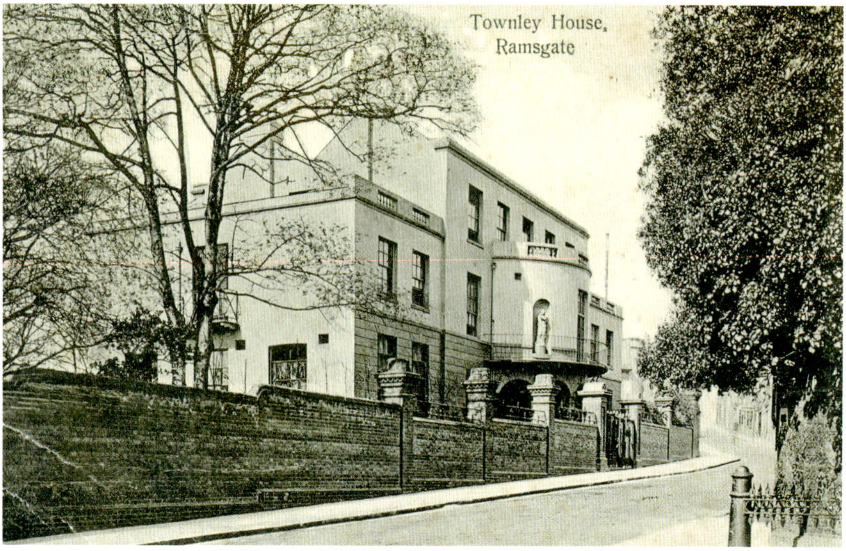

FIGURE 1.9 Townley House, Ramsgate, designed and built by Mary Townley in 1797. Photo dating to the twentieth century. Courtesy of Terry Wheeler/Ramsgate Historical Society.

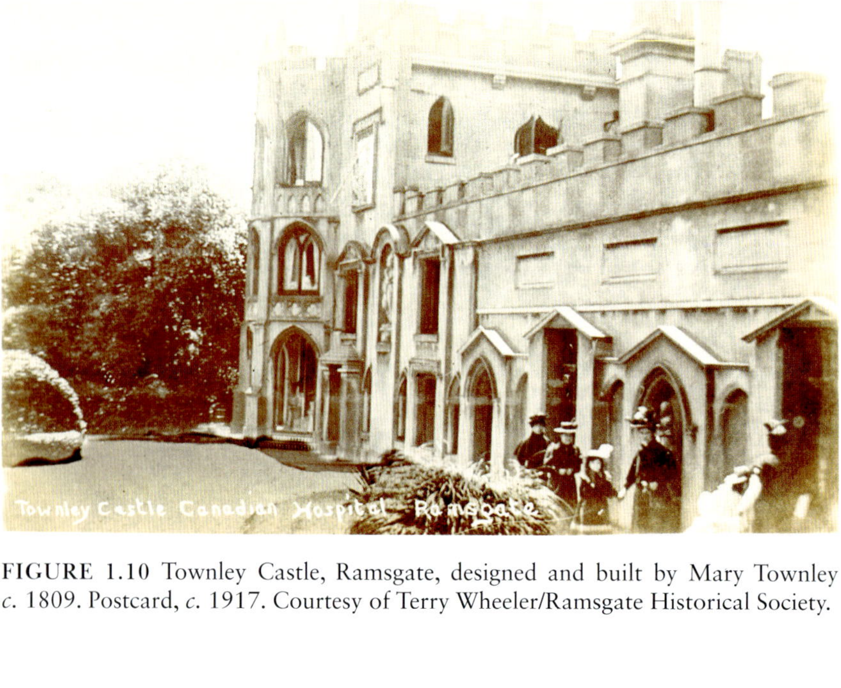

FIGURE 1.10 Townley Castle, Ramsgate, designed and built by Mary Townley *c.* 1809. Postcard, *c.* 1917. Courtesy of Terry Wheeler/Ramsgate Historical Society.

Female architectural patronage

When considering female architectural patronage, it is useful to first define what constitutes architecture within the context of this book. The definition of architecture employed here is broad and encompasses all instances in which an individual engaged with the built environment. Naturally, it will consider the commissioning and financing of new building projects and the modifying of existing constructions, but it will also cover less-permanent expressions of architecture, such as interior design and decoration. If we were to exclude interior design from our definition of architecture, many valuable examples of female patronage would be overlooked.[53] Furthermore, although modern notions tend to place interior design below other architectural expressions in importance, this was not the case in the eighteenth century. For architects such as Robert Adam and Sir John Soane, interior design was as important as the architectural design itself. Interior design enabled individuals to display their knowledge of the latest decorative fashions, introduce personal innovation and express their taste and learning.

Similarly, when defining architectural patronage, not only will the definition cover those women who directly financed a project themselves but will also include any instances in which women possessed the agency to autonomously influence a building project. This influence could take many different forms, ranging from superintending a building scheme on behalf of a family member, through to commissioning entirely new buildings for themselves. Crucially, where a woman liaised with architects, contractors, craftsmen, friends or relatives in order to influence their architectural surroundings, she will be considered a patron. This will then allow the contributions of previously discounted women, particularly wives, to be acknowledged.

Book structure

The architectural endeavours of our female patrons will be explored by building type, namely country houses, town houses, suburban villas, estate buildings, as well as garden design and follies. Women built across this wide spectrum of architecture, but due to the hugely costly nature of building, most engaged with either one or two building projects during their lifetimes. There were, of course, exceptions to this rule, such as the indomitable Sarah Churchill, Duchess of Marlborough (Figure 1.11), who was perhaps one of the most remarkable architectural patronesses of the first half of the eighteenth century.[54]

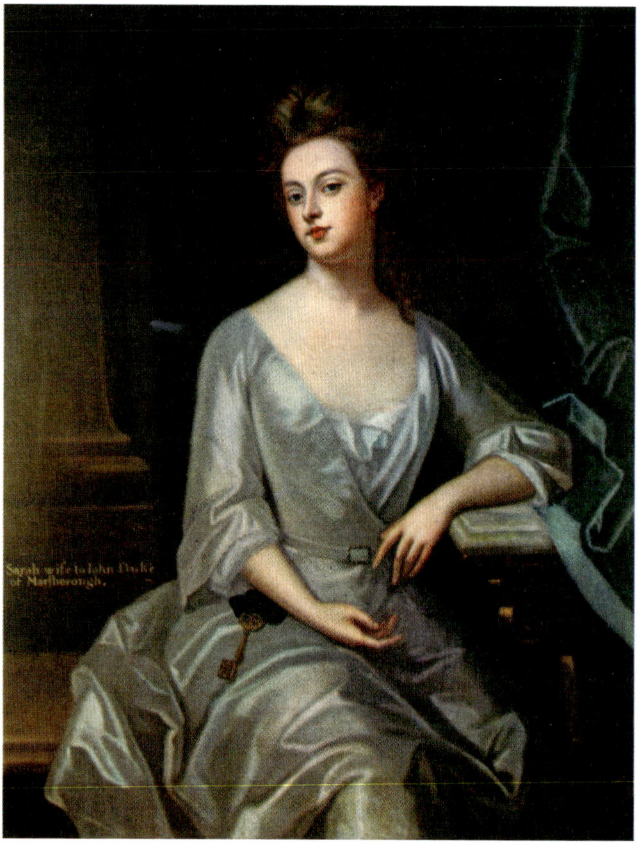

FIGURE 1.11 After Sir Godfrey Kneller, *Sarah Churchill, Duchess of Marlborough*, *c.* 1702, oil on canvas. Charles Phelps Cushing/ClassicStock/Getty Images

Born in 1660, the daughter of Richard Jennings (or Jenyns) and Frances Thornhurst, Sarah married John Churchill, later 1st Duke of Marlborough, in the winter of 1677–8. An ambitious power couple, the Churchills forged highly successful careers and became extremely influential during their lifetimes. Apparently unrestricted by her gender, the Duchess of Marlborough regularly and forcefully expressed herself through her architectural schemes. This was made possible by her incredible affluence, which was accrued predominately through her own tireless efforts, making her one of the wealthiest women in England, worth over £1 million – approximately £130 million today.[55] Such was her financial power that she 'held a controlling interest in the national debt' and on more than one occasion the 'fate of the Bank of England lay in her hands'.[56]

As a result of her immense wealth, privileged social status and unfailing self-confidence, the Duchess was easily able to engage with building projects. During her long life (she died aged eighty-four), she commissioned the remodelling of her ancestral home, Holywell House in St Albans; she managed the building of Blenheim Palace during her husband's absence; commissioned the remodelling of Ranger's Lodge in Windsor Great Park; commissioned a magnificent London town house; built a suburban villa in Wimbledon and almshouses in St Albans.[57]

It is without doubt that Sarah Churchill was a prolific patron of architecture, even when compared to male patrons of the period. To enact her many architectural visions, she naturally hired the best architects that money could buy, including William Talman, Sir Christopher Wren, Nicholas Hawksmoor, Roger Morris and Francis Smith of Warwick. These men, together with an army of talented craftsmen, allowed the Duchess to shape her surroundings and declare to the world that she was a woman of taste, power and influence. So, although we cannot consider her patronage to be the norm for eighteenth-century women, we can regard her as an outstanding example of what women could achieve architecturally when endowed with status and opportunity. As such, we will of course encounter her again in subsequent chapters.

For those women who lacked the Duchess's extraordinary social and financial resources, it was often necessary to exercise their architectural agency in subtler ways, often operating in the shadows, side-stepping, mollifying or even fawning to their male counterparts in order to succeed. Despite this, women still pursued their architectural ambitions with enthusiasm, influencing building schemes of all shapes and sizes.

The country house

The country house, the first building type to be considered within this book, was the grandest and arguably the most important type of building for eighteenth-century land-owning families. Built to reflect ideals of patriarchal wealth, status and power, it is perhaps the most surprising that women were as eager to engage with this legacy as their male contemporaries. The first chapter will show that women regularly and eagerly participated in country-house building projects and asserted their own architectural preferences. They did so for many reasons, as this book will soon explore. When it came to country-house building, women were as passionate and discerning in their architectural endeavours as their male peers and were just as influential in shaping the fabric of these magnificent buildings.

The London town house

When in town (London), grand town houses served as bustling social headquarters for the fashionable and political elite. Women were often at the heart of the social scene and built and modernized their own town houses accordingly, utilizing them as loci for social and political activity, to enhance their own social status or to launch their family members and friends into society.

The second chapter of this book will investigate the town houses of a number of remarkable women, all of whom were determined to express their architectural and aesthetic tastes in order to enhance their standing in society. The construction and modification of the London town house transcended architectural expression and was often used by women to attain concrete goals, such as making social, political and cultural statements, or to further their commercial ventures. In so doing, great sums of money were spent on hiring the best architects to create the most fashionable and luxurious homes, within which polite society could be entertained with *éclat*.

The villa

The third chapter of this book will consider the popularity of the villa amongst eighteenth-century women. To escape the commotion and pollution of London, women often leased, bought or built suburban villas, a form of residence that offered tranquillity and arcadian delight. Since villas were more private, affordable and convenient than larger country houses, women regularly used them as a platform upon which they could demonstrate their architectural sophistication, often advocating the latest in stylistic and aesthetic fashions.

In establishing a more secluded house away from society, the women discussed in this chapter were determined to satisfy their own notions of comfort, convenience and taste. Moreover, because the villa was usually separate from the patriarchal estate, they were seen by women as an attractive means by which they could provide a legacy for a younger child or female relative who would otherwise have been overlooked by primogeniture. As will be made evident, such architectural endeavours were not uncommon. The villa was, in many ways, the most accessible building that women could shape entirely according to their own desire.

The wider estate, garden design and ornamental buildings

While the country house was the nucleus of patriarchal authority, the wider estate played an essential role in the presentation of wealth, status and architectural discernment. Estate buildings, ranging from schools to family churches, were just as important in the expression of dynastic power and legacy. This, together with carefully landscaped gardens, beautiful parks and fashionable follies, signalled erudition and taste. As will be explored in this final chapter, women also enjoyed augmenting their estates, parks and gardens. They commissioned fashionable landscape designers to transform their parks, they built schools and almshouses to show their benevolence, and they erected ornamental diaries, grottoes and Chinese temples to beautify their gardens.

* * *

Although women's legal status in eighteenth-century society was highly restrictive, this book will show that women had a practical and intellectual interest in the field of architecture. Since women could not practise as architects, it was natural for them to channel their architectural ambition into commissioning building works as highly engaged patrons. In doing so, women circumvented the societal restrictions of the age and had a substantial and enduring impact on Britain's architectural heritage.

2

The country house

The country house was traditionally promoted as the dynastic seat of a wealthy, landowning family; a power base from which they could radiate control over their lands, tenants and political interests.[1] The management of the family estate was the preserve of men, while the management of the country house was perceived as the female domain.[2] Although the role that women played within the eighteenth-century country house has received greater attention in recent decades, female architectural patronage still remains relatively obscure.

Country house architecture is inextricably intertwined with the concept of dynasty, which in the eighteenth century was defined by the system of male primogeniture. More than mere residences, country houses were manifestations of patriarchal succession and landed power. They were the canvasses upon which powerful families could display their dynastic connections, wealth, status and taste. Women, on the whole, were excluded from inheriting such country houses, which dramatically limited their opportunity to engage with country house architecture. However, despite this curtailing of opportunity, women still found numerous ways in which they could influence the design, form and decoration of the country houses in which they lived.

For instance, when one considers Blenheim Palace in Oxfordshire (Figure 2.1), the grand, palatial country house of the Marlborough family, it is often thought of as the magnificent Baroque creation of John Churchill, 1st Duke of Marlborough and his architect, Sir John Vanbrugh. After all, it only exists because a grateful nation wished to reward Marlborough, Commander-in-Chief of the Forces, for his great military victory at the Battle of Blenheim in 1704.[3] However, what is generally not remembered is that the Duchess of Marlborough was also highly influential in the building of Blenheim Palace.

Throughout the project the Duke and Duchess worked together to create a magnificent home befitting their hard-won rank and status. The Duke regularly relied on his wife to progress the building when he was

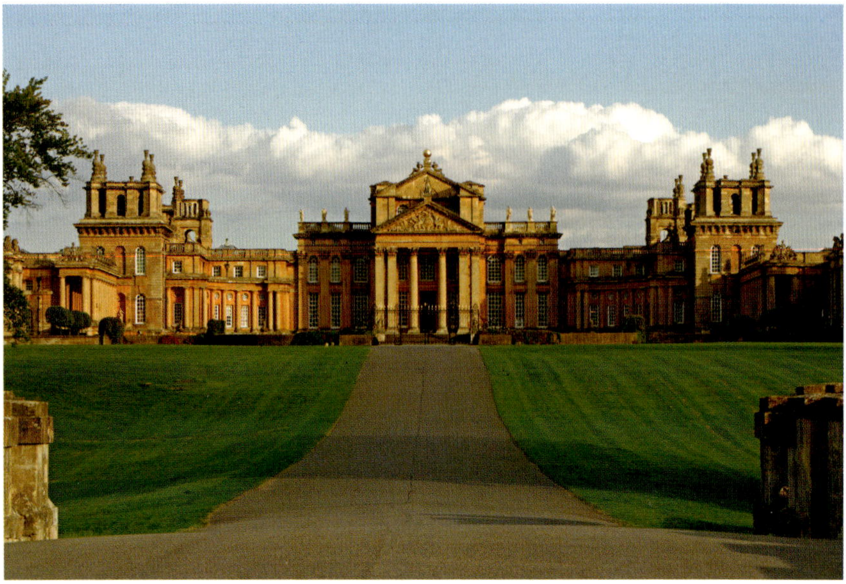

FIGURE 2.1 Blenheim Palace, Oxfordshire. DeAgostini/Getty Images.

engaged on the Continent with military duties and left many key decisions in her capable hands, much to the irritation of Vanbrugh.[4] On one occasion Marlborough wrote, 'I leave it intierly to you to order what you think is best, and what pleases you I am sure I shal like',[5] and on another, 'As to the house and bridge, whatever you judge best, I shall be well pleased with'.[6] The Duchess's architectural judgement was respected and followed indicating that although her husband was certainly the lead patron, in his absence she, *ipso facto*, assumed this role.

Sarah Churchill's influence over the building of Blenheim increased significantly when the Duke suffered a terrible stroke in 1716, which rendered him unconscious for a full three days and left him partially paralysed with impaired speech.[7] This tragedy propelled the Duchess forward in her quest to complete Blenheim as soon as possible, protecting her husband from the awful stresses that it caused. Describing the building works as a 'chaos that turns one's brains but to think of it' in *c.* 1716, Sarah only proceeded with it for her husband's sake.[8] In the midst of this turbulent time the Duchess's notoriously volatile relationship with Vanbrugh finally broke down beyond recovery, culminating in his sensational resignation on 8 November 1716, in which he vigorously defended himself against her accusations of mismanagement, wastefulness and extravagance:

> These papers Madam are so full of Far-Fetched, Labour'd Accusations, Mistaken Facts, Wrong Inferences, Groundless Jealousies and Strain'd Construction: That I shou'd put a very great affront upon our

> understanding if I suppos'd it possible you cou'd mean anything in earnest by them; but to put a Stop to my troubling you any more. You have your end, Madam, for I will never trouble you more Unless the Duke of Marlborough recovers so far, to shelter me from such intolerable Treatment.[9]

The Duchess, unmoved by Vanbrugh's actions and undaunted by the challenge of completing Blenheim, quickly assembled an elite team behind her, headed by James Moore, the cabinet-maker, who she described as 'a miracle of a man'.[10] With a focused determination and a seemingly endless vigour, she succeeded in completing the east wing sufficiently enough for the Duke to at last move in to by August 1719. Despite this remarkable effort the Duchess's beloved husband died only three years later without fully realizing his grand architectural ambition.

In his will, the late Duke dedicated a lump sum of £50,000 (about £6 million today) towards the completion of Blenheim Palace, together with £10,000 (about £1.2 million today) 'a year to Spoil Blenheim, her own way', as Vanbrugh believed.[11] The Duchess, now saddled with the hollow task of completing Blenheim alone, rehired Nicholas Hawskmoor, Vanbrugh's assistant, and together they finally finished the state apartments, stable block and chapel.

The Duchess was also determined to commemorate her husband's achievements, as well as her own, and built a huge triumphal arch (Figure 2.2)

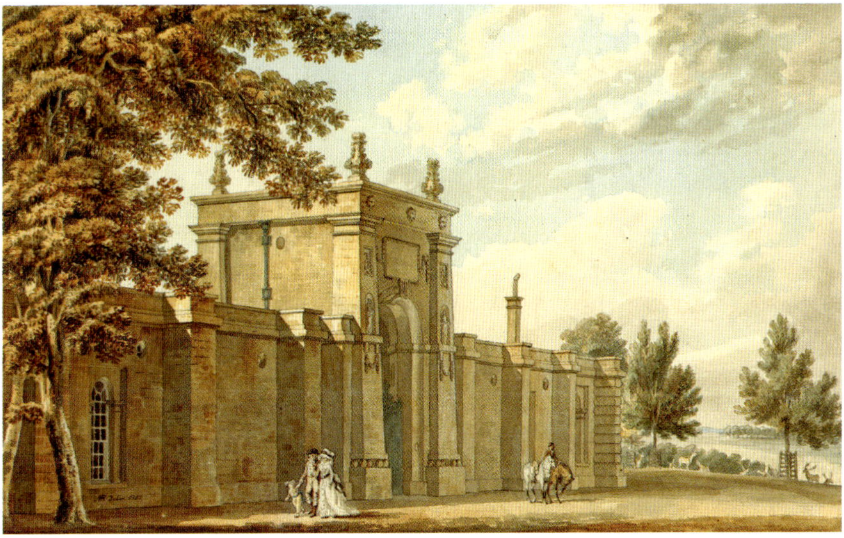

FIGURE 2.2 Michael 'Angelo' Rooker, *The Gate at Blenheim*, 1787, watercolour and grey ink. Yale Center for British Art, Paul Mellon Collection, B1986.29.463. Courtesy of the Yale Center for British Art, Yale University.

as an appropriate entrance to the park, on which she recorded her own instrumental involvement:

> This gate was built the year after the death of the most illustrious John Duke of Marlborough by order of Sarah his most beloved wife to whom he left the sole direction of many things that remained unfinished to this fabric.

She proudly proclaimed that it was she, and not Henrietta Godolphin, her estranged daughter and heir, who brought Blenheim to its conclusion. Known for her difficult relationship with her daughters and grandchildren (which caused her to re-write her will twenty-six times) this prominent and very public inscription also allowed the Duchess to further bolster her own architectural legacy.[12]

The themes exhibited in the Duchess of Marlborough's narrative, in which she oversaw the construction of a patriarchal country seat, exerted her influence over its design and finished the building project after her husband's death, are also present in the stories of many other elite eighteenth-century women. This chapter, therefore, will explore the impact that women had on country house architecture, beginning with those instances where women possessed the least opportunity and influence, and culminating with examples of women who, by virtue of their marital status, social standing and financial situation, wielded complete control over country house design and construction.

First and foremost, a woman's ability to engage with the fabric of the country house was strongly determined by her marital status. The least likely category of woman to make any discernible impact upon the country house was the unmarried daughter, as she was usually utterly dependent upon her father (or male relative) for everything. Nevertheless, even within these restrictive circumstances some women still endeavoured to influence country house architecture. This often manifested itself in the form of superintending works commissioned by their male relatives. By acting as a deputy, women were still provided with the chance to shape their homes, despite not allowing for individual architectural expression.

In contrast, the architectural opportunities available to married women were far greater, as the creation of the marital home was often a collaborative affair between husband and wife. Within this context, interior design was the predominant avenue through which wives could influence the aesthetic of the patriarchal country house. Interior decoration could vary substantially in scope, ranging from the introduction of new wallpaper through to the encompassing of major architectural elements, such as the insertion of new walls, staircases, chimneypieces, ceilings and doors.

Similarly, when a new country house was commissioned or when an existing house was substantially remodelled, spousal collaboration was often integral to the success of the project. Husbands and wives discussed, argued and collaborated over every design aspect of their new houses. They talked with architects and craftsmen and debated with family and friends, all with the aim of building a country house that was modern, fashionable and comfortable. In the creation of such houses some wives dutifully limited their architectural scope to the interiors, while others eagerly and forcefully pushed for their preferred architectural scheme to be commissioned.

In the few instances in which a woman inherited her family's ancestral seat (in the absence of a male heir) the task of maintaining, improving or remodelling the seat fell to her. If she was married, a degree of spousal compromise was needed, as her inheritance was legally controlled by her husband. If unmarried or widowed, a woman's architectural scope was limited only by the amount of money she was able to or wished to spend. As will become apparent, heiresses felt a keen sense of familial pride regardless of marital status and were just as eager as their male peers to improve their ancestral seats. In doing so, they were conscious of honouring their ancestors' architectural legacies, whilst also immortalizing their own contributions through the inclusion of inscriptions, monograms and coats of arms. Indeed, under these circumstances, women played an integral role in the shaping of their country houses and were crucial in ensuring their long-term survival.

Lastly, the many and varied ways in which widows influenced country house architecture will be explored. Firstly, in some instances widowed women could inherit their late husband's estates for the remainder of their lives, providing them with unprecedented architectural opportunity. This was sometimes coupled with the formidable responsibility of completing their husband's palatial country seats, an undertaking which could take years to complete. Secondly, when the heir to an estate had not yet reached his majority, the management of his lands and houses often fell to his widowed mother. In these cases, women were conscientious about protecting their son's inheritance and engaged in country house building only as a means of enhancing the patriarchal estate. Thirdly, when they had the desire to do so, widows often chose to build or remodel country houses (dower houses) for their own personal use. In doing so they confidently pursued their own architectural and aesthetic agendas. Across this spectrum of opportunity widows could vastly influence the design and form of the country houses in which they lived.

Chatelaine of a male relative's country house

While marital status played a pivotal role in a woman's standing in society, marriage was not a universal state in eighteenth-century Britain. Often, women were relegated to the undignified shelf of spinsterhood due to circumstance rather than choice, perhaps caused by their lack of a dowry, the inclination of their family or the paucity of suitable men. Their single status placed them at the bottom of the pecking order, sometimes condemning them to a life of familial dependency and exploitation.

In some rare instances, however, unmarried women were presented with the opportunity to run the households of their unmarried male relatives. When Sir Francis Willoughby gained control of his estate in 1687, he asked his seventeen-year-old sister, Cassandra (1670–1735), to manage Wollaton Hall, Nottingham, for him, which she did until her marriage in 1713 (Figure 2.3).[13] Cassandra's role as mistress of the house was emancipating, as she herself acknowledged, 'This proposall I was much delighted with, thinking it would be no small pleasure for me to be Mrs of Wollaton, and to doe whatever I had a mind to'.[14] As mistress of Wollaton, Cassandra not only had the same social status as a married woman, but she also had the opportunity to engage with architecture for the first time. Wollaton, an impressive Elizabethan house designed by the prominent architect Robert Smythson, had been vacant since 1643 and was in great need of repair. However, it was not until 1688, when her younger brother Thomas inherited the house, that a series of improvements were commissioned.[15] Cassandra was integral to this rebuilding project, overseeing the works and ordering new suites of furniture from London.[16] Although unable to commission architectural works in her own name, Cassandra's contributions to Wollaton Hall were significant.

A similar situation occurred with the Hon. Anne Robinson (1742–after 1812), a single lady who held the prestigious position as chatelaine of Saltram House, Devon, for over twenty years. Anne was the daughter of Thomas Robinson, 1st Baron Grantham, of Newby Park, Yorkshire, and Frances Worsley. Following the untimely death of her younger sister Theresa Parker in 1775, Anne was invited by her brother-in-law, John Parker, later 1st Baron Boringdon, to become mistress of Saltram and surrogate mother to his two young children. Before her death, Anne's sister had been heavily involved in redesigning Saltram's interiors, working with Robert Adam to create a sumptuous suite of fashionable rooms, complete with appropriate artwork.[17] Indeed, Lord Boringdon was a country squire at heart, more interested in the pursuit of game and the breeding of his racehorses, than in the minutiae of interior design. When Lord Boringdon died in 1788, Anne continued as chatelaine for her nephew, John 'Jack' Parker, for the rest of her life.

Throughout her time at Saltram, Anne ran the household and directed various forms of maintenance and improvements. In July 1791, while her nephew was away on his Grand Tour, she ordered a series of minor repairs to Saltram, in which she took great pride:

> I have a long story to tell about the repairs of this House ... I have compromised, and agreed with Mr Parlby that only the south west front, of the south Bow, shall be new done entirely from top to bottom and the sashes of the upper floor to be painted outside ... so that at the moment we are all litter and scaffolding and stink.[18]

Later, when Jack reached his majority in 1794, he soon set about adding his own aesthetic to Saltram, the direction of which he often left to his capable

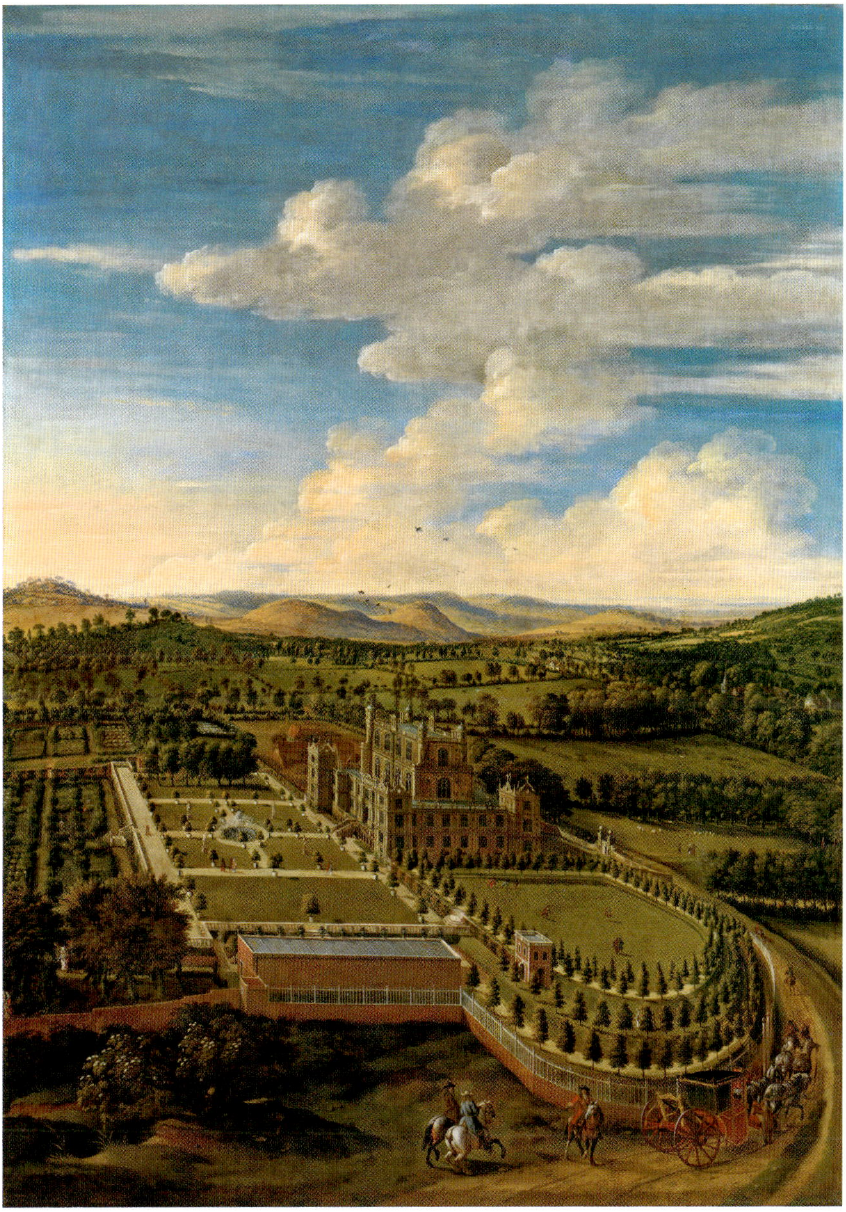

FIGURE 2.3 Jan Siberechts, *Wollaton Hall and Park, Nottinghamshire,* 1697, oil on canvas. Yale Center for British Art, Paul Mellon Collection, B1973.1.52. Courtesy of the Yale Center for British Art, Yale University.

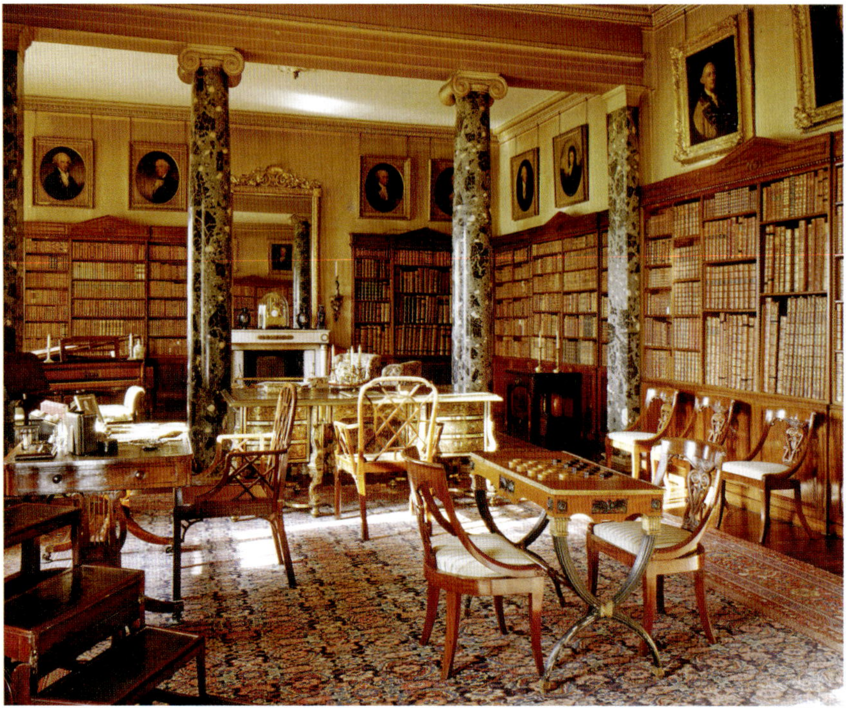

FIGURE 2.4 The Library at Saltram House, Devon. Photo: Andreas von Einsiedel/ Getty Images.

aunt. Anne was delighted with the flurry of activity, joyfully writing that 'I am very busy, or at least think so, in superintending a great work which is nothing more than the entire allteration of the library' (Figure 2.4).[19] She further details every aspect of the alteration, which included a new chimney piece and new bookcases 'to make more room for the books'.[20] Although Anne was greatly limited in her architectural influence, she evidently possessed an interest and took great enjoyment in the orchestration of Saltram's architectural schemes. Both Anne's and Cassandra's limited participation suggests that even within the most conventional of circumstances, women were able to interact with the architecture of country houses. They both eagerly embraced the opportunity to improve their respective country houses and each felt invigorated by the challenge.

Interior decoration

Just as the unmarried Cassandra Willoughby and Anne Robinson enjoyed exerting their limited influence over the improvements of their country houses, married women also endeavoured to participate by introducing new decorative schemes to their homes. On entering their role as the new mistress of the patriarchal country seat, it was often expected that a new wife would want to exert her taste upon its interior decorative scheme.[21] The benefit of this was twofold: firstly, it provided the perfect opportunity to update outmoded décor from previous generations, and secondly, it allowed the wife to create an aesthetic of her choosing. The timescale for this could vary significantly, from immediately after the wedding to years later, depending on the family's financial situation, social commitments, and personal interest. Equally, when a new family home was purchased, the task of making the interiors tasteful and comfortable fell to the wife. For example, when the Scottish businessman Sir Lawrence Dundas bought Aske Hall in Yorkshire from Lord Holdernesse, he left the interior design and furnishing entirely to his wife Margaret, Lady Dundas (1715/16–1802), daughter of Alexander Bruce of Kennet:

> I beg you will take time and look minutely through every part of the house to see what is wanted; some of the furniture is old and should be changed, particularly the Yellow Silk Drawing room below stairs, but everything of this sort I leave to your taste which is the best I ever met with.[22]

Lady Dundas was responsible for examining every room in detail, including the state of the soft furnishings, the quality of the furniture and the tastefulness of the ornamentation. Every chimney piece, ceiling, door, window, wall and piece of furniture would have been carefully examined by Lady Dundas to check whether it needed to be repaired, replaced or beautified. Such a task fell within the female domain and was one that allowed women to express themselves artistically, display their fashionable taste and ultimately shape the country houses that they inhabited.

Naturally, the extent to which women were involved in the process of interior design varied depending on their character. For many, the chance to direct and oversee every aspect was an liberating experience. When Mary Delany (1700–88), daughter of Colonel Bernard Granville and Mary Westcombe, married her second husband, Dr Patrick Delany, she was delighted to redecorate her new marital home, Delville House, located outside Dublin. Writing to her sister Anne, in 1744, Mary gushed about the hive of activity under her control: 'I have workmen of all sorts in the house – upholsterers, joiners, glaziers, and carpenters – and am obliged to watch them all, or their work would be but ill-finished'.[23] We can imagine Mary walking from room to room checking the progress of her workmen and correcting them when she spotted something amiss. Mary directed absolutely everything, including the colour of the rooms, which for her 'English room' she chose 'a sort of olive ... for the sake of my pictures, because the room is very light'.[24] For the ornamentation she ordered the frieze to be 'painted with festoons of flowers and shells alternate'.[25]

Throughout her marriage, Mary continuously updated the interiors, with her most ambitious shellwork project taking place in 1759 when she decorated her husband's private chapel:

> My chief works have been the ceiling of the chapel, which I have formerly described, done with cards *and shells* in imitation of stucco. In the chancel are four Gothic arches, two on each side, made *also of shells* in imitation stucco, that arches no deeper than the thickness of the shells, to take off the plain look the walls would have without them. The wreath round the window is composed of oak-branches and vines made of cards; the *grapes*, *nuts*, and *large periwinkles*, the corn, *real wheat* painted, all to look like stucco.[26]

Mary's enthusiasm for interior design and her love for and mastery of shellwork provided her with constant occupation. Her autonomy over the decorative scheme at Delville was absolute and permitted her to actively influence the aesthetic of her home, imprinting it with her own personality and stylistic judgement. This agency was shared by many of Mary's contemporaries, who utilized it to introduce the latest fashions into their musty, tired country houses.

When Emily FitzGerald, Countess of Kildare (1731–1814) (later Marchioness of Kildare and then Duchess of Leinster), daughter of Charles Lennox, 2nd Duke of Richmond and his wife Sarah Cadogan, was visiting London in 1757, she was jealous of the fine, fashionable interiors that her family and friends had. She wrote discontentedly to her husband, James FitzGerald (created Marquess of Kildare in 1761 and then 1st Duke of Leinster in 1766), lamenting the decorative state of Irish houses, including their own, Carton House, in Co. Kildare:

> My Jemmy, won't you have the bookcases taken down at Carton and the moulding carved, ready to put up in the new library. I shall long to go about it the minute I come, for I shall wish to have our house look *sprucish*. Every mortal's house here is so pretty, and smart, and well furnish'd, that I do long to have ours so too a little.[27]

Now a decade into her marriage and with six children (two had sadly died), Lady Kildare was impatient to update Carton House to suit her taste. A woman of persuasive talents, Lady Kildare was not one to be refused by her husband, and thus two years later she was busily engaged in updating the interiors with new wallpapers and reupholstered furniture:

> [T]his morning I am setting out for Carton, where I hope to find a great deal done in my absence ... My dear Lord Kildare, don't let Louisa [her younger sister] forget the India paper, and if you see any you like buy it at

> once, for that I have will never hold out for more than three rooms, and you know we have four to do; for I have set my heart upon that which opens to the garden being done, for 'tis certainly now our best and only good living room. I really think Carton House when 'tis spruced up will be vastly pretty and full as fine as I wou'd ever wish a country house to be. I have seized upon the blue paper that was for the great room here. Don't be angry, you may have enough for that before winter, and it will make one of the middle apartments at Carton so pretty, with the fine chintz furniture lined with blue silk, that I have taken out of the old beds.[28]

Despite her husband's reluctance to overspend, Lady Kildare's interiors were lavish and adventurous. Her 'India paper' refers to a beautiful hand-painted Chinese wallpaper that depicts scenes of everyday life and landscapes.[29] The Chinese or Chinoiserie aesthetic was highly popular in Britain and Ireland in the mid-eighteenth century and was fuelled by the exploits and adventures of trading companies, such as the East India Company.[30] The luxury imports they brought back from China, Japan and other Asian countries, including wallpapers, textiles, porcelain and lacquerware, together with publications such as Jean Baptiste du Halde's *A Description of the Empire of China* (1736 and 1738–41), succeeded in popularizing a world that was perceived as exciting and exotic.

Lady Kildare's Chinese wallpaper was intended for a family drawing room, and was cut by her into panels, ovals and cartouches and then pasted directly onto the walls and surrounded by intricate Chinese borders. The room was completed with an ornate gilded Rococo overmantle beautifully carved with little brackets that would once have held decorative Chinese jars and figurines.[31] The overall effect was, and still is, complex, sophisticated and dazzling. Lady Kildare's Chinese room is the earliest extant example of this form of decoration in Ireland, which signifies that her taste was very much *en vogue* for the period.

Lady Kildare's younger sister, Lady Louisa Conolly (1743–1821) (Figure 2.5), was equally instrumental in the decorative scheme of her marital home, Castletown House, located just a few miles away (Figure 2.6). Following her marriage to Thomas Conolly in 1758, she arrived at Castletown to find the interiors incomplete and hopelessly outdated, having been barely touched for thirty years.[32] Lady Louisa immediately sought to change this and, aged only fifteen, embarked upon a major redecoration campaign that would last throughout the 1760s and 1770s. Under her direction, a grand cantilevered staircase was inserted into the double-height space located beyond the entrance hall, complete with ornate brass banisters (Figure 2.7).[33] The beautiful Rococo plasterwork that adorns the walls was executed by the Swiss-Italian Lafranchini brothers, who had also worked for her sister at Carton House.[34] Stucco cameos of Lady Louisa and her

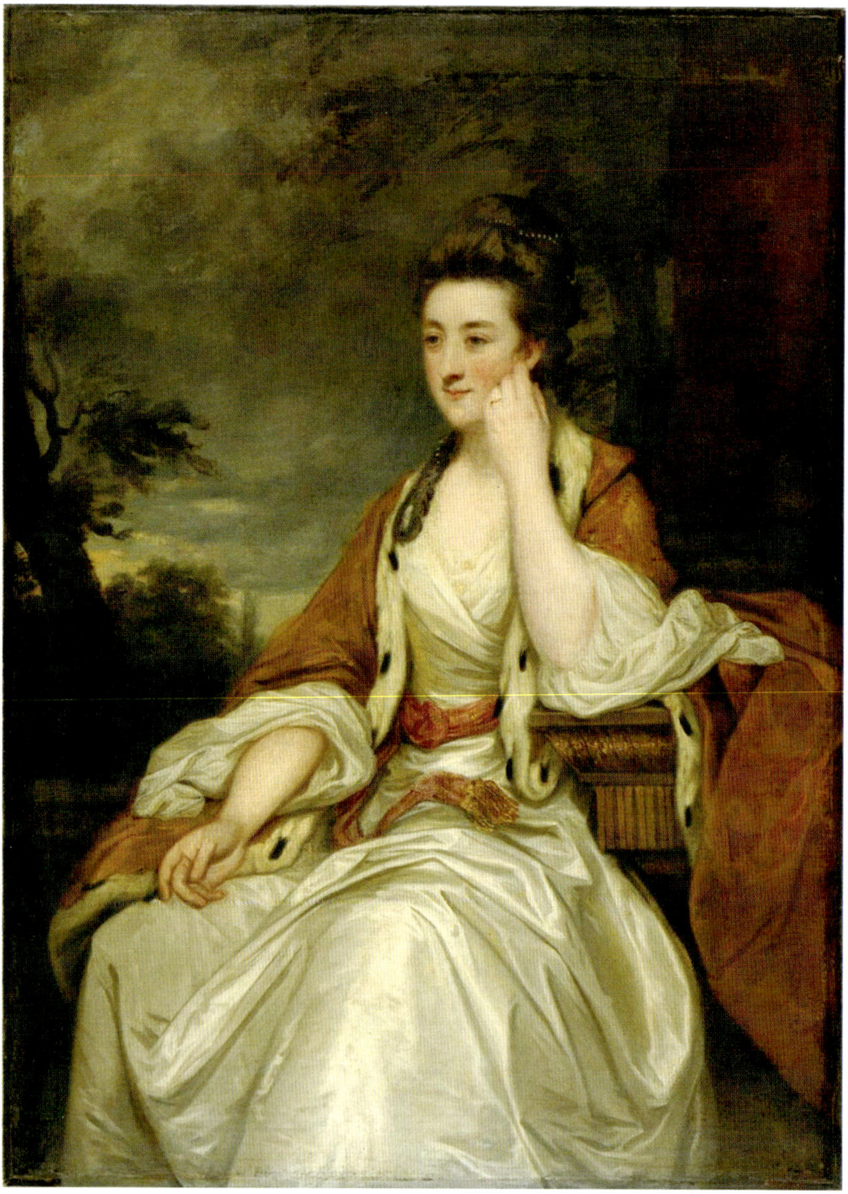

FIGURE 2.5 Sir Joshua Reynolds, *Lady Louisa Conolly,* 1775, oil on canvas. Harvard Art Museums, 1970.112. Photo: Danvis Collection/Alamy Stock Photo.

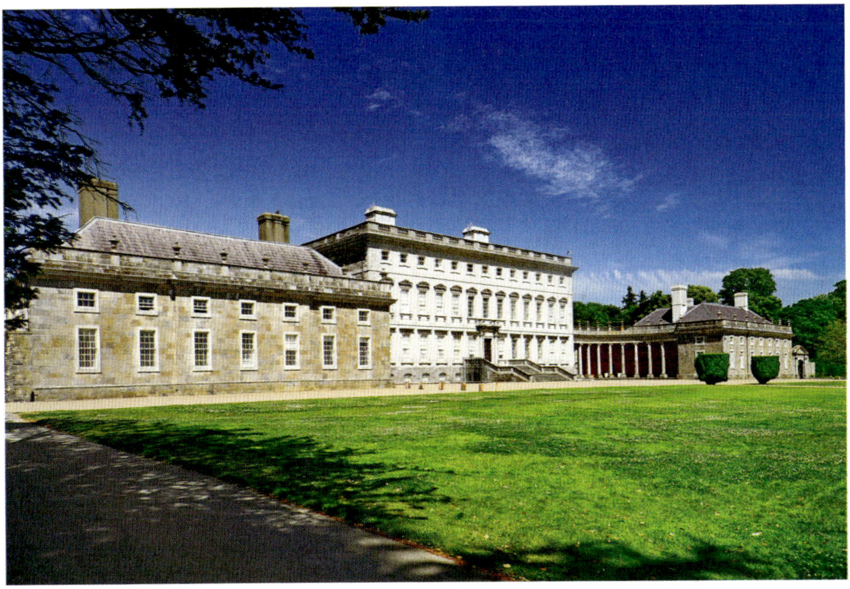

FIGURE 2.6 Castletown House, Co. Kildare. Photo: Eye Ubiquitous/Getty Images.

husband, Thomas Conolly, sit at the head of the stairs, opposite whom are cameos of her sister, Lady Kildare, and her husband, and on the adjacent wall sits a cameo of Lady Sarah Lennox, their younger sister.[35] The inclusion of her own family members represents Lady Louisa's personalization of Castletown and was an effective way of weaving herself and her inner circle into the fabric of the building.

Lady Louisa was responsible for every detail of the project, directing the insertion of new sashes, shutters, mahogany doors, carved architraves, doorcases, cornices, friezes and dado rails, particularly for the dining room and the red and green drawing rooms. The new decorative scheme was strictly Neo-Classical, the designs for which have been attributed to Sir William Chambers.[36] As well as furnishing her new rooms with luxury furniture, Lady Louisa also reinvigorated existing objects, including the picture frames which she re-gilded in the dining room, gleefully telling Lady Sarah: 'this finishing work is very entertaining, I am as busy as a Bee, and that you know is mighty pleasant'.[37]

One of Lady Louisa's greatest aesthetic triumphs, however, was the creation of the Pompeian Long Gallery on the first floor, with its sumptuous painted walls inspired by the ancient Roman decorative schemes discovered at Pompeii and Herculaneum (Figure 2.8). In 1773 when vising her brother, the 3rd Duke of Richmond, at Goodwood House, Lady Louisa observed Charles Reuben Riley's (*c.* 1752–98) work in the library. Riley (also Ryley)

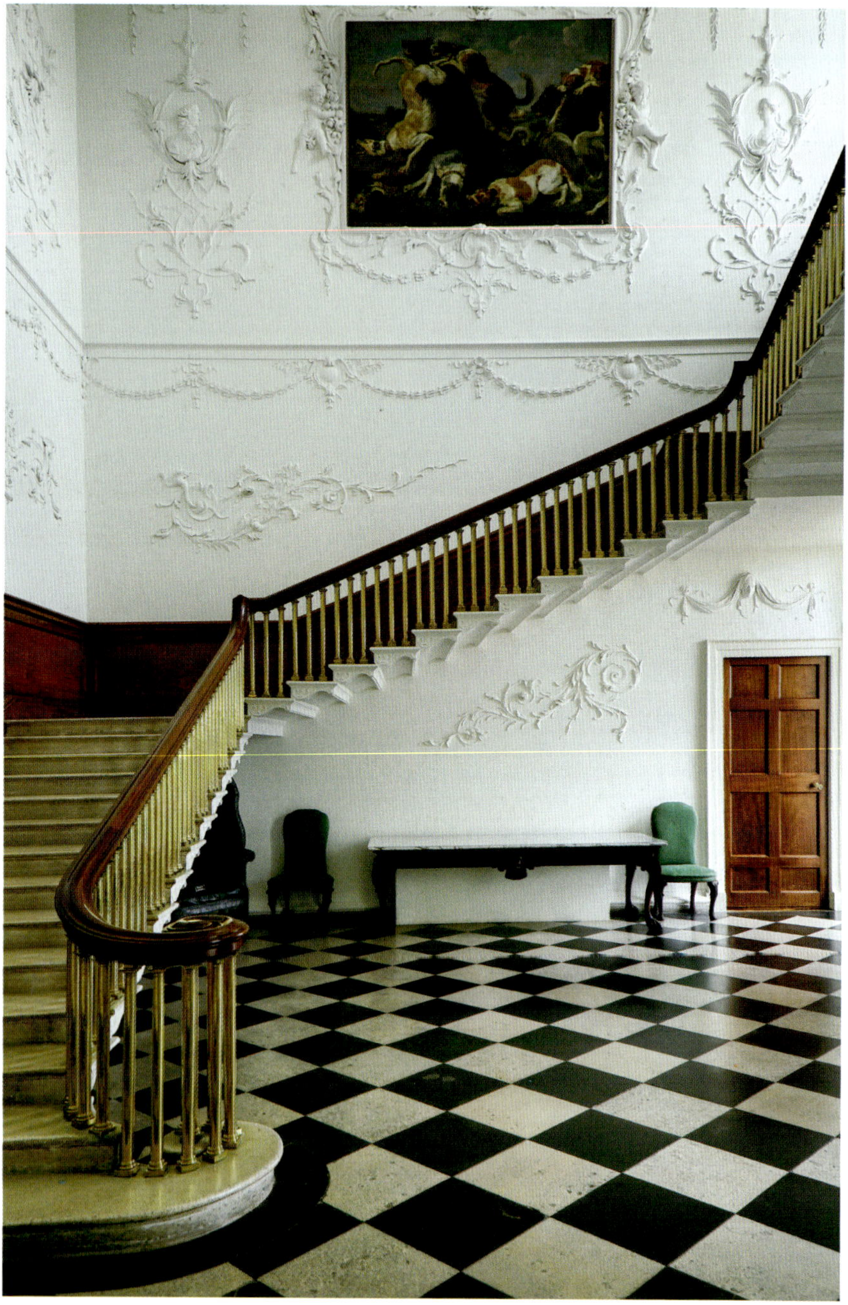

FIGURE 2.7 The staircase at Castletown House. Photo: Hugh Rooney/Alamy Stock Photo.

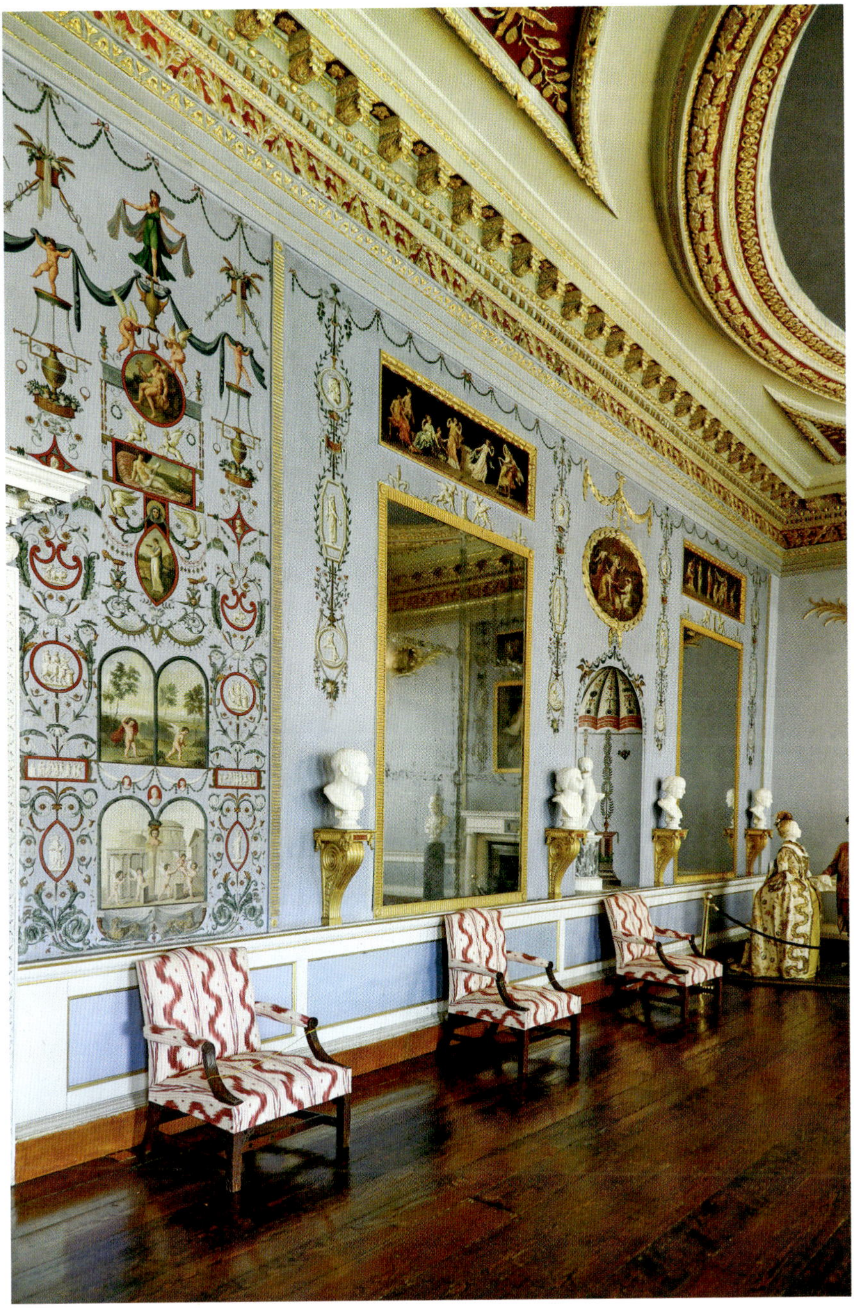

FIGURE 2.8 The Long Gallery at Castletown House. Photo: Hugh Rooney/Alamy Stock Photo.

worked as a decorative painter in the latest Neo-Classical tradition. Lady Louisa instantly fell in love with his style, writing that the library was 'to my taste ... one of the prettiest rooms I ever saw' and that 'if Mr Conolly approves, I shall wish mightily to finish our gallery in the same manner'.[38] She made her brother solemnly promise to send Riley over to Ireland once he was finished at Goodwood, but the Duke was slow in doing so and even a year later Lady Louisa was still waiting:

> I wish my brother would send me Mr Reily for I am impatient to get our room finished; Six weeks or two months are as long as I should want him what has been done is in the style you intended it, for I have painted the ceiling in scarlet grey and white and gold and it really looks much better than I expected. If I am not to go to England pray send me Mr Reily directly je petille d'impatinece.[39]

Eventually Riley came over in the Spring of 1775 and began work, assisted by Thomas Ryder (1746–1810), painting the gallery 'in the most beautiful way'.[40] Lady Louisa involved her younger sister in the design of the gallery's murals, joyfully writing that 'Sarah's taste in putting the ornaments together, and mine in picking them out, so that *we* flatter ourselves that it must be charming, as Mr Riley executes them so well'.[41] The sisters would have spent hours and hours poring over the latest books relating to the excavations at Pompeii and Herculaneum, such as Bernard de Montfaucon's fifteen volumes of *L'antiquité expliquée et représentée en figures* (1719–24). Even their nephew, the Marquess of Kildare, while on his Grand Tour in Italy, sent back books to provide further decorative inspiration for his aunts. In 1767 he wrote of his desire to purchase 'the book of Etruscan vases' as he thought it would be a 'pleasant book to dip in, as there [are] very pretty figures, and vases to draw from', which he thought his aunt would appreciate, 'I am sure it is a sort of think she would like, as she is fond of pretty ornaments, etc'.[42]

The iconographical programme of the gallery consisted of themes of love, marriage and family; a happy reflection upon the Conollys' successful marriage. Above each fireplace, situated at either end of the gallery, were portraits of Lady Louisa, by Sir Joshua Reynolds (1775), and Tom Conolly, by Anton Raphael Mengs (1758); a further representation of their equal and blissful marriage. Significantly, throughout the whole course of the redecoration, Tom Conolly was content to trust his young wife's stylistic judgment. In fact, even when he did think an alternative aesthetic arrangement might be better, he only ventured an opinion when asked:

> I am doing much more than I intended, that pretty grey, white and gold look that I admired in the ends of the room, did look a little naked by the painted compartment when finished, upon asking Mr Conolly's opinion

> about it, he meekly told me, he had always thought it would be much prettier to have painting, but thought I knew best. Did you ever hear anything so humble?[43]

Such a charming exchange amply indicates that Conolly was more than happy to let his wife transform their home to suit her taste. Indeed, Lady Louisa's decorative exploits, together with Mary Delany's and Lady Kildare's, demonstrate that, while women were constrained by a lack of opportunity and by the restrictive ideals of femininity, they eagerly and skilfully undertook interior design projects to imbue their surroundings with their own distinct personalities. The scale of such projects could be vast and entirely transformative, thereby allowing the patroness to exert considerable influence over their country house aesthetic. These ventures were exciting and were widely discussed amongst female correspondents, indicating that women enjoyed the social and intellectual aspects of such endeavours.

Spousal collaboration in the creation of country houses

Whereas interior design was usually considered to fall within the female sphere of influence, the decisions relating to the architectural design and plan form of a country house have traditionally been seen as the male preserve. Sometimes, however, when a married couple were in pursuit of a new or updated country seat, the design process was regularly a shared enterprise between husband, wife and architect. For example, on 17 June 1809, Sir John Soane went to Coombe House to visit the 2nd Earl of Liverpool, presumably to discuss architectural plans, and 'breakfasted with [both] Lord and Lady Liverpool', indicating that Louisa, Lady Liverpool (1767–1821), was engaged in the process from the beginning.[44] Indeed, a few years later in September 1813, Soane went to visit Lady Liverpool alone where he 'shew'd her the proposed alterations'.[45]

Such collaboration between husband and wife in the architectural process was the norm in many instances. Considering that the building or remodelling of a country house was no small undertaking, it is understandable that married couples would work together to achieve their vision. Within this context women were able to influence building schemes to suit their needs and design preferences. As such, there are numerous examples of wives liaising with architects directly, of wives taking sole control over building projects during their husbands' absence and of husbands deferring to their wives' desires and opinions in the design process.

An excellent example of this cooperative approach to country house building is the marriage of Frances (Fanny) Boscawen (1719–1805), and her

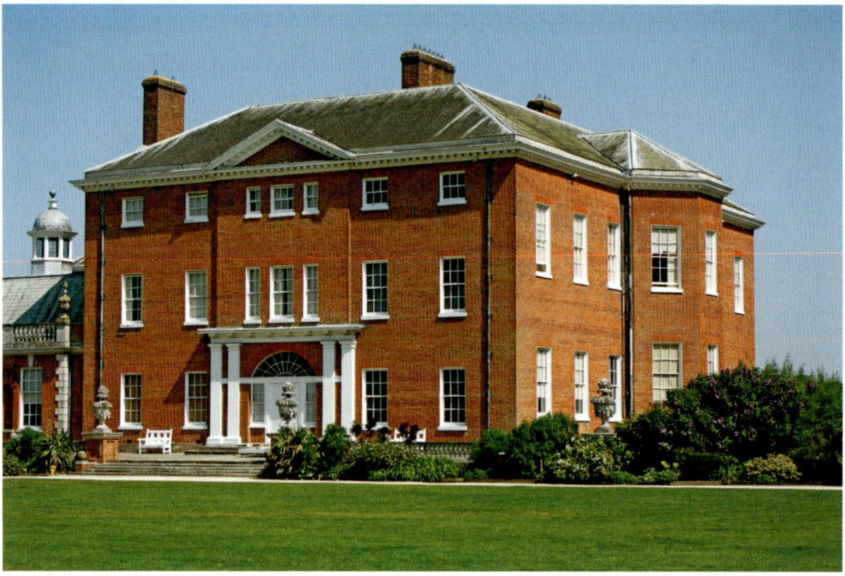

FIGURE 2.9 Hatchlands Park, Surrey. Photo: Hugh Rooney/Alamy Stock Photo.

husband, the renowned naval officer, Admiral Edward Boscawen. Born in 1791, Fanny was the daughter of William Evelyn and Frances Glanville; she married Edward in 1742. Whilst her husband was at sea, Fanny directed and managed the building of their new country seat, Hatchlands Park in Surrey (Figure 2.9). During the spring of 1756, preparations for building were well underway, with Fanny acting as the crucial lynchpin between her husband and their potential architect, Stiff Leadbetter. Whilst aboard the 74-gun ship, the *Invincible*, Boscawen wrote of his hope that Fanny had managed to commission Leadbetter, because 'if we get Mr. Ledbeater to promise, we may hope to have a comfortable house'.[46] Leadbetter proved harder to pin down than expected, but Fanny was instrumental in eventually securing his services for their country house, just as Boscawen was instrumental in securing the funds: 'I flatter myself to make the French pay for this building this summer.'[47]

In the building of Hatchlands, Fanny was happy for her husband to take the architectural lead and diligently ensured that his specification was followed by Leadbetter. She managed the whole project, liaising with their architect and sourcing building materials when necessary: 'I have agreed for 50,000 bricks brought in from Peas Marsh at 25 sh. pr. thousand' which 'was a shilling cheaper than I expected to get them'.[48] The construction of Hatchlands was thus a collaborative project that suited both husband and wife. A letter from Edward dated August 1756 specifies a clear distinction in their roles:

> I am very sensible in your condescension in letting me have the direction of our building, and much more so for you owning you do not understand

> it. Most wives meddle with all concerns, understanding or not. In return, you shall have the principal hand in furnishing, that is in directing all that is to be new.[49]

Fanny, at some point, had declared that she did not understand the principles of architecture, which allowed him to take charge of the design and plan form. In exchange, Fanny was to have sole control over the interior design, an arrangement that conformed to the gendered norms of the time. Fanny's proclamation that she did not understand architecture can be readily understood as a concerted effort on her part not to stray outside the bounds of feminine propriety. Indeed, Fanny's professed ignorance is almost certainly affected modesty, bearing in mind that she was a prominent member of the Bluestocking society whose members regularly embarked upon architectural exploits of their own.

The Bluestocking society was established in the 1750s by Elizabeth Montagu (1718–1800), daughter of Matthew Robinson, and Elizabeth Vesey (*c.* 1715–91), daughter of Sir Thomas Vesey, 1st baronet, and was an informal social group of largely privileged women who placed emphasis on female education and intellectualism.[50] Bluestocking salons were held regularly by the leading members of the group, including Fanny, at which educated men and women were invited to join in rational conversations on various topics, such as the arts, literature and the natural sciences. In 1779, the prominence of the Bluestocking society was such that Richard Samuel exhibited *The Nine Living Muses in Great Britain* at the Royal Academy.[51] In this painting nine prominent Bluestockings were depicted, each presiding over a different art, sacrificing not to Apollo but to Britannia. Together these women formed a network of famous intellectuals who engaged in cultural activities, ranging from writing poetry and political pamphlets, to performing arias and exhibiting paintings.[52]

Fanny was an integral member of this group and possessed an intellectual interest in architecture. Her subscription to Robert Adam's *The Ruins of the Palace the Emperor Diocletian at Spalatro in Dalmatia* (1764) hints at a deeper interest in architecture than her husband allowed. Despite the increasing celebrity of the Bluestocking women, architectural learning, much like education in the Classical languages, was still widely seen as central to elite male culture and education, which therefore made women vulnerable to criticism and disapproval.[53] For example, when William Napier discovered that his niece, Mary Hamilton (1721–71), was learning the Classics, he begged her to 'keep it a dead secret from your most intimate friends, as well as from the rest of the World, as a Lady's being learned is commonly looked on as a great fault – even by the learned'.[54]

Fanny, it seems, was perfectly content to downplay her intelligence in order to facilitate a blissful marital dynamic. She happily directed the interior design and, as an arbiter of fashion and taste, sought to commission a decorative scheme that was fresh and innovative. The current trend for 'neo-Palladian pomposity', as she called it, did not impress Fanny, but she found Robert Adam's Neo-Classical style refreshing, describing it as one 'of simplicity improved by art and care'.[55] As such, the Boscawens' commissioned Adam for what has been described as his earliest country house commission following his return from the Grand Tour.[56] The interiors at Hatchlands, for which a number of Adam drawings survive, were a triumph of Neo-Classical decoration, enhanced with befitting nautical motifs. The ceiling of the drawing room (now the library), for instance, boasts an array of naval trophies, together with the classical figures of Neptune, Justice, Fame and Victory (Figure 2.10).[57] Such elegant and refined detailing not only looked beautiful, but also spoke of the Boscawens' accomplished taste, thereby solidifying their standing amongst elite society.

Tragically, the Boscawens did not have long to enjoy their new house because Edward suffered an attack of typhoid fever while at sea near Quiberon Bay, off the east coast of France. Although he made it back to Hatchlands, and despite Fanny's constant nursing, he died in January 1761. Fanny's loss was acute; she lived the first year of her widowhood in almost complete seclusion. For Fanny, without her husband by her side, Hatchlands irrevocably lost its appeal. Despite its fashionable interiors, she chose to re-establish herself in London, eventually selling Hatchlands in 1770. She went on to become a celebrated Bluestocking hostess, regularly holding literary salons at her Audley Street house, which she had tastefully remodelled in the 1740s.[58]

Her final tribute to her beloved husband was to commission Adam to design a funerary monument for the Church of St Michael Penkevil in Cornwall – Edward was from Cornwall and thus he was buried in the Boscawen family tomb. In commissioning this monument Fanny was conforming to a long-established tradition in which women commemorated their late relatives and themselves through funerary monuments. In the seventeenth century, for instance, Catherine Roper (d. 1625), daughter of John Seborne of Sutton St Michael, commissioned the sculptor Epiphanius Evesham to produce a glorious monument for her late husband Christopher Roper, 2nd Lord Teynham, at Lynsted in Kent.[59] Eighteenth-century women were no different, commissioning the best architects and sculptors, such as the Duchess of Marlborough who hired William Kent to design her late husband's monument for the chapel at Blenheim and engaged Michael Rysbrack to execute it.[60]

For the Admiral's monument a mixture of fourteen (unexecuted) preliminary and finished drawings of the monument survive at the Soane Museum, of five variant schemes.[61] The sheer number of drawings suggests that Fanny was a discerning patron who took considerable care in designing a suitable monument for a national hero and a beloved husband. The final scheme, as executed, featured a bust of the Admiral in Roman robes, surrounded by nautical trophies including an anchor and trident, placed upon a pedestal against a flat pyramid (Figure 2.11).[62] A large inscription written by Fanny commemorates the Admiral's life and laments his death.

Fanny Boscawen's restrained involvement in the designing of Hatchlands was a trait she shared with many of her female contemporaries. Even when

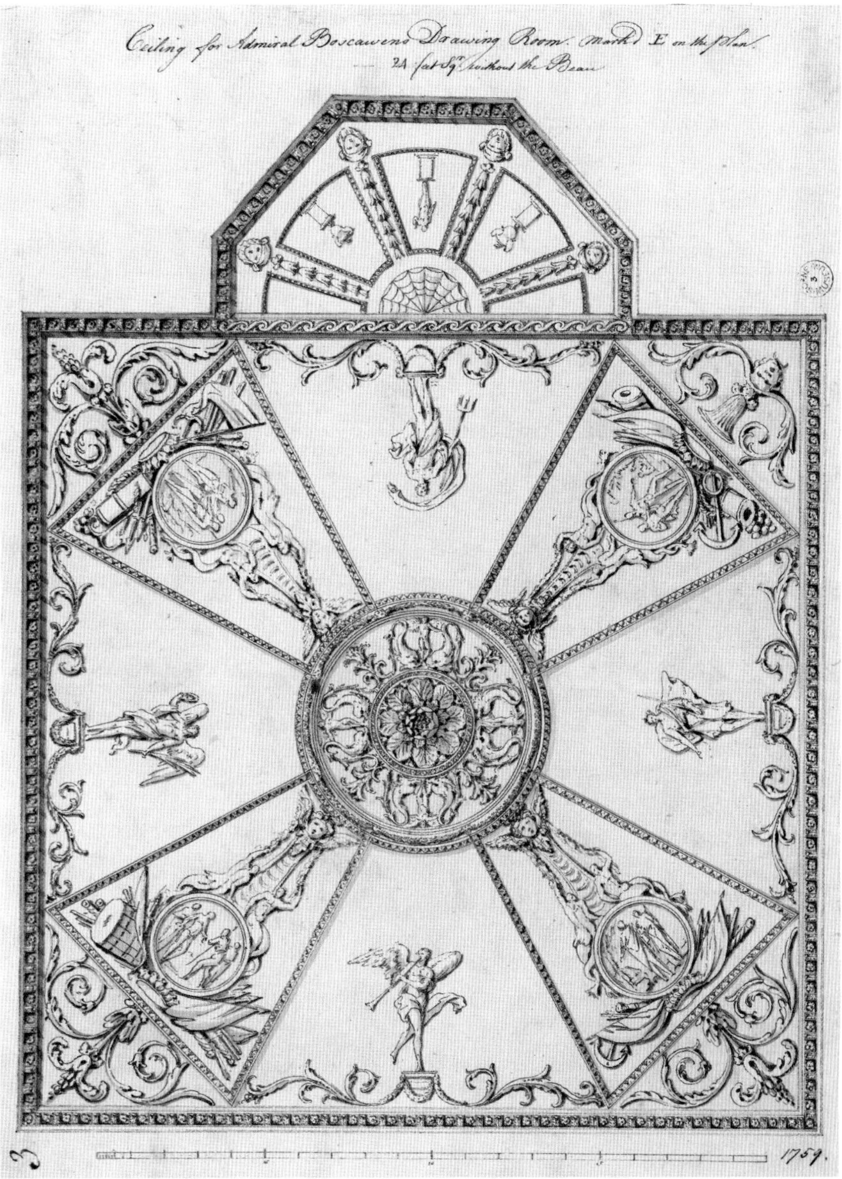

FIGURE 2.10 Adam Office hand, design for a ceiling for Admiral Boscawen's Drawing Room, as executed, 1759. SM Adam 11/3. © Sir John Soane's Museum, London. Photo: Ardon Bar-Hama.

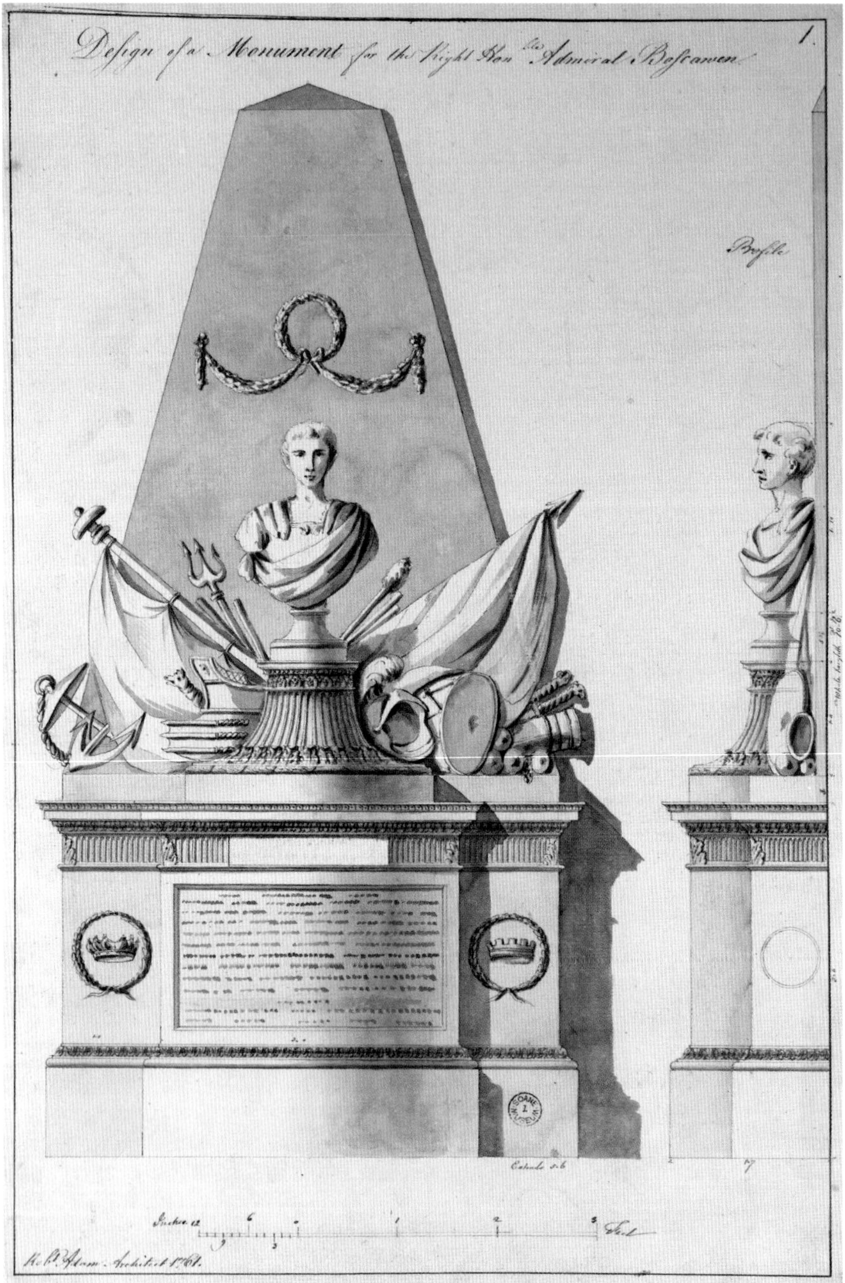

FIGURE 2.11 Robert Adam, 'Design for a Monument for the Right Hon[oura]ble Admiral Boscawen', 1761. SM Adam 19/1. © Sir John Soane's Museum, London. Photo: Ardon Bar-Hama.

women possessed a keen understanding of architecture or had experience of managing building projects, it was often assumed that their husbands would still take the lead in designing and commissioning architectural works. This was even more likely when the husband was an amateur architect who wanted to design his own country house.[63] This was the case for Thomas Robinson, 2nd Baron Grantham (brother of Theresa Parker and Anne Robinson), and his wife, Mary Robinson, Baroness Grantham (1756–1830) (Figure 2.12), who was more than happy to allow him to take charge. Lady

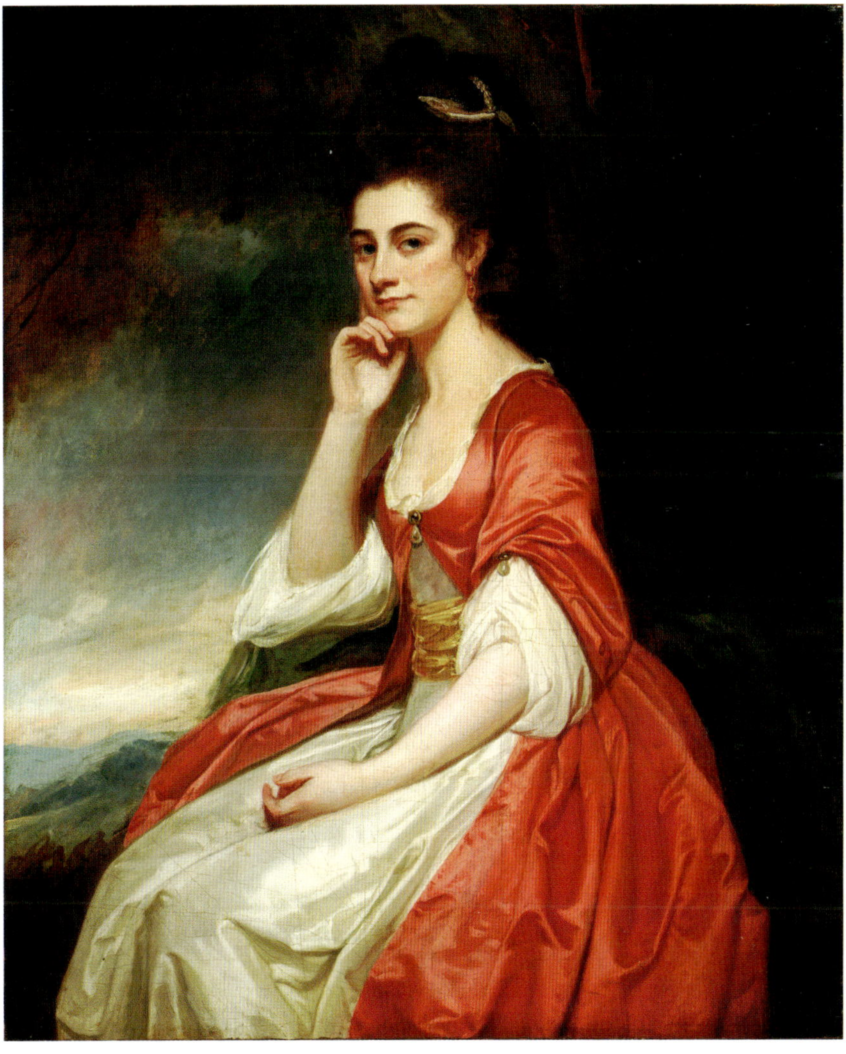

FIGURE 2.12 George Romney, *Portrait of Lady Grantham*, 1780–1, oil on canvas. Philadelphia Museum of Art: The John Howard McFadden Collection, 1928, M1928-1-36. Courtesy of the Philadelphia Museum of Art.

Grantham was the daughter of Philip Yorke, 2nd Earl of Hardwicke, and his wife, Jemima, Marchioness Grey, whom we have already briefly met.

Even though Lord Grantham took the lead on the design of their marital home, this did not diminish his wife's integral role in the remodelling of Newby Park (now Baldersby Park), Yorkshire, their marital home (Figure 2.13). In fact, due to Lord Grantham's roles as President of the Board of Trade between 1780 and 1782 and Foreign Secretary from July 1782 to April 1783, which regularly took him away to London, they appointed 'a Mr Belwood, a Yorkshire Architect', as the executant architect.[64] In her husband's absence, Lady Grantham managed the entire project, which consisted of a great number of alterations as she expressed to her sister Amabel, Lady Polwarth:

> I regret much not having shown you the plans as without them I shall make a very awkward hand at description ... among other amendments, all the windows must be covered, for with modern ideas it is impossible to bear them: a Hall of entrance will be a very good Room when boarded & covered & a very long Gallery which opens into it is to be made a Library & promises to be a very comfortable Room, & some Day or other I hope to see you take a Run in it: a very pretty Apartment over it is next year to be fitted up for me.[65]

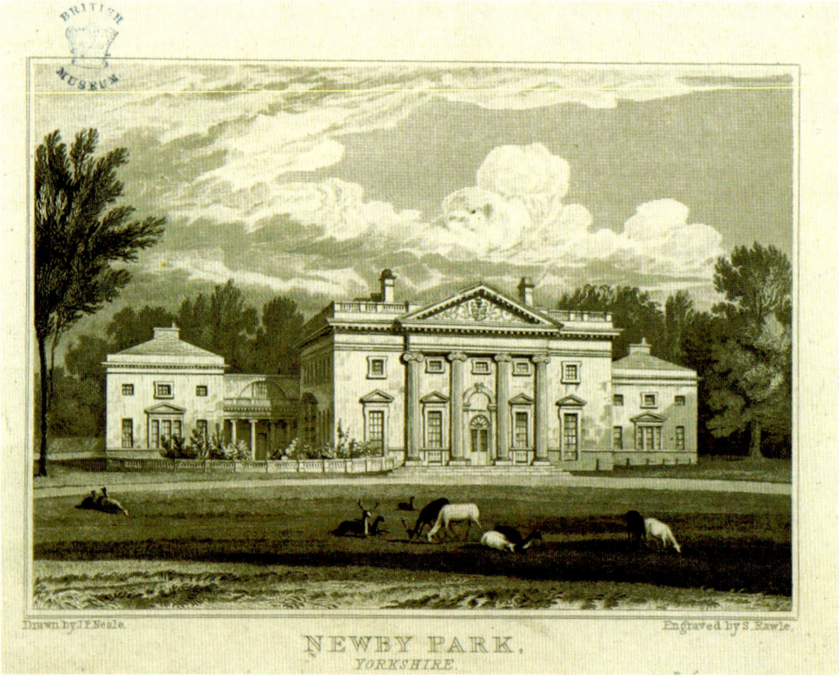

FIGURE 2.13 Samuel Rawle, after John Preston Neale, *Newby Park*, 1822, etching. Photo: Historic Images/Alamy Stock Photo.

Even when Belwood fell ill a few months later, Lady Grantham was undaunted by the challenge, and took to hastening the workmen 'as much as possible'.[66] Thus, even though the designs for the alterations were not her own, she was still the driving force behind the execution of the alterations and could therefore claim joint ownership over the modernization of Newby Park.

In 1781, however, when her new bedroom apartment was to be designed and built, Lady Grantham was naturally in charge of every detail. When describing it to her sister, she enclosed 'a miserable scrawl to give a very inadequate idea of the disposition of the rooms which are very conveniently disposed' (Figure 2.14).[67] She also included the

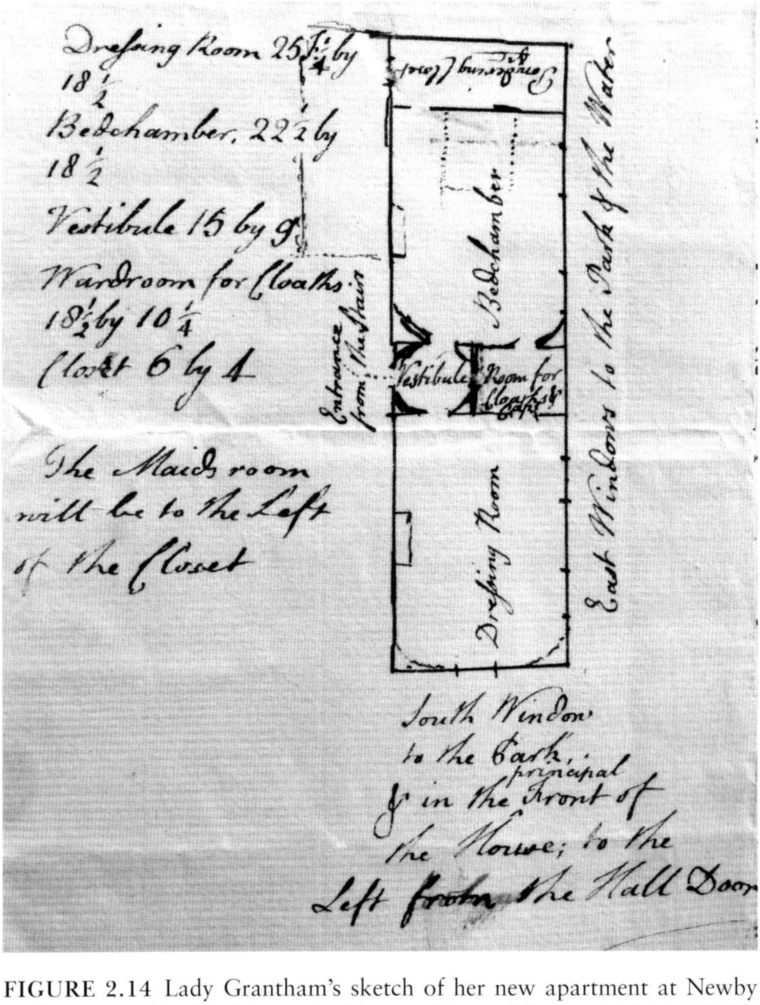

FIGURE 2.14 Lady Grantham's sketch of her new apartment at Newby Hall, 1781. Bedford and Luton Archives and Record Service, L30/11/240/18. Courtesy of the Bedford and Luton Archives and Record Service.

measurements of each room so that 'Mrs J Yorke', her aunt, 'may amuse herself in disposing them right, for I do not suppose I have kept to any proportion in the plan'.[68] This plan still survives and depicts the locations of the dressing room, bedchamber, powdering room, 'Room for Cloaks & Caps', vestibule and the maids' room. Lady Grantham also indicated the position of the windows on the south and east fronts, as well as all doorways, fireplaces, and the proposed location of her bed. Her sketch is detailed, illustrating her sense of pride and ownership over the design and execution of the apartment.

The inclusion of the plan is significant because it indicates that women of this period drew architectural plans/sketches for friends and family as a means of conveying architectural information. These plans did not require the professional's precision, but still required some level of knowledge regarding proportion and scale. By including the exact measurements, Lady Grantham demonstrated her intimate involvement in the execution of her design and provided her aunt with the means of drawing of an accurate plan.

Lady Grantham was heavily involved with shaping Newby Park into a modern, fashionable family home and by 1783, with two young sons to accommodate, she was responsible for further alterations, which among other things consisted of 'rooms for the Children, near my own, which is much wanted'.[69] However, in a terribly similar fate to that of the Boscawens at Hatchlands Park, Lord Grantham died before the great alterations could be completed, aged only forty-six. His grief-stricken widow, despite her love for Newby, packed up and took her children to London, never to live there again. It seems that for both Fanny Boscawen and Lady Grantham, they saw the building of their family homes as collaborative affairs, which could only be truly enjoyed together with their husbands. The expensive nature of running a country house may also have been a determining factor in the decision to dispose of the houses in question.

Female influence over country house design

Evidently, married women could play a crucial role in the design of country house interiors and in overseeing the construction phase of country houses. But it is also true that they could wield considerable influence over country house design in its entirety, choosing the architectural style and plan form. This level of influence tended to manifest when patronesses were especially passionate about a particular architectural style, were financing the building scheme through their dowry, or when they were simply the more forceful spouse. In the case of Elizabeth Lyttleton, Lady Lyttelton (1716–95), daughter of Sir Robert Rich, 4th baronet, and the building of Hagley Hall in Worcestershire, all three reasons applied (Figure 2.15). When her husband, Sir George Lyttelton, 5th Baronet, created 1st Baron Lyttelton in 1756,

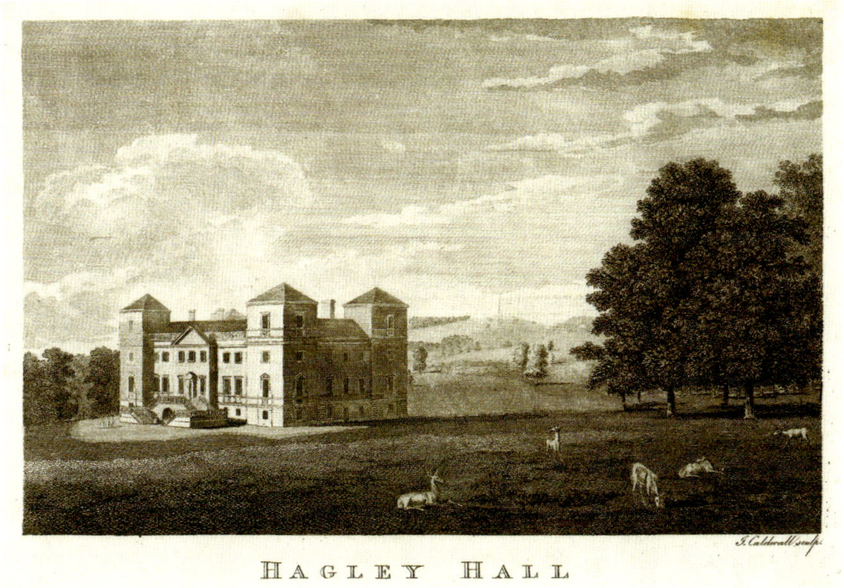

FIGURE 2.15 Print made by James Caldwall, *Hagley Hall*, undated, etching. Yale Center for British Art, Paul Mellon Collection, B1977.14.14751. Courtesy of the Yale Center for British Art, Yale University.

set about building his new country seat, his original intention to pursue a Gothic aesthetic was overruled by his wife:

> Dear Miller – Upon showing the Plan of the House to my wife she finds it so different from what she desired of Mr. Barrett, and so inconvenient in many respects, that I believe that no alterations that can be made in it will answer our purpose. We therefore desire that you will try your skill in the Greek Architecture, being persuaded that no other Gentleman Architect will have so great a regard to the convenience as you, or know so well how to give us the rooms that we want. We are pretty indifferent about the outside, it is enough if there by nothing offensive to the eye; but Lady Lyttelton insists upon dark closets and back stairs. She wishes too for a small room of separation between the eating room and the Drawing room, to hinder the Ladies from hearing the noise and talk of the Men when they are left to their bottle, which sometimes happen even at Hagley.[70]

Lady Lyttelton objected so strongly to the Gothic designs proposed by Sanderson Miller, that she prevailed upon her friend Thomas Barrett Lennard, 17th Baron Dacre, to enlist his cousin John Chute, an amateur architect who helped design Horace Walpole's Strawberry Hill House in Twickenham, to produce designs in the Classical tradition.[71] Horace

Walpole (1717–97), the youngest son of Sir Robert Walpole, was one of the eighteenth century's most famous writers, collectors and socialites. Chute, described by Walpole as 'an able geometrician and an exquisite architect, of the present taste, both in the Grecian and Gothick styles', subsequently did produce an abundance of Classical designs for Hagley Hall, presumably at Lady Lyttelton's request.[72] Chute's plans were later incorporated by Miller to create the Classical house that stands there today, built between 1754 and 1760.[73]

Lady Lyttelton's influence over the design was significant, leading Lord North to comment in 1751, that 'If an Italian House is built at Hagley, it is by my lady'.[74] Evidently, in this instance, Lady Lyttelton was responsible for changing the entire stylistic direction of the design, from Gothic to Classical, as suited her preference. Her influence was such that Sir George gave her free reign over the improvement and modification of the plan, as demonstrated in his letter to Miller: 'I can trust you and my wife in making any alterations you please in the Plan'.[75] Although Sir George was commissioning a new patriarchal seat for the Lyttelton family, and was therefore considered the overall patron, Lady Lyttelton's crucial influence and her helpful £20,000 (approximately £2.4 million today) dowry should not be overlooked.

In fact, a wife's dowry often played a significant part in the enabling of country house building and this sometimes afforded her a say in the design and building process. This was also apparent at Saltram, Devon, when Lady Catherine Parker's (1706–58) large dowry enabled the rebuilding of the house in the 1740s. As the daughter of the 1st Earl of Poulett, Lady Catherine knew her worth and advocated her preference for a Palladian design, as evidenced by a surviving presentation drawing inscribed with 'To The Rt Honble Lady Katherine Parker at Saltram' (Figure 2.16).[76]

For the Lyttletons, mutual satisfaction was clearly very important, with Lady Lyttelton expressing as much in her letter to Miller: 'At last Hagley

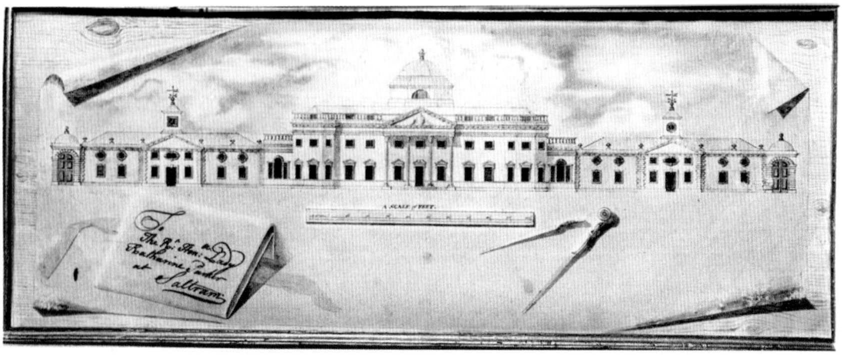

FIGURE 2.16 Unknown hand, presentation drawing of a proposed elevation for Saltram House, 1740s. National Trust, NT 871169. Saltram © National Trust/ Sophia Farley & Denis Madge.

House is absolutely set upon, both as to the inside and the outside and perfectly to the satisfaction of Sir George and myself'.[77] It is perhaps all the more astonishing therefore, that despite Lady Lyttelton's clear enthusiasm for building, she never actually got to enjoy the country house she had helped to design. In 1759, before Hagley was completed, she and Sir George (now Lord Lyttelton) formally separated when her notorious affair with George Durant, the son of the Rector of Hagley, came to light, and when her love letters to Signor Tenducci, an opera singer, were exposed.[78]

This shocking twist in the tale of Lady Lyttelton may suggest that because she was not in love with her husband, she felt less of a need to compromise with him over the architectural style and design of their country house. She certainly did not think it necessary to absent herself from the design process as other married women sometimes did. In fact, Lady Lyttelton's determination to build in a style of her choosing was a trait shared by Lady Ann Ward (d. 1789) at Castle Ward, Co. Down. There, the two principal façades sport differing architectural styles; the entrance front and the rooms behind are staunchly Palladian (Figure 2.17), as advocated by Lady Ann's husband, Bernard Ward, later 1st Viscount Bangor, while the garden front and the rooms to the west are distinctly Gothic, as advocated by Lady Ann

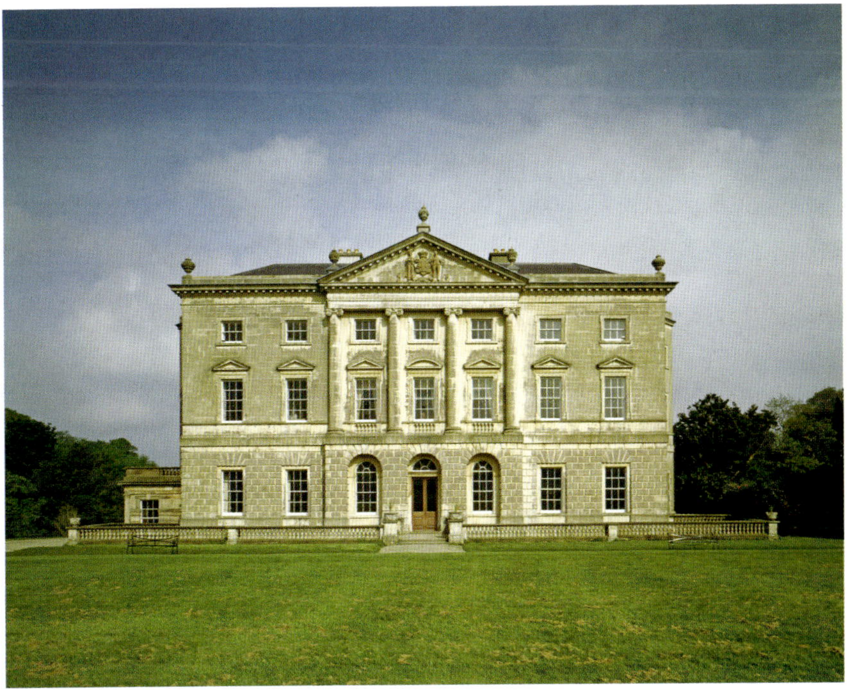

FIGURE 2.17 Classical façade of Castle Ward, Co. Down. National Trust Photo Library/Matthew Antrobus /Alamy Stock Photo.

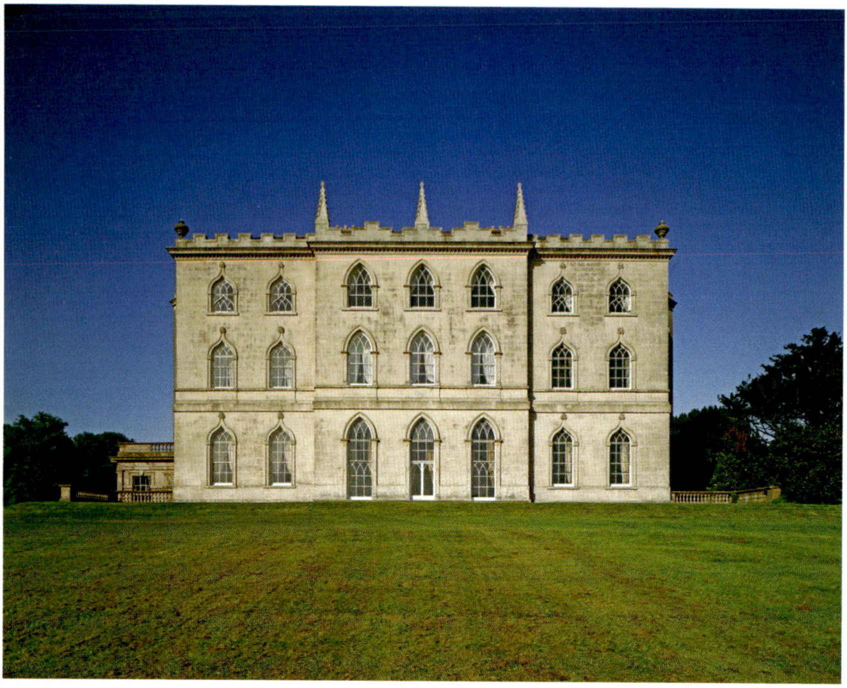

FIGURE 2.18 Gothic façade of Castle Ward, Co. Down. National Trust Photo Library/Matthew Antrobus /Alamy Stock Photo.

(Figures 2.18 and 19). Mary Delany remarked in 1763 that 'Mr. Ward is building a fine house ... *He* wants taste, and *Lady Anne Ward* is so whimsical that I doubt her judgement'.[79] Lady Ann's determination to enforce her architectural preference was seen by Delany as unusual, particularly as she advocated a style that did not conform to the fashionable norm of the day.

Lady Ann's confidence in her own architectural agenda possibly stemmed from her illustrious lineage. She was the daughter of John Bligh, 1st Earl of Darnley and Theodosia Hyde, Baroness Clifton (of Leighton Bromswold). Her grandfather, the 3rd Earl of Clarendon, was the nephew of Anne Hyde, Duchess of York, wife of James II, and was therefore a first cousin of Queen Anne. Queen Anne was the godmother of Lady Ann's mother, Lady Theodosia, who was permitted to marry in Westminster Abbey and was later buried in the Clarendon family vault in the Abbey. Lady Ann was evidently proud of her royal connections and sought to remind her contemporaries and descendants of this fact, and even went so far as to create a beautiful fan-vaulted ceiling in her morning room, based upon the Gothic ceiling of the Henry VII Chapel in Westminster Abbey.

Lady Ann's 'whimsical' nature and forthrightness were characteristics shared by her eccentric family. Her grandfather, while Colonial Governor of New York, allegedly acted out his official duties in women's clothing,

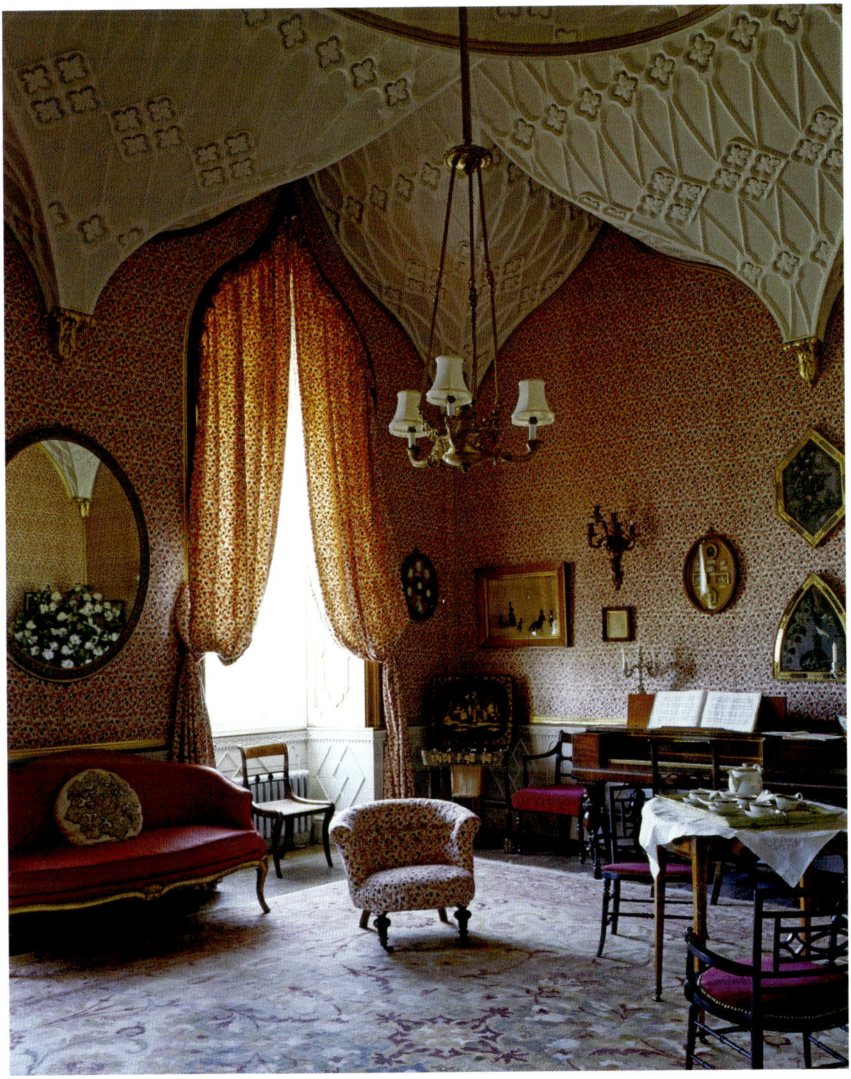

FIGURE 2.19 Lady Ann's Gothic Boudoir, Castle Ward. The National Trust Photo Library/Andreas von Einsiedel/Alamy Stock Photo.

scandalizing society,[80] and her brother, the 3rd Earl of Darnley, supposedly suffered from the strange delusion that he was a 'fine China tea pot' and upon the night of his marriage 'was under great fears, lest the spout should be broken off before morning!'.[81] In addition, her son Nicholas, 2nd Viscount Bangor, was declared a lunatic in 1785, resulting in the Castle Ward estate being vested with the Court of Chancery.[82] Lady Ann herself was described as having 'a shade of derangement in her intellects', but this comment was likely in reference to her bold behaviour, an attribute that was largely condemned by society as unfeminine.[83]

Even more appalling to society was her eventual separation from her husband, which took place shortly after the completion of Castle Ward. Apparently, even with the conspicuous display of architectural compromise, the marriage of the Wards had long been floundering. There is some speculation that prior to her marriage Lady Ann had enjoyed a six-year romantic relationship with Letitia Bushe, a gentlewoman some fifteen years her senior, suggesting that the discord between the Wards went deeper than their architectural tastes.[84] Lady Ann's decision to leave her marital home, her husband and her seven young children was one that would certainly have been met with societal disapproval, and yet, as with her unwavering architectural agenda, it seems that little prevented Lady Ann from pursuing what she wanted. In this sense both she and Lady Lyttelton were very alike. They both advocated an architectural forthrightness that was perceived as unusual by their contemporaries, as was their attitude towards marriage. Each woman dramatically demonstrated that wives could be as influential over country house design as their husbands, especially when possessed of a vast dowry or a strong sense of familial pride.

Heiresses preserving the ancestral seat

When the male line of an ancient family ended, large estates, great wealth and the responsibility of continuing on the family name sometimes transferred to a female relative. Although this did not necessarily suit the patriarchal nature of inheritance, it was the only way to prevent an established family from becoming extinct. Under these circumstances, an heiress's property rights and assets were tightly guarded, usually by trusts or as stipulated in the marriage settlement, to prevent the breaking up of the estate. If an heiress married, the ancestral home that came with the marriage, although legally the husband's due to coverture, was usually respected as the joint property of husband and wife, to be inherited by their heir. The architectural endeavours of heiresses provide a unique insight into the opportunities available to women who, under these unusual circumstances, acquired a rare measure of financial and legal independence. With this freedom many heiresses decided to dedicate their time, energy and resources to updating and improving their ancestral seats. These women felt the pull of ancestral glory as keenly as their male counterparts and did everything in their power to preserve their ancestral homes and further their families' interests.

Jemima Yorke, Marchioness Grey (1722–97) (Figure 2.20) was one such heiress, who inherited her grandfather's (the 1st Duke of Kent) vast estates in 1740.[85] When the Duke's last surviving son George Grey, Earl of Harold, died in his infancy, Jemima became the heir to the barony of Lucas of

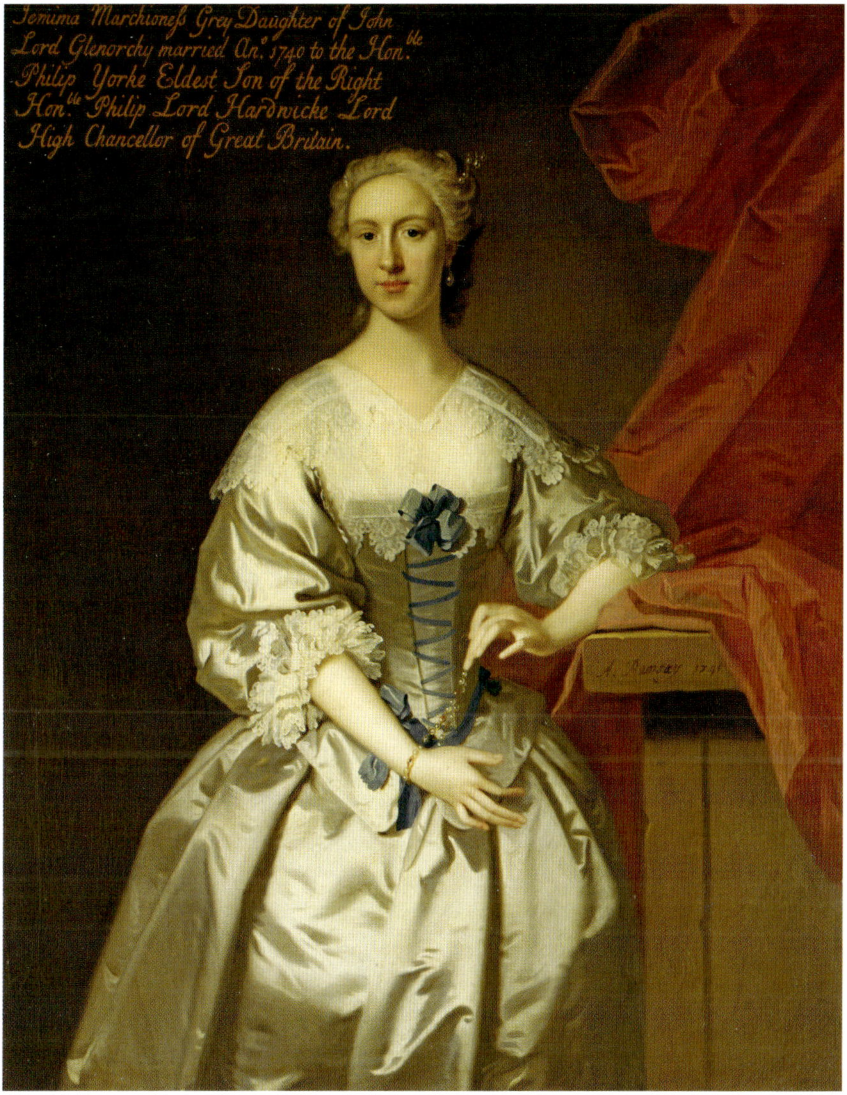

FIGURE 2.20 Allan Ramsay, *Jemima Yorke, Marchioness Grey,* 1741, oil on canvas. National Trust Photo Library/Roy Fox/Alamy Stock Photo.

Crudwell; a title that could be inherited by women. At this point, to prevent the Grey name from dying out, the Duke decided that his granddaughter should become the sole heir to his estates. In May 1740, therefore, the title of Marquess Grey was created at the Duke's behest with remainder to the 'heirs male of his body; and in default of such issue, the dignity of Lady Grey to Jemima Campbell'.[86] Consequently, when the Duke later died on 5 June

1740, not only did Lady Grey succeed to the marquessate, she also inherited the vast Grey estates which included the ancestral country seat at Wrest Park, Bedfordshire, and a London house in St James's Square.

Later that year, Lady Grey married Philip Yorke, the eldest son of Philip Yorke, Baron and later 1st Earl of Hardwicke, Lord Chancellor, and owner of the Wimpole Hall estate in Cambridgeshire. The marriage was a dynastic affair with the aim of uniting the long-established Greys to the socially ambitious Yorkes. It was a very happy, affectionate marriage which produced two children, both of whom we have already met: the Ladies Amabel (later Lady Polwarth) and Mary (later Lady Grantham). In 1743 the Yorkes finally settled into Wrest Park, a grand old rambling house that had been built in a piecemeal fashion since the sixteenth century.[87] In fact, the house itself had been little altered since its seventeenth-century remodelling, and was therefore in desperate need of modernizing.[88] Consequently, in a conscious effort to improve Wrest and create a more fashionable home, the Yorkes commissioned a constant succession of alterations throughout their fifty-year marriage.

Firstly, they commissioned Henry Flitcroft to design and construct a large new dining room on the south front of the house. Lady Grey took great enjoyment from her first foray into architecture, and regularly updated her correspondents on its progress. When writing to her kinswoman Lady Mary Gregory, she stated that 'we came to look after our Workmen' indicating that she felt a joint responsibility for the building works, continuing on with 'The new Room is begun, & that part of the poor Old House which has come down for this modern new-fangled Thing to rise looks indeed a little ruinous'.[89] Lady Grey clearly felt a great sense of affection for her old house and rather than tearing it down and starting again, as her grandson later did, she was determined to modernize it and ultimately save it for future generations.

Following a period of concentrated improvements to the Wrest gardens, Lady Grey and her husband later decided to make further alterations to the south front of Wrest. A letter to Philip dated 13 October 1763 from John Smith, Clerk of Works at Kensington Palace (1761–83), includes an 'Estimate for rebuilding the Drawing room' for £294 7s. 0d.[90] A final presentation drawing (Figure 2.21) of the proposed elevation, ground-floor and first-floor plans dated 'Novem^{r} the 1st 1763', together with an updated estimate of £429 5s. 0d., demonstrates how the project had quickly expanded to ensure that the most appropriate arrangement was achieved.[91] The purpose of the alteration was to create a large, elegant, modern drawing room, adjacent to their fashionable dining room, together with a smart bedchamber apartment above. The project served to create an additional entertainment space, which simultaneously improved the garden front by unifying the façade.

An undated bill in Lady Grey's hand, for the hanging of Indian wallpaper, may well relate to this remodelling project (Figure 2.22).[92] It is of particular

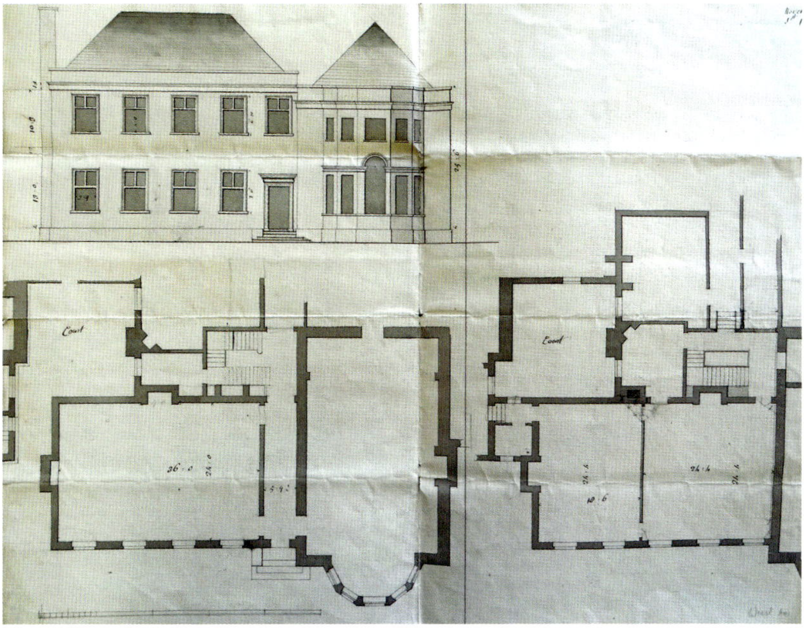

FIGURE 2.21 John Smith, final presentation drawing of the new drawing room, *c.* 1763. Bedford and Luton Archives Service, L31/263. Courtesy of Bedford and Luton Archives Service.

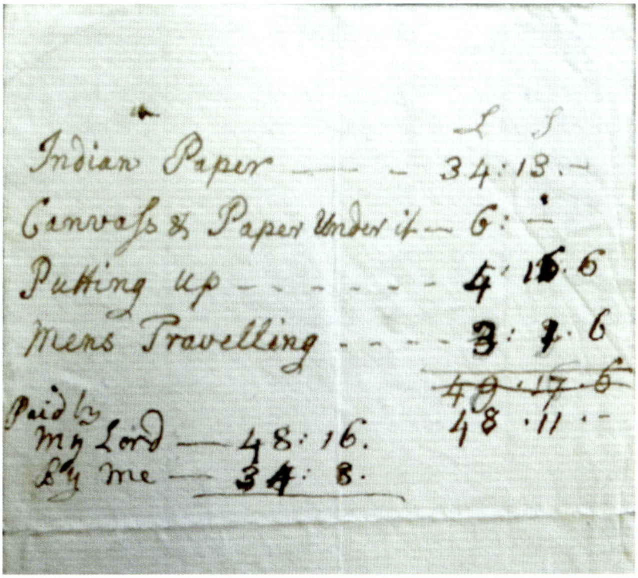

£ s
Indian Paper —— – 34:13.–
Canvass & Paper Under it — 6: –
Putting up - - - - - - 4: 15.6
Mens Travelling - - - - 3: 7.6
~~40:17.6~~
48 :11 .–
Paid by
my Lord — 48:16.
by me — 34: 8.

FIGURE 2.22 A bill in Lady Grey's hand, *c.* 1760s. The Bedford and Luton Archives Service, L31/273. Courtesy of Bedford and Luton Archives Service.

interest because she recorded that her husband, 'My Lord', paid £48 16s. and that she paid £34 8s., clearly proving that although architectural drawings, estimates and bills were often sent to Philip, this did not preclude her from being involved in the building schemes. This bill signifies that Lady Grey and her husband shared the responsibility for their architectural endeavours and shared the financial costs accordingly. Thus, although married women were usually not able to finance projects independently, they were often directly involved in their design and direction.

Lady Grey was so passionate about modernizing her ancestral seat that she embarked on a whole-scale remodelling of Wrest Park when she was widowed; the estimate for the works totalled the sum of £4,888 (approximately £400,000 today).[93] This project included constructing new high-status rooms, modernizing ancient parts of the house, demolishing an underused and outdated bedchamber apartment, inserting new water closets, redecorating unfashionable rooms, regularizing the south front, as well as updating the vast gardens.[94] The purpose of this scheme was not only to preserve her ancestral home, but also to make it as comfortable and convenient as possible for her daughter and heir, Lady Polwarth, who succeeded her in 1797. Interestingly, despite Lady Grey's mission to update and renovate, she left some of the grander 1670s rooms untouched, including the old library. It is likely that she wished to preserve some of her predecessors' architectural legacy for future generations. Unfortunately, her grandson, Thomas Philip de Grey, 2nd Earl de Grey, did not feel quite so beholden to his ancestors, and tore down Wrest to build an entirely new house in the French château style between 1834 and 1839.

A similar reverence for the ancestral seat was displayed by the widowed Henrietta Harley, Countess of Oxford and Mortimer (1694–1755) (Figure 2.23), who commissioned an extensive remodelling of Welbeck Abbey, Nottinghamshire, between 1741 and 1755 (Figure 2.24).[95] Lady Oxford was the only daughter of John Holles, 1st Duke of Newcastle-upon-Tyne and his wife, Lady Margaret Cavendish, daughter of Henry Cavendish, 2nd Duke of Newcastle-upon-Tyne. Welbeck Abbey formed part of Lady Oxford's Cavendish inheritance, which only came to her in 1716 after lengthy litigation, together with Bolsover Castle in Derbyshire. Just as Lady Grey possessed a great respect for her illustrious lineage and ancestral home, so too did Lady Oxford for her own, which instilled in her a similar passion for building and a desire to preserve her ancestral seat.[96]

Lady Oxford's ancestors before her had likewise shared an enjoyment for building, particularly Lady Oxford's great-great-great-grandmother, Elizabeth Talbot, Countess of Shrewsbury, commonly known as Bess of Hardwick.[97] Bess is famous for amassing an immense fortune through a series of advantageous marriages and for constructing Hardwick Hall in Derbyshire, one of the greatest houses of the Elizabethan age.[98]

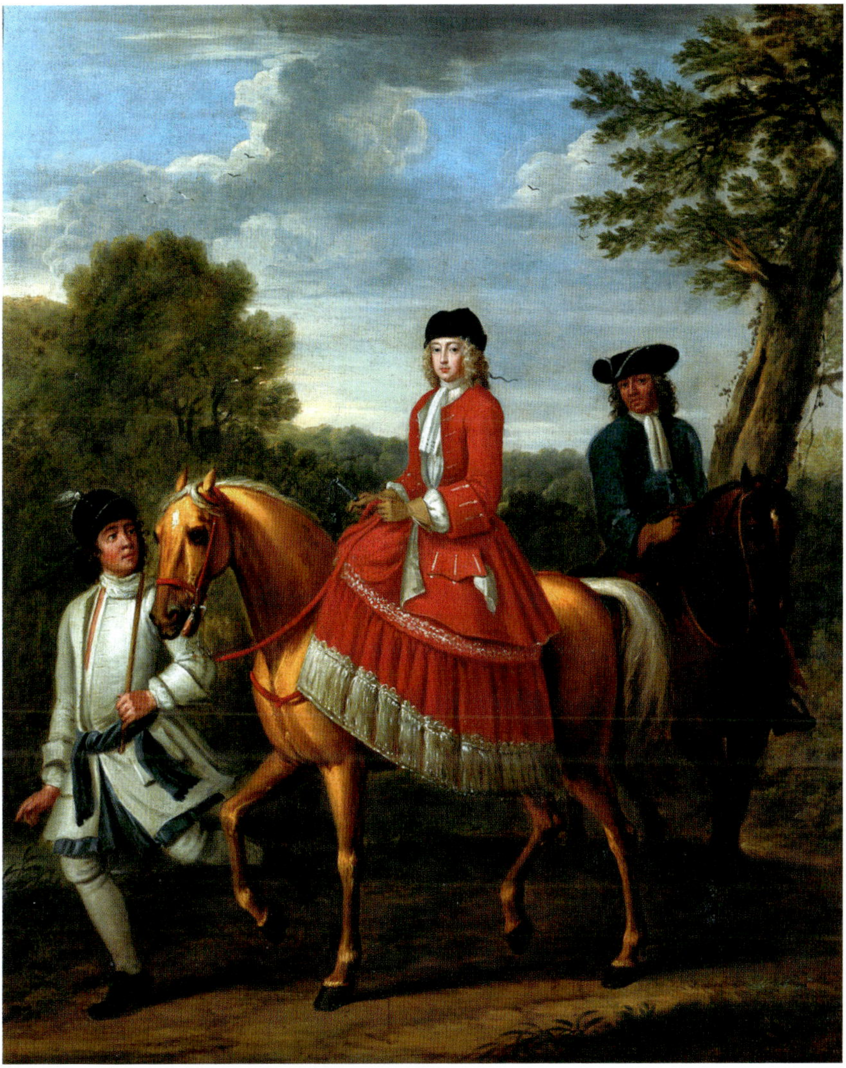

FIGURE 2.23 John Wootton, *Henrietta Harley, Countess of Oxford and Mortimer*, 1716, oil on canvas. The Harley Gallery, Welbeck Abbey. The Portland Collection. The History Collection/Alamy Stock Photo.

Thus, when Lady Oxford set about her own architectural project, she was nobly following in her forebear's footsteps. When writing to her friend Lady Mary Wortley Montagu (1689–1762), she opined: 'I confess I retard ye paym^{t} of y^{e} Great Debts by indevouring to incline my Family to reside at y^{e} only Habitable Seat of my Ancesters, it being my opinion y^{e} Estate reduced, will still bear maintaining one House upon it.'[99] Lady Oxford felt

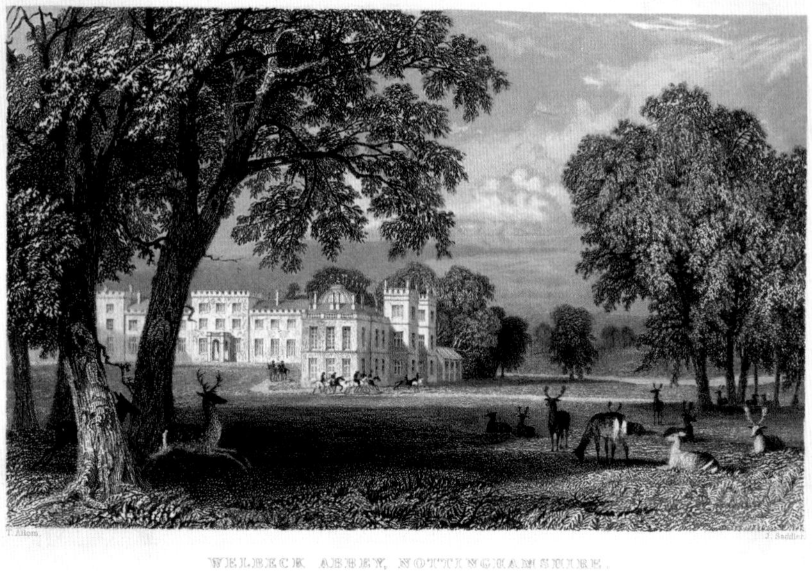

FIGURE 2.24 J. Saddler, after Thomas Allom, *Welbeck Abbey, Nottinghamshire*, 1836, engraving. Chronicle/Alamy Stock Photo.

some trepidation about spending such sums of money on her architectural projects, but was still determined to do so, later declaring that 'Y^{e} censure of others will not make me uneasy'.[100] It will become clear throughout this book that when women spent large sums on architectural projects they were often vulnerable to public criticism. Female patrons could either decide that public opinion was unimportant to them, or they attempted to disguise their ambition as feminine virtue, thereby rendering it more palatable. Lady Oxford evidently chose the former option, though it is possible that her show of familial piety softened society's opinion.

In further letters she wrote of her pleasure in knowing that her family 'seemed much pleas'd wth ye improvem^{ts} I have made here for thence I flatter my selfe this Place will not returne to allmost Ruines, as I found it, as likewise it having a probable chance to have my scheme finisht, after I cease to be'.[101] By improving her ancestral seat, Lady Oxford hoped that her family, particularly her grandson, the future 3rd Duke of Portland, would be encouraged to live there after her death. She was eagerly supported in her endeavour by Lady Mary who believed that it was Lady Oxford's duty to preserve her ancestral pile:

> I think it extreme reasonable that you should take that of embellishing your Paternal seat ... which I think one of the most rational as well as agreeable you can take. Indeed it is a sort of Duty to support a Place

> which has been so long dignify'd and distinguish'd by your Ancestors, and I believe all people that think seriously, or justly, will be of that Opinion. I hope your Ladyship will live to see it finish'd, and enjoy many years, the Beautiful Improvements you are making.[102]

Lady Oxford's project was substantial and included the creation of new lodges, a service block, a driveway, a great hall, as well as two new bedchamber apartments. Throughout this scheme she advocated three distinct styles, namely Gothic, early English seventeenth-century Revival and Classicism, indicating that although Lady Oxford revered her ancestors, she did not feel bound by their architectural precedents. In fact, when building her daughter and son-in-law's new bedchamber apartment, she chose the fashionable Palladian style, as befitted the modern young couple.[103] However, her penchant for the Gothic style showed a deep appreciation for antiquarianism and historicism, which was perhaps most dramatically illustrated in the Gothic Hall, a remarkable room which boasts an extraordinary ceiling of pendant-fan tracery (Figure 2.25). Her advocation of this style stemmed from her interest in her past, her heritage and ultimately her desire for the continuity of her family at Welbeck.

Throughout her decorative scheme at Welbeck, Lady Oxford was able to commemorate her heritage with the inclusion of her family emblem, the Cavendish stags' heads, throughout her Gothicized rooms. Bills for carving 'Bucks Heads and Horns' indicate that they were also gilded: '6 staggs

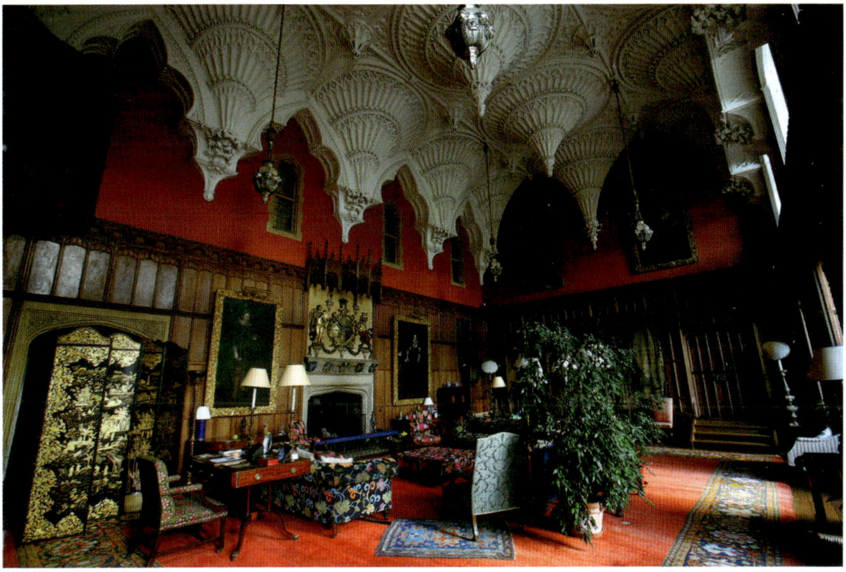

FIGURE 2.25 The Gothic Hall at Welbeck Abbey. Photo: Dave Thompson/Stringer/Getty Images.

Heads Gilt in Gold', thereby attracting the most attention.[104] This conscious display of lineage and familial piety was reinforced with the dining room ceiling, which was 'Painted wth ye Armes of my Family & ye Marriages into it in proper Colours to be Hung wth whole Length Pictures in Cedar Frames'.[105] For the entrance hall she commissioned a new 'Gothick Chimney Piece Designed partly from a Fine one at Bolsover, but composed of great Variety of English Scotch & Irish Marbles & Alabaster & not one bit of Foreigne in it'.[106] Her arms were carved prominently above this chimneypiece, while numerous heraldic devices and family crests adorned the Welbeck interiors at her direction.[107] Such display signified Lady Oxford's evident pride in her forebears, whilst simultaneously consolidating her own status and pedigree. This is further evident through the inclusion of her initials 'H.C.H.O.M' upon the north Gothic apartment.

Both Lady Grey and Lady Oxford were undeniably proud of their ancestral seats and shared a keen desire to preserve them for future generations. Their interaction with country house architecture was expected and praised by contemporaries, which may have lent them further confidence to be ambitious in their building schemes. Similarly, for Lady Elizabeth Hastings (1682–1739), the heiress of Ledston Hall in Yorkshire (Figure 2.26), the

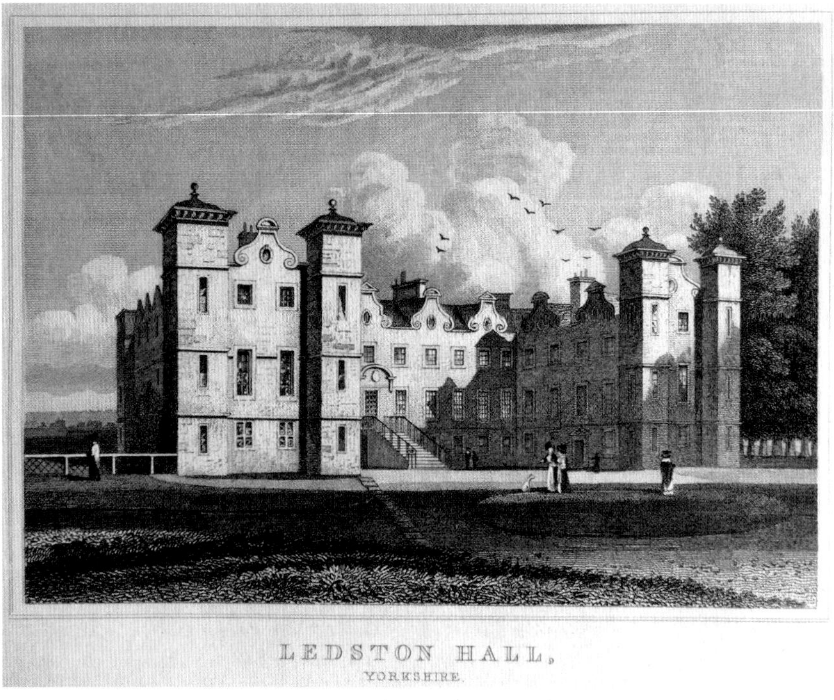

FIGURE 2.26 J. Lacey, after John Preston Neale, *Ledston Hall, Yorkshire*, 1822, engraving. Photo: author's own.

desire to modernize her ancestral seat was tempered only by her dedication to charity and her religion.[108] Following the unexpectedly early death of her beloved brother, George Hastings, 8th Earl of Huntingdon, in 1705, Lady Betty (as she was known) inherited the Ledston estate, the seat of her grandfather, Sir John Lewis, which yielded £3,000 per annum (approximately £321,000 today).[109] Despite her eligibility, Lady Betty never married, preferring instead to dedicate her time to her house and estate where she became renowned for her piety, philanthropy and intelligence. She generously took in her four impoverished half-sisters, the Ladies Ann, Frances, Catherine and Margaret; together they lived in pious harmony, attending prayers four times a day.[110]

Lady Betty's fortune, which was 'not so great as to be called splendid, yet sufficient to enable her to afford an illustrious example of active goodness and beneficence', enabled her to remodel her outdated seventeenth-century country seat.[111] Indeed, a survey drawing inscribed with 'Lord Bingley's plan for finishing Ledstone' indicates that Lady Betty may have originally considered a large-scale rebuilding programme in the Palladian style.[112] Given her subscription to William Kent's *Designs of Inigo Jones* (1722) and her contemplation of a new Palladian scheme, Lady Betty was evidently eager to elevate the status of her ancestral seat by using the most fashionable architectural style of the day. In the end however, the cost must have been too great, because she proceeded with a series of smaller changes, commemorating her work by including her initials on various lead rainwater heads on the east front and on the intricate wrought iron railings on the entrance flight of steps. This feature, which we have previously seen at Welbeck Abbey, similarly served to immortalize Lady Betty's architectural contributions to the patriarchal country seat.

With the assistance of William Thornton, a York carpenter-cum-architect, and her friend and neighbour William Benson, Lord Bingley, of Bramham Park, she redecorated the principal rooms and refenestrated the principal elevations.[113] Lady Betty transformed the appearance of the principal façade overlooking the entrance courtyard by replacing the old first-floor cross-mullioned windows with huge 24-pane sashes. These fashionable windows, as well as the twelve-pane sashes inserted on the second floor, instantly updated the exterior while allowing light to flood into her most important suite of rooms. Within these rooms, Lady Betty significantly altered the decoration: she panelled the rooms and installed high-quality fireplaces, some of which still retain their original shelves for the display of porcelain. The dining room was the most lavishly decorated with an elaborate marble buffet and fireplace, moulded from grey fossiliferous Derbyshire marble, ornamented with fine *trompe l'oeil* work and enriched architraves.[114] While Lady Betty's scheme was certainly more cautious than those seen at Welbeck and Wrest, she still succeeded in enhancing the comfort and fashionableness of Ledston for herself, her sisters and for future generations.

Widows and the country house

Like heiresses, widows represent another category of women who were, on average, much less financially and legally constrained than their single and married counterparts. Their relative freedom provided them with increased opportunity to engage with architecture, resulting in a greater variety of commissions relating to country houses.

Widows inheriting a life interest in a country house

Occasionally when there was a lack of a suitable heir, or when a husband felt great affection for his wife, a widow could inherit a life interest in the patriarchal estate. This life interest provided women with incredible opportunity and power: as well as providing them with increased political influence, it also allowed them to shape the country houses within which they lived, perhaps for the first time in their lives. For instance, in 1718, after a twelve-year marriage, Sir John Germain died and left his Drayton estate in Northamptonshire to his widow Lady Elizabeth (Betty) Germain (1680–1769), for life. Although Lady Betty predominantly lived in London and in her own apartments at Knole House (the seat of her close friends the Duke and Duchess of Dorset), in Kent, she diligently maintained the Drayton estate in her absence.

During her fifty-year tenure, although she largely left Drayton House untouched, she did commission the remodelling of the chapel, for which an undated bill from George Worrall, Master Plasterer at the Office of Works, survives, entitled: 'The Prizes of the Plast^{er} work to be Done For ye Lady Germain att Drayton house in Northamptonshire'.[115] A rough plan of the chapel floor also exists, specifying the number of 'whole', 'half' and 'q^{er} stones' required to complete the geometric pattern of white and black squares and diamonds.[116] An accompanying note further records the number of tiles needed for paving the 'Counting Room' and the 'New Eating Room', suggesting that Lady Betty commissioned various updates throughout the house.[117]

Of particular interest is a rough pencil sketch of the combined 'arms of Sir John Germaine' and 'L^{y} Elizabeth Berkeley', indicating that Lady Betty actively sought to immortalize the alliance between herself and her late husband.[118] As the daughter of Charles Berkeley, 2nd Earl of Berkeley and his wife Elizabeth, daughter of Baptist Noel, 3rd Viscount Campden, Lady Betty evidently wished to celebrate her lineage. This coat of arms was designed to be prominently displayed upon the wall of the new chapel, as evidenced by an accompanying sketch of the chapel walls.[119] Thus, although Drayton was not her ancestral home and despite her hardly living there, Lady Betty still wished for her architectural contribution to be remembered and appreciated by future Drayton occupants. Furthermore, her subscriptions to William Kent's *Designs of Inigo Jones* (1722) and Robert Castell's *Villas of the Ancients* (1728) indicate that she kept abreast of the latest architectural trends, which may have influenced her modest commissions at Drayton.

For women such as Lady Betty Germain, widowhood represented the opportunity to engage with architecture in a way that was often denied them as unmarried daughters or wives. In exceptional cases, however, widows were given no choice in the matter and were simply handed the immense responsibility of completing great country houses, as specified in the wills of their late husbands. Within this context widows could exert their own influence over the building scheme by hiring new architects and workmen to follow their orders, by updating the building scheme as they saw fit, and by commemorating their architectural achievements through the inclusion of inscriptions and their marital coats of arms. When Thomas Coke, Earl of Leicester, died in 1759 he charged his widow, Margaret Coke, Countess of Leicester (1700–75) (Figure 2.27), to complete Holkham Hall, his Palladian masterpiece in Norfolk (Figure 2.28).[120]

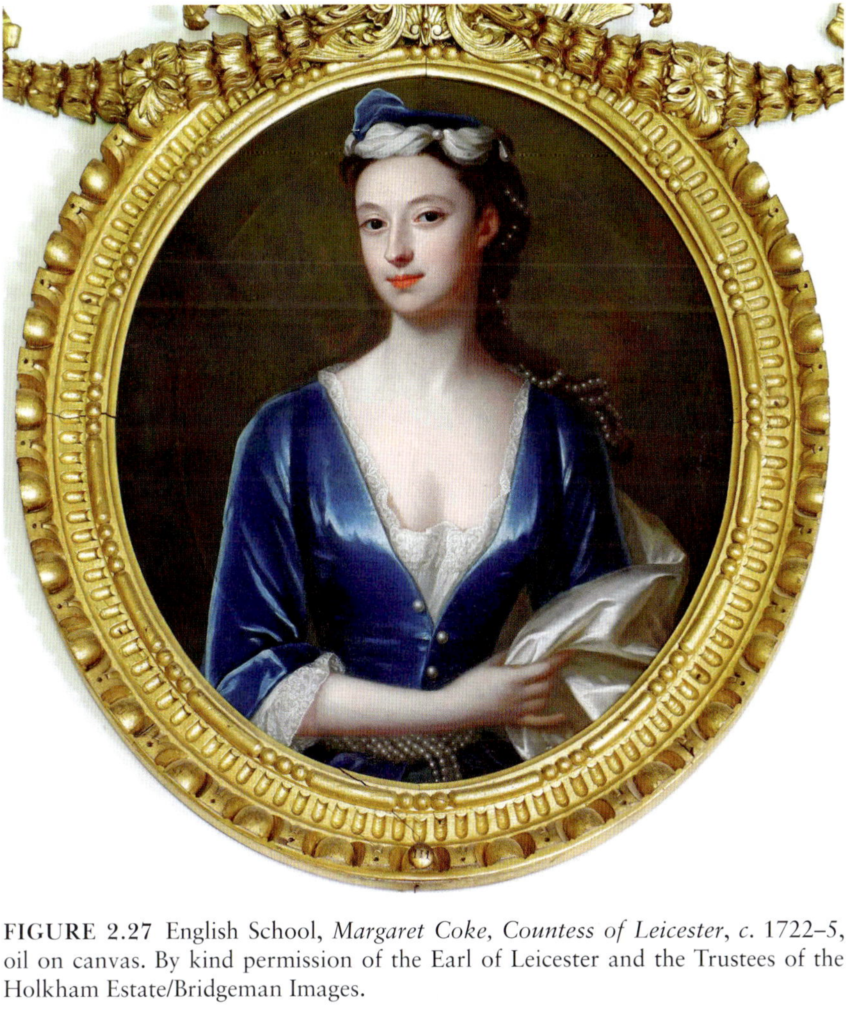

FIGURE 2.27 English School, *Margaret Coke, Countess of Leicester*, *c.* 1722–5, oil on canvas. By kind permission of the Earl of Leicester and the Trustees of the Holkham Estate/Bridgeman Images.

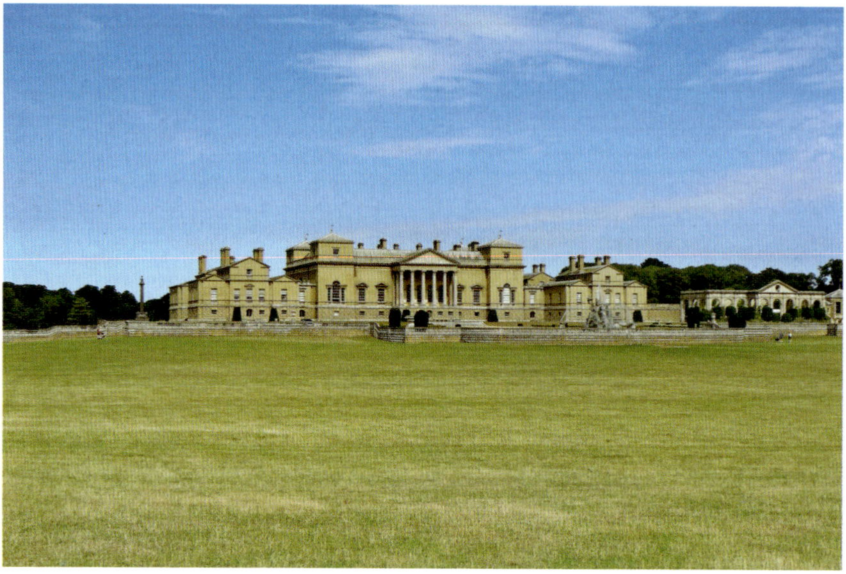

FIGURE 2.28 South front of Holkham Hall, Norfolk. Photo: author's own.

Born in 1700, Lady Leicester was the third daughter of Thomas Tufton, 6th Earl of Thanet, and Catherine, daughter of Henry Cavendish, 2nd Duke of Newcastle-upon-Tyne. After over four decades of marriage Lady Leicester was now faced with an immense task. In his will, Lord Leicester left the entirety of his estate to his 'deare wife ... to be used occupied held and enjoyed ... during her life', and directed that £2,000 per annum was to be used for the completion of Holkham Hall.[121] He appointed her as a trustee to complete the building, decoration and furnishing of Holkham, together with Ralph Cauldwell his steward, Matthew Lamb his lawyer, and Wenman Coke his nephew and heir.

One of the first decisions that Lady Leicester made during her widowhood was to dismiss her late husband's executant architect, Matthew Brettingham, and replaced him with James Miller, a carver who had been on site since 1748. Lady Leicester likely felt it necessary to hire someone with whom she was familiar, and who she was confident would not challenge her decisions. For the next six years the two worked well together, bringing Holkham to its glorious conclusion. In doing so, not only did she diligently ensure that her late husband's vision was realized, she also pursued her own architectural and aesthetic goals where possible. She oversaw the completion of the magnificent Marble Hall, the entirety of the Strangers Wing, the Chapel, Portico Room, as well as the Stewards Lodge and Stables in the park. She also spent over £3,000 (approximately £310,000 today) of her own money on the furnishing of Holkham, ensuring that it was finished to the highest specification.[122]

Lady Leicester evidently felt great pride in her late husband's architectural legacy and was determined to complete it and commemorate it. The need to immortalize Lord Leicester's achievement was likely motivated by the fact that the newly created Leicester earldom, for which the Cokes had worked so hard, was already extinct. Their only child, the hopeless Viscount Coke, had died years earlier (probably due to alcohol poisoning) which meant that the weight of completing Holkham and of preserving the Coke legacy fell to the widowed Lady Leicester. In a bid to do so, she commissioned a marble inscription to be placed above the Marble Hall entrance:

THIS SEAT, on an open and barren Estate,
Was planned, planted, built, decorated,
And inhabited the middle of the XVIIIth Century
By THO^{S} COKE EARL of LEICESTER

For this, Miller received payment for '3 Books of Gold' for gilding the inscription in 1764.[123] Notably Lady Leicester decided not to include her own name in the inscription or to record her own essential involvement in Holkham's completion. This reticence was seen throughout the project, indicating that she was careful not to steal the architectural limelight and was conscious of conforming to the traditional ideals of feminine modesty. Interestingly, however, the only times that Lady Leicester did record her contributions with inscriptions was on the Holkham Almshouses, which she built in 1755, and on a window in the Church of St Withburga (on the Holkham estate), which she extensively restored in 1767–8.[124]

Poignantly, her patronage of these two charitable and religious architectural projects fell within the accepted sphere of feminine virtue, which thus allowed Lady Leicester to commemorate her involvement. This is perhaps why Lady Leicester felt confident to significantly update her late husband's approved design for the chapel, as published in Matthew Brettingham the elder's publication, *The Plans, Elevations and Sections of Holkham in Norfolk*, 1761.[125] Instead of following Lord Leicester's original design, Lady Leicester altered almost every aesthetic detail of the chapel. On the east wall behind the altar, for example, she reduced the number of Corinthian columns intended to flank Guido Reni's *Assumption of the Virgin* from four to two columns and two pilasters.[126] This alteration provided space for the two flanking paintings of St Cecilia and St Anne (the patron saints of music and motherhood) that Lady Leicester commissioned from Giovanni Battista Cipriani in 1764.

Equally, on the west wall, she increased the size of the family gallery to include a convenient fireplace as well as a gib door to allow access from the Chapel Wing bedchamber apartments, indicating that she considered comfort and convenience as necessary as architectural flair and correctness.[127] Above the gallery, prominently placed for all to see, Lady Leicester included her marital coat of arms, with her supporting Clifford wyvern standing proudly

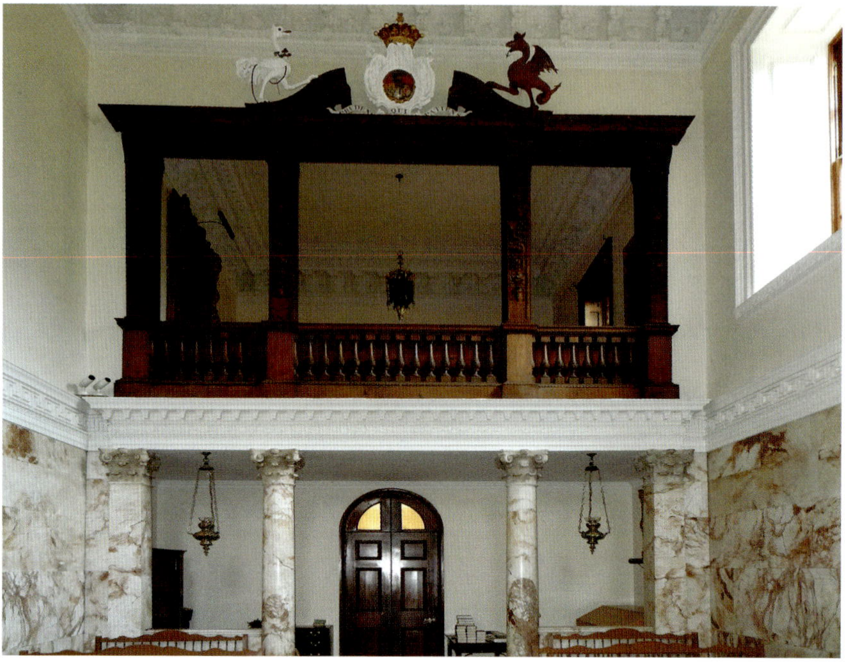

FIGURE 2.29 West end of the Holkham Hall Chapel. Photo: author's own.

on equal terms with the Coke ostrich (Figure 2.29).[128] The inclusion of the Clifford wyvern is particularly important because in 1734 Lady Leicester had successfully campaigned to George II for the termination of the abeyance of the Barony de Clifford in her favour, thus becoming the 19th Baroness Clifford in her own right. By including her marital coat of arms in the chapel, just as Lady Betty Germain had done at Drayton House, she was able to ensure that her own architectural contribution to Holkham would not be forgotten.

Evidently, the inheritance of a life interest in the patriarchal estate represented a remarkable opportunity for a woman to influence the architectural design and aesthetic of the country houses under her control. Moreover, it seems that with the absence of their husbands and without an heir to support, there was a reduced need to constantly promote the patriarchal line and a slightly greater freedom to commemorate their own architectural contributions.

Managing the estate for the heir during his minority

When the family patriarch died whilst his heir was still a minor, the guardianship of the heir and the management of his estates sometimes fell to his widow. During these periods of tenure, it was the widow's responsibility to ensure that her son's estates were managed appropriately and that the properties in her care were maintained to a suitable standard. In these instances, widows were able to commission new buildings, purchase others and complete unfinished architectural schemes, all of which were done for the good of the estate, in the name of the male heir.

Following the untimely death of her husband in 1786, Mary Robinson, Lady Grantham (whom we have met previously when creating her marital home) was charged with the upbringing and education of her three young sons, Thomas (who was now the 3rd Lord Grantham), Frederick and Philip. Despite her fondness for Newby Park, her marital home in Yorkshire, Lady Grantham immediately moved her young family to London. The tenancy of Newby Park was taken over by her brother-in-law, Frederick 'Fritz' Robinson, who was also the joint guardian of her children. Fritz and his wife Catherine continued to improve Newby, much to the delight of Lady Grantham, who, upon receiving her annuity in July 1790, wrote of her generous intention to spend some of it on furnishing the dining room:

> It has long been my wish, but til now never so near in my power, to shew my regard for Newby by furnishing some one object there from some one design of Lord Grantham's; the one that occurred to me was the Tables in the Dining Room, with the vases & all the ornaments as made out in the design that you I believe kept; that would complete one Room, & be observed by those who saw it.[129]

Lady Grantham sought to commemorate her late husband's memory by bringing some of his furniture designs to life.[130] As such, she commissioned a pair of pedestals with vases and two side tables to his designs from the renowned furniture-maker, Thomas Chippendale.[131] It seems extraordinary that Lady Grantham would wish to finance the remodelling of a dining room in a house that she no longer occupied. However, because the owner of Newby Park, Sir Norton Robinson, 5th baronet, had been certified insane in 1770 and did not have any children, Lady Grantham's eldest son, Thomas, had a strong claim to the estate, meaning that it is possible that she was keeping an eye on his potential inheritance.

In 1792 both Sir Norton Robinson and Uncle Fritz unexpectedly died, which caused uncertainty about whether the ten-year-old Lord Grantham was the rightful inheritor of the Newby Park estates. This was compounded by the sudden death of William Weddell of Newby Hall, a distant cousin of the Robinsons, resulting in Lord Grantham's sudden inheritance of Newby Hall, North Yorkshire.[132] This quick succession of unforeseen deaths meant that the issue of Lord Grantham's inheritance was referred to the Court of Chancery for clarification. During this lengthy and tiresome period of litigation both the Newby Park and Newby Hall estates were entrusted to Lady Grantham's care. This was significant, as it meant that she was now a considerable landowner with two substantial country houses under her management – albeit in her son's name.

The management of the Yorkshire estates was not straightforward, however, because the Court of Chancery placed strict financial restrictions upon both estates until the case was settled. This substantially limited Lady Grantham's ability to commission architectural works and allowed only for the bare minimum of repairs and maintenance to be carried out. Her management of Newby Hall was rendered even more difficult by the obstinate 'Mr Bernard', the land steward, who refused to cooperate:

> I find this house in good order, the Plantations grown, & the walks in middling condition; the Steward is like his master, & with a specious appearance has refused me impertinently some accounts I wanted for my future plans; so I have been in a rage, & have written him down in the black book.[133]

Lady Grantham was justifiably outraged at Mr Bernard's defiance and insubordination, even more so given that she was legally in charge of the estate. The reason for his uncooperative nature is unknown, and he apparently refused to provide her with the required accounts even after his name was put down in her black book of grudges. Judging by Lady Grantham's reaction, she was not one to suffer such dismal behaviour lightly, and yet, curiously, she did not dismiss him, and he was still at Newby Hall two years later.[134]

Despite these trials and tribulations and after seven long years of campaigning, Lady Grantham's patience and careful management were finally rewarded as she was granted complete control of Newby Hall in 1799. She was delighted with the result, writing excitedly to her sister-in-law: 'Now I must inform you, that the High Court have directed Newby Hall to be put into my hands at Christmas'.[135] Almost immediately, she set about commissioning a series of improvements to the house and park on behalf of her son: 'I have employed myself here in looking over our improvements, alas spending the savings of the High Court in fitting rooms, & building dog Kennels; besides thinning Plantations; with all which I am well satisfied'.[136] Soon afterwards, Lady Grantham was also awarded complete control of the Newby Park estate, which was a clear testament to her capable management and intelligent campaigning.[137] Until Lord Grantham reached his majority in 1802, Lady Grantham diligently continued to maintain, improve and manage the Yorkshire estates with her customary proficiency.

A similarly restrained interaction with country house architecture can also be seen in the case of the widowed Albinia Brodrick, Viscountess Midleton (*c.* 1731–1808), granddaughter of Charles Townshend, 2nd Viscount Townshend. Lady Midleton competently guarded her son's inheritance during his minority, although in this instance she also oversaw the completion of Peper Harow, Surrey, the patriarchal country seat.

In 1752 Lady Midleton had married George Brodrick, 3rd Viscount Midleton, after which numerous plans were made for the construction of a new house at the Midleton's family seat, Peper Harow.[138] Various drawings were submitted, including a set from Lancelot 'Capability' Brown in 1752,[139] as well as others by John Vardy in 1753 and an undated pair attributed to Henry Flitcroft.[140] In the end, Sir William Chambers won the commission, but this was not until 11 March 1765, when the contract drawings were signed with Lord Midleton.[141] The contract stipulated that the house was to be completed in three years 'for a sum of £8,190 to be paid as the Building proceeded by 12 different payments'.[142]

Unfortunately, Lord Midleton died a few months later of an abscess in the spleen, with his new house only 'raised to the Ground Floor'.[143] Lady Midleton was widowed with a young family and her son George, the new Lord Midleton, was aged only eleven. In a similar situation to Lady Grantham's, it was Lady Middleton's responsibility to ensure that the Brodrick estates were managed appropriately until George reached his majority. As such, a new account book was established entitled 'The Right Hon Lady Viscountess Midleton, in account with her son Lord Viscount Midleton'.[144] The book covers the accounts of all the Brodrick estates in England and Ireland and spans George's entire minority during 1765–76. On page 6 it states that, as the executrix of her late husband's will, Lady Midleton was:

> [A]t Liberty to have terminated the Contract [with Chambers] upon payment of the Penalty being only £200 but advised if the building was not compleated the money which had been expended would be lost to the prejudice of the present Lord who inherits this Estate under his Father's Marriage Settlement; wherefore Lady Midleton by the advice of her Councel and Friends Resolved as Executrix out of the Personal Assetts of her Late Lord to make up the sum of £1,239 16s 10d advanced before his Lordship's death £3,500 which compleated the five First payments of the Contract.[145]

Thus, Lady Midleton decided to continue the contract with Chambers so that the new house was completed for her son. In a parallel ledger that spans 1765–71, written by Lady Midleton herself, regular payments were made to Chambers between 17 October 1765 and 4 March 1768.[146] According to her ledger, Lady Midleton made a series of additional payments in her capacity as executrix in February 1766 for the work done at Peper Harrow, including £67 7s. 6d. to the plasterer Thomas Collins, £96 19s. to the stone mason George Mercer and £22 8s. to James Palmer, a blacksmith.[147] Other than these payments, there is little mention of the building progress at Peper Harow throughout the following years; presumably all other payments were covered within Chambers' contract. There are two supplementary entries, however, where Lady Midleton authorized payments to Chambers that were not included in his contract, both of which were written under the heading of 'My Son the Ld Visc^{t} Midleton'. The first was made on 7 March 1767 to Thomas Collins for £14 15s. 6d., for his 'plaisterers work done at the new house', the second was made on 8 February 1768 for 'Slating the Stables' costing a further £18 19s. 7d.[148]

It would seem that Lady Midleton's interest in architecture was largely practical, but her purchase of '16 Numbers of an add^{l} Volume to Vitruvius Britannicus' would suggest that she did seek to improve her knowledge of the subject.[149] Although Lady Midleton did not involve herself directly with the building scheme at Peper Harow, she was still indispensable to its progress and completion. Her careful management of the accounts demonstrates that she followed the progress with a keen eye and was willing to authorize additional payments if the need arose. It is also likely that her lack of aesthetic direction was borne out of respect for her son's taste, who, upon coming of age, completed the interiors to his own preference between 1775 and 1777.

Dower houses

In the eighteenth century, it was customary for a widow to vacate the marital home to allow her son or heir to assume his position as the head of the family. As the marital home was usually the patriarchal ancestral seat, this move was seen as essential in allowing the heir to fully embrace his responsibilities. This was not always an easy transition, and some widows found it difficult to leave the home that they had lived in and governed for years. This was the case at Wivenhoe Park, Essex, where the strong-willed mother of Isaac Martin Rebow proved difficult to remove upon his marriage to his cousin Mary Martin in *c.* 1775. His mother had enjoyed being the undisputed mistress for forty-six years and was in no hurry to relinquish power to her new daughter-in-law.[150] Such was her influence that her son's engagement dragged on for seven years, during which time she refused to move until her new residence or dower house was refurbished to her exacting standards.

Dower houses were smaller country houses built or remodelled specifically for and by widows. As such, widows often took charge of these building projects directly, as it enabled them to create a country house that suited their architectural preferences entirely. They were able to choose the style, plan form, decoration and furnishings, as well as the architect and craftsmen that they wished. Although these were not grand ancestral seats, dower houses still allowed for architectural display, and enabled widows to live fashionably, comfortably and independently.

When the widowed Georgiana Spencer, Countess Spencer (1737–1814) (Figure 2.30), mother of the famed Georgiana Cavendish, Duchess of

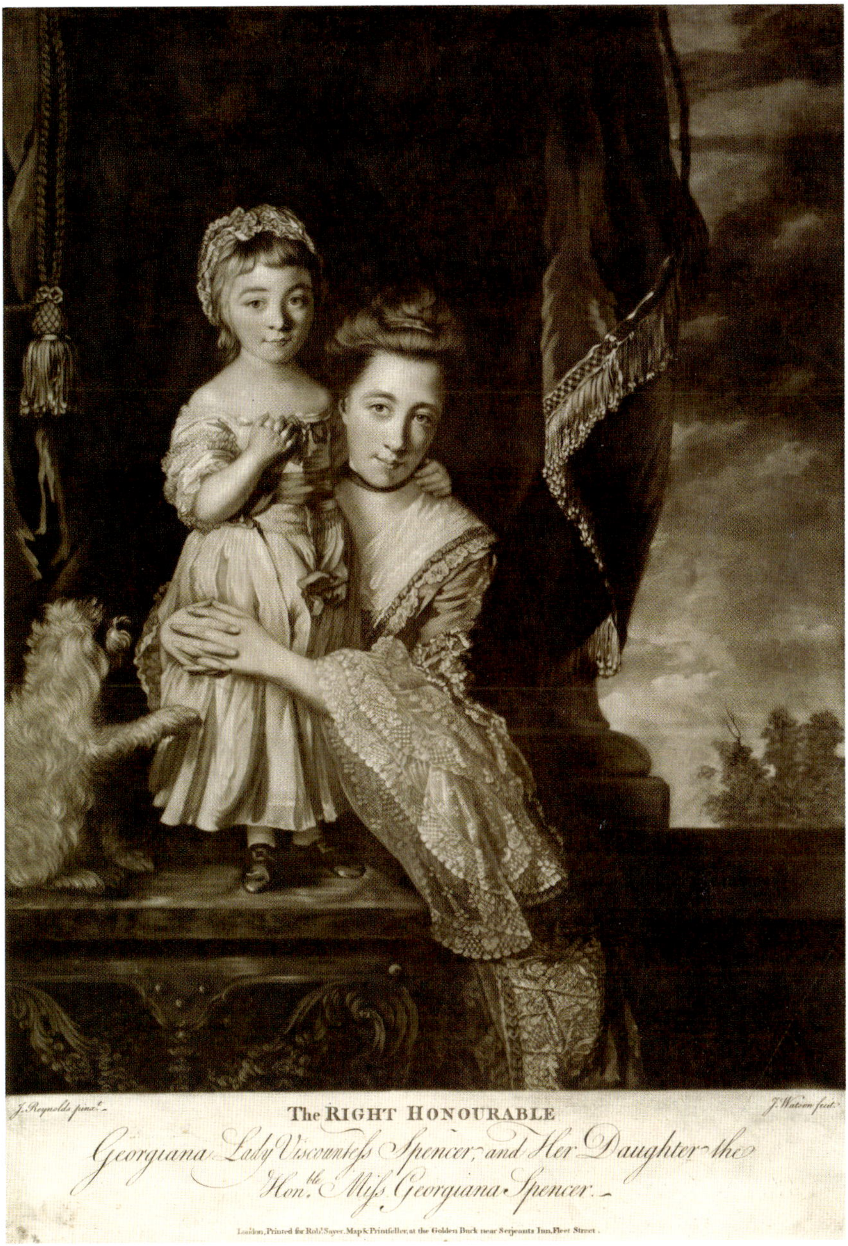

FIGURE 2.30 James Watson, after Sir Joshua Reynolds, *The Right Honorable Georgiana Lady Viscountess Spencer, and Her Daughter the Honorable Miss Georgiana Spencer*, 1769, mezzotint. Yale Center for British Art, Paul Mellon Collection, B1977.14.12902. Courtesy of the Yale Center for British Art, Yale University.

Devonshire, arrived at her designated dower house, Holywell House in St Albans, she found it to be in a bad state of neglect. Holywell House was the ancestral home of Sarah Churchill, Duchess of Marlborough, and had thus been incorporated into the Spencer estate following her death in 1744. Little in the way of modification had been done to the house since her time which rendered it a cold, dilapidated and unwelcoming house. The eminent writer and philanthropist Hannah More (1745–1833), while staying in 1784, remarked upon the terrible heating at Holywell: 'It [the house] is at present a very cold one, though my lady has just told me there are twenty fires in it'.[151] Consequently Lady Spencer decided to restore the house and, under her direction (but at the expense of her son), she oversaw the renovation and transformation of the old, decayed house into a comfortable, stylish Gothic dower house.[152]

From the beginning of the project, Lady Spencer was concerned with the architectural design, lamenting to her friend Mrs Caroline Howe ('Dear Howey') about the inadequate deigns proffered by her architect George Shakespear. She wrote how Shakespear had made 'a strange hodge-podge of Gothic & Modern in his design for the Garden front', which prompted her to refer him on to her friend Lord Harcourt (who also consulted Lord Camelford), because she knew 'little more than my own ignorance in these matters'.[153] Her noble friends both agreed 'that Shakespear's design was detestable, but have settled nothing, so that all is at a stand, & Shakespeare of course violently out of humour'.[154]

Once more, the need for female modesty in relation to architectural projects is apparent. Just as Fanny Boscawen downplayed her knowledge of architecture, so too did Lady Spencer when discussing her plans with her male friend. After the meeting with Shakespear, Harcourt went so far as to state that Shakespear's design 'could not be endured by any eyes the least conversant with picturesque effects'.[155] He commented that 'Shakespear's heavy regular parapet was a most abominable idea' and that 'it was not possible that either the drawing room end of the House, nor the opposite end could have been suffered to remain as Shakespear drew it'.[156]

As Lady Spencer desired a house that conformed to the correct principals of Gothic, she sent Lord Harcourt a series of questions regarding various stylistic detailing, ranging from the size of the bow window, to the form of the arches, to asking his opinion about stuccoing the fronts.[157] Such detailed questions clearly illustrate that although Lady Spencer deferred to Harcourt's judgement in this instance, she was able to converse with him as an equal upon the subject. The following extract consists of Lady Spencer's questions on the left, with Lord Harcourt's answers on the right and note at the bottom:

Shall the arches be of the present form, or do you prefer any other	To remain as they are at present except, that I should advise, their being converted into real arches by removing the lower part of the brick work.
Shall the part under the bow window be inclos'd or open	Certainly open, I think.
Shall the bow of the window be 20 feet or 24 feet wide, the height can be but 12 feet 4	This is a question to which you alone can reply. Since I wrote the above no answer I have seen the plan and am rather inclined to 20 than to 24 feet.
Shall the Town & garden fronts be whiten'd & the roof slated instead of til'd	The Town front I care not about; that to the Garden would be much improved by being stuccoed, and that whole front should have an embattled parapet over it.
If the arches below are of a Gothic form should the windows above be made to correspond with them – or be plain sashes	The windows above, undoubtedly ought to correspond with the lower arches, but they may have sashes in them, and should be lofty: the arches mitred ones without any ornament over them; but in order to give an ancient & corresponding appearance to the whole front, the tow windows in the Drawing room & those in your intended dressing room, though they may without objection remain in their present form, ought to have the following sort of ornament; & a plain gothic moulding around them would be a great improvement.

* When I answered the above queries, I had not seen Shakespear's plan. If you are partial to the old Arches, which I believe are really Gothic, because I have seen similar ones in other places, decide, at once, to retain them.[158]

In a further letter, Harcourt determined that if these alterations were included 'I think your Gothic front will be pretty picturesque & tollerably chaste, which is more than can be said for every part of the house on Strawberry Hill'.[159] Shakespear, however, proved to be obstinate in following his patroness's orders, especially on the height of the bow window room, which he refused to increase despite Lady Spencer thinking that it would 'spoil the room' if he did not.[160] Understandably, Caroline Howe became increasingly angry on Lady Spencer's behalf and sought to provide her with encouragement and architectural solutions:

> I am quite provoked at Shakespear, why had not you Holland my dear Lady Spencer: that I have always heard is clever in contrivances, for my part I wd give up any alterations rather than that room & I would have it thus, away with the dressing room that prevents the whole being equally heightened, the great outward room above might serve as a dressing room

> occasionally to that bedchamber, & I would have the Gallery all in one room, the height need not be above 13 feet, it will light that whole room I'll answer for it with 4 candles ... I beg you will not determine hastily, nor let Shakespear get the better of you unless he convinces you, pray do not think of expence in it, does not your son wish you to be pleased?[161]

Howe's forthright opinions regarding Lady Spencer's architectural project were a common occurrence amongst female correspondents, who regularly sought to offer their friends architectural advice and suggestions. In contrast to Harcourt's stylistic advice, Howe's principal points of argument concern that of comfort and convenience, suggesting that for women the eventual use of the rooms played a significant role in their construction. Howe's suggestion that Henry Holland would have been a better choice of architect is telling and again signifies that women had the capacity to promote worthy architects into their circles.

Nevertheless, despite Lady Spencer's difficulties with Shakespear, she did manage to convince him to raise the bow window room to her desired 12 feet 4 inches, but they later quarrelled over the proportions of the window.[162] Her perseverance eventually paid off, as the house was completed to her specification. The ensemble was pleasingly Gothic and featured arches, battlements, Gothic window mouldings as well as the much-debated bow window (Figure 2.31).

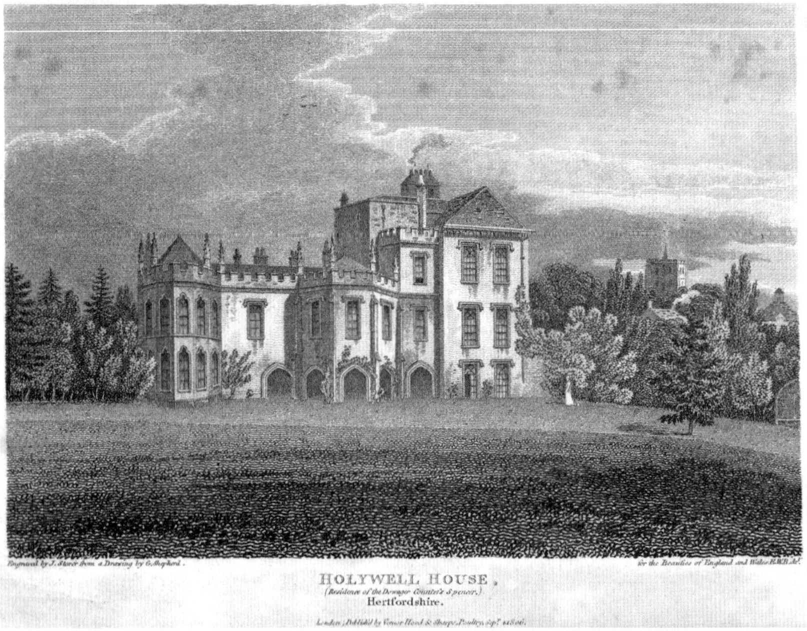

FIGURE 2.31 J. Storer, after G. Shepherd, *Holywell House, St Albans*, 1808, engraving. The Print Collector/Getty Images.

The design was met with mixed opinions, which prompted Lady Spencer to defend her choices, writing 'the best plea I have, [was] that it was Convenient & I lik'd it'.[163] Once again, it would seem, when declaring their architectural taste, women felt vulnerable to criticism and had to justify themselves accordingly.

In contrast to Lady Spencer's complete transformation of Holywell House, Elizabeth Somerset, Dowager Duchess of Beaufort (*c.* 1713–99), took a different approach to her dower house – Stoke Park (Figure 2.32) in Somerset, which she inherited in 1770 from her brother Norborne Berkeley, 4th Baron Botetourt.[164] As the only surviving child of John Symes Berkeley and Elizabeth Norborne, the inheritance of her family seat must have prompted a mixture of emotions in the Duchess. Naturally, she felt some sense of pride at owning such an estate, but this must have been mingled with a sense of sadness, given that she was the last of her family line. It also held a deeper sadness, because ten years earlier her second daughter, Lady Elizabeth Somerset, whilst out riding on a spring day, was tragically thrown from her spooked horse and fatally broke her neck. Aged only eighteen, the young girl died on the spot. This tragedy was followed only three years later by the deaths of the Duchess's eldest daughter, Anne, Countess of Northampton, who died in Naples of tuberculosis aged just twenty-two, and of her son-in-law, Lord Northampton, who died of the same disease five months later in Lyon aged twenty-six.[165] Six years later, as if she had not already experienced her fair share of grief, of her three surviving children

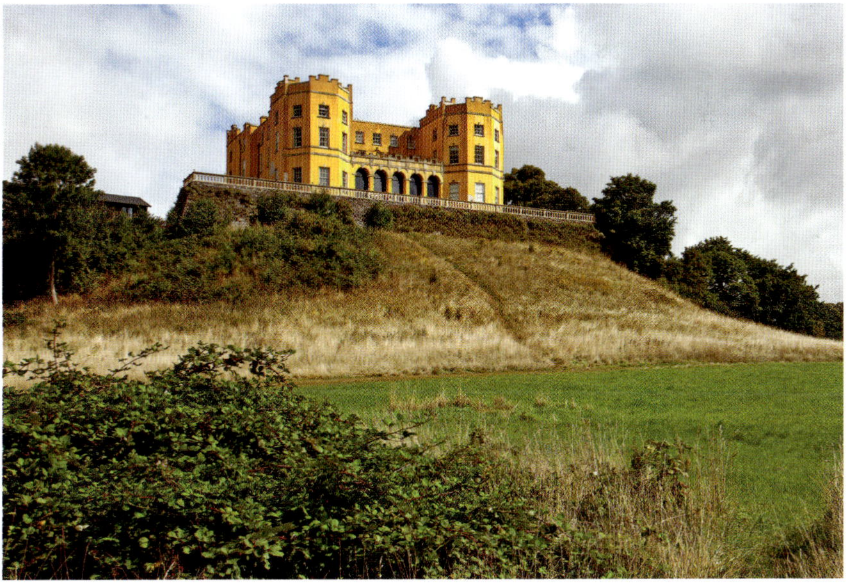

FIGURE 2.32 Stoke Park, Gloucestershire. Redorbital Photography/Alamy Stock Photo.

another daughter, Lady Henrietta Somerset, sadly died aged twenty-one, only three months after her wedding to Sir Watkin Williams-Wynn.

Seemingly haunted by death, the Dowager Duchess continued stoically on, taking up residence in her new country seat in 1770. As Stoke Park had undergone a succession of improvements commissioned by her late brother, to the designs of Thomas Wright of Durham, there was little in the way of improvements to be made.[166] Arguably, therefore, the Duchess had little need to involve herself with architecture during her twenty-nine-year tenure at Stoke. Nevertheless, the surviving Stoke estate papers document a series of constant and varied building works. Her commissions consisted of the continuous repairs required to maintain the large estate as well as others that fulfilled her aesthetic and architectural desires. Between 1776 and 1777, the Duchess commissioned the complete redecoration of Stoke's interiors as documented by a number of surviving letters between herself and her trusty steward, Silas Blandford.[167] A letter dated 17 July 1776 from an apologetic Blandford provides an insight into the flurry of works being carried out:

> I ... am very sorry that the backwardness of the Alterations in the Rooms should be a means of keeping Your Grace from coming to Stoke as soon as you intended and (hope as the Carpenters work will be quite done by the latter end of this week all but the planeing of the floors and putting on the Locks, which is not to be done till after the upholsterers and Painter have done their work) it will not be long before it will be quite finish'd.[168]

Although absent from the day-to-day management in 1777, the Duchess kept a careful eye on the project, trusting her deputies to follow her instructions to the letter. When it was time to paint the principal rooms, she sent specific commands detailing the exact colour she desired for each room:

> Let the painter know I w'd have the rooms that are intended to be painted, namely the great Eating room, & drawing room below & the best bed Chamber & a Bow window above stairs, to be painted a dead white: the little closet between the Octagon & drawing room exactly in the same manner & colours with the Octagon, & the passages & little stair cases of a stone colour. The stucco of the vestibule & great stair case must be cleaned & that of ye vestibule that has already been painted should be painted again as a stone Color: the Ceiling of the Vestibule must be white washed.[169]

The Duchess's taste was for everything to be white and stone coloured; popular choices for the time, as they allowed decorative mouldings and motifs to be elegantly highlighted. She was keen to present a tasteful home, and thus regularly patronized a range of famous craftsmen throughout her widowhood to furnish her homes with elegant and costly furniture, including William Ince and John Mayhew, the leading London cabinetmakers. For the next three decades she constantly purchased luxurious pieces from them, such as a mahogany lady's dressing table in 1778, a pair of Neo-classical pier tables painted grey and white with inlaid marble tops in 1779, a satinwood and marquetry Pembroke table in 1785 and six 'cottage pattern' chairs with feather ornament backs, japanned green and white in 1790.[170] Further accounts detailing payments to other noted craftsmen, including Chippendale and Haig, cabinetmakers, in 1793; Jefferys & Jones, silversmiths, in 1795; and Wedgwood, potter, 1792–5, all suggest that Elizabeth Somerset regularly sought to augment her interiors, and that no expense was spared in achieving her ideal aesthetic.[171]

In keeping with her drive for aesthetic improvement, she ordered a succession of modifications, some of which were recorded in memorandums written by the carpenter-cum-architect Charles Evans in 1782 and 1789.[172] The works were largely cosmetic, but were still closely monitored by the Duchess, as her annotations delineate: 'Could not the Dairy be made more commodious?'[173] Her careful attention extended beyond the house into the gardens and park, where she commissioned numerous projects, including a new Lodge at Broom Hill gate,[174] new greenhouses and cucumber frames[175] and new cottages for her tenants.[176]

Although the Duchess's dower house did not necessitate the architectural overhaul that Lady Spencer's did, she still lavished great sums of money in moulding it to suit her stylistic preferences. Through the commissioning of new decorative schemes and the ordering of bespoke pieces of furniture and luxury objects, she was able to create a home that was both convenient and fashionable. Elizabeth Somerset's architectural legacy contributed to Stoke Park eventually becoming the designated dower house for the widowed duchesses of Beaufort during the nineteenth century. Lady Spencer's dower house fared less well however and was unfortunately demolished in 1837. Despite these differing fates, each house proved to be greatly important to their widowed occupants, who, each in their differing ways, relished the chance to create a home that suited their architectural tastes.

* * *

The myriad ways in which women engaged with country house architecture are a facet of architectural history that has hitherto been under-researched. However, it is abundantly evident that women passionately undertook their own country house building projects, while working within the scope of social propriety, architectural opportunity and financial autonomy. Although country houses have traditionally been perceived as being part of the male domain, female patrons confidently influenced their design and construction and were instrumental in shaping their interiors. We have also seen that women contributed to country house architecture in part because, like their male peers, they felt a strong sense of familial pride and used architectural detailing such as initials, inscriptions and coats of arms to commemorate their involvement in the preservation of their country seats.

Much of the impact women had on the evolution of the country house has been obscured because they had to realize their ambitions by working through their male relatives, and because the spirit of the times incentivized them to downplay their own involvement. Evidently, women had an indispensable impact on the history of the British country house, although the stories behind their involvement are only now coming to light.

3

The London town house

From the medieval period onwards, elite members of society have created grand metropolitan residences, located close to the centres of power and commerce. Since the capital was the principal location to conduct private business, including 'commercial and industrial interests, as well as seeking the professional services of lawyers, brokers, conveyancers and architects', most members of the eighteenth-century social elite, whether they were landed aristocrats or wealthy merchants, had a town house befitting their status.[1] Extended stays in London were necessary for parliamentary and Court attendance, for 'maintaining close ties with social and political factions', and for seeking avenues of social, political and financial advancement.[2] The capital was also the centre of cultural activity, with numerous modes of entertainment on offer, such as the theatre, shops, galleries, parks and assembly rooms.

The sizes of town houses could vary considerably, ranging from free-standing aristocratic palaces, such as Spencer House in St James's Place, through to more modest terrace houses, such as those on Brook Street in Mayfair – the home of Handel from 1723 until his death in 1759. Regardless of size, the layout of such houses often followed a similar plan, with suites of reception rooms for entertaining on the ground and first floors, with a prominently designed staircase providing access between floors. Private accommodation was placed on the upper floors, with services either located in the basement or in ancillary buildings.

Many new terraces and squares were built speculatively during this period, with landowners 'disposing of blocks or, more usually, single plots for long terms (leaseholds), and mainly to numerous building tradesmen', who then erected houses with the purpose of selling them on to wealthy buyers.[3] Such was the case with Grosvenor Square (Figure 3.1), Mayfair, developed between 1725 and 1731, where 'no fewer than thirty builders or partnerships were lessees or sublessees at the fifty-one sites'.[4] Of the first fifty-one ratepaying residents of Grosvenor Square, there were thirty-five titled individuals, including sixteen peers, six children of peers, four baronets, four knights and five titled widows.[5]

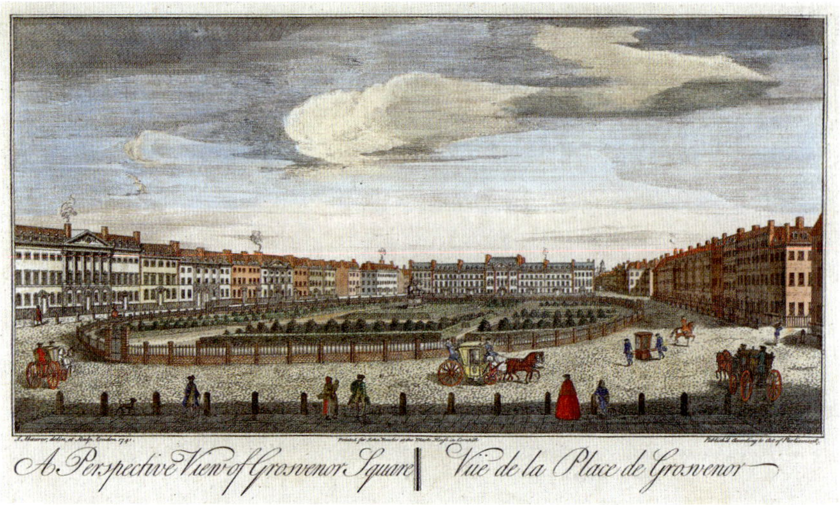

FIGURE 3.1 John Maurer, *A Perspective View of Grosvenor Square*, 1741, hand-coloured engraving. Yale Center for British Art, Paul Mellon Collection, B1977.14.16782. Courtesy of the Yale Center for British Art, Yale University.

Of course, speculative terraces and squares also sprung up in many major cities during this period, with some of the most famous being found in Bath, Brighton, Dublin, Edinburgh and Liverpool. In Liverpool, a notable property developer of the mid-eighteenth century was an unmarried heiress called Sarah Clayton (1712–79) (Figure 3.2). Born into a prominent family of merchants in 1712, she gained financial independence on the death of her mother in 1745, and then went on to establish a thriving coal mining and property development business. From 1752 she began to lay out a handsome new town square, Clayton Square (demolished 1986), reserving the largest house for herself. She also laid out the adjacent Leigh, Tyrer, Houghton, Parker and Cases streets, named after her mother's maiden name and the married names of her sisters. Perhaps to commemorate her achievements, Sarah commissioned her portrait from Joseph Wright of Derby in *c.* 1769, in which she is depicted pointing to a ground-floor plan of the Acropolis in Athens, denoting her architectural knowledge and interest.[6]

Interestingly, because many town houses were leaseholds, rather than freeholds, there was usually a high turnover of occupants, which meant that such houses were less associated with ancestral reverence and dynastic display.[7] The first occupants of Grosvenor Square in London, for example, stayed for just under thirteen years on average.[8] As such, town houses often became the focal point of an individual's (or married couple's) architectural display, designed as social spaces to showcase exemplary aesthetic taste and judgment.[9] Interiors of exquisite and innovative designs were regularly created to amaze and impress visitors, to advocate the latest fashions and to display impressive art collections.

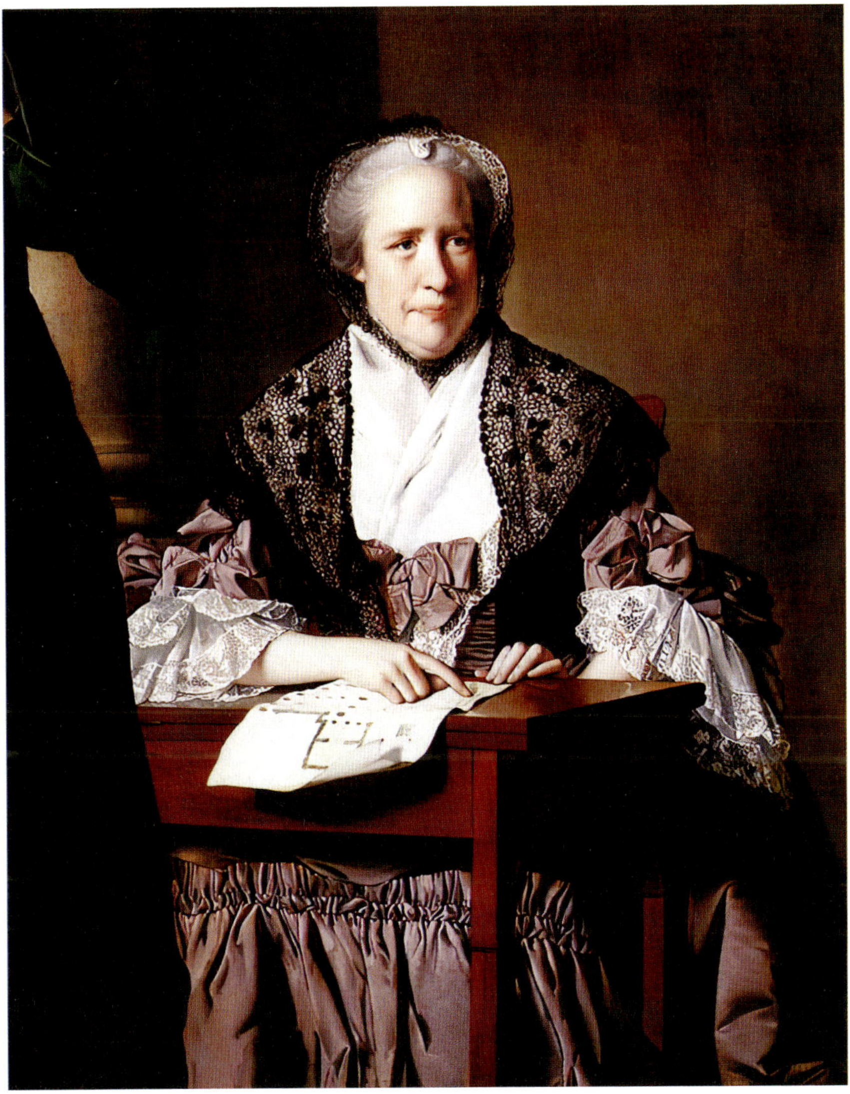

FIGURE 3.2 Joseph Wright, *Mrs Sarah Clayton*, 1769, oil on canvas. Fitchnurg Art Museum, Fitchburg, Gift of Louise I. Doyle, 1953.1. Artefact/Alamy Stock Photo.

For women, whether married or single, the establishment of a fashionable abode in the city was an attractive prospect, as it was less restrictive than the country and boasted greater culture and sociability.[10] As noted by the writer of *Common Sense* (1738), 'every fine Woman, who comes to Town in January, comes heartily tired of the Country and her Husband'.[11] Single women made up a significant proportion of London house owners and occupiers during this time, as seen in Grosvenor Square, where during the period 1720 to 1760 there were nearly thirty single women in residence, which contrasts significantly with the number of single men, of which there were only two.[12] Of these single women most were widows, but there were also large numbers of unmarried aristocratic daughters, estranged wives and royal mistresses.[13] It is clear from these numbers that it was more common for women to own or occupy grand town houses, in comparison to country houses. There was a societal expectation that women would want to partake in the social scene of London, and since the town house was the location for most entertainments, it stood to reason that women also bought and commissioned town houses of their own.

Indeed, whether building brand new houses or remodelling and redecorating existing ones, women were often at the heart of town house creations. Married women eagerly participated in the establishment of fashionable town houses if allowed to do so, but, as with country houses, their influence could be dependent on their husbands. In contrast, for those elite women who possessed their own financial and legal autonomy, namely unmarried heiresses, courtesans and widows, the building of a town house was a logical step. As this chapter will show, these women built for a great variety of reasons. For some, the building of a town house provided them with the chance to pursue their own architectural agenda, with styles carefully chosen to either conform to existing trends or consciously go against them.

This chapter will also highlight how other women chose to build town houses to further their own socio-political agendas. Lavish town houses provided the perfect stage upon which politically minded hostesses could exercise their influence in a variety of ways, including endorsing favoured politicians, dispensing patronage, cultivating powerful connections and instigating political debate.[14] Other houses were built purely as places to entertain, designed to host sumptuous parties, lavish dinners or erudite salons. As we shall see, even women of precarious social standing, such as wealthy courtesans, also shaped their town houses into spaces of luxury.

Wives and the creation of town houses

This chapter predominantly considers the town houses of women who were legally and financially independent. Much like with country houses, while wives did engage in the building of town houses, their involvement has been obscured by the fact that their husbands were the ones responsible for financing such building schemes. Consequently, although many married women were intimately involved in the commissioning, management and completion of town houses, unless they financed such projects from their own private funds or corresponded about them, their contributions have now mostly been forgotten. Moreover, the architectural ambitions of married women were more likely to be constrained by the restrictive social ideals of submissive femininity in the eighteenth century, and as such they often focused on interior design or acted as their husbands' deputies, which was traditionally considered to overlap with the domestic sphere.

Even when moving into an existing town house, a wide range of architectural and decorative improvements was usually necessary, which often fell under the wife's jurisdiction. For instance, when Lady Grisell Baillie (1665–1746), daughter of Sir Patrick Hume (later 1st Earl of Marchmont), and her family moved into an unfurnished house in London in 1715, she recorded all the payments for the repairing, decorating and furnishing of the property.[15] The very first payments were for essential maintenance including the 'scouring all the wanscote of new house at 20d a day', 'For white washing the House'[16] and 'Repairing the Rooff of the new house'.[17] Further payments recorded by Lady Grisell for glazing, painting, joinery, smith's work and the transportation of pictures all indicate that such works were her responsibility.[18]

Naturally, Lady Grisell's influence extended to the interiors, which included great sums spent on upholstery, such as £36 'for 6 pices Green Damask for hangins, chairs and window curtins from Piter Hambly' and £26 paid to John Sanderson, a London upholsterer, for 'makeing 8 Damask window Curtins with 4 seats'.[19] As well as purchasing luxury pieces of furniture including a walnut tree writing desk and a Japan tea table,[20] she also commissioned an order of furniture from the renowned cabinet-maker James Moore, thereby placing her interiors among the most fashionable in London.[21] Lady Grisell's accounts make it clear that in her conventional capacity as 'mistress of the house' she was able to control far more than just her household and children. She had the sole responsibility of creating a fashionable London town house for her family which shows that even within the traditionally accepted role as wife and household manager, women could exert power over the formation of their homes.

Surviving archival evidence also shows that wives could be responsible for facilitating payments for the building of town houses. In 1766, Margaret, Lady Dundas, the wife of the wealthy Scottish businessman Sir Lawrence Dundas, paid Robert Adam the sum of £203 3s. for a large list of designs and drawings that he had made for their London house, 19 Arlington Street, and Moor Park.[22] Lady Dundas was involved and interested in the design process relating to her houses and was entrusted by her husband to make the necessary payments when he was absent. She also subscribed Adam's *Ruins of the Palace of the Emperor Diocletian* (1764) further demonstrating her intellectual interest in the latest Neo-Classical aesthetic.

Similarly, at Norfolk House, St James's Square, the exceptional Rococo interiors were certainly the collaborative achievement of both Mary Howard, Duchess of Norfolk (1701–73), and her husband, the 9th Duke.[23] The Duchess's progressive aesthetic taste was likely the driving force behind the chosen designs, as suggested by her ownership of a set of engravings by two leading Rococo designers, Gilles-Marie Oppenord and Juste Aurele Meissonnier, one of which she annotated with 'French Designs of Finishing of Rooms'.[24] We can imagine the Duchess flicking through the latest books and engravings for inspiration and annotating those that she liked the most. Her involvement in the design process is obvious and is further indicated by the incorporation of the Duke and Duchess's entwined initials in an elaborate cypher displayed prominently in the magnificent white and gold panelled Music Room (Figure 3.3), now on display at the Victoria and Albert Museum.

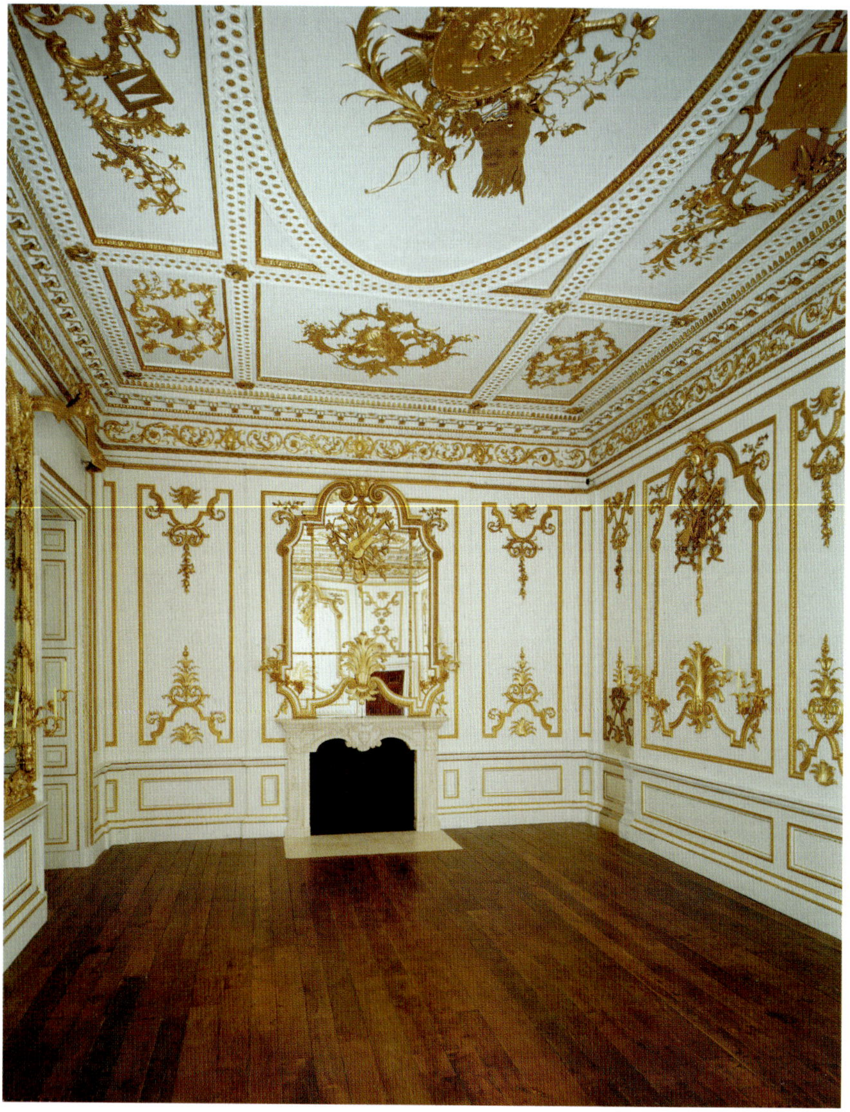

FIGURE 3.3 The Music Room at Norfolk House. V&A Images/Alamy Stock Photo.

Upon the grand opening of Norfolk House in 1756, Horace Walpole wrote of the effect that the glorious interiors had on its guests: 'You would have thought there had been a comet, everybody was gaping in the air and treading on one another's toes. In short, you never saw such a scene of magnificence and taste. The tapestry, the embroidered bed, the illumination, the glasses, the lightness and novelty of the ornaments, and the ceilings, are delightful'.[25]

Conversely, and perhaps exceptionally, Sarah Churchill, Duchess of Marlborough, was the sole and undisputed patron of Marlborough House, Pall Mall – the Marlboroughs' London house (Figure 3.4). When it became clear that her relationship with Queen Anne was rapidly deteriorating, the Duchess decided to make a grand architectural statement by building a new town house as close to St James's Palace as was possible. The Duke, who was at this time preoccupied with the building of Blenheim, agreed to give £7,000 towards the building of the house, provided that she bequeathed it to their heir after her death.[26] He also gave his wife complete control over the design, aesthetic direction and choice of architect, as the Duchess herself recorded:

> [T]he Duke of Marlborough was so good as to give me leave to make this house precisely as I liked to have it and to employ who I pleased, upon which I sent for Sr C. Wren and told him I hoped it would bee no great trouble to him to look after the building I was going to begin.[27]

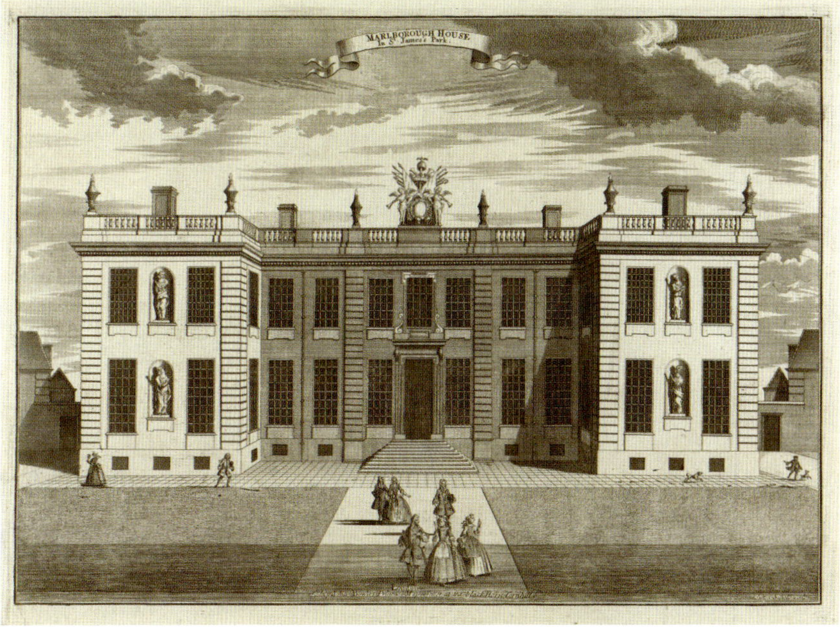

FIGURE 3.4 Sutton Nicholls, *Marlborough House in St James's Park*, active 1725, engraving. Yale Center for British Art, Paul Mellon Collection, B1977.14.9653. Courtesy of the Yale Center for British Art, Yale University.

Wren was in his late seventies and, in this project as with others, he was assisted by his son Christopher.[28] Wren was probably *the* most famous architect of the time and as he had previously been employed by Queen Anne in 1703, for whom he had built a range of state apartments, the Duchess no doubt felt that nothing less than the royal architect would do.[29] By commissioning such a prominent architect, the Duchess was sending a clear message to all that she was seeking to reassert her position within Court and within elite society.

With her husband absent and uninterested in the project, she enthusiastically set about designing the perfect London house for her family. Almost as a reaction against the Baroque flamboyance of Blenheim Palace, she took inspiration from the distinctly unornamented façades of the 1st Duke of Buckingham's newly built Buckingham House, Pall Mall. In line with the Duchess's character, she was particular about the style of her house, and instructed Wren accordingly, stating that:

> [H]e must promise me two things, First that hee would make the contracts reasonable and not as crown work … The other article was that hee must make my hous strong plain and convenient and that he must give me his word that this building should not have the least resemblance of any thing in that called Blenheim which I had never liked but could not prevail against Sr John.[30]

Not all was plain sailing however and by 1711 the Duchess's relationship with her architects had soured to the point that she halted all works until their issues were resolved.[31] She unceremoniously dismissed them soon afterwards and took charge of the completion of Marlborough House herself. In later life she explained her actions: 'I began to find that this man [Wren] from his age was imposed upon by the workmen and the prices for all things were much too high for ready money and sure pay, upon which I took the finishing part myself'.[32] She directed the execution of the interiors, commissioning Louis Laguerre to paint eight battle scenes from the Duke's military campaigns to decorate the grand staircase and the entrance hall (now the saloon), which were consciously designed to remind all visitors of the prominence and glory of the Marlborough family.[33] In a time when the Marlboroughs' political clout at Court was quickly diminishing, the Duchess succeeded in building a town house that served to remind their contemporaries of the integral role that they had played in British and European politics.

Women commissioning new town houses

Sarah Churchill was not unique in her desire to build a grand London town house, although she certainly had greater freedom than most to pursue her architectural ambition. In general, when women had the capital, opportunity and the inclination, they were free to build sumptuous town houses of their own. They were motivated by many things, but ultimately they sought to please themselves by creating a home that was to their satisfaction.

Architectural statements

One of the simplest and most obvious reasons for building was to create a house that suited the patroness's own ideas of convenience and style. As such, some women pursed their own architectural preference regardless of whether their choices were deemed fashionable or not. Two such women were the widowed Molly Hervey, Baroness Hervey (1700–68) and Henrietta Fermor, Countess of Pomfret (1698–1761). Lady Hervey was the daughter of the naturalized Dane, Brigadier-General Nicholas Lepel, and Mary Brooke, whereas Lady Pomfret had a grander parentage, being the only surviving child of John Jeffreys, 2nd Baron Jeffreys, and Lady Charlotte Herbert, daughter and heiress of Philip, 7th Earl of Pembroke and Montgomery.

Both women, in their younger days, had held prominent positions in Caroline of Ansbach's household; Lady Hervey, when still Miss Lepel, was fêted as one of the beautiful Maids of Honour to Caroline when Princess of Wales, and Lady Pomfret held the more senior position as one of the Ladies of the Bedchamber for over ten years. Both women benefited from the sophistication of Caroline's Court, where the arts, literature, science and the Enlightenment were celebrated and promoted. With such a prominent patroness of the arts leading the way before them, the Ladies Hervey and Pomfret were no doubt inspired to become daring patronesses themselves. Thus, when they each decided to build a town house of their own during their widowhoods, they deviated from the popular and prevailing style of Palladianism (the architectural style rigidly based on the work of the sixteenth-century Italian architect Andrea Palladio) and instead decided to follow their own architectural preferences.

When Lady Hervey (Figure 3.5), the widow of the famous courtier and political writer John Hervey, 2nd Baron Hervey, commissioned her town house at No. 25 St James's Place, she was determined to please only herself with its architectural style and form. For this great project she hired one of the most fashionable architects of the day, Henry Flitcroft, yet still insisted on designing every aspect of the building herself, as she proudly declared to her eldest boys' tutor Reverend Morris in 1747: 'I have a dozen plans, a compass, ruler, &c. lying before me, and expect Mr. Flitcroft every instant ... Here comes the executor, so the architect must give her directions'.[34] Here we can imagine Lady Hervey surrounded by drafts, plans and drawing equipment, excitedly designing her new house, and eagerly waiting to discuss it with her architect. A year later, she again reasserts her role in designing the house:

> At present, my thoughts are greatly taken up with the plan of my house, which I have made entirely myself, and is to be executed next April. Perhaps you'll think I ought to begin such a plan the first day of that month: but though it may be, and certainly is, contrary to all palladian

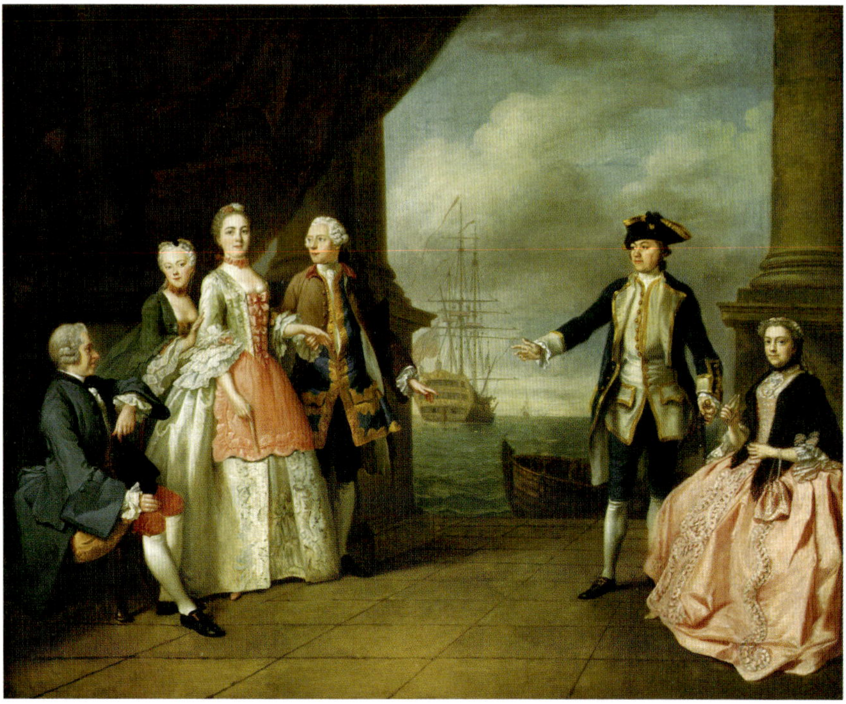

FIGURE 3.5 Hubert Gravelot with Jean-Etienne Liotard and possibly Francis Hayman, *The Hon. Mrs Constantine Phipps being led to greet her Brother, Captain the Hon. Augustus Hervey, later 3rd Earl of Bristol, with Molly, Lady Hervey seated*, 1750, oil on canvas. National Trust, Ickworth, NT 851727. © National Trust.

> rules, yet, as it is for myself, and not for others, that I build it, I think I ought to consider my own convenience and taste in it.[35]

Lady Hervey confidently explains that the house she builds is for herself, and thus, her architectural preferences are the only ones of significance. After over twenty years of marriage to a man who considered her 'little more than a child-bearing irrelevance',[36] and after years of being regularly trapped with her hateful mother-in-law at Ickworth, the Herveys' country seat in Suffolk, Lady Hervey was now finally free to live her life as she wished.[37] Her life experience, intelligence and learning allowed her to reject the most conventional style of the time and pursue her own aesthetic, that of the French style, or Rococo. It is likely that the exterior of her house was conventionally Classical, with the interiors acting as the focus of her stylistic talents.

Lord Chesterfield, a long-time admirer of Lady Hervey, respected her 'easy good-breeding', noting that 'She has all the reading that a woman should have; and more than any woman need have; for she understands Latin perfectly well, though she wisely conceals it'.[38] Lady Hervey was well-read and owned a substantial library that covered numerous topics, including history, politics and religion. More than five hundred of her books survive at Ickworth House, all of which have her armorial plate pasted into the front. She was also one of Voltaire's earliest subscribers and several of his works still exist in her book collection.[39]

Lady Hervey was fluent in French, visited Paris regularly, and was known to be an unabashed Francophile. Her interest and passion for Rococo interiors were no doubt fuelled by the latest publications on the subject, such Jean Mariette's *L'Architecture Française* (1738), as well as the fine French-inspired Rococo interiors of Chesterfield House (1747–52), Westminster, which was under construction contemporaneously.[40] Lord Chesterfields house is often touted as one of the earliest to contain Rococo interiors in England, but it seems that Lady Hervey's can also claim that accolade.

Despite Lady Hervey's great enthusiasm for building her house, she did still worry about the great cost, fearing that it was 'a very dear one'.[41] She was well aware that she would face some societal censure for embarking upon such a conspicuous and expensive project, but in her usual feisty manner, she defended herself well, stating:

> If I am contented with two dishes rather than four, and with four servants rather than eight, and choose to make that diminished expence in a good house, I please myself, and injure no one; – after that, let them condemn, wonder or ridicule – 'tis indifferent to me; for so much I know of human nature, that, in general, most people are more prone to find faults than beauties.[42]

Indeed, such expenditure would have been a cause of concern for most widows, as they were often solely dependent on the annuity provided by their jointures, and Lady Hervey's was shockingly meagre. When Lord Hervey died he left his devoted wife only £300 (approximately £35,000 today) a year, writing waspishly in his will: 'Whatever I am obliged to leave my wife by the writing signed at our marriage she must have. I leave her nothing more'.[43] Such callous treatment did not go unnoticed by society with one commentator, Fanny Russell, declaring that 'Lord Hervey's will has made a great noise, and he has finished his charming character by it. Lady Hervey has made the best of wives and mothers, yet he leaves her nothing but her jointure'.[44]

Despite her late husband's harsh treatment, Lady Hervey rallied and may possibly have used the £4,000 (approximately £470,000 today) that was given to her in 1730 by Stephen Fox (later 1st Earl if Ilchester), who was her husband's lover.[45] Lord Hervey's bisexuality was well known amongst his contemporaries, with Lord Pulteney publicly labelling him a 'delicate Hermaphrodite' and 'a pretty, little *Master-Miss*'.[46] Lord Hervey's male favourites included Stephen, with whom he had a ten-year relationship between 1726 and 1736, and Count Francesco Algarotti, the beautiful and charming Italian polymath.[47] As well as fathering eight children with Lady

Hervey, he was also known to have had numerous mistresses, including Anne Vane, Maid of Honour to Queen Caroline, who was allegedly later stolen from him by Frederick, Prince of Wales.[48] The £4,000 from Fox, therefore, was presumably given to Lady Hervey in exchange for her interest in the Herveys' marital town house in Great Burlington Street, the lease of which had been reassigned to Stephen by her husband.[49] The reason why Lady Hervey was paid the sum instead of Lord Hervey is unclear, but it may have been provided so that she could independently lease, buy or build a new town house for herself, thereby allowing Lord Hervey and Fox to live together.

Given the length of time that Lady Hervey had waited to be financially independent, it comes as no surprise that she was determined to control every aspect of the building. She clearly enjoyed the process, and had a good working relationship with Flitcroft, writing to Rev. Morris in 1748: 'I now quit you, Middleton and Horace, for Mr. Flitcroft, angles, feet, Greystock bricks, cornice, fascias, copeings'.[50] Her house was a labour of love that took over a decade to build and, although no contemporary depictions or descriptions of the house survive, it is known that she furnished her principal room with a fashionable set of Gobelins tapestry chairs, as befitting a stylish Rococo interior.[51] Suites of Gobelins furniture were the epitome of taste in France, a fashion led by Madame de Pompadour, mistress to Louis XV, who ordered a set of Gobelins furniture in 1751, and another between 1754 and 1756, and again in 1760.[52]

Lady Hervey would have filled her house with luxurious furniture and works of art that she had collected and commissioned throughout her life, such as the beautiful silver spice box engraved with her arms and the Hervey motto '*je n'oublierai jamais*' ('I will never forget') (Figure 3.6), and the pretty porcelain scent flask decorated with a portrait of Prince Charles Edward Stuart, the Young Pretender, and her arms.[53] Lady Hervey was also a life-long Jacobite sympathizer and apparently wore a white rose, the Stuart colours, on 10th June, the Old Pretender's birthday.

She would also have hung the conversation piece that she commissioned in Paris in 1750 from Hubert Gravelot featuring herself, her favourite son Augustus Hervey (the future 3rd Earl of Bristol), and two of her daughters, Mrs Lepel Phipps (later Lady Mulgrave) and Lady Mary Fitzgerald with their respective husbands (Figure 3.5).[54] Lady Hervey was an exacting patroness, because although Gravelot painted the bodies and most of the heads in this group painting, Jean-Etienne Liotard bizarrely painted the heads of the Phipps', and later, apparently still dissatisfied, Lady Hervey had her own head and that of her son's repainted back in England!

The rooms in Lady Hervey's house, we can imagine, were highly decorated, with the 'great room' described as the 'pleasantest room in town'.[55] Lady Hervey became a renowned hostess, holding regular dinner parties and engaging with everything French. She hired a French chef, Jacques Lalliet, who delighted guests with excellent cuisine. William Douglas, 3rd Earl of March, upon returning from the 'Hôtel de Milady', wrote eagerly to his

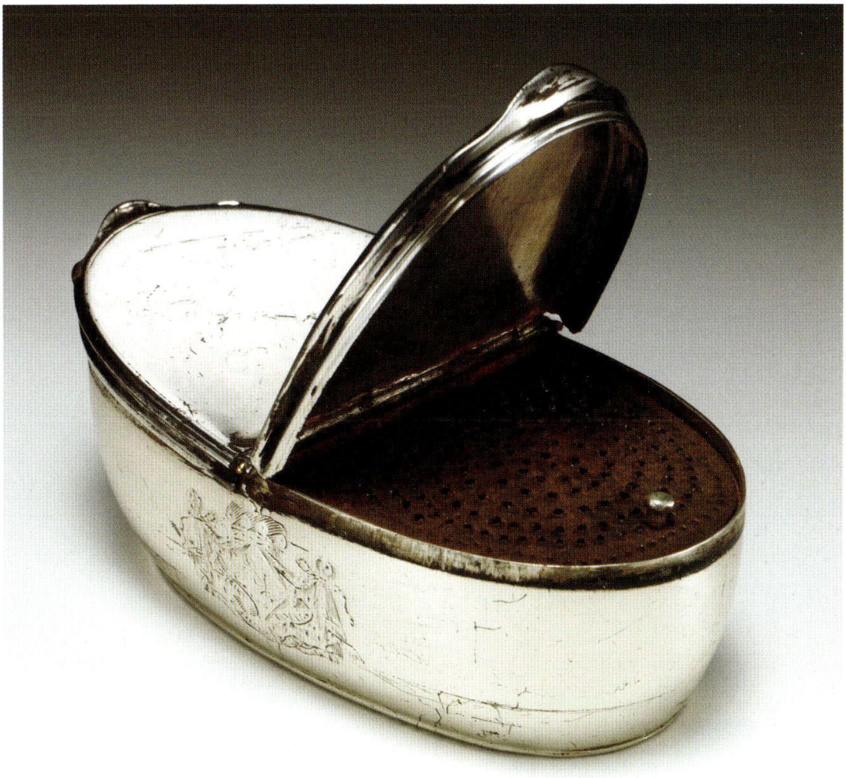

FIGURE 3.6 Nutmeg or spice box with arms of Mary, Lady Hervey, 1743–68, silver. The Metropolitan Museum, New York, 14.58.193. Courtesy of The Metropolitan Museum.

friend George Selwyn in October 1762 that 'Never was anything so French as her dinner and the manner of being served. It is a charming home, and as I have rather a partiality for the French I am very glad of the entré'.[56]

Her sophisticated soirées were well-respected, and introductions were eagerly sought. Edward Gibbon, the English historian and author, was thrilled to gain entry in 1758, stating '('tis true, though wonderful) there is no card-playing but very good Company and very good Conversation'.[57] This type of assembly was a forerunner to the renowned salons held by the famous Bluestockings later in the century. Cards, gambling and excessive amounts of alcohol were cast over in favour of intelligent conversation and lively debate. In later life, Gibbon reflected fondly upon his evenings at Lady Hervey's 'French house in St. James's Place', writing that 'her dinners were select: in the evenings drawing-room was filled by a succession of the best of company of both sexes and all nations; nor was I displeased at her preference and even affectation of the books, the language, and manners of the Continent'.[58]

Lady Hervey achieved her ambition in creating a beautiful home that championed the French style. Although Lady Hervey ran the risk of appearing affected and a little conceited in her near obsession of France, it seems that she cared little about what her contemporaries thought in this regard.

Lady Hervey's confidence to pursue her own style was shared by her near neighbour, Lady Pomfret (Figure 3.7), in Arlington Street. Pomfret Castle, as Lady Pomfret's house was later dubbed, was a celebration of

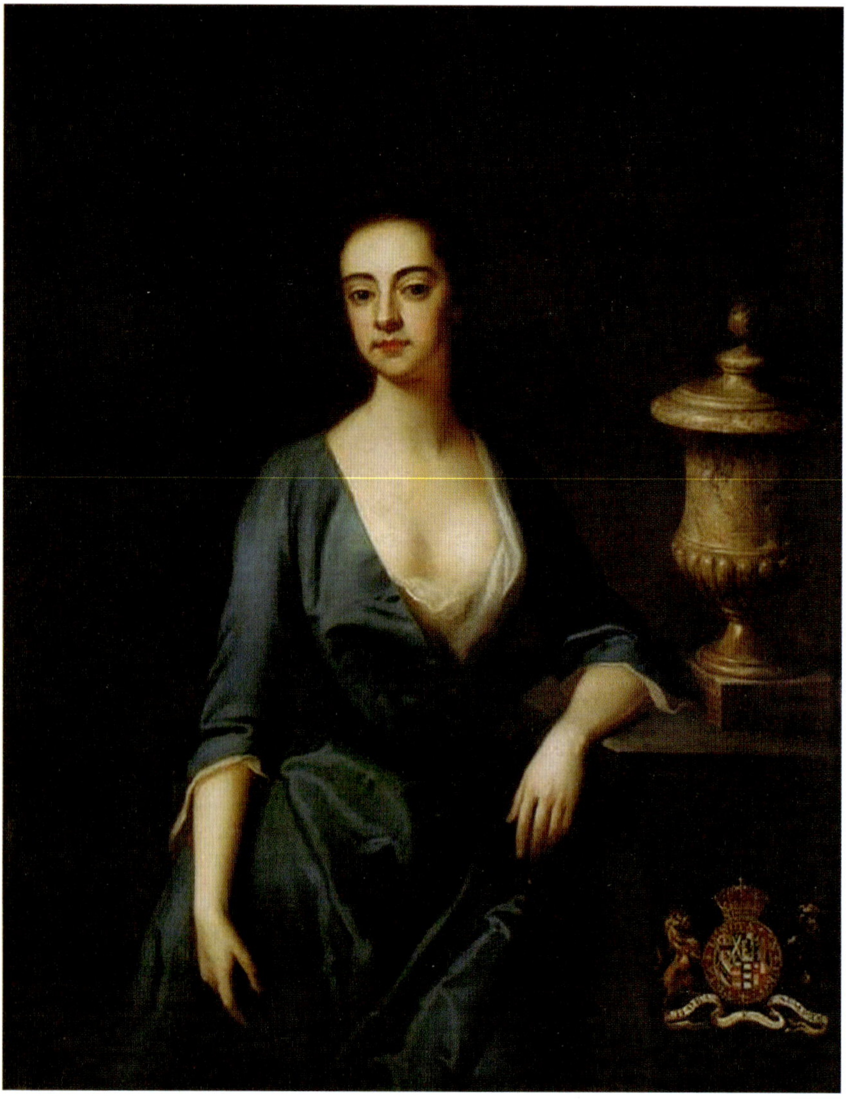

FIGURE 3.7 Enoch Seeman, *Henrietta Louisa Jeffreys, Countess of Pomfret*, *c.* 1720, oil on canvas. Private collection. Signal Photos/Alamy Stock Photo.

British Gothicism, complete with a gatehouse, bold interiors and specially commissioned Gothic furniture.[59] The British penchant for Gothic Revival was only just beginning to take hold in the 1750s, and yet this was the time that Lady Pomfret, now in her widowhood, chose to build the only Gothic town house in London between 1757 and 1759 (Figure 3.8). Gothic, at this

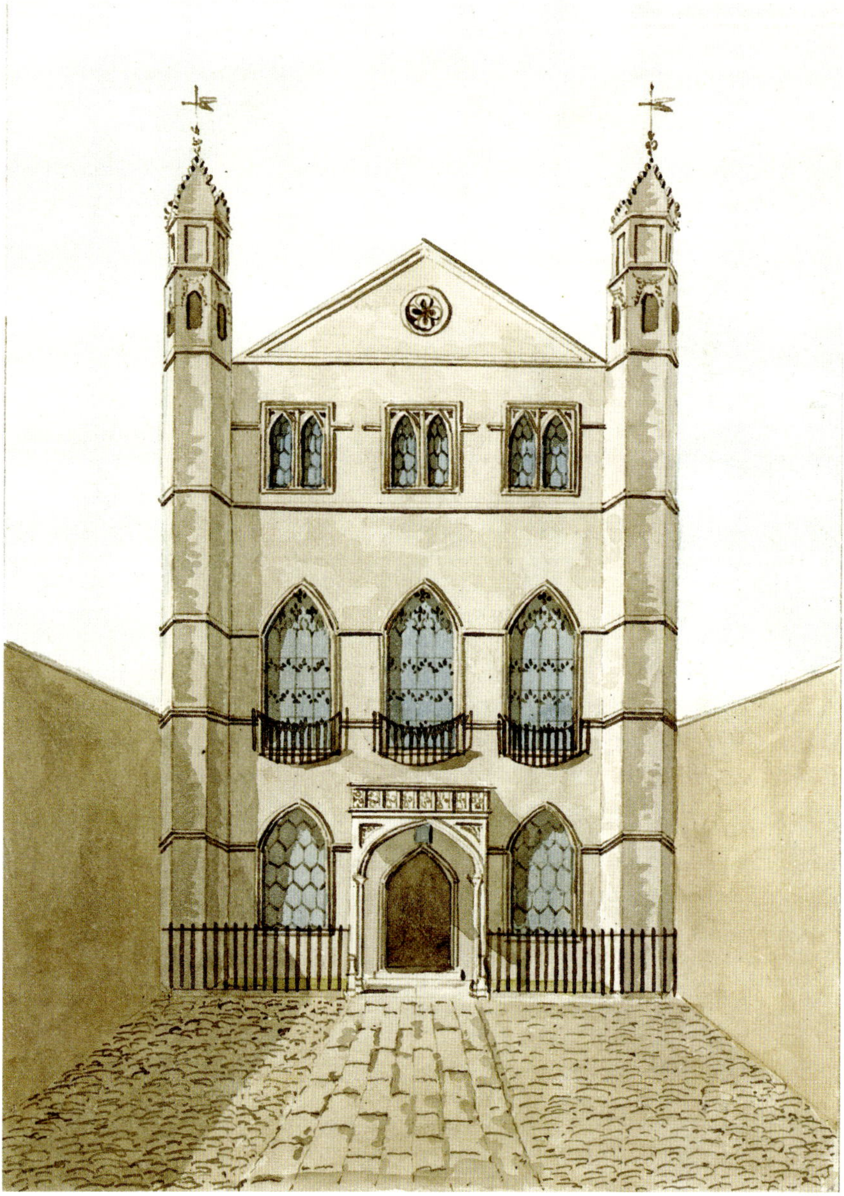

FIGURE 3.8 Sir John Pender, *Pomfret Castle's Courtyard Façade*, 1860, watercolour. Westminster Archives, Gardner Box 48 No 28. Courtesy of Westminster Archives.

time, was a style more often used for the restoration of old buildings or for the construction of garden architecture and follies. It was not used for entirely new building schemes, which is why Lady Pomfret's choice of style is all the more fascinating.

During her life Lady Pomfret had developed a deep passion for antiquarianism and historicism, advocating a desire to return to the true antiquarian roots of medieval Gothic architecture. She subscribed to Samuel and Nathaniel Buck's *Perspective Views of the Ruins of the Most Noted Abbeys and Castles of England* (1726–39) and wished that old buildings were better preserved for future generations:

> I am always glad to hear of any remains of the old English grandeur; and am both amazed and provoked when I hear of people destroying those magnificent structures (made to last for ages) in order to erect some trifling edifice, whose chief merit consist in the vast expense, which often renders the builder unable to inhabit it when he has done; whereas to repair an abbey or castle in the same way as it was first built is a worthy monument both of the owner's piety to his ancestors, and care of his posterity.[60]

Her mention of 'some trifling edifice' signifies her condescension and dismissal of the conventional architectural styles of the day, namely Classicism and more specifically, Palladianism. Perhaps curiously, despite Lady Pomfret's European tour, which she underwent with her husband and three eldest children between 1738 and 1741, she remained steadfast in her preference for Gothic architecture.[61] In fact, her exposure to the best architectural landmarks and collections in Europe served only to retrench her appreciation for medieval architecture and fostered in her an interest in the preservation of ancient buildings and their collections. Not only did this interest later manifest itself in the building of her town house, but also in her bequest of the antique Arundel and Pomfret marbles to Oxford University in 1755.[62]

This significant bequest of statues, taken from Easton Neston, was rendered necessary because of the reckless, scandalous and irresponsible character of the Pomfrets' heir, George, Lord Lempster, who had proved himself to be a disreputable gamester, dueller and a man of violent temper.[63] Lord Lempster's uncontrollable spending and mounting debts forced his father to rewrite his will so that upon his death in 1753 all of his personal property, including his valuable art collection, was disposed of for the benefit of his two unmarried daughters.[64] When Lord Lempster heard of his father's death and his reduced inheritance, instead of wearing mourning as was customary, he callously 'produced himself in a suit of crimson velvet, that he may be sure of not being mistaken for being in weepers'.[65] In light of such outrageous behaviour, Lady Pomfret bought the valuable marbles herself, determined to keep the collection intact and well cared for.

As for Lady Pomfret's interest in Gothic architecture, it is probable that as a Lady of the Bedchamber she would have been influenced by the Gothic garden follies pioneered by Queen Caroline in the gardens of Richmond Lodge, particularly Merlin's Cave, built in 1735. Merlin's Cave, designed by William Kent, was a thatched Gothic-inspired folly, built as a conscious declaration of Caroline's British patriotism, celebrating the ancient origins of the British monarchy.[66] Lady Pomfret was equally interested in the origins of her family, and in *c.*1750 she commissioned a beautiful pedigree tracing her ancestry and that of her husband back to the two wives of Edward I, which was produced in the style of a richly illuminated medieval manuscript.[67]

Before Lady Pomfret had settled on building her town house, she had first considered commissioning a small country house in Bedfordshire for which she asked Sir Roger Newdigate for sketches that 'you think wou'd suit my Gothick Imagination'.[68] Sir Roger was married to her niece, Sophia Conyers, and was an amateur architect and fellow connoisseur of medieval architecture. From 1750 he remodelled his ancestral home, Arbury Hall, Warwickshire, in the Gothic Revival style, thereby providing Lady Pomfret with the perfect advisor and collaborator in all matters relating to building. In the end, however, this country house project never materialized.

It was not until February 1757, therefore, that Lady Pomfret secured the necessary land in Arlington Street from her former son-in-law John Carteret, 2nd Earl Granville.[69] This allowed her to finally embark upon her Gothic Revival vision, for which she involved two architects, as recorded in her diaries. As early as April 1756, she recorded that she 'went alone to Mr Leadbetter to settle my place for Building' and later in 1757 she noted that 'Mr Biggs came about my plans'.[70] Both architects were well versed in Gothic design: Stiff Leadbetter was soon to design the first complete Gothic Revival country house in England, Elvills in Englefield Green; and Richard Biggs was Clerk of Works at Windsor Castle.

The completed house was an astonishing creation. The façades consisted of all the essential Gothic tropes including machicolations, turrets, embattled parapet, Gothic tracery and arched windows and doorways.[71] The house was set back from the road, enclosed by a single-storey gatehouse comprising two octagonal towers, topped with battlements (additional storeys were added in the nineteenth century) (Figure 3.9). The interiors were equally dramatic (Figure 3.10), boasting a range of medieval-inspired decorative motifs such as *fleur-de-lis*, rosettes and quatrefoils, as well as Perpendicular tracery panelling upon the main staircase that was directly copied from Windsor Castle.[72] Lady Pomfret commissioned bespoke pieces of Gothic-styled furniture for her house, including an exquisite library writing desk, which has been attributed William Hallett, one of the most prominent cabinet makers of the time.[73]

Unfortunately, after years of planning and building, Lady Pomfret died in 1761 before having been able to enjoy her newly completed house. Lady Pomfret's final wish was to be buried next to her husband in the family vault

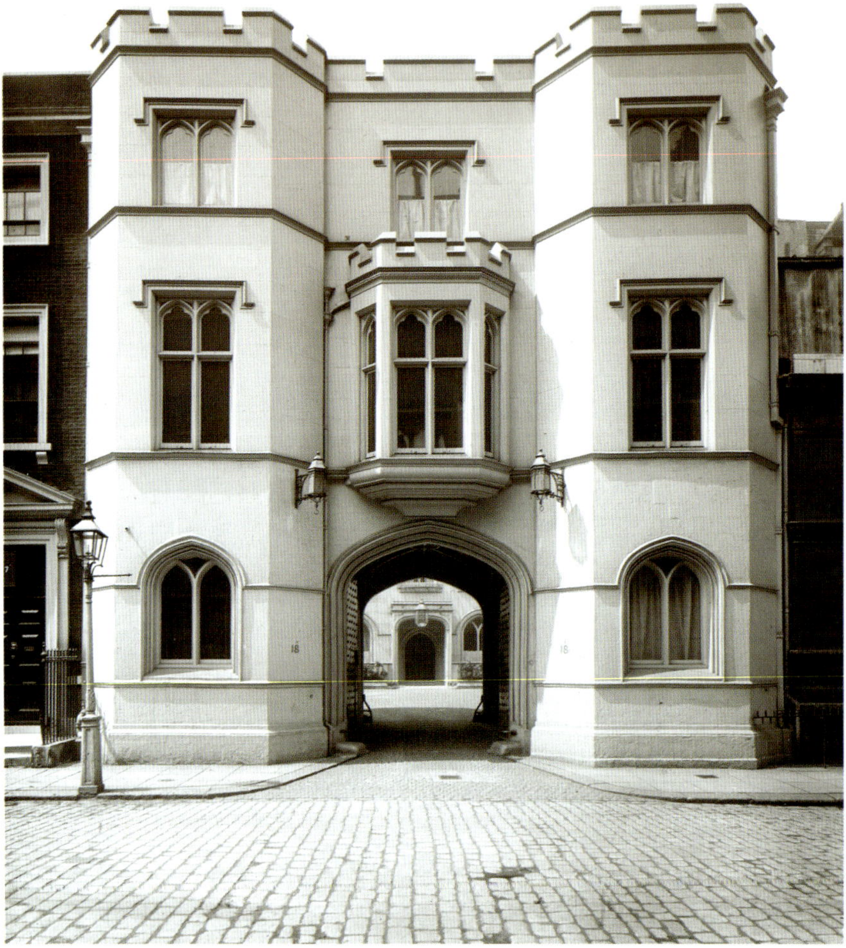

FIGURE 3.9 The gatehouse to Pomfret Castle, 1894. Bedford Lemere and Company. Historic England Archive: BL12821. Courtesy of Historic England.

at Easton Neston, but her son was spiteful to the last and flatly refused. After some last-minute scrambling, her daughters arranged for her to be laid to rest in St. Mary's Church, Oxford, which seems fitting given her generous bequest.[74]

The architectural styles chosen by Lady Hervey and Lady Pomfret, although bold, were considered to be departures from 'uniformity and proportion' and were thus perceived of as 'feminine and undisciplined or effeminate and corrupt'.[75] Lady Pomfret's Gothic Revival house, therefore,

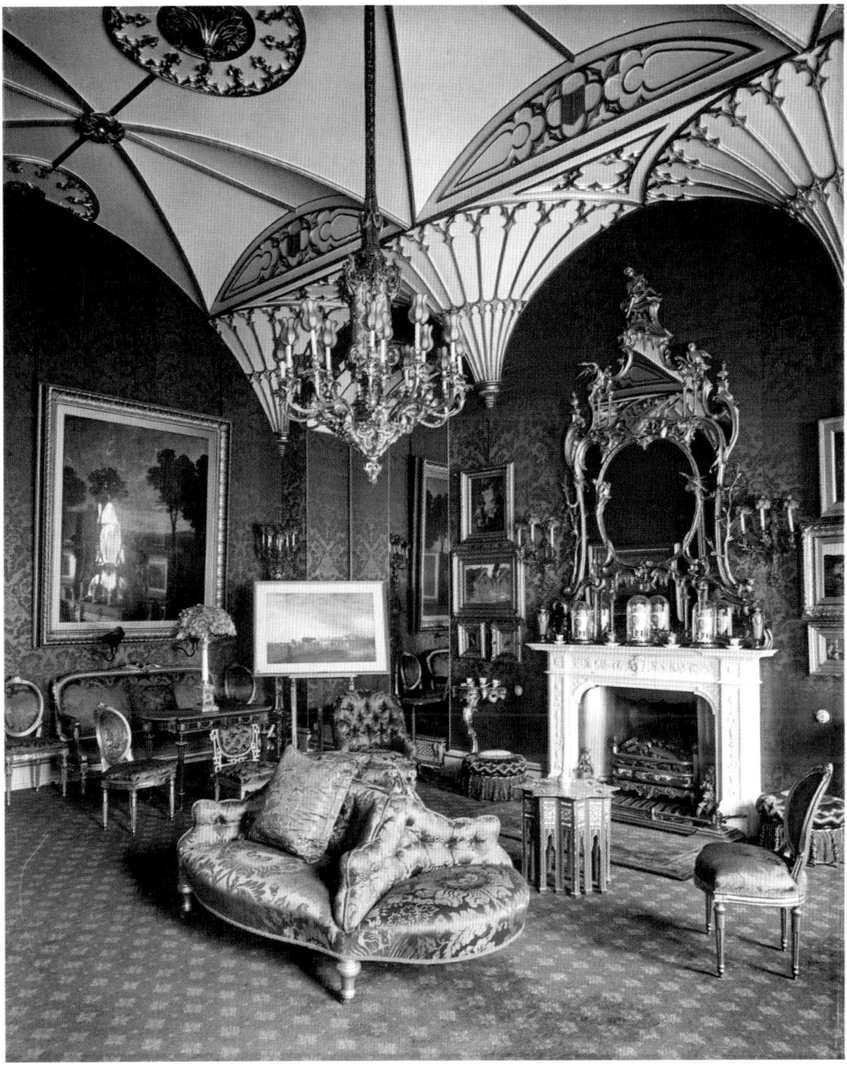

FIGURE 3.10 The Great Room at Pomfret Castle, 18 Arlington Street, 1894, Bedford Lemere and Company. Historic England Archive: BL12824. Courtesy of Historic England.

was most likely perceived by her contemporaries as a playful build, but certainly not a serious one. Similarly, Horace Walpole's Gothic Revival villa, Strawberry Hill House in Twickenham, was also seen as an experimental, unusual interaction with architecture, explained away by his eccentric and effeminate nature.[76] Nonetheless, Lady Pomfret's deliberate patronage of the Gothic Revival demonstrates that she wished to inspire in her fellow countrymen an appreciation of the past, and a desire to look beyond the architectural norm. In this sense it is possible to state that both Lady Pomfret and Lady Hervey were stylistically pioneering and did much to promote these fledgling architectural styles in mid-eighteenth-century London.

Political houses

As well as being platforms for architectural display, the London town house was often at the centre of eighteenth-century politics, built by some of the greatest political families of the era to host elaborate dinners and parties to further their political ambitions. Many women engaged in socio-political activities, with several acting as grand political hostesses, such as the famous Whig hostess, Georgiana Cavendish, Duchess of Devonshire and the Tory hostess, Jane Gordon, Duchess of Gordon.[77] Some women chose to build town houses to maintain their elevated positions amongst the political and societal elite. A fashionable town house also allowed ambitious women to host political gatherings, form powerful social networks, influence leading statesmen, promote their favourites, and further their own political and social agendas.

Lady Cecilia Isabella Finch (1700–71) exerted political influence through the entertainments that she hosted in her new town house at 44 Berkeley Square. Lady 'Bell' Finch, as she was known, was the daughter of Daniel Finch, 2nd Earl of Nottingham, later 7th Earl of Winchelsea, and his second wife Anne Hatton. From about 1730 she was appointed to wait on the three eldest daughters of George II,[78] and following the death of Queen Caroline in 1737, Lady Bell was appointed as the first Lady of the Bedchamber to Princess Amelia; a lucrative position yielding a salary of £400 per annum (about £50,000 today).[79] This provided Lady Bell with financial independence and allowed her to remain unmarried for the entirety of her life. Her intelligence and competence in business matters soon saw her acting as Princess Amelia's personal and business secretary. She regularly corresponded with the 1st Duke of Newcastle, Secretary of State, successfully representing the Princess's interests, as well as dealing with other matters such as patronage and politics.[80] In 1761, in a letter to Newcastle, the true extent of Lady Bell's influence is apparent: 'Her RHss. Places an intire confidence in me as to what relates to her Finances'.[81]

Thus, Lady Bell's construction of a town house served to consolidate her position as one of the most eminent ladies at Court while also allowing her to enhance her social and political networks within London society, thereby furthering her influence. In accordance with her visions of grandeur, she commissioned the renowned architect William Kent between 1742 and 1744.[82] Lady Bell may have been influenced in her choice of architect through her connections at Court, as Kent had been a favoured architect of Queen Caroline, but she may also have been encouraged by her close connection to Richard Boyle, 3rd Earl of Burlington, who had married her half-niece Lady Dorothy Savile in 1721. Burlington was a fierce champion of English Palladianism and was instrumental in propelling Kent into the architectural spotlight.

The cost for building No. 44 was substantial, approximately £7,000 (about £830,000 today), which was made possible by the £5,000 in trust that she inherited from her father's estate upon his death in 1730.[83] The building accounts entitled 'Artificers Employ'd on the Rt. Honble the Lady Isabella Finch's Acct. at her new House in Berkeley Square London', though incomplete, provide a detailed insight into the construction and decoration of the house.[84] No. 44 consisted of two principal rooms of display, namely the staircase hall (Figure 3.11), famously described by Horace Walpole as 'a beautiful a piece of scenery, and considering the space, of art, as can be imagined', and the Great Room on the first floor (Figure 3.12).[85] Both spaces were designed to impress; the top-lit staircase, which covers three floors, is full of theatrical Classical detail, with an Ionic-columned screen (on the first floor), Vitruvian scrolled wrought iron railings and a magnificent domed ceiling.[86]

The Great Room is equally impressive, with the ceiling consisting of a combination of 'octagons, lozenges and squares in the coving', which was 'painted in grisaille' with a series of Classical figures.[87] A surviving drawing of the coffered ceiling is inscribed with the names of the intended figures, with 'Jupiter' intended for the central octagon, flanked by 'Appollo' and 'Diana' (Figure 3.13).[88] The surrounding lozenges are filled with representations of the elements and seasons. The iconographical arrangement of the ceiling was inspired by Lady Bell, who 'almost certainly [owned] a copy of the *Metamorphoses*' and identified with the goddess Diana, insofar as Lady Bell remained unmarried all her life and was a skilled huntress.[89]

Kent and Lady Bell clearly had a successful relationship, because in his will he bequeathed her his 'veined Alabaster Vase with brass ornaments gilt ... together with my four models of Newton, Lock, Woollaston and Doctor Clark'.[90] These were the modellos of Queen Caroline's statues that she had selected for her Richmond Hermitage (1730), as part of her 'pantheon of Worthies, representing British excellence in science and philosophy'.[91] Kent's bequest contributed to Lady Bell's self-presentation by alluding to her interest and understanding of philosophical debate and by emphasizing her personal relationship to Queen Caroline.[92]

Lady Bell's desire to present herself as an educated and learned woman was realized in the creation of her library, located on the second floor. Although the contents of Lady Bell's library remain unclear, it is known that she had an extensive collection of antique texts,[93] and paid for various subscriptions, including Archibald Bower's *The History of the Popes, from the Foundation of the See of Rome to the Present Time* (1750), Elizabeth Carter's 1758 translation of the works of Epictetus, and James Stuart and Nicholas Revett's *The Antiquities of Athens* (1762).[94]

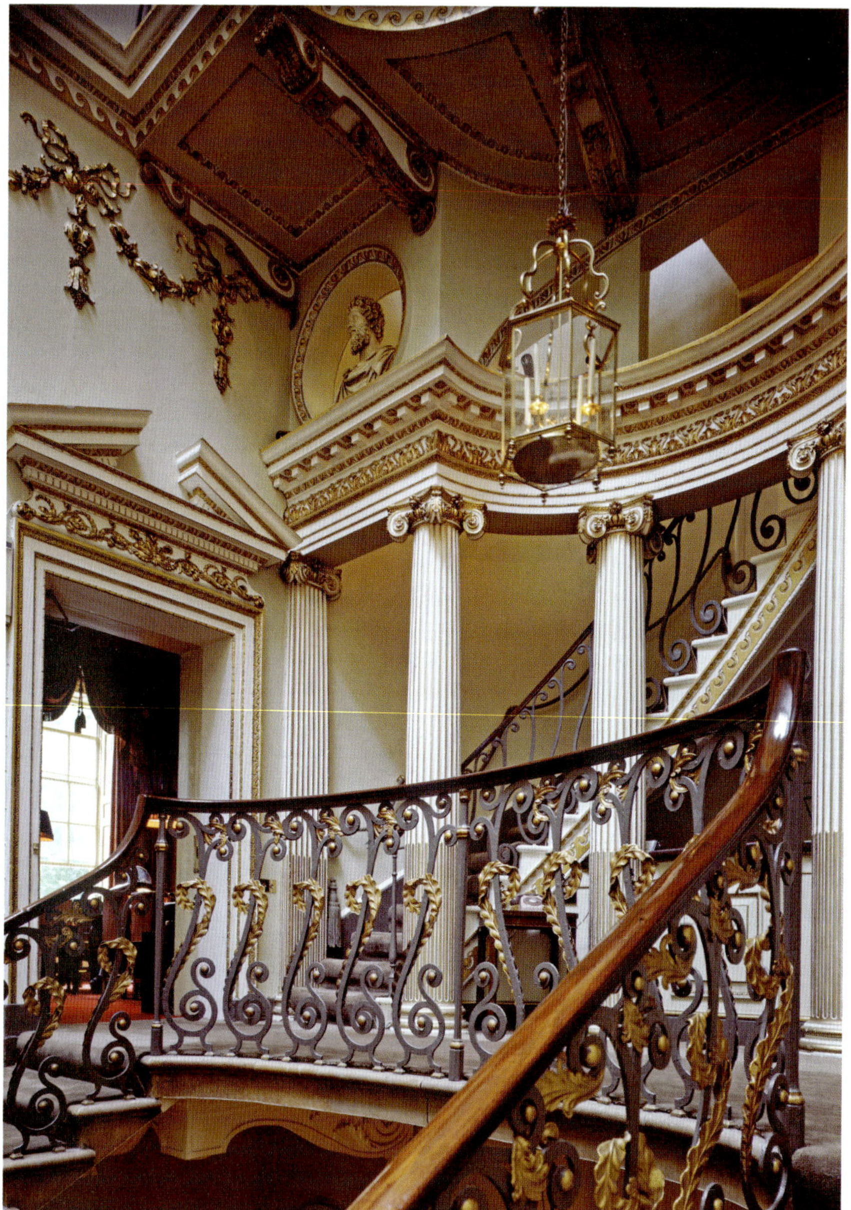

FIGURE 3.11 The staircase at No. 44 Berkeley Square. Photo by G. Nimatallah/ De Agostini Picture Library via Getty Images.

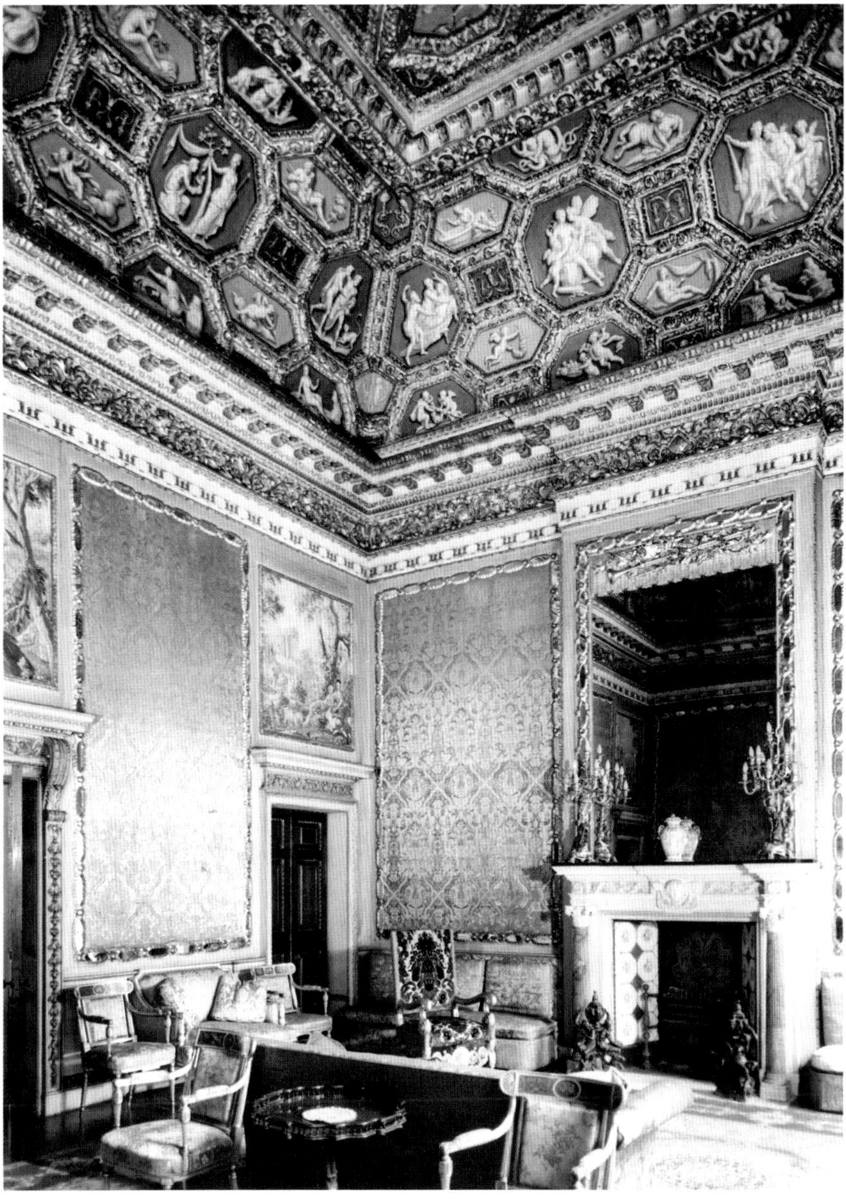

FIGURE 3.12 The Great Saloon at No. 44 Berkeley Square, 1953. Sydney W. Newbery. Historic England Archive, No: 3688_101. Courtesy of Historic England Archive.

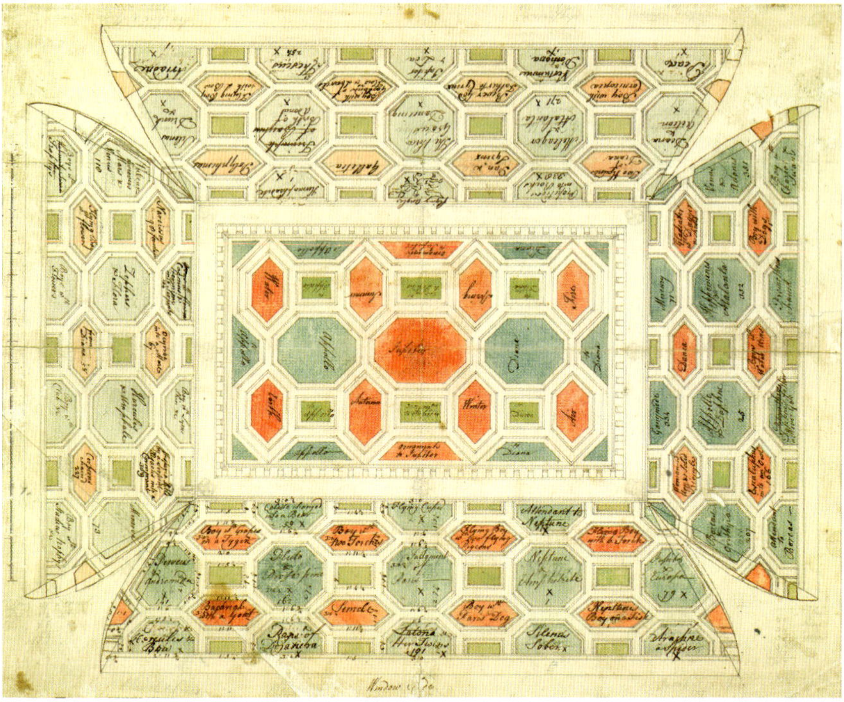

FIGURE 3.13 Stephen Wright, drawing to show the layout of the ceiling of the Great Saloon at No. 44 Berkeley Square, *c.* 1742–4. Pen, black and grey inks, watercolour. RIBA Collections, SC50/2. Courtesy of Royal Institute of British Architects.

Lady Mary Wortley Montagu later remarked in 1752 that Lady Bell was 'the only Lady at Court that has [a Library]'.[95] Care should be taken with this comment, however, as Lady Mary was famously waspish in her commentary, and it is likely that far more libraries belonging to women existed but have since been dispersed and forgotten. Indeed, many of the women discussed in this book had private libraries and regularly augmented them with the latest publications. Queen Caroline, for instance, famously commissioned Kent in 1737 to build her a vast, magnificent library at St James's Palace, which she filled with nearly three thousand titles and envisaged as the setting for her intellectual salons.[96]

Following the completion of No. 44, Lady Bell entertained in great style, hosting regular gatherings that often included Princess Amelia. She was exceptionally proud of her house, believing it to rival those of her male counterparts, and in 1745 she remarked that her saloon trumped Robert Walpole's at Houghton Hall in Norfolk, stating that there was not 'such a Room as I will show you in my House of but 30 odd feet in front which people go to see as a curiosity'.[97] Her house was frequented by some of the most influential politicians in the country, including Walpole and Lady Bell's old friend the Duke of Newcastle. Her property enabled her to informally sit at the centre of the political world, from which she exerted power and influence through her social networks. In 1764, when hosting Sir Brook Bridges, a Whig politician and friend of the Finches, she succeeded in persuading him to vote in a parliamentary debate on warrants, much to the satisfaction of Newcastle who had sought her assistance.[98]

Such was her status that when her sister-in-law, Lady Charlotte Finch[99] (the daughter of Lady Pomfret), attempted to present an illegitimate daughter of Lady Bell's brother, John Finch, to Princess Amelia, Lady Bell flatly refused to allow it, causing a family rift. This 'excellent civil war in the house of Finch' culminated in Lady Bell banishing William Finch (her brother and Lady Charlotte's husband) from No. 44.[100] When responding to her brother's insulting accusation that she wished to cause the pregnant Lady Charlotte to miscarry, she retorted with imperious indignation: 'This is not the place to be indecent, and therefore I shall *only* tell you, that you are a rascal and a villain, and that if ever you dare to put your head into my house, I will kick you downstairs myself'.[101]

Lady Bell's strong will and prominent house gave her the power to decide who she associated with and who she entertained, with non-admittance being the ultimate mark of displeasure. The pride that Lady Bell felt for her residence was also apparent in her will, in which she was determined that the beneficiary 'make no Alteration in the building or disposition of the rooms on the first and second Floors of the said house or in the Furniture of the said Rooms'.[102] Lady Bell was successful in not only forging an independent life, but also in creating a house from which she could subtly, and sometimes not so subtly, choreograph the socio-political world around her.

For others, the desire to influence fashionable society was essential, particularly if they wished to make new allegiances, forge beneficial friendships or repair damaged reputations. The creation of a new, tasteful town house, designed by the most fashionable architects of the day, was a means by which disgraced individuals could seek to regain their place amongst society. This scheme was employed by Elizabeth Greville, Countess of Warwick (*c.* 1721–1800), and her lover, General Robert Clerk, when they commissioned Robert and James Adam to build their new mansion in Mansfield Street.[103]

Lady Warwick was the daughter of Lord Archibald Hamilton and his second wife Lady Jane Hamilton, a mistress to Frederick, Prince of Wales. In 1742 she married Francis Greville, Lord Brooke (created 1st Earl of Warwick in 1760), but after two decades of marriage the two seemed to have grown apart. By the early 1760s it was rumoured she was in a relationship with Clerk, which resulted in a shocking formal separation that deprived her of a London residence and damaged her social status.[104] To remedy this the Adam brothers were quickly hired to design a new house and in July 1768 Lady Warwick made the first cash payment of £500, following which she paid £250 every quarter until 1776.[105] Lady Warwick's ownership over the project is clear, with her son Robert Fulke Greville later annotating the building accounts with: 'Disbursements incurred & paid for the House built by The Countess Dow^r of Warwick' with a further comment stating that the house was paid for by 'the monies belonging to Ly W. herself'.[106]

As well as financing the scheme, a first-floor plan of the house inscribed with 'Drawn & written by herself' suggests that she was also intimately involved in the design process (Figure 3.14).[107] Lady Warwick also noted on the plan that the 'building is with arches, & is the first and only one so built in London to this present year 1775'.[108] Lady Warwick later gave the plan to her niece, the courtier and diarist Mary Hamilton (1756–1816), which suggests that they shared an interest in architecture and design. Surviving Adam drawings dating to 1779 allude to a highly sophisticated early Neo-Classical interior, indicating that Lady Warwick and her now-husband wished to be at the forefront of architectural fashion.[109] They finally took possession of their beautiful home in 1780, some six years after they had married, and seven years since Lord Warwick had died. Thus, after many years of living apart, they were at last able to set up home together and relaunch themselves into polite society as a married couple.

Building a brand-new house that showcased the owner's refinement and ability to host extravagant entertainments was perhaps one of the best ways to regain societal acceptance for those who were shunned. This was one of the motivating factors for the widowed Elizabeth Home, Countess of Home (1703/4–84), who built a lavish town house in Portman Square to host glittering entertainments for the disgraced Duke and Duchess of Cumberland.

Lady Home was a Jamaican-English heiress, the only child of William Gibbons, a West Indies merchant. In 1732 she had moved to London with her first husband James Lawes, but he died the following year leaving his young widow a vast jointure of £7,000 per annum (approximately £830,000 today), which, together with the Jamaican plantations that she had inherited from her father, made Elizabeth an immensely wealthy widow.[110] In 1747 Lady Home was listed as the owner of Snow Hill, St Andrew, with 1373 acres and 194 enslaved people, and the joint owner of Townwell and Temple Hall, also in St Andrew, with 2000 acres and 229 enslaved people.[111] According to the Jamaican Quit Rent books of 1754 Lady Home was listed as the owner of 1215 acres in St Andrew, 500 acres in St George, 765 acres in St Mary, 600 acres in St Elizabeth, 1000 acres in Clarendon, 1085 acres in Vere and 112 acres in St John; a grand total of 5287 acres.[112] The number of enslaved people toiling on these plantations is not listed, but it is clear that there would have been hundreds.

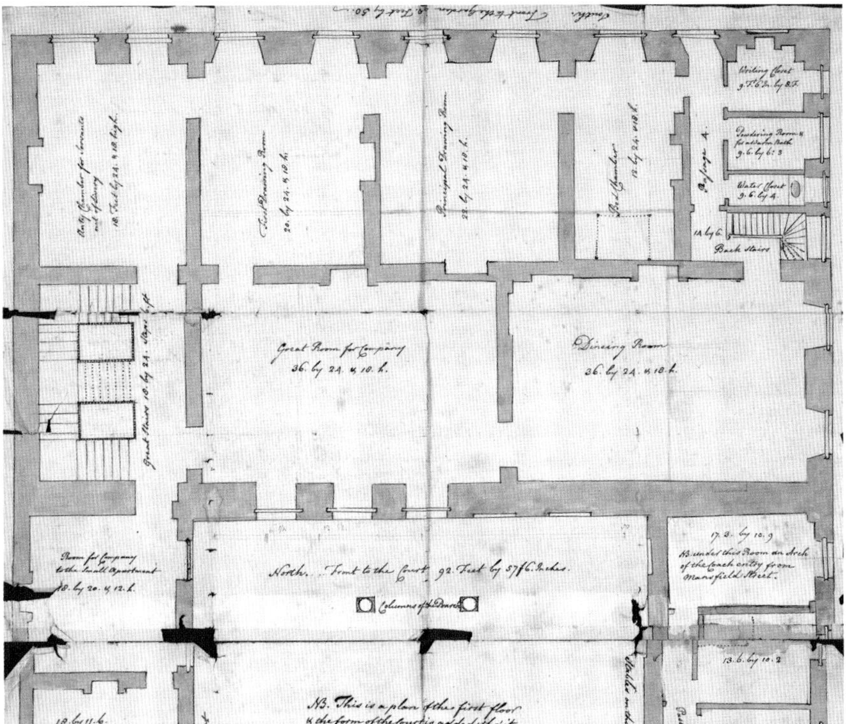

FIGURE 3.14 Lady Warwick's first-floor plan of her house in Mansfield Street, 1775. The John Rylands Library, University of Manchester, Mary Hamilton Papers, GB 133 HAM/1/5/4/1. Copyright of the University of Manchester.

Lady Home was not unique in her role as an absentee female plantation and slave owner.[113] Another was Anna Eliza Elletson (1737–1813), who inherited Hope Plantation in Jamaica from her first husband, Roger Hope Elletson, and was an active absentee manager and owner of her 385 enslaved men, women and children.[114] Anna's Jamaican fortune made her an attractive marriage prospect, so much so that in 1777 she married the 3rd Duke of Chandos. Upon her death in 1813 she bequeathed her estates and enslaved people to her daughter Anna, Duchess of Buckingham and Chandos.

On 25 December 1742 the widowed Elizabeth had also joined the ranks of the aristocracy, marrying the 8th Earl of Home. The Earl, evidently only interested in his wife's fortune, deserted her only two months later, choosing to pursue his military career, later dying in 1761 in Gibraltar. The income provided from slavery made heiresses such as Elizabeth and Anna lucrative catches for British aristocratic families, who often needed cash injections to sure up their estates or embark on new architectural projects, such as the building of country houses. It is a sad historical fact that a number of Britain's most beautiful houses were partially or wholly funded by the dismal practice of slavery; this important subject has received greater attention in recent years.[115]

For Lady Home, the money she received from her plantations was channelled into luxurious living and grandiose display. Following the death of her first husband she engaged John Cheere to sculpt a grand marble monument in his memory, and at the same time she also commissioned another to honour her late mother. Both monuments were substantial in size, the one to her husband measuring two and a half meters in height, the largest monument to be shipped from England to the West Indies at the time.[116] Such display hints at Lady Home's social pretentions and inclination to ostentation; traits that further manifested in 1772, when she unexpectedly commissioned James Wyatt to build a palatially large new town house on the north side of Portman Square (despite her already living on the south side).[117]

The reason for this commission was to provide a suitably extravagant establishment for the entertainment of the recently married, and subsequently disgraced, Duke and Duchess of Cumberland.[118] In 1771 H.R.H. Henry Frederick, Duke of Cumberland and Strathearn, had greatly angered his brother, George III, by marrying a beautiful young widow, Anne Horton, without his consent. The Cumberlands' marriage caused a huge scandal, triggering the Royal Marriages Act of 1772, which resulted in them being banished from Court and shunned by society.[119] Anne was the daughter of Lady Home's sister-in-law, Judith Maria Luttrell (*née* Lawes), later Countess of Carhampton, so it would seem that Lady Home hoped to assist her disgraced relatives by providing a suitably grand setting in which they could establish their own alternative quasi-royal Court. By doing so, Lady Home risked social suicide herself because it was made clear by the royal

Court that if anyone dared to receive the Cumberlands, they themselves would also face banishment from Court. Being in her late sixties and with immense wealth at her disposal, Lady Home appears to have cared little about such threats and was more concerned about helping her kinswoman than offending the king.

James Wyatt was responsible for building the relatively plain shell of Home House, which was dramatically juxtaposed with the magnificent suite of Neo-Classical reception rooms. Unfortunately, although Wyatt had made progress enough to design ceilings by 1773, Lady Home was dissatisfied with his work and in 1775 she dismissed him.[120] The reasoning for this is unclear, but was probably due to Wyatt's somewhat dilatory approach to his work.[121] Lady Home's frustration with Wyatt is clear in a letter to Robert Adam dated 24 February 1775, in which she complains that, 'Mr Jam^{s} Wyatt, & Mr Daval are trying which of them can be most troublesome to me in their hasty demands for irregular payments'.[122]

Lady Home quickly exchanged Wyatt for Robert Adam, who succeeded in replacing and enhancing his competitor's interiors with his own, for which there are seventy-three surviving Adam drawings in the Soane Museum. Perhaps his most breath-taking achievement was the construction of the circular staircase hall and Imperial stair, inserted into the square-shaped shell previously designed by Wyatt (Figure 3.15).[123] Rising the full height of the house, the staircase is ornamented with fine stucco trophies and medallions by Joseph Rose and large grisaille paintings of fictive bas reliefs by Anthony Zucchi; the whole is topped with a dome and skylight (Figure 3.16).[124]

On the *piano nobile* the Music Room was one of the most opulent of Adam's creations, designed to host private musical parties, such as the one attended by William Beckford, the novelist and art collector, in 1782:

> I accepted yesterday [an invitation from] no less a personage in short that the Countess of Home, known amongst all the Irish chairmen and riffraff of the metropolis by the name, style, and title of the Queen of Hell ... Aware of my musical propensities she determined to celebrate my accession to Portman Square by a sumptuous dinner and a concert of equal magnificence. Last evening it took place and you never beheld so splendidly heterogeneous a repast as the dinner nor ever heard such a confounded jumble of good and bad music – such a charivari in fact – as the Concert.[125]

Despite Beckford's unflattering (and somewhat ungrateful) description of the raucous event, it was nonetheless hosted in the most sumptuous suite of rooms. Dubbed the 'Queen of Hell' because of her 'irascible behaviour and lavish parties', Lady Home knew how to entertain in style.[126] The exquisite decoration of the Music Room, for example, consists of six apses, three along the north wall and three along the south, framing the windows, all

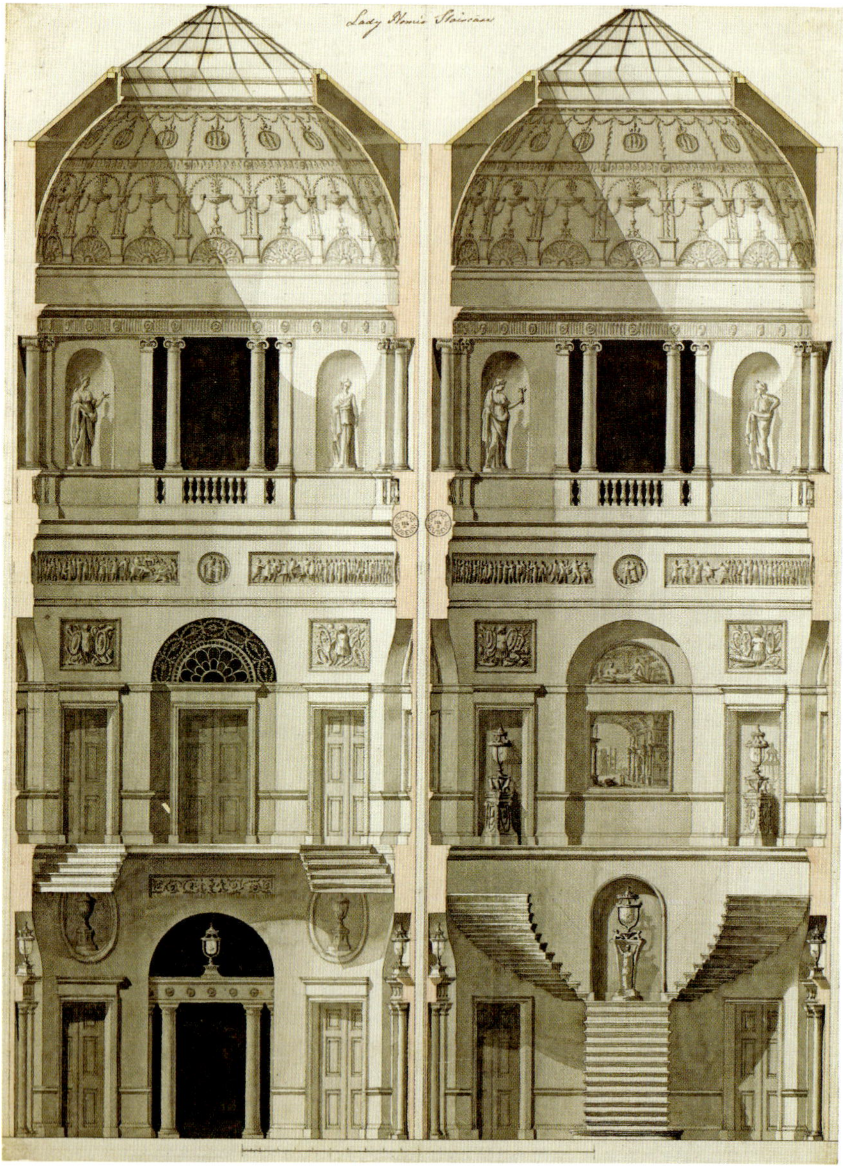

FIGURE 3.15 Adam Office hand, stairwell sections for Home House, *c.* 1775, pen, pencil, wash and pink wash on laid paper. Adam Volume 14/116. © Sir John Soane's Museum, London. Photo: Ardon Bar-Hama.

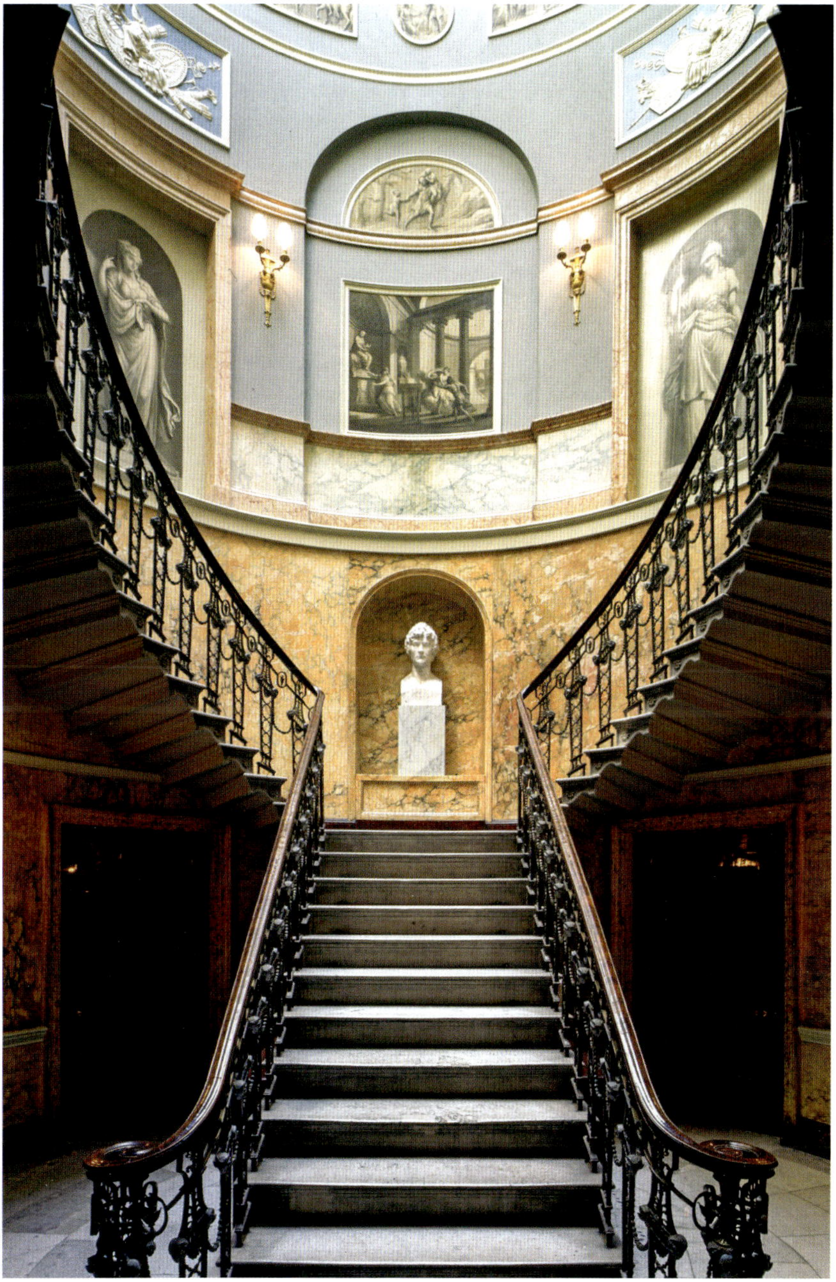

FIGURE 3.16 The staircase at Home House. Florian Monheim/Roman von Götz/ Alamy Stock Photo.

of which are tied together with a beautiful ceiling of circles with musical-related paintings in the centres, painted by Zucchi (Figure 3.17).[127] The whole room is dominated by an elaborate organ designed by Adam.[128]

Beyond the Music Room lay the 'Second Drawing Room', which once displayed Lady Home's treasured state portraits of the Duke and Duchess of Cumberland, by Sir Thomas Gainsborough.[129] These portraits, now at Buckingham Palace, were gifted to Lady Home by the royal couple, which she proudly recorded in her will: 'their Royal Highnesses the Duke and Duchess of Cumberland were graciously pleased to present me with their portraits at full length and which are now hung in my Capital Room'.[130] They were mounted in elaborate custom-made gilt frames with ducal coronets, also designed by Adam.[131] Lady Home was profoundly proud of these portraits and it is likely that the commissioning of her house centred around the need to create a room grand enough to accommodate the royal paintings. By doing so Lady Home was able to celebrate her royal connection, assist in the repairing of the Cumberlands' damaged reputations and launch herself into society as a leader of architectural fashion.

Upon its completion, Lady Home's house was one of the most extravagant London houses created in the later eighteenth century. Her determination to build a venue fit to receive members of the royal family ensured that she hired the greatest architects, painters and artisans of the time, at immense cost to herself.[132] Before she died in 1784, Lady Home had only seven years to enjoy the fruits of her labour, reinforcing the fact that this commission was of great importance to her, and centred around the Cumberlands' reintroduction into fashionable society. Interestingly, upon her death, Lady Home gave specific instructions relating to the Cumberlands' paintings, bequeathing them to the 'Lord Mayor Aldermen and Commonalty of the City of London' so that they could be 'hung up in some proper place in the Mansion House London there to remain and to be deemed and considered as ornamental fixtures'.[133] It seems that even after death Lady Home wished to continue promoting the Cumberlands. The Mayoral office, however, did not accept this bequest (perhaps wishing to stay out of the political drama) and they instead reverted to the Cumberlands. In 1808, the Duchess of Cumberland bequeathed the portraits to William IV in her will and thus they became part of the Royal Collection.[134]

Lady Home's foray into architectural patronage is testament to the fact that town houses were important status symbols that enabled women to freely engage in the socio-political sphere. Just as Lady Bell used her house to host illustrious guests to forward her own political agenda, so too did Lady Home, albeit with a focus on influencing Court politics. In a similar vein, although Lady Warwick did not necessarily seek to engage in politics of any kind with the building of her house, she was still determined to improve her social status and relaunch herself into society free from the taint of scandal. Town houses, therefore, afforded their patronesses both political and social influence, the latter of which will now be explored in greater detail.

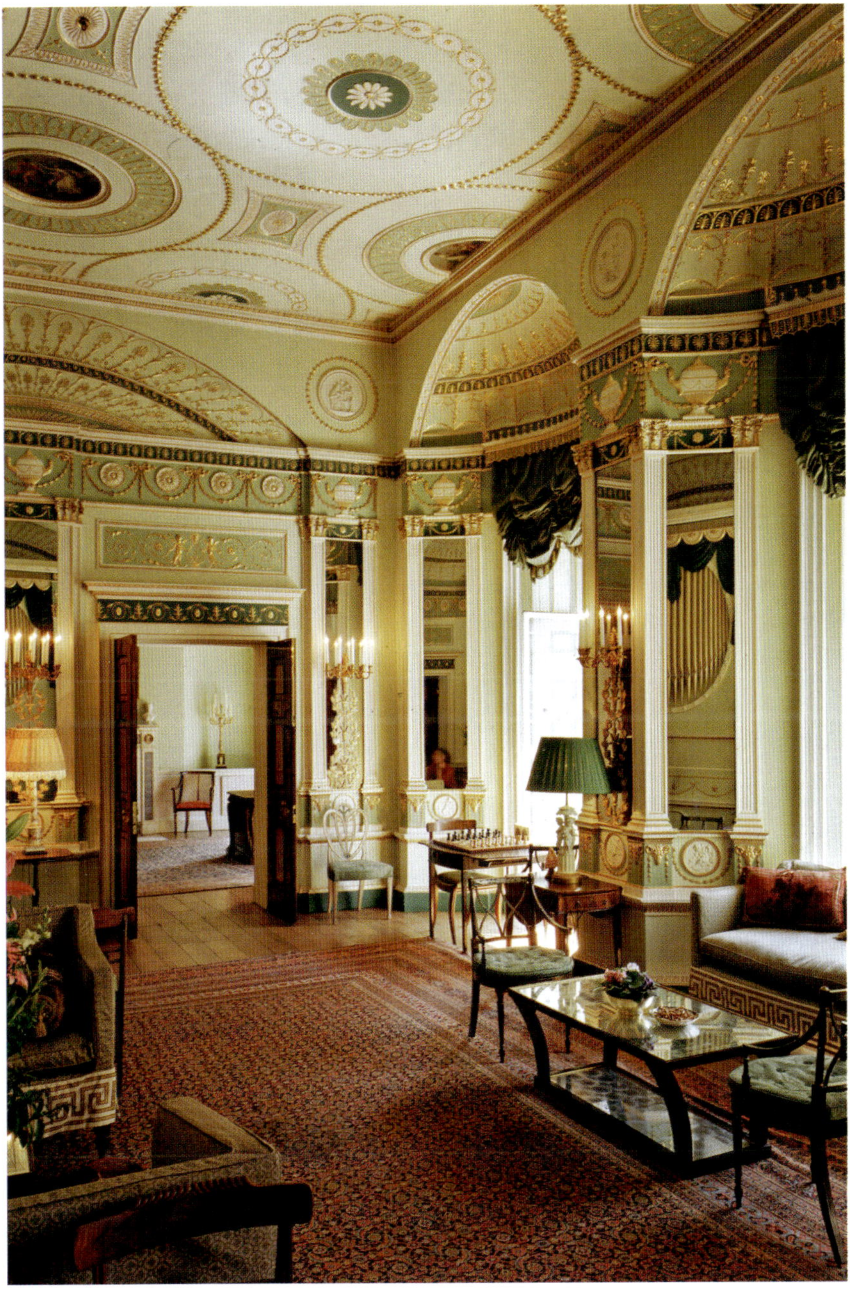

FIGURE 3.17 The Music Room at Home House. Florian Monheim/Roman von Götz/Alamy Stock Photo.

The social house

In addition to working as a political stage, the London town house also served an important social function, often designed with circuits of receptions rooms intended to host sumptuous entertainments. Women were at the heart of the eighteenth-century social scene, with many determined to host the most sophisticated, the most extravagant and the most memorable soirées of the season. We have already seen how Lady Hervey, Lady Bell Finch and Lady Home succeeded in creating beautiful homes that allowed them to entertain in style. Another patron that deserves our attention is the famous Bluestocking and *salonnière*, Elizabeth Montagu (1718–1800) (Figure 3.18). Elizabeth, the daughter Matthew Robinson and Elizabeth Drake, was an extremely wealthy widow with commercial property and estates in London, Berkshire and Northumberland, which, at her death in 1800, were reputedly worth £10,000 (approximately £450,000 today) a year.[135] Her wealth came from her late husband's Northumberland coalmines, which she had successfully managed from 1766, eventually owning them outright upon his death in 1775.[136]

Just as Lady Home decided to build a grand new town house in her sixties, so too did Elizabeth (Figure 3.19). In fact, she also built her house in Portman Square and patronized the fashionable architects James Stuart and James Wyatt.[137] From the very beginning of her project, Elizabeth intended her house to be a hub of social gatherings, a stage upon which polite intellectual society would congregate: 'I shall be wishing my great room finished & the Lustres glittering in it & my self sitting in the Center, beaux spirits in one hand, some gentlemen & fine ladies (without any esprit at all) on the other, feathered nymphs & great – maccaronies circulating about'.[138] Not only did she wish to throw glittering soirées, but in contrast to the raucous events organized by her neighbour, she also intended to host refined Bluestocking salons which aimed to bring together the greatest minds and wits of the age.

Elizabeth played a central role within the sophisticated, cultured Bluestocking community.[139] Her regular salons were strictly hierarchical, with the seating arranged in a semi-circle, with herself sat at the apex of the curve and with those of the greatest social prominence sat next to her.[140] Elizabeth set the topic of discussion and chaired the conversation, the aim of which was to assimilate the variety of participants' ideas into collective knowledge. Elizabeth was so successful in creating the perfect salon that Dr Samuel Johnson crowned her the 'Queen of the Bluestockings' and Fanny Burney, a fellow Bluestocking, described her to be 'Brilliant in diamonds, solid in judgement, critical in talk'.[141]

Therefore, as a leader of the Bluestockings and as a woman of the Enlightenment, Elizabeth took her role as an architectural patroness seriously. Having cultivated her image as a sociable intellectual through her letter writing and assemblies, Elizabeth was experimental in her choice of

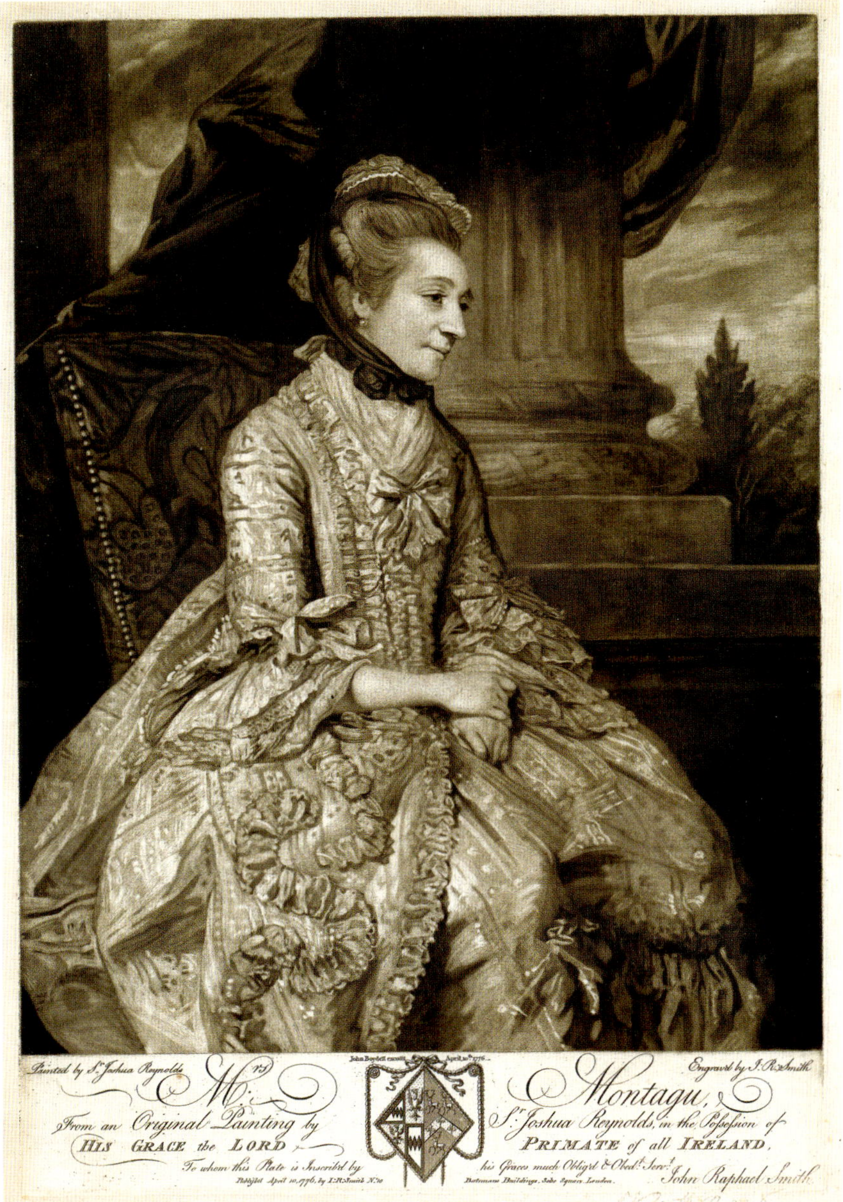

FIGURE 3.18 John Raphael Smith, after Sir Joshua Reynolds, *Mrs. Montagu*, 1776, mezzotint. Yale Center for British Art, Paul Mellon Collection, B1977.14.10115. Courtesy of the Yale Center for British Art, Yale University.

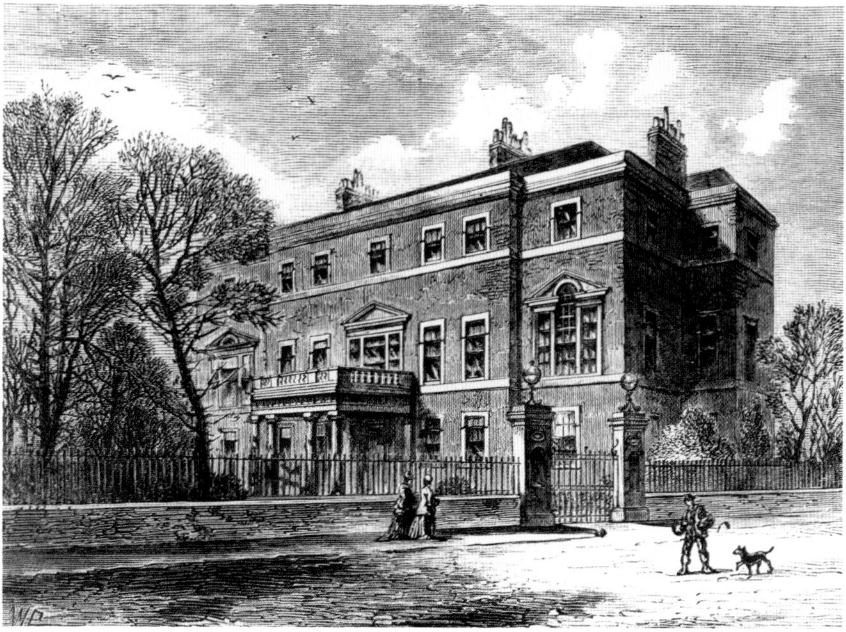

FIGURE 3.19 Unknown artist, *Mrs Elizabeth Montagu's house in Portman Square*, *c.* 1880, engraving. Hulton Archive/Getty Images.

styles and always sought to be the leader of aesthetic fashions.[142] In her first London town house, at 23 (now 31) Hill Street, Elizabeth distinguished herself as a trend-setter by being one of the first to commission an entire room in the Chinoiserie style between 1748 and 1752.[143] Her Chinese room was a celebration of all things Chinese, which she described to her sister, Sarah Scott, as a 'Temple of some Indian God ... The very curtains are Chinese pictures on gauze, and the chairs Indian fan-sticks with cushions of japan satin painted: as to the beauty of colouring, it is carried high as possible'.[144]

This celebrated room was of her own design, filled with objects, furniture and textiles made and sourced by her friends and family. Her brother, William Robinson, who was a captain in the East India Company, regularly brought back Chinese objects to decorate the room, leading Elizabeth to describe her house as an 'Indian warehouse'.[145] In 1752 Elizabeth commissioned a suite of japanned furniture from William and John Linnell, cabinet-makers of distinction, of which two pieces survive.[146] The first is a secrétaire-commode with open lattice work and jappaning, which depicts Northern Song-style scenes, the second is a cabinet on a stand with latticework doors with painted scenes of rocks and flowers.[147]

Elizabeth's correspondence indicates that the Linnells also supplied her with a large, elaborate pier mirror and a glass chimneypiece, both in the

Chinoiserie style.[148] This suite of furniture is one of the earliest known Chinoiserie commissions associated with the Linnells, thereby highlighting Elizabeth's trendsetting taste in interior decoration. In fact, the latticework on the cabinet bears a strong similarity to the Chinoiserie cabinet made two years later for the Elizabeth, Duchess of Beaufort for Badminton House.[149]

At her new house, No. 22 Portman Square, Elizabeth commissioned the most *à la mode* Neo-Classical interiors, with a determination to achieve an authentic antique style, perhaps in direct contrast to Lady Home's more fantastical interiors. Elizabeth's house was to consist of five principal reception rooms located on the *piano nobile*, accessed by a grand cantilevered staircase. In a rough sketch (Figure 3.20) of this floor, drawn by Elizabeth in 1780, she labelled the entertaining rooms as the 'Gallery', 'Great Room', 'Antiroom', 'Dining Room' and 'Room for Morning Company'.[150] Located beyond these rooms, to the west of the house, was her bedchamber and an accompanying dressing room.

The architect appointed to realize Elizabeth's true antique dream was James 'Athenian' Stuart, whom she had previously hired at her Hill Street house. Stuart was considered a pioneer in the authentic Neo-Classical style and was well-known for introducing the new 'Greek Style' to Britain. In 1762 he and Nicholas Revett published *The Antiquities of Athens*, which was the first accurate survey of ancient Greek architecture based on archaeological excavation.[151] Elizabeth subscribed to this publication, as well as to Adam's *Ruins of the Palace of the Emperor Diocletian* (1764), indicating that she was

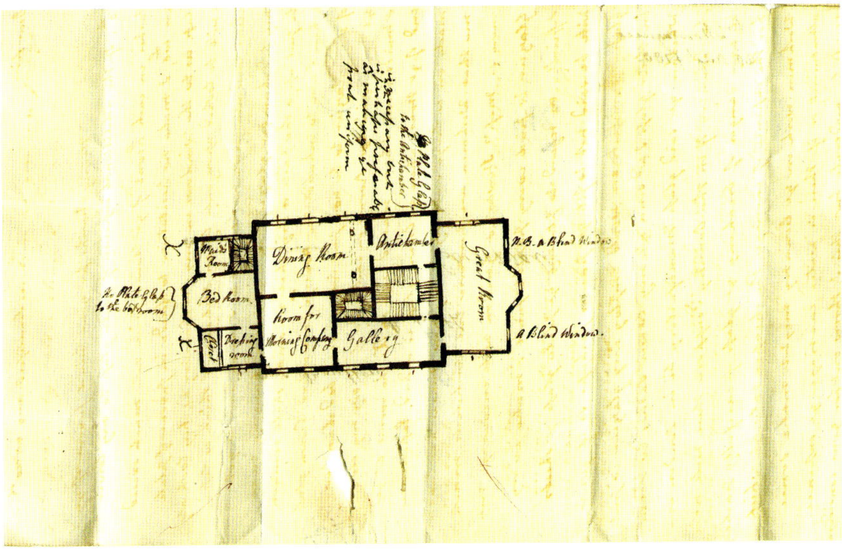

FIGURE 3.20 Elizabeth Montagu's sketched plan of the first floor of Montagu House, 1780. Birmingham Central Library, Matthew Boulton and Family Papers, MS 3782/12/93/17. Courtesy of the Birmingham Assay Office.

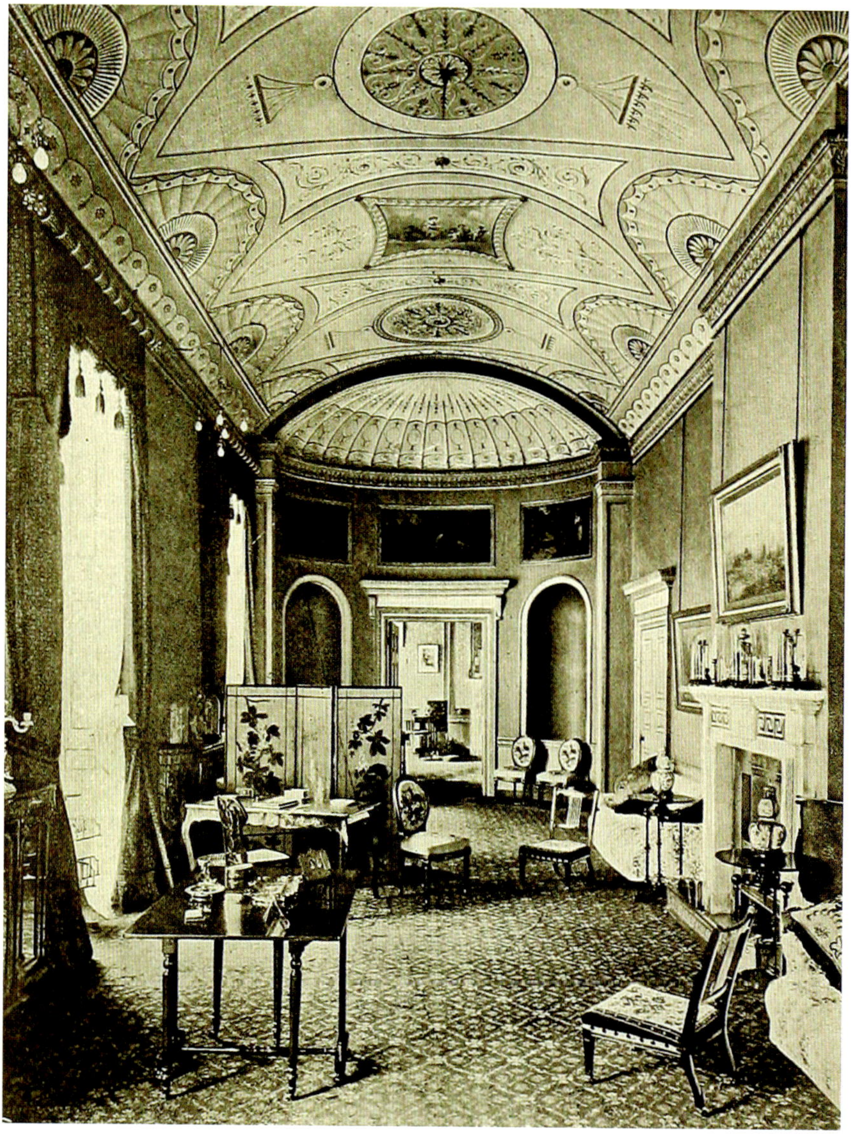

FIGURE 3.21 The Gallery at Montagu House, as it was in *c.* 1915. The Reading Room/Alamy Stock Photo.

already interested in the latest in Neo-Classical trends. Elizabeth, together with her cultured guests, would no doubt have studiously consulted the drawings of ancient Greek temples and other public edifices, which had hitherto seemed remote and unreachable. Thus, with Stuart as her architect and with the leading architectural treatises at her disposal, Elizabeth must have felt confident that she could create one of the best houses in London (Figure 3.21).

However, although Stuart had a promising start at Montagu House, he soon became increasingly incompetent in his management of the project as a whole. His delays, escalating costs, inability to provide designs for his workmen and his rampant alcoholism eventually resulted in his replacement with James Wyatt in 1780.[152] Ironically, only five years earlier, Wyatt had been dismissed by Lady Home and replaced with his rival, Robert Adam. With a new architect who could be relied upon, progress was swift, and in 1782 Montagu House was sufficiently complete to host a small housewarming party. Horace Walpole was amongst the guests and was greatly impressed with what he saw, writing that he 'thought it so magnificent a house' with 'not a morsel of gilding'.[153] He relished its sophisticated interiors, further stating that 'It is grand, not tawdry, nor larded and embroidered and pomponned with shreds and remnants, and clinquant like all the Harlequinades of Adam, which never let the eye repose a moment'.[154] He was perhaps comparing Elizabeth's refined Neo-Classical taste to that of the more ostentatious interiors of Lady Home's house, suggesting that there was a desire amongst the *beau monde* for a less fussy interior.

Another visitor who admired Elizabeth's accurate recreation of the antique was James Harris, the literary intellectual and grammarian, who was so impressed that he wrote that he had:

> seen an Edifice which for the time made me imagine I was at Athens, in a House of Pericles, built by Phidias. I felt a more solid satisfaction ... that, the genius of Phidias could still produce an architect, and the genius of Pericles still produce a Patroness.[155]

Elizabeth would no doubt have been extremely gratified to know that her careful pursuit of the true Classical style had been a success, and perhaps even more pleased that she had been likened to Pericles, the great Greek statesman and patron of the arts. She had triumphed and managed to capture the spirit of ancient architecture.

Although Elizabeth had already opened her house to guests, her house was by no means finished: two principal rooms, the Morning Room and the Great Room, still remained incomplete. The Morning Room, which at this point already boasted a beautiful ceiling by Stuart, was later hung with a set of remarkable feather wall hangings, a scheme of Elizabeth's own invention. She asked friends and family to send her colourful feathers from home and abroad, which were then woven into tapestries by Elizabeth Tull at Sandleford.[156] Later renamed the 'Feather Room', it was described in the *St James's Chronicle* as 'wholly covered with feathers, artfully sewed together, and forming beautiful festoons of flowers and other fanciful decorations. The most brilliant colours, the produce of all climates, have wonderful effects on a feather ground of a dazzling whiteness'.[157] Such was the novelty of the scheme and the renown of its creator that Elizabeth was honoured with a visit by Queen Charlotte and five of her daughters in 1791. Such a visit not only publicly acknowledged Elizabeth's refined aesthetic taste, but also served to enhance her reputation further as a patron of the arts and a prominent member of fashionable society.

The Great Room was also completed in 1791 and, although started by Wyatt years earlier, it was adapted and finalized by yet another architect, Joseph Bonomi. Bonomi's proposal for the room, which survives, shows a heavily Neo-Classical room with a barrel-vaulted ceiling with inset paintings, *vert antique* scagliola columns with gilded Corinthian capitals, walls hung with white damask, window frames of solid white marble, chiaroscuro over-door paintings by Biagio Rebecca and a magnificent carpet (Figure 3.22).[158] Upon its grand opening the Great Room received all the praise and approval that its patroness could have hoped for. It was lauded as:

> [A] magnificent drawing-room, designed by Bonomi; the centre piece of the ceiling charmingly painted by Rigaud; the beautiful columns of verde antico executed by Bartoli; the chimney-piece by Westmacott; the carvings and gildings by Nelson and Borgnis. The room is hung with white figured damask; the curtains are of white satin fringed with gold; the chandeliers and large looking-glasses are superb; and the whole is an assemblage of art and magnificence which we have never witnessed in a private room.[159]

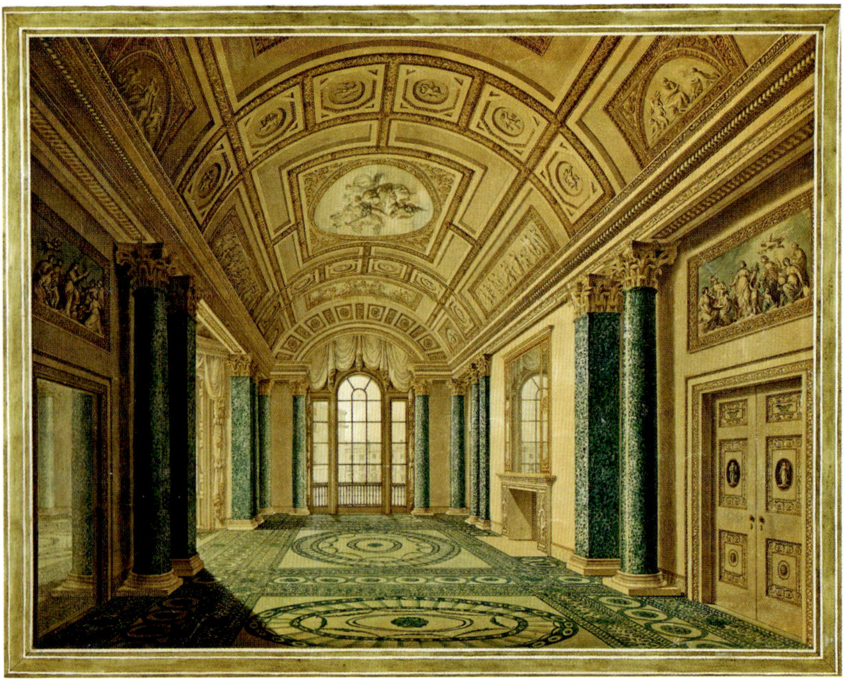

FIGURE 3.22 Joseph Bonomi, proposal for the Great Room at Montagu House, 1782. RIBA Library Drawings Collection, BONOMI [19] 10 SOS/A/IO. Courtesy of RIBA.

Once again Elizabeth succeeded in creating a remarkable interior space that was publicly extolled as exceptional. Given Elizabeth's talent for pursuing perfection in each architectural style that she chose, it is satisfying to see that even at the age of seventy-two she was still a leader in the field of architectural patronage and design. Indeed, until her death in 1800 Elizabeth continued to use her beautiful house to host gatherings, including an annual May Day feast for the chimney sweeps of London.[160]

Women remodelling existing town houses

For women who could not afford to build an entirely new house or did not wish to, the alteration of an existing one was an acceptable method of displaying one's taste. For example, between 1797 and 1799 the widowed Elizabeth Herbert, Countess of Pembroke (1737–1831), Lady of the Bedchamber to Queen Charlotte, commissioned John Soane to remodel No. 49 (formerly 44) Grosvenor Square, costing the sum of £2,189 (approximately £100,000 today).[161] Similarly, at the turn of the nineteenth century, the widowed Elizabeth, Lady Heathcote (d.1813) commissioned Thomas Chippendale Jr. to transform the interiors of her town house at No. 49 Upper Brook Street, spending £747 12s. 11 ½d. (approximately £35,000 today) for the supply of fashionable furnishings and furniture.[162] Although the alteration of an existing house did not provide the same level of control over the architectural design as a new build, it still allowed a great number of women to engage in architectural patronage. In fact, due to the lower costs and the faster time to completion, it is arguable that it allowed more women from a wider social background to shape the London town house.

For those women who did not come from the privileged landowning classes, but still possessed wealth, the desire to mould their town houses was no less great than that of their social superiors. Entrepreneurial women such as courtesans and businesswomen could sometimes become astonishingly wealthy, which provided them with the means and opportunity to embark upon architectural projects of their own. Despite their lack of formal education and limited access to the latest architectural treatises of the day, they could be just as ambitious and innovative in their architectural pursuits.

Town houses of courtesans and enterprising women

The eighteenth century could arguably be described as *the* era for celebrity courtesans. The seventeenth century had of course seen many women vie for the exalted position as royal mistress to Charles II, but beyond the royal circle mistresses were less celebrated. Conversely, the nineteenth century, with its retrenching of family ideals and the general return to Christian values, meant that the sex industry was driven further underground. The eighteenth century, however, was the age of celebrity, with print shops, newspapers and artists clamouring to make their fortune from the images and exploits of the nation's latest obsession. Fanny Murray, Kitty Fisher, Nelly O'Brien, Sophia Baddeley, Mary 'Perdita' Robinson, Charlotte Hayes, Emma Hamilton and Elizabeth Armistead were some of the most famous courtesans of the age. Their fame was garnered not only from their beauty and notoriety, but also from their meteoric ascent from obscurity to the height of wealth and fame.

Many courtesans began their careers in the brothels or bawdy houses of London, the conditions of which could range significantly.[163] At the upper end, such establishments were known as seraglios, convents or nunneries, which were exclusively female-run, as the German traveller Archenholz noted in the late eighteenth century: 'A little street called King's Place is inhabited by nuns of this order alone, who live under the direction of several rich abbesses'.[164] The women of these residences lived a life of luxury, albeit of the gilded cage variety. They wore the very best clothes, had liveried servants, travelled about in carriages and lived in extravagantly furnished rooms – ultimately, however, they were indentured to the 'Madams' or 'Mother Abbesses' who ran the establishments.[165]

Mother Abbesses, such as the notorious Jane Douglas, Jane Goadby and Charlotte Wells, ran these enterprises with ruthless efficiency. They rented town houses in popular areas of London, including St James's and Covent Garden, transformed them into opulent dens of delight and filled them with a constant stream of young girls. Douglas's bawdy house, for instance, located in the north-east corner of the Covent Garden piazza, was expensively furnished and was allegedly decorated with old master pictures in gilt frames.[166] Goadby's high-end nunnery in Great Marlborough Street was equally famous for its exuberant interiors, extortionate prices and its vast array of beautiful young girls. In 1773, a letter from 'Curioso' to the editor of *The Covent Garden Magazine* wrote excitedly about the upcoming season:

> Mrs G – dby, that celebrated Lady Abbess ... having fitted up an elegant nunnery in Marlborough-Street, is now laying in a choice stock of *Virgins* for the ensuing season ... As Mrs. Cornely's [Cornelys] has been justly stiled the empress of taste in the regions of *decent* amusements; so may Mrs. G – dby with equal propriety be termed *the most favourite priestess of Venus*.[167]

Admittance to such establishments was 'so exorbitant' that only the richest men could 'aspire to the favours of such venal divinities'.[168] Young sex workers hoped to secure for themselves a wealthy benefactor, who would take her into high keeping, providing her with all the necessary trappings. Sir Richard Atkins, 6th Baronet of Clapham, did just that when he took the celebrated Fanny Murray (1729–78) as his mistress around 1746, by providing a 'splendid equipage, a numerous retinue, an elegant furnished house, and a handsome allowance'.[169] Atkins later purchased the lease of 'an elegant country house near Richmond, which he suitably furnished' for Fanny, indicating that she was also able to enjoy the pleasures of both town and country life as much as any of her social superiors.[170]

Successful courtesans could amass great wealth which they used to increase their visibility by establishing grand, fashionable households in the capital. They competed with one another 'in ostentatious displays of extravagance, to attract ... the richest and most prestigious lovers'.[171] An appropriate residence, therefore, was clearly a mark of status and of the utmost importance to a courtesan who wished to retain her place at the forefront of the *bon ton*. Her house provided her with the veneer of respectability, which allowed her to host fashionable assemblies and to entertain her lovers extravagantly. In *A St James's Beauty* (Figure 3.23) we are offered a rare glimpse into the material world of the eighteenth-century high-class courtesan.[172] Here, a beautifully dressed courtesan sits in her elegant room, which is tastefully decorated, filled with luxury furniture and complete with a cabinet of books. This is a room in which she could entertain her elite clients, and perhaps she just has, as she is sniffing a rose left by one of her lovers.

Two famous society women, Sophia Baddeley (1745–86) and Teresa Cornelys (1723–97), are outstanding examples of self-made women who used architecture to further their goals. They both came from obscure backgrounds but used their beauty, charms and wit to build large enough fortunes to establish themselves in fashionable London abodes. They were flamboyant in their architectural display, and during their lifetimes used their town houses to attract future lovers and patrons. Both were mistresses to wealthy men at various points in their lives and thus the architectural opportunities available to them were predominately constrained to the interiors of their London houses. There are two main reasons for this. Firstly, while courtesans were often able to accrue significant wealth, their funds were not ample enough to purchase leaseholds or freeholds outright, which significantly diminished their opportunity to build. Secondly, they were expected to keep up the appearance of luxurious living, which consumed most of their income and left little for long-term goals such as building new houses.

The beautiful Sophia Baddeley was a famous actress and singer, who, following the separation from her husband, realized that she could sustain

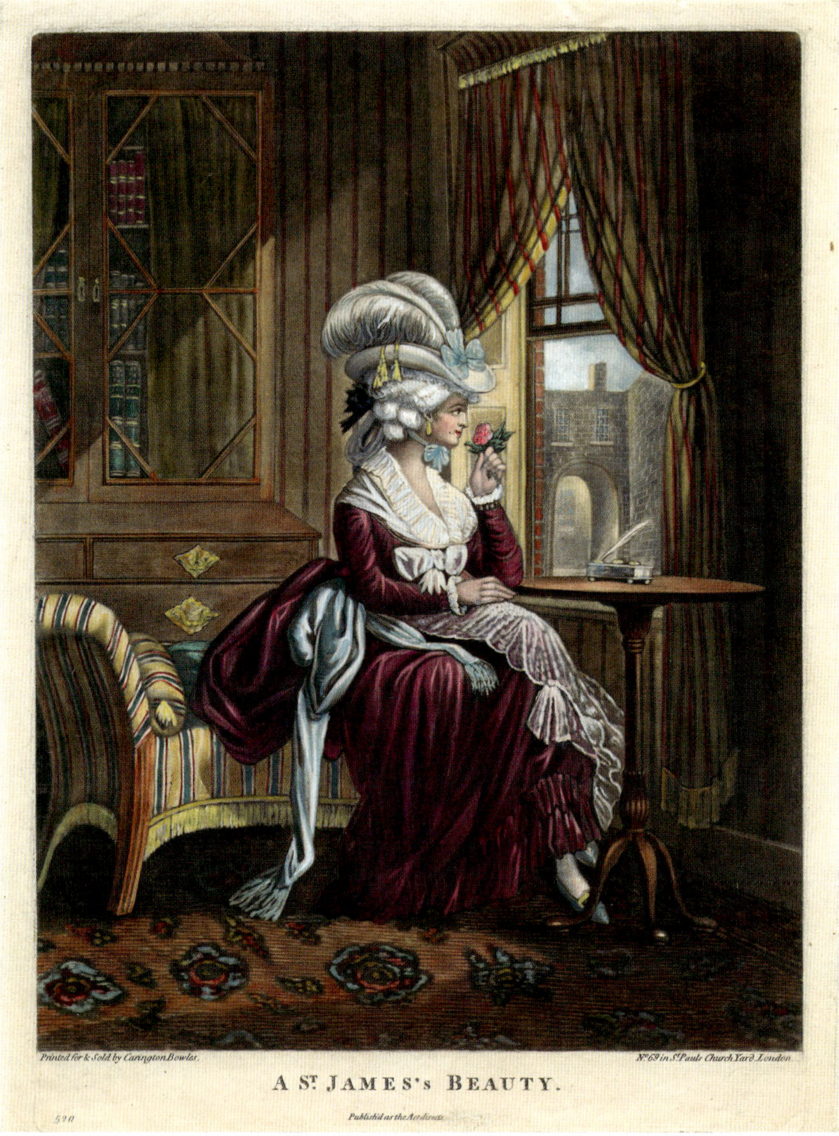

FIGURE 3.23 *A St James's Beauty*, published by Carrington Bowles, 1784, hand-coloured mezzotint. The Colonial Williamsburg Foundation, 2009–22. Courtesy of the Colonial Williamsburg Foundation.

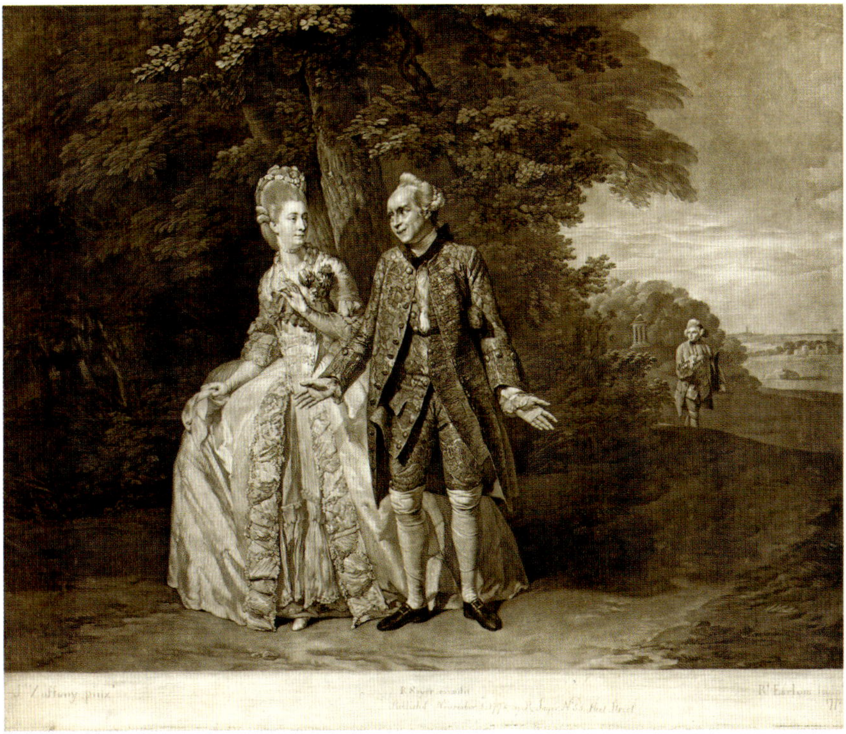

FIGURE 3.24 Richard Earlom, after Johan Joseph Zoffany, *The Clandestine Marriage*, 1772, mezzotint. Yale Center for British Art, Paul Mellon Collection, B1977.14.14614. Courtesy of Yale Center for British Art.

herself with the assistance of wealthy lovers (Figure 3.24). Born in London, Sophia was the daughter of Valentine Snow, the sergeant-trumpeter to George II. Sophia's first serious patron was the Hon. John Hanger who immediately took a 'handsome lodging in Dean Street, Soho, [and] hired her a carriage at his own expence'.[173] This dalliance ended in disaster. Sophia fell hopelessly in love with Hanger, who promptly abandoned her when his father demanded he return home. Disgracefully, he left Sophia to deal with their debts of £700 (approximately £72,000 today).[174] Sophia's was utterly betrayed and heartbroken upon hearing this news, causing her to fall 'senseless to the floor'.[175] She then called a hackney chair to take her to an apothecary where she asked for 300 drops of laudanum, which, as soon as she returned home, she allegedly drank in one go.[176] Although she was later saved by a maid who ran out to get medical help, Sophia's health suffered terribly from this suicide attempt, and even after six weeks she was still barely able to walk.[177]

Shortly after this tragic episode, Sophia set up home with her old school friend Mrs Elizabeth Steele, in St James's Place.[178] Elizabeth was also separated from her husband (who had been declared bankrupt), and it seems as though the relationship was of mutual satisfaction, with Sophia bringing in the money and Elizabeth running the household and managing the finances.

Although not fully recovered from her heartbreak, Sophia soon began to accept visits from her admirers. She received numerous offers, including many proposed financial settlements which would have cleared her debts and provided her with an annuity, but she rejected them all, allegedly declaring that 'she would never *wholly* be at the disposal of any man'.[179] This did not prevent her from accepting gifts of money and neither did it prevent her suitors from trying to win her over. Many were so desperate to gain access to Sophia that they forcefully gained admittance to her house, which sometimes resulted in humorous situations. Lord Palmerston, for example, barged into a lightshow performance and fell over the camera obscura; Lord March was pushed down the stairs by a protective servant and covered with contents of the of the pail she was carrying; and the Neapolitan Ambassador, who was 'an eternal plague' and would 'take no denial', got locked in a closet for half an hour for being so annoying.[180] In all such instances, Sophia's town house was central to her image as one of the most desirable and fashionable women about town. By presenting herself as a member of elite society, she successfully attracted the wealthiest men, which in turn allowed her to maintain her independence.

One of her most persistent admirers was the newly married and very wealthy Peniston Lamb, 1st Viscount Melbourne. During his campaign to win Sophia he gave numerous presents of money, including £300 (approximately £31,000 today) on one occasion, and on another, before leaping out the parlour window to avoid detection by Elizabeth, he gave a further £200 (approx. £21,000 today).[181] These vast sums of money led to lavish spending sprees, during which Sophia spent over £900 (nearly £80,000 today) outright in one day on luxurious jewellery, as well as buying a diamond necklace on credit, costing £450 (approx. £40,000 today) – which was promptly paid for by Lord Melbourne.[182] Shortly after, in about 1771, Sophia left the stage to become Melbourne's mistress, and moved into an elegant house in Grafton Street, with a rent of £200 a year covered by Melbourne.[183] With her new-found financial stability Sophia embarked on an extravagant lifestyle, filled with an endless cycle of spending sprees, outings, parties and entertaining – anything that would increase her visibility and preserve her celebrity status.

Sophia's desire to present herself as a leader of fashion extended to the interior decoration of her new house, which she constantly updated:

> At times she was rather whimsical; she would one day put up furniture in the house, and next day pull it down, and was always changing. Nothing, either of dress or furniture pleased her long. We had workmen of some denomination always in the house, such as upholsterers, painters, carpenters and the like.[184]

Sophia's extraordinary wealth during this period allowed her to remain at the forefront of decorative taste, which probably accounts for the constant change of furniture and furnishings. On another occasion she sought to imitate the interiors of Louis XV's mistress, Madame du Barry, at Versailles:

> Her house in town was as elegantly furnished as a good taste and money could make it; the walls of her drawing-room were hung with silk curtains, drawn up in festoons, which she had done, in imitation of Madame du Barre's room, at Versaille, Lewis the Fifteenth's mistress, and every thing proportionally elegant and costly; so that she lived, and made an appearance equal to a woman of the first rank.[185]

Sophia's status had catapulted her into elite society, so much so that she was able to present herself as the near equal of the highest born ladies in the country. She adorned her walls with artworks purchased from sales at Christie's, including a painting of 'a miser', purchased for her by a Mr Thomas Stanley, and two paintings of fruit purchased for her by Sir Cecil Bishopp.[186] By displaying these artworks she was thus pleasing her benefactors as well portraying herself as a connoisseur of the arts.

The purpose of the Grafton Street residence, therefore, was for Sophia to entertain her male admirers in a suitably glamorous fashion. Her principal reception rooms consisted of a drawing room and a parlour, which proved very useful when, occasionally, Sophia's admirers would arrive at the same time. For example, on one occasion the 4th Duke of Queensberry and a 'Captain Fawkner' arrived together and were shown into the parlour, where 'a harpsichord being in the room, at the joint request of the gentlemen, Mrs. Baddeley sung them a song'.[187] However, in the interim (as fate would have it), two further admirers arrived, so they were tactfully shown into the drawing room to await Sophia.[188]

Within these reception rooms Sophia hosted a variety of intimate entertainments for her admirers, including morning concerts 'with accompaniments by people of fashion', where she would sing songs from different operas, all with 'great taste and judgement'.[189] In the evenings she would host sumptuous dinners where her table 'was set out with elegance' with 'all sorts of French and Spanish wine' to entertain her 'nobler friends'.[190]

Unfortunately, Sophia's success was not to last, and when Melbourne's attentions waned, so too did her fortunes. Having grown accustomed to a limitless stream of money and credit Sophia had racked up debts totalling an eye-watering sum of £7,000 (approx. £720,000 today), which she could never hope to pay off without the assistance of a wealthy benefactor.[191] In 1776, having been abandoned by her patrons, she was forced to return to acting, performing in London, Dublin, York and Edinburgh, while battling laudanum addiction, ill health and poverty.[192] She sadly died of tuberculosis in July 1786 aged only forty-one.

Another woman with a similar tale of fame, fortune and eventual downfall was Teresa Cornelys. She was remarkable, daring and innovative in her architectural endeavours, using her London town house to make her fortune by hosting magnificent assemblies for the elite. Teresa's architectural patronage differs from that of other architectural patronesses during this era because she utilized architecture to heighten the success of her commercial venture. Where Sophia Baddeley spent her money on maintaining the appearance of an extravagant lifestyle, Teresa purposefully set money apart for architectural schemes to further her business goals.

Teresa Cornelys is famous for having taken London by storm with her lavish subscription balls and concerts for the nobility and gentry during the 1760s and 1770s.[193] An Italian-born opera singer, Teresa moved permanently to London in 1759, and soon enjoyed a meteoric rise to fame and fortune.[194] With her 'sound judgement … uncommon taste and an imagination inexhaustible of inventions', she became the 'fairy queen' of London, committed to 'gratifying the English nobility with entertainments'.[195] Observing the success of outdoor entertainments enjoyed by the *beau monde*, such as Vauxhall and Ranelagh Gardens, Teresa spotted a lucrative opportunity to create an indoor equivalent. Thus, she leased the out-dated seventeenth-century Carlisle House in Soho Square (Figure 3.25) and transformed it into a 'fairy palace, for balls, concerts, and masquerades'.[196]

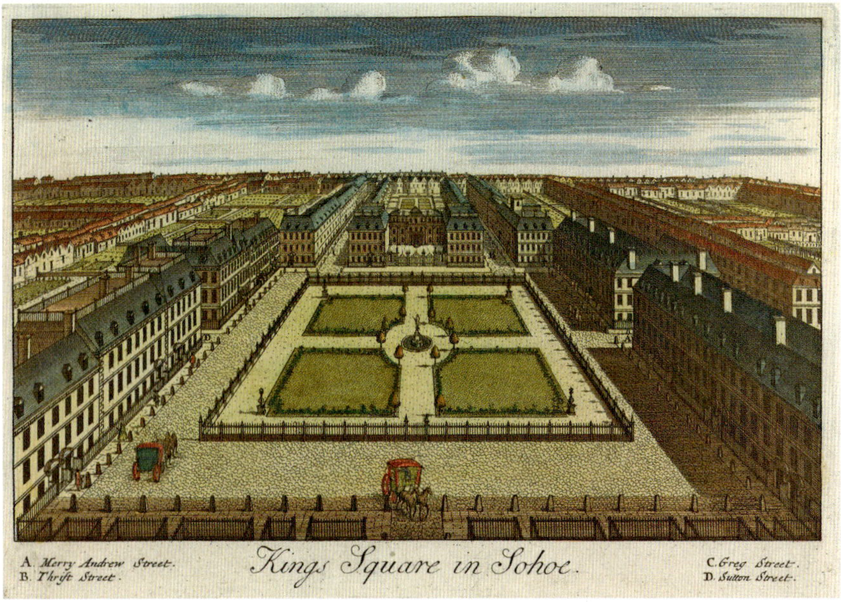

FIGURE 3.25 Unknown artist, *King's Square in Soho*, mid-eighteenth century, hand-coloured engraving. Yale Center for British Art, Paul Mellon Collection, B1977.14.18315. Courtesy of Yale Center for British Art.

When Teresa moved to London she came as the mistress of John Fermor, a married clergyman. She had left her husband in Italy and brought her daughter Sophie with her, a child of the infamous Casanova. Although Teresa's marital status was less than favourable, she was determined to make her fortune among London's society. Far from constraining Teresa's ability to succeed, these factors, together with her determined character, served to fascinate the elite. Consequently, Teresa soon had the friendship and patronage of the notorious Elizabeth Chudleigh, a society beauty and Maid of Honour to Augusta, Princess of Wales. In Chudleigh, Teresa found a kindred spirit, as Chudleigh was equally ambitious and equally risqué, posing as an unmarried lady to maintain her position at Court, whilst being secretly married to Augustus Hervey, later 3rd Earl of Bristol. Elizabeth later created a sensation of her own, when she became the mistress of Evelyn Pierrepont, 2nd Duke of Kingston-upon-Hull, and then his bigamous wife in 1769.

With Elizabeth's encouragement, Teresa set about establishing her subscription balls and quickly decided that Carlisle House, with its vast interconnecting reception rooms and impressive grand staircase, was a fitting venue to entice the upper echelons of society.[197] With Fermor's financial assistance, she negotiated a lease in April 1760 for the house.[198] During the summer Teresa set about updating the interiors of Carlisle House as swiftly as possible, ensuring that it would be ready to receive its guests by late November. On 22 November 1760 the first meeting was announced on the front page of the *Public Advertiser*.[199] Elizabeth Chudleigh headed a committee of ladies that decided who was eligible to subscribe to Teresa's exclusive balls and concerts and soon people were clamouring to be allowed in. The first meetings of cardplaying and dancing proved highly successful, which encouraged Teresa to embark on a wholescale remodelling project at Carlisle House (Figure 3.26).

Enthused by her initial success, Teresa purchased the leasehold of Carlisle House in 1761 for £1,950 (approximately £200,000 today).[200] She then engaged Samuel Norman, a carver, gilder, cabinetmaker and upholsterer, to draw up plans for the enlargement and improvement of the house.[201] The principal purpose of the works was to demolish the adjoining buildings at the back of the house that ran along Sutton Street. In their place was to be erected a new building which would consist of a large concert room on the first floor, with a supper room underneath.

By all accounts the exterior of the new building was unremarkable, constructed from 'good sound Bricks' with the 'whole to be Covered with the best Tavistock Slates'.[202] Instead, it was the interior that was to be the focus of Teresa's creative efforts. In addition to the new concert and supper rooms, the building project created a 'Waiting Room [at the] Gable End of [the] New Building', with music rooms above, two tea rooms, a 'large Front Card Room', and a 'Yellow Waiting Room', as well as a renovated marble hall and grand staircase.[203]

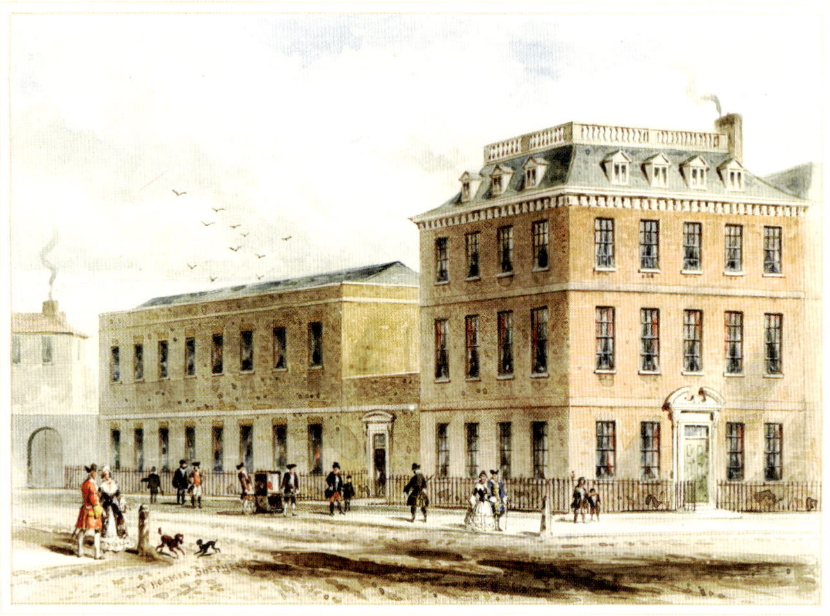

FIGURE 3.26 Thomas Hosmer Shepherd, *Carlisle House*, 1850, watercolour. British Museum, London, 1880,1113.4469. © The Trustees of the British Museum.

The scale of the new rooms was astounding, intended to impress from the outset, with the concert room alone measuring '80 Feet long and 35 feet wide in the Clear and 30 Feet high in the Clear'.[204] This room, the grandest of all of them, was arranged with symmetrically lined windows on the north and south walls which drew the eye towards a magnificent coffered semi-dome on the east wall (Figure 3.27). This impressive architectural feature crowned the space for the orchestra, which was raised on a wooden dais 'out of a good stone Colour'.[205] The walls were finished with festooned garlands draping from the entablature and the flat ceiling was decorated with Rococo stucco-work.[206] The supper room underneath was equally lavish, decorated with 'Cullums in the middle of the Room with Doric Capps and Bases on a Portland Stone'.[207]

Teresa's taste in furnishing her new rooms was expensive, with Norman supplying £730 7s. 9d. (approximately £75,000 today) worth of goods for the concert room, including 'a fine large glass ... in a glass bordered burnished gold frame' costing £262.[208] The supper room was supplied with goods costing £124 17s. and the 'Grand Waiting Room [with] Octagon Glass Doors' was supplied with £100 5s. 6d. worth of goods. Although Fermor was still financing the works, this project was very much Teresa's.

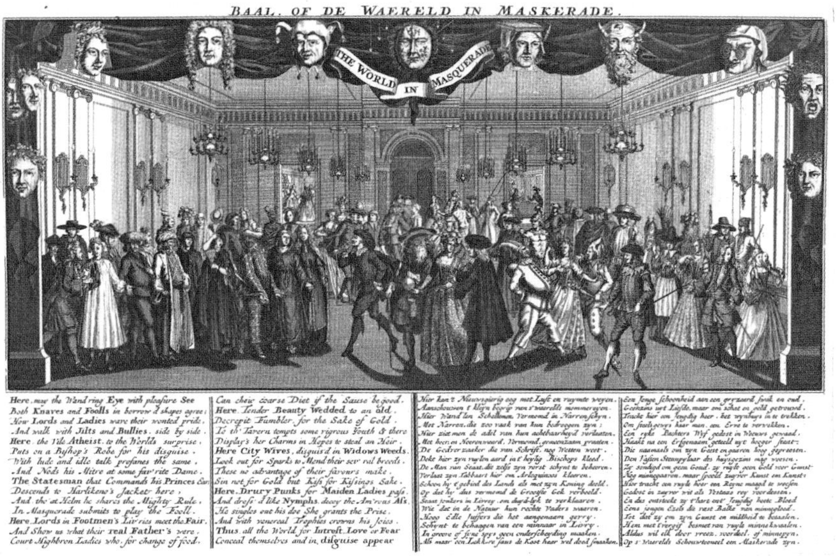

FIGURE 3.27 James Cole, *The World in Masquerade*, *c*. 1771, engraving. BTEU/RKMLGE/Alamy Stock Photo.

When laying the foundations in 1761 she added a copper plate with the following inscription:

> Not Vain but Grateful In Honour of the Society [of her first subscribers] and my first Protectress Ye Honble Mrs. Elizabeth Chudleigh is Laid the First Stone of this edifice June 19 1761 by me Teresa Cornelys.[209]

Teresa was evidently very proud of her achievement and felt a great sense of optimism for her entertainment business. As a single woman with a precarious social status, she was defying the odds and proving that it was not just well-born women who could make an architectural impact.

When Teresa's assembly rooms were completed, they were celebrated and exalted. When Count Friedrich von Kielmansegge's, a German soldier, visited London in 1761, he went to one of Teresa's assemblies and described the evening as follows:

> On the 26th we went to Court, and in the evening to an assembly at Soho. This consists of a concert and a ball, which take place every fortnight in a fine room, which has been much improved this year … The rooms in which they play, as well as the large ballroom, are very fine and beautifully lighted, and exceedingly well furnished. The vocal and instrumental music, by an orchestra at the end of the room, begins at

> seven o'clock and lasts until nine; dancing afterwards goes on until one or two. Tea, lemonade, and cake are served in two rooms.[210]

From this point onwards Teresa enjoyed a decade of great success, with her assemblies regularly and prominently advertised and subscriptions constantly sought after. She held assemblies once or twice a month and played hostess to the most prominent names in society. Such was the general approval of Teresa's assembly rooms and her ability to orchestrate extravagant balls, that Carlisle House was often chosen as the venue for grand society and royal events. On 24 January 1764 Carlisle House was used for a subscription ball hosted by the Dukes of Devonshire and Grafton in honour of the marriage of Princess Augusta, elder sister of George III, to the Hereditary Prince of Brunswick:

> The ball, last night, at Carlisle-house, Soho, was most magnificent: one hundred and fifty men subscribed, at five guineas each, and had each three tickets. All the beauties in town were there, that is, of rank, for there was no bad company. The Duke of Cumberland was there too; and the Hereditary Prince so pleased, and in such spirits, that he stayed till five in the morning.[211]

Teresa had succeeded in establishing Carlisle House as the go-to venue for the most prestigious events in London. When Johann Wilhelm von Archenholz was visiting England, he was amazed by Teresa's 'genius', remarking that she 'knew how to vary her entertainments in a thousand different shapes'.[212] Teresa's flair for interior design also impressed him, particularly the variety of aesthetic styles that she chose:

> A whole *suite* of rooms were richly furnished, so as to imitate the manners and luxury of foreign nations, in the Indian, Persian, and Chinese stiles, while nine thousand wax-candles, placed with great art, produced a fine effect to the spectators.[213]

In 1764, whilst Teresa was enjoying her newfound fame and fortune, a potential threat arose. William Almack, a merchant and tavern owner, set about building new assembly rooms in King Street, St James's, in purposeful rivalry to Carlisle House. He intended it to be open to both sexes of the nobility and gentry, whose entry would be controlled by a committee of ladies. Such a blatant poaching of Teresa's successful formula prompted her to respond by commissioning further architectural improvements to her venue. In October, a letter from 'Curious' to the editor of the *Public Advertiser*, stated that they wished to know the 'nature and design' of Teresa's plan, 'as well as the motives for erecting a second set of rooms' when 'her's are universally allowed, by all who have seen them, to be so magnificently elegant, and so commodiously complete'.[214]

Teresa was determined not to be outdone by Almack and sought to improve Carlisle House by adding a further suite of rooms. By December she was once again open for business, with Horace Walpole reporting that, 'Mrs Cornelis, apprehending the future assembly at Almack's, has enlarged her vast room, and hung it with blue satin, and another with yellow satin'.[215] Remarkably, in October 1765 she was again directing further embellishments:

> It is said, the alterations and additions to Carlisle house in Soho-Square, performing by Messrs. Phillips and Shakespeare, together with all the new embellishments and furniture adding thereto by Mrs. Cornelys, will this year alone, amount to little less than 2000*l.* [about £205,000 today] and that, when finished, it will be, by far, the most magnificent place of public entertainment in Europe.[216]

Teresa placed this announcement in the *London Chronicle* as a clever means of advertising to her subscribers that Carlisle House would, once again, be offering something new for the upcoming season. She was determined to maintain her spot as the best hostess in London, and as such no expense was spared. To entice her subscribers further, in November she placed another tantalizing announcement in the papers: 'We are told that Mrs. Cornelys, amongst her other elegant alterations, has devised the most curious, singular, and superb ceiling to one of the rooms that ever was executed, or even thought of'.[217] By constantly experimenting with interior design, Teresa ensured that her venue was still the most fashionable in London.

Once the alterations were complete, Carlisle House and its hostess received every form of praise and approval. Her interiors were celebrated for their 'matchless Elegance' and Teresa was lauded for having 'eminently distinguished herself for her superior Taste' (Figure 3.28).[218] Subscribers thought that her raising of the subscription price to a guinea (approximately £110 today) was perfectly acceptable, as Teresa's 'Taste, Improvement, and *extraordinary* Expences, amply demand such a trifling Return'.[219] A report in the *London Chronicle* in March 1766 would even suggest that Teresa had finally won the battle against Almack's:

> A lady of fashion, who subscribes both to Mrs. Cornelys's, and to Mr. Almack's ... being asked the other day, by a great personage, her opinion of each place, readily replied, "Going to Almack's, Sir, is only like going to Church, but going to Mrs. Cornelys's, is like going to Heaven at once".[220]

Still not satisfied with her triumph over Almack's, Teresa redecorated two of her rooms in the Chinoiserie taste and commissioned a wooden 'Chinese bridge' to connect the main house to the new building.[221] Thomas Chippendale, the fashionable cabinet-maker, may have been responsible for the bridge and for furnishing Teresa's Chinese rooms, as he was later listed

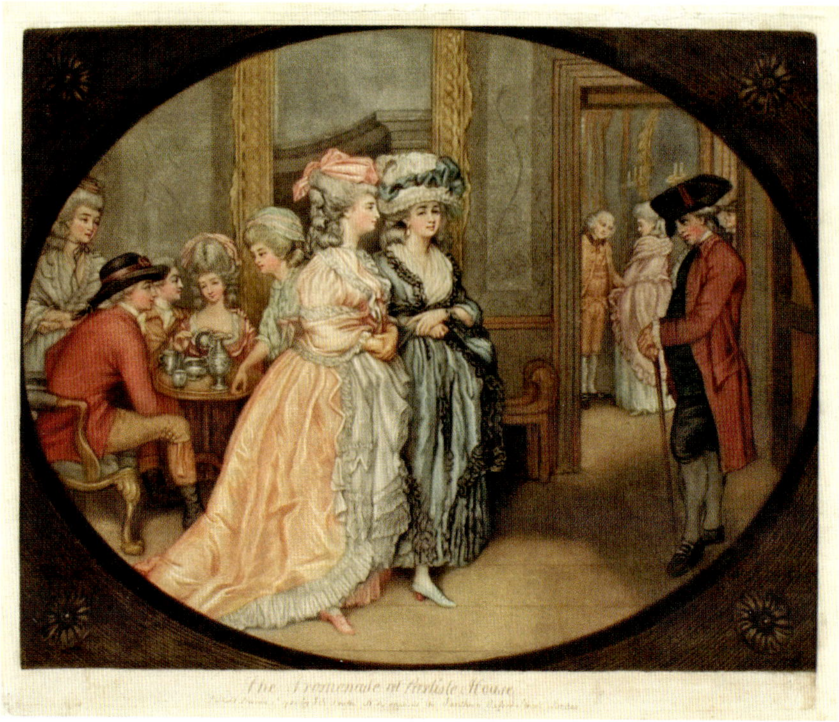

FIGURE 3.28 John Raphael Smith, *The Promenade at Carlisle House,* 1781, mezzotint on paper. The Clark Art Institute, 1955.2027. Courtesy of the Clark Art Institute.

as one of her main creditors.[222] Teresa experimented even further by later incorporating a grotto which contained, 'natural evergreens planted round the walls' as well as 'a natural well, with a living spring'.[223]

Teresa's success allowed her to live a life of luxury. At the height of her fame, as well as owning Carlisle House, she also had a country retreat in Hammersmith, kept six horses and had a large household including two secretaires, a female confidante and thirty-three ordinary servants.[224] Yet, still not content, Teresa soon began a series of masquerade balls which became her most successful venture yet. Every person of rank and beauty flocked to Carlisle House in costumes of the most elaborate and expensive nature. The famous courtesan Sophia Baddeley, mentioned previously, was naturally present at many of these balls, as her friend Elizabeth Steele recorded: '[A]s a masquerade was to be at Carlisle-house in a few days, we proposed to go to it. Mrs. Baddeley's dress was that of a shepherdess; mine, a domino, with a man's hat and feather … The rooms were crowded'.[225]

An engraving by James Cole entitled 'The World in Masquerade' depicts one of Teresa's famous masquerades (Figure 3.27).[226] Here we see Teresa's sumptuous concert room filled with guests all decked out in fantastical costumes. The room is elaborately decorated in the Classical style, with Ionic pilasters lining the walls, a coffered semi-dome at the far end, and the whole glittering party is illuminated with hundreds of candles hanging from the ceiling in beautiful chandeliers and adorning the walls in fashionable sconces.

In 1772 however, Philip Elias Turst opened his elaborate assembly rooms, the Pantheon, on Oxford Street, again in direct competition with Teresa's Carlisle House. Unlike Almack's, the Pantheon posed a real threat to Teresa's near monopoly of the entertainment market. Its principal room, the rotunda, was designed by James Wyatt and contained a spectacular coffered dome, around which on the east and west sides were grand colonnades that screened the aisles and first-floor galleries.[227] The purpose-built assembly rooms were met with widespread excitement and approval, with Horace Walpole exclaiming the following year that 'the Pantheon is still the most beautiful edifice in England'.[228] Naturally, in response to this threat, Teresa commissioned further alterations to Carlisle House. This time she embarked upon the task of 'changing the position of her fine long gallery from that of the North and South to East and West'.[229] Described by the press as a 'female Hercules' many speculated whether this ambitious plan could be carried out successfully.[230] When it came to protecting her establishment as the most fashionable in town, there was apparently nothing that would stand in Teresa's way.

Sadly, however, despite Teresa's continued conspicuous display of wealth and grandeur, in reality she was facing bankruptcy, and by 1772 her creditors finally caught up with her. Her atrocious grasp of financial management resulted in her confinement in the King's Bench debtor's gaol. Teresa's property was seized by her creditors and an attempt was made by them to sell the lease of Carlisle House and all its contents at auction.[231] The auction failed to attract potential buyers, so a consortium of Teresa's creditors clubbed together to purchase the lease and contents for the greatly reduced price of £15,000.[232] This marked the end of Teresa's monopoly over London's party-goers and effectively triggered the beginning of her gradual decline. Although she did return to Carlisle House to manage assemblies and concerts for her creditors, she was never able to replicate the great successes of the previous decade. Plagued by continued debts and increasing competition Teresa's heyday was gone – she eventually ended up in Fleet Street prison, where she died alone in 1797 aged seventy-four.[233]

Despite Teresa's ignoble and tragic demise, her architectural schemes at Carlisle House provide a valuable insight into what enterprising women could achieve architecturally within the town house. Teresa exploited the most fashionable architectural styles, including Neo-Classical, Rococo and Chinoiserie, to ensure that she continued as the leader of taste in London. Her ability to transform the interiors of Carlisle House so regularly and so profoundly suggests that she had a remarkable skill in architectural and aesthetic direction. She was pioneering in her architectural schemes which allowed her to make a vast fortune (at least initially) and become one of the most famous figures in London.

Town houses, much like country houses, served a very public function. They were designed to be seen, inspire awe and serve as status symbols. In contrast, the building type that will be explored in the next chapter, the villa, was a more private affair where the prime object was not ostentation, but tranquillity and comfort.

4

The villa

In 1734, the Duchess of Marlborough, at the age of seventy-four, was busily completing her latest architectural project – her suburban villa in Wimbledon (Figure 4.1):

> I have been at Wimbledon and when the house is furnished it will be a delightful place to my taste. And I do think it is a great addition to have it within an hour's driving to London upon a good road.[1]

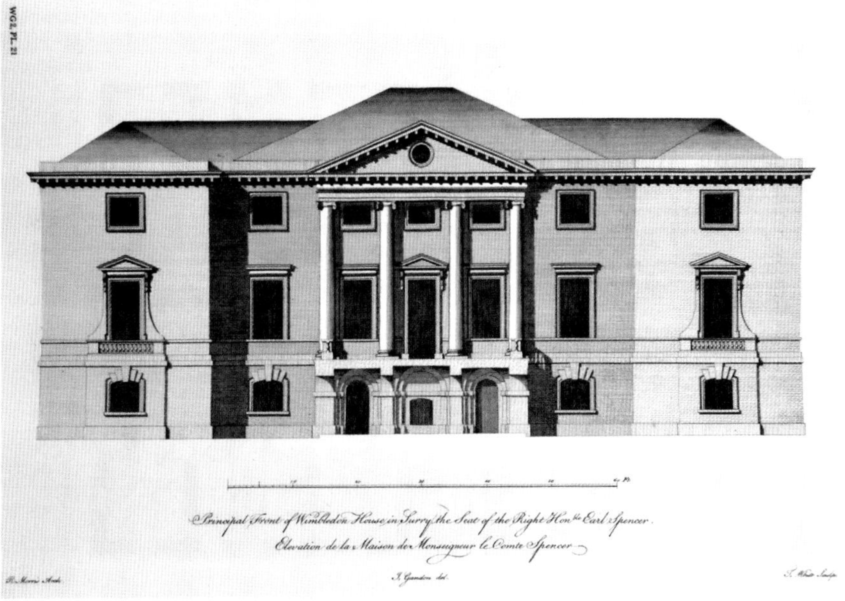

FIGURE 4.1 Principal front of Wimbledon House in Surrey, 1771, as published in *Vitruvius Britannicus* vol. v, plate 21. Photo: author's own.

Following the death of her husband in 1722, she purchased Wimbledon Manor from Sir Theodore Janssen (a director of the failed South Sea Company) for £15,000 (approximately £1.8 million today).[2] Having no love for Blenheim Palace and knowing that Rangers Lodge in Windsor – her favourite rural retreat – would return to the Crown upon her death, she decided to build a Palladian villa to suit her own tastes.

Sarah Churchill employed Henry Herbert (later 9th Earl of Pembroke), whom she later described as 'often mad and always very odd', and his assistant, Roger Morris, to build a villa that was to be plain, convenient and comfortable.[3] She wanted no 'Gimmeny Gommenys', as she termed any kind of modish ornamentation, and due to her arthritic legs, she sought to place the *piano nobile* at ground level, to prevent the necessity for steps.[4] Herbert's response to this conundrum was to sink the house into a moat-like depression, so that the Duchess could access the first floor easily via a bridge. The end result was rather unique, with the Duchess lamenting that the house 'looked as if it was making a Curtsie'.[5] Contemporary accounts were equally perplexed, with Lady Mary Wortley Montagu ridiculing the Duchess's design: 'The D of Marlborough used ... [to say] one might always live upon other people's follies, yet you see she built the most ridiculous house I ever saw'.[6] This unusual scheme, together with other building-related frustrations, led the Duchess to once again dismiss her architects, complaining that she 'always had the misfortune to suffer very great mischiefs from the assistance of architects'.[7]

Despite this setback, the Duchess was content with the plan of her villa's *piano nobile*, which was compact and convenient, as designed by herself and her favourite granddaughter, Diana Russell, Duchess of Bedford. A surviving plan drawn by the Duchess of Bedford, 'my Paladio Dye ... done at my Request, to oblige me', depicts the arrangement of the principal floor (Figure 4.2).[8] The Duchess was obviously delighted with her granddaughter's scheme, writing that 'I must do her the Justice to say that I believe she would not have done it for any other body in the World, being so great an Architect, that she loves nothing but Shew and Italian Building'.[9] Grandmother and granddaughter shared an interest in architecture, and enjoyed collaborating over the design and building of Wimbledon House. Tragically, just as her new villa was nearing completion in 1735, the Duchess of Bedford died at the tender age of twenty-five from tuberculosis, rendering the entire project futile in the eyes of her grandmother. Despite having spent £70,000 (approximately £8.3 million today),[10] the Duchess refused to live there (at least initially), believing it to be damp and unhealthy 'and consequently I have thrown away a vast sum of money upon it to little purpose'.[11]

In building her villa, Sarah Churchill was conforming to the fashionable trend established by the urban elite, which popularized small, compact villas with beautiful gardens that were situated in a peaceful rural setting within a

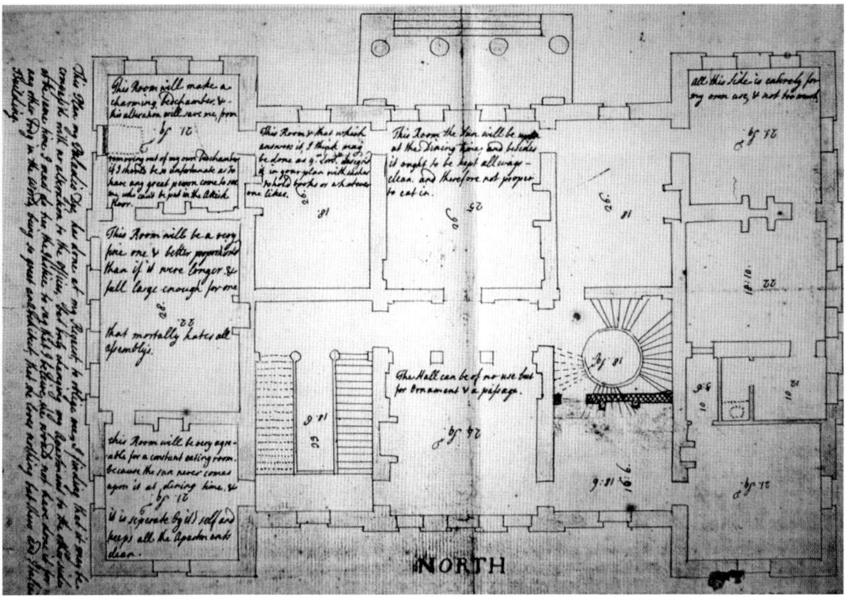

FIGURE 4.2 The Duchess of Bedford's plan of Wimbledon House, *c.* 1730s. Wiltshire Record Office, 2057/Fb/14. Courtesy of the Earl of Pembroke, Wilton House, Wiltshire.

day's ride from the metropolis. These villas were inspired by Roman luxury models, such as Villa Poppaea, situated between Naples and Sorrento, as well Andrea Palladio's Renaissance villas of the Veneto, such as Villa Capra 'La Rotonda' in Vicenza.[12] Thus, as London rapidly expanded, and the heat, dust and clamour became unsavoury, accessible rural idylls were eagerly sought. Sarah chose Wimbledon Common, but Twickenham and Richmond also became extremely fashionable areas during the eighteenth century, as they boasted tranquillity, open green spaces, riverside walks and views from Richmond Hill (Figures 4.3 and 4.4).

Throughout the eighteenth century a succession of villas were erected in this area, including Alexander Pope's famous riverside villa with its accompanying grotto and garden; Sir Joshua Reynolds's villa, Wick House, commissioned from Sir William Chambers in 1771; Garrick's Villa, the country seat of the celebrated actor David Garrick and his wife Eva; and Strawberry Hill House, the Gothic masterpiece of Horace Walpole.[13] Due to their smaller size and upkeep, patrons were able to partake in lavish architectural display and experimentation. For instance, Richard Boyle, 3rd Earl of Burlington, together with William Kent, famously built Chiswick House, the first Palladian villa in England, completed in 1739.

Compared to country and town houses, villas were much more economical, which allowed a greater number of women to own property

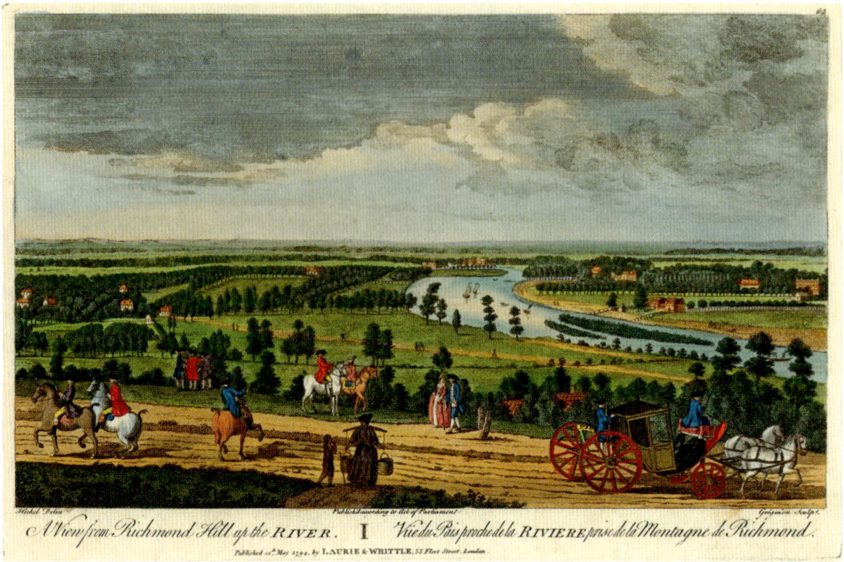

FIGURE 4.3 Charles Grignion, after Augustin Heckel, *A View from Richmond Hill Up the River*, 1794, line engraving and etching with hand colouring. Yale Center for British Art, Paul Mellon Collection, B1977.14.11728. Courtesy of Yale Center for British Art, Yale University.

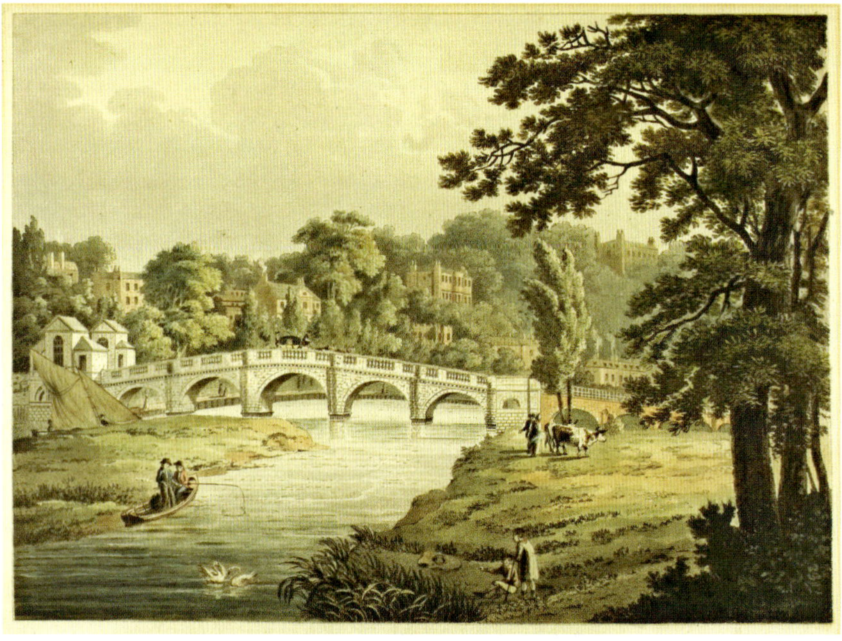

FIGURE 4.4 Thomas Sutherland, after John Gendall, *View of Richmond Bridge*, 1819, aquatint, heightened with watercolour. Art Institute Chicago, Bequest of Marie S. Budd, 1985.1120. Courtesy of Art Institute Chicago.

and engage in architectural patronage. The penchant amongst noble women to possess a villa is evident in the Countess of Hertford's remarks in 1741:

> The duchess of Manchester has taken a house, no bigger than a nut-shell, upon Englefield Green ... She has added a wooden porch bigger than the house, and furnished all her rooms with paper. The duchess of Kent has bought my Lord Weymouth's, at Old Windsor; and the duchess of Beaufort has taken the Hermitage on St. Leonard's Hill.[14]

For these women, the buying, renting, building and altering of a villa provided them with the opportunity to establish their own independent country seat whilst maintaining a convenient distance from the social life of the city. As with country and town houses, villas could be built for a multitude of reasons. First and foremost, they were recreational in nature and were built as green retreats, where women could enjoy the peace of the countryside, entertain their friends in suitable arcadian surroundings, recover their health in the cleaner air or enjoy the delights of gardening. Since villas were so personal in nature, female patrons were largely unconcerned about public perception, and were more uninhibited in following their own preferences. This type of building is therefore somewhat unusual, since women were free to pursue their own agendas without societal censure.

A woman's desire to escape the city could also be driven by the need to escape an abusive husband. For these harried women, the creation of a suburban retreat represented independence, relief and safety, and allowed them to establish a separate household away from their husbands. As we shall see, only women of independent means could afford to embark on such schemes, but if they could they truly relished the chance to create a beautiful residence of their own. Equally, villas could provide a retreat away from the public eye, particularly if one was suffering from grief or from the humiliation of a family scandal.

Villas were particularly popular amongst widows, who, having vacated the patriarchal country seat, sought a pleasant, affordable country residence of their own. The generally reduced costs (Sarah Churchill's villa was exceptionally expensive) associated with building and maintaining villas were persuasive factors for many women, as it allowed them to express their architectural taste and live fashionably. At the same time, the creation of a small villa estate allowed widowed women to establish a tangible legacy for a relative or friend, as Sarah Churchill had sought to do for her granddaughter. In many cases women were able to bequeath villas to those of their choice, and thus were able to provide a suitable inheritance for those who would otherwise be overlooked by primogeniture, such as younger sons or daughters.

Finally, villas were sometimes utilized by women to enhance their status. For courtesans villas represented another means by which they could engage in conspicuous consumption and ostentatious display. The possession of a fashionable, well-appointed country villa enhanced their social status and also provided a welcome respite from the constant whirl of the London social circuit. In addition, villas could be used to further commercial interests. Perhaps uniquely, Eleanor Coade (1733–1822) used her seaside villa, Belmont House, to advertise her product, Coade stone, in a prominent and fashionable location.

A rural retreat for comfort, convenience and economy

The rural nature of most villas, and the promise of peace and tranquillity, proved to be an attractive prospect for many single women such as widows and courtesans. Through the acquisition of a villa, financially autonomous women could escape the city, live more privately and establish a small estate of their own. When the celebrated beauty Elizabeth Armistead (1750–1842) (Figure 4.5) purchased a villa in Chertsey, it signalled the end of her courtesan days.[15] Together with her lover, the politician Charles James Fox, she set about creating a delightful idyll, away from the prying eyes of London society.

Although Elizabeth had been born into relative obscurity, she had experienced a spectacular rise to fame and fortune through her life as a courtesan. She began her career in Jane Goadby's notorious high-end 'nunnery' in Great Marlborough Street, and possibly in the other high-end brothels such as Sarah Pendergast's on 3 George Street and Charlotte Hayes's at 5 King's Place.[16] Elizabeth's beauty soon resulted in a succession of lovers, initially including the Duke of Ancaster, the Duke of Dorset and the Earl of Derby.[17] The Earl of Derby was particularly generous in his provisions for Elizabeth, setting her up in considerable style, by taking 'a house for her in Hampstead, allow[ing] her his own equipage, besides two very handsome saddle horses'.[18] Derby was succeeded by a string of paramours including Viscount Bolingbroke, Lord George Cavendish, General Richard Smith and even the Prince of Wales (future George IV). Smith and possibly Cavendish provided Elizabeth with annuities which enabled her to purchase the freehold of a town house in Bond Street in *c.* 1776.[19]

In stark contrast to the lavish spending of Sophia Baddeley, Elizabeth was sensible with money. Although she lived fashionably, she also lived within her means, which allowed her to later invest in a second property, No. 46 Clarges Street, Mayfair.[20] No records of Elizabeth's town houses survive with regard to style and furnishings, but she no doubt appointed them in a tasteful and attractive manner, as befitting her high status. In 1781, Elizabeth began to seek a property in the country, settling upon a villa called St Anne's Hill, in Chertsey, which she leased from the Duke of Marlborough until 1785, when she bought it for £2000.[21]

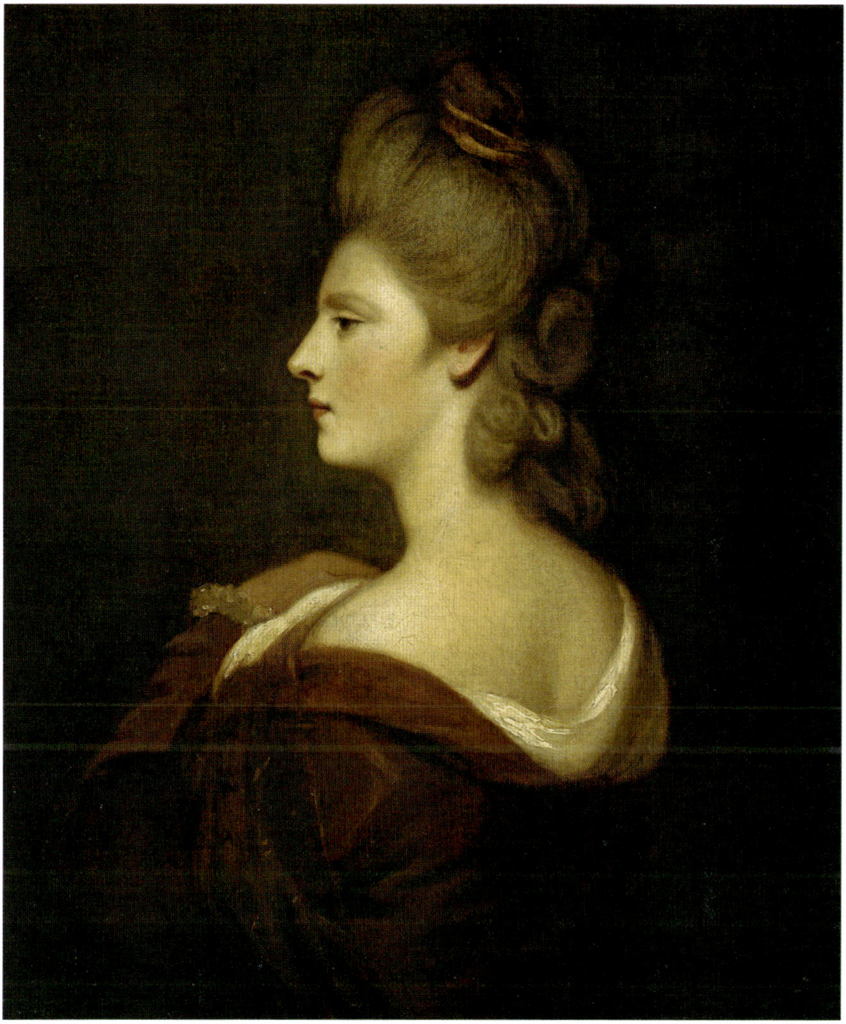

FIGURE 4.5 Circle of Sir Joshua Reynolds, *Mrs. Charles James Fox*, *c.* 1780, oil on canvas. Sepia Times/Universal Images Group via Getty Images.

In 1783, after a ten-year friendship, Elizabeth became the mistress of Charles James Fox. The couple soon fell in love and it was because of him that Elizabeth retired from her profession, gave up her town houses and moved permanently to St Anne's Hill. Together they transformed St Anne's Hill into the perfect suburban retreat, where they lived in domestic bliss until Fox's death in 1806. A mid-nineteenth-century survey of the St Anne's Hill estate indicates that it was a sizeable estate, with about ninety acres of land, most of which was rented out to local farmers.[22] According to contemporary opinions, the villa itself was unremarkable, with the poet Samuel Rogers

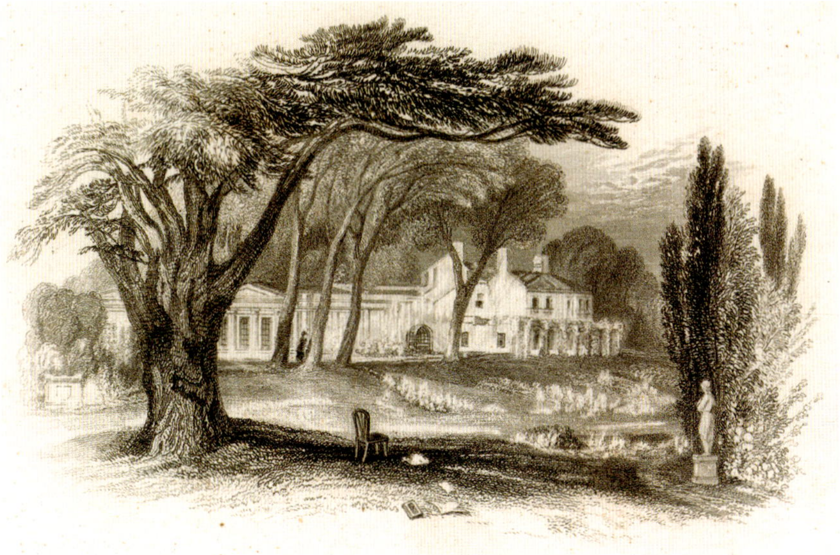

FIGURE 4.6 Edward Goodall, after J.M.W. Turner, *St. Anne's Hill, I,* 1834, line engraving. Yale Center for British Art, Paul Mellon Collection, B1977.14.7331. Courtesy of Yale Center for British Art, Yale University.

describing it as 'a low white house on the brow of a hill'.[23] J. M. W. Turner's vignette (Figure 4.6) of St Anne's Hill shows a small white house happily situated in amongst an abundance of trees and greenery, emphasizing its picturesque effect.[24]

Elizabeth and Fox adored their home and furnished it with all of their treasured possessions. Unlike the showy town houses of London or the grand dynastic houses in the country, Elizabeth's villa was unpretentious and cosy.[25] When Rogers visited in 1803 he conveyed the sense of tranquil domesticity that prevailed at St Anne's Hill:

> In the small drawing room, Sir Joshua Reynolds's Girl with the mouse-trap. In the hall books and statues. The library on the first floor – small and unadorned – the books on open shelves. Engraved portraits, principally after Sir Joshua Reynolds, all over the house. In the garden-passage a copy in black marble of the Eagle at Strawberry hill; and a bust of Hippocrates, with a Latin inscription by Lord Holland, found in Italy. In the eating room a portrait of Lord Holland sitting, carefully painted by Reynolds; and of Lady Holland sitting, by Ramsey. Several old good pictures ... The drawing room prettily furnished with pink silk panels, inclosed with ebony bead, and a frame of blue silk; made of old gowns.[26]

The statues, family portraits, selected engravings and piles of books can be imagined scattered throughout the house, creating an informal and comfortable atmosphere. The use of Elizabeth's recycled gowns for the drawing room walls indicates that she was happy to economize, and perfectly content not to be a slave to the latest aesthetic trends. Fox was always at his most content when he was at home with Elizabeth. When writing to his nephew, he wrote of the peace that he had found: 'Here I am passing a most comfortable week of holidays, the weather delicious, and the place looking beautiful beyond description, and the nightingales singing, and Mrs. A. as happy as the day is long'.[27] The couple enjoyed their country life, dedicating their hours to reading, gardening and entertaining. Fox provides another glimpse into their blissful situation in 1794: 'I am perfectly happy in the country, I have quite resources enough to employ my mind; and the great resource of all, literature, I am fonder of every day; and then the Lady of the Hill is one continual source of happiness to me. I believe few men, indeed, ever were so happy in that respect as I'.[28]

The charm of St Anne's Hill rested on its successful integration of the villa and the garden, in true arcadian fashion (Figure 4.7). The gardens, by

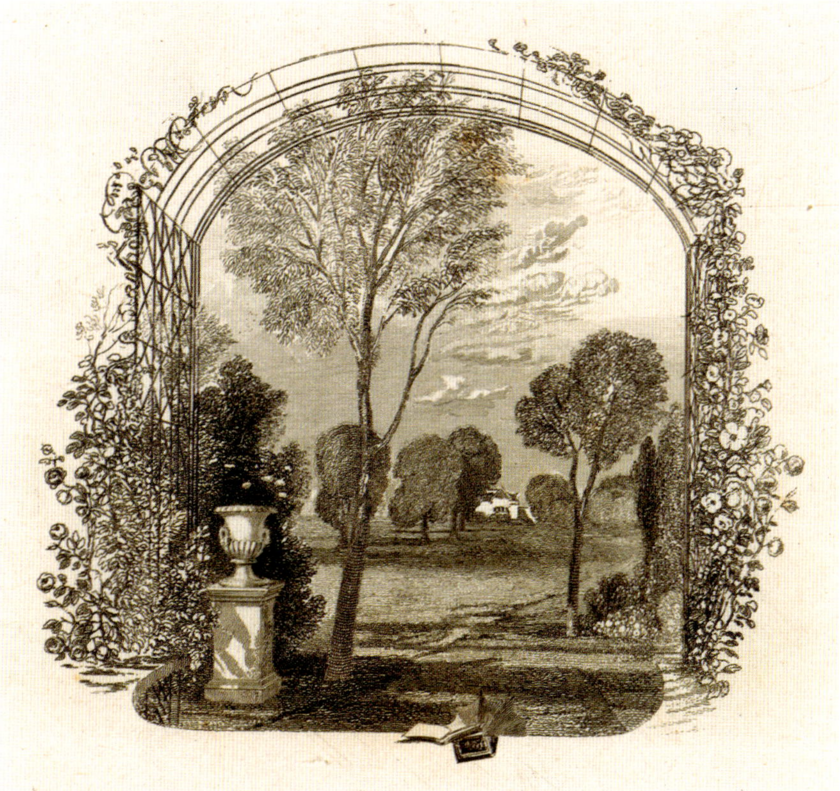

FIGURE 4.7 Edward Goodall, after J.M.W. Turner, *St. Anne's Hill, II*, 1834, open etching and line engraving. Yale Center for British Art, Paul Mellon Collection, B1977.14.7356. Courtesy of Yale Center for British Art, Yale University.

all contemporary accounts, were spectacular. When Lady Chatterton (1806–76), author and traveller, visited in the early nineteenth century she wrote gushingly of the beauty that she found:

> The sunny dells and shady groves, the cool mid-day seat and evening bower, seem all calculated to afford repose and enjoyment to a spirit wearied with political cares. Antique statues are placed exactly where their graceful forms adorn the surrounding scenery, without ... disturbing the eye by a want of harmony with the scene ... Every successive grotto, seat or temple, commands a view quite different from the preceding; yet the whole garden covered but a small space.[29]

The whole ensemble at St Anne's Hill allowed Elizabeth and Fox to escape the prejudices and vices of the world. Their retreat was especially warranted in 1802 when they publicly announced that they had secretly married in 1795, thereby causing some degree of scandal. On the whole however, Elizabeth's new status as a respectable wife was accepted, particularly amongst the Whigs, with whom she had been involved for years. Elizabeth naturally excelled in her new role as a statesman's wife, but it was at St Ann's Hill, the 'seat of true happiness', that the Foxes always found the greatest contentment.[30]

Their contentment was not to last for long, however, because Fox died in 1806, leaving behind a broken-hearted widow. Elizabeth outlived Fox by thirty-four years, dedicating her life to improving her small estate and to philanthropic causes in the local community. At her funeral, although she intended it to be private, such was her popularity that 'persons of all classes were anxious to show their respect for one who has been so long and justly beloved, and who by her urbanity, kindness, and excessive benevolence, has acquired the esteem of the inhabitants of the neighbourhood of her own residence, St. Anne's Hill'.[31] By this account it would seem that despite Elizabeth's obscure beginnings, she had successfully transcended social boundaries to become an esteemed member of society. Through her careful financial management, Elizabeth succeeded where many of her contemporaries had failed, in reinventing herself as a prominent lady of quality, complete with a respectable suburban villa and estate.

The establishment of a comfortable rural retreat was also popular amongst widows of independent wealth. This was particularly true for the widowed Yorke sisters. By 1786, both Lady Polwarth and her younger sister, Lady Grantham, were widows, aged only thirty-five and thirty respectively. Both were financially independent and had moved to London following the deaths of their late husbands, where they enjoyed a busy social life of visiting friends and family, as Lady Polwarth's diary entry for November 1786 reveals:

> Thursday, Nov. 23rd. Went to Mrs Francis, visited Mrs Maddox. Went at night to Ldy Grantham's. Ldy Eliza, Mr & Mrs Robinson were all there.

Friday 24th. Dined at Ld Hardwicke's: visited Ldy Beauchamps.

Saturday, Nov 25th. Visited Ldy Yorke, & went to Ldy Grantham's. N.B. Mrs Robinson & Miss Harris visited me in the morning.

Sunday Nov 26th. Din'd at Ld Hardwicke's, went to Ldy Grantham's.[32]

Lady Polwarth (Figure 4.8) established herself at No. 49 Upper Brook Street and Lady Grantham had a life interest in Grantham House, Whitehall

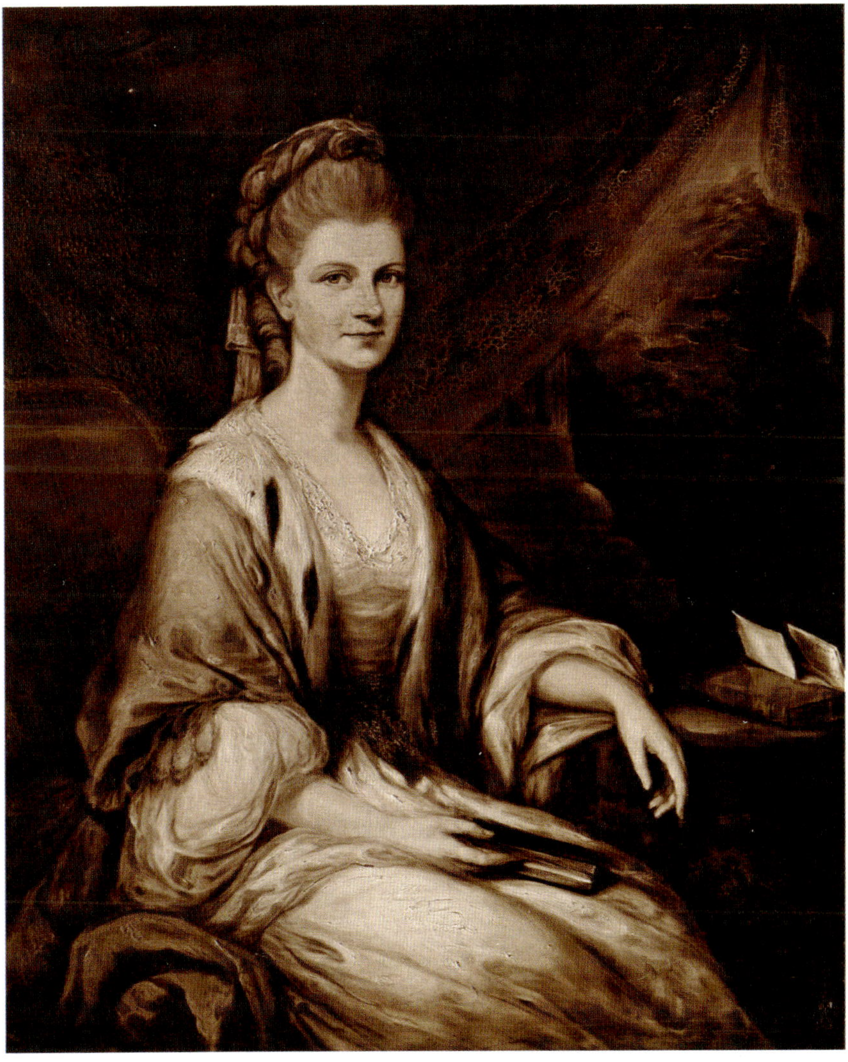

FIGURE 4.8 Richard Cosway, after Anne Forbes, *Amabel Hume-Campbell, Lady Polwarth*, c. 1776. National Portrait Gallery, NPG Z16761. © National Portrait Gallery, London.

Yard.[33] Both were in close proximity to their parents' town house in St James's Square, which was often the location for family gatherings. The Yorkes had always been a close and affectionate family, with the sisters sharing a particularly warm and supportive relationship throughout their lives. Such was their sisterly bond, that in 1791 Lady Polwarth purchased a villa right next door to her sister's villa, Grantham House, on the north side of Putney Heath.

Having been raised at Wrest Park, where they had witnessed their mother's (Marchioness Grey) regular and varied architectural commissions, both sisters possessed an interest in building. As we have seen, Lady Grantham had already experienced commissioning and managing building works at her marital country house at Newby Park, but Lady Polwarth had not yet had the opportunity. During the 1790s both sisters commissioned John Yenn to alter their respective villas to suit their tastes. These villas effectively became their dower houses, providing them with fashionable suburban homes set in extensive gardens. Indeed, villas were often appealing as dower houses, especially for women who did not want to be constrained to a familial estate far from the social hub of the city, or for those who did not want to be pushed into an outdated or dilapidated dower house, or for those who simply could not afford the upkeep of larger country houses.

Due to their relatively compact size, the remodelling and improvement of existing villas was an affordable way through which the sisters could engage in architectural patronage. For both, the ambition of their building schemes was to create a comfortable and tasteful home. Lady Polwarth was the first to embark on her remodelling scheme, paying John Yenn £200 in August 1791 to survey the property 'on account of the intended Addition & Alteration to her Ladyships House on Putney Heath'.[34] Work was soon underway, with her sister reporting in December 'that yr Buildings were near covered in a Week ago'.[35] Progress was swift and a year later Lady Polwarth was pleased to record that she 'Went to Putney to meet Mr Yenn ... All is in a manner finish'd except the papering'.[36]

Lady Polwarth was responsible for almost doubling the size of her villa, building extensions to the east and west with canted bays on the north elevation, together with a large projecting central room with a bow window. A surviving ground-floor plan and elevation drawn by Yenn reveal that a suite of reception rooms were created, including a drawing room, breakfast parlour, library and an anteroom (Figure 4.9).[37] Lady Polwarth's taste for the interior was fashionably Neo-Classical, as indicated by the surviving drawings for beautifully carved marble chimney pieces (Figure 4.10).[38]

Interestingly, whilst Yenn was engaged with enlarging Lady Polwarth's villa, her sister also decided to commission him to enlarge and remodel

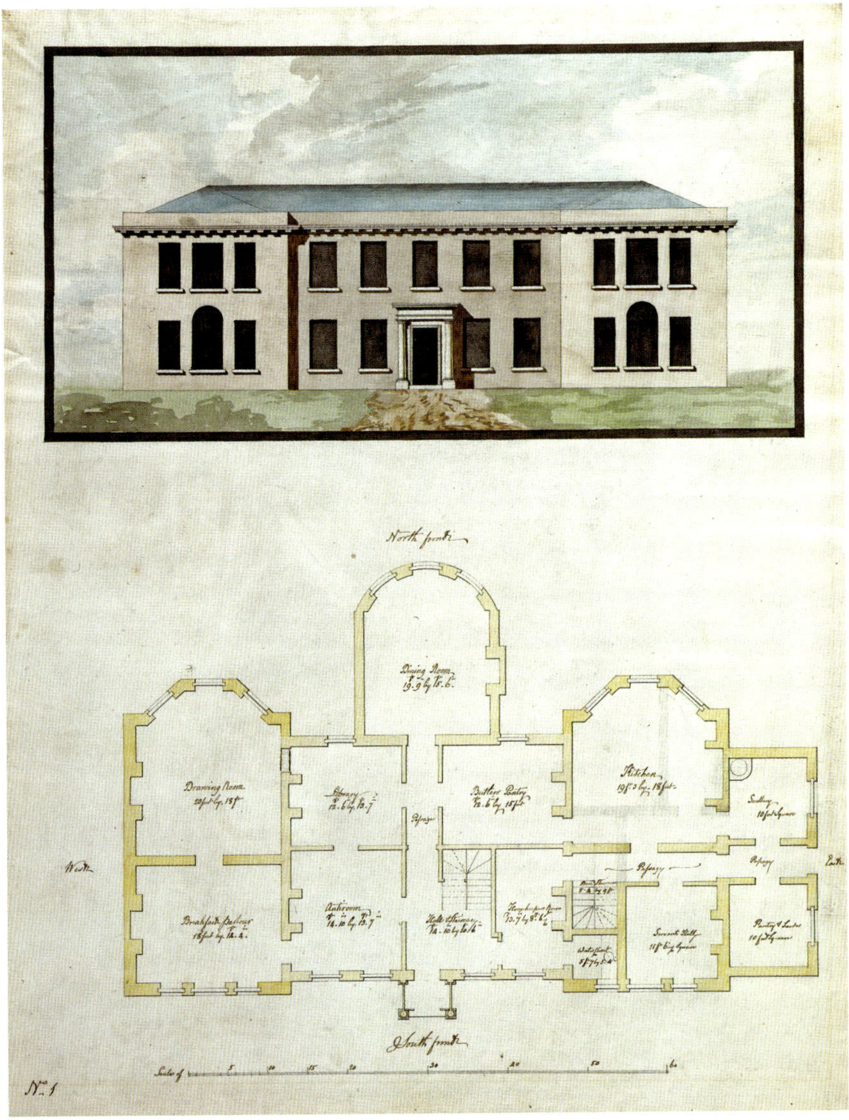

FIGURE 4.9 John Yenn, ground-floor plan and south elevation of Lady Polwarth's villa, *c.* 1780. Royal Academy of Arts, 09/440. ©Royal Academy of Arts, London; photographer: John Hammond.

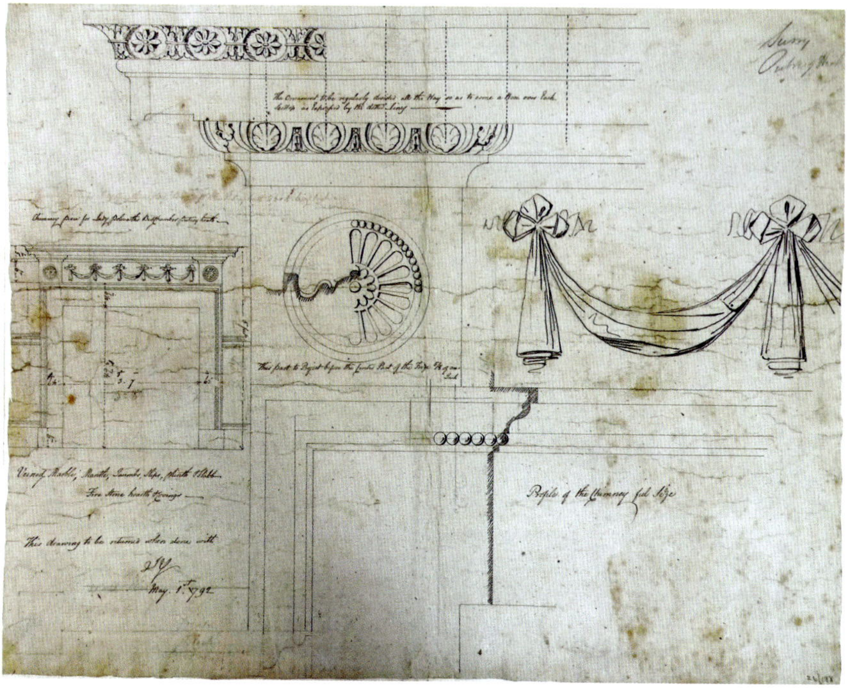

FIGURE 4.10 John Yenn, chimney piece details for Lady Polwarth's bed chamber, 1792. Lambeth Archives, LP 26/188/POL7. By kind permission of London Borough of Lambeth, Archives Department.

Grantham House (Figure 4.11). In March 1792, Lady Polwarth lent her sister £4000 (approximately £310,000 today) so that she could purchase and improve Grantham House.[39] In December 1793, Lady Polwarth lent her sister a further £700 'for her Buildings at Putney', signifying that she was instrumental in Yenn's continued employment, and essential in helping her sister to embark on her own scheme of architectural improvements.[40]

Lady Grantham also extended her villa substantially and shared her sister's Neo-Classical taste, commissioning stylish interiors and ornamentation.[41] For her 'Bow Room Drawing Room', one of her best reception rooms, the surviving drawing for the cornice and frieze shows a profusion of sophisticated detailing, including acanthus leaves, egg and dart, acorns, and reed and ribbon mouldings, for which an annotation instructs that 'Mr Rose must keep these Ornaments Light and Thin' (Figure 4.12).[42] The Mr Rose presumably refers to the leading master stuccoist Joseph Rose Jr. (1745–99) who worked closely with Robert Adam for many years. His mastery of the Neo-Classical style was renowned and thus his patronage at Lady Grantham's villa suggests that she wished to fashion an interior of

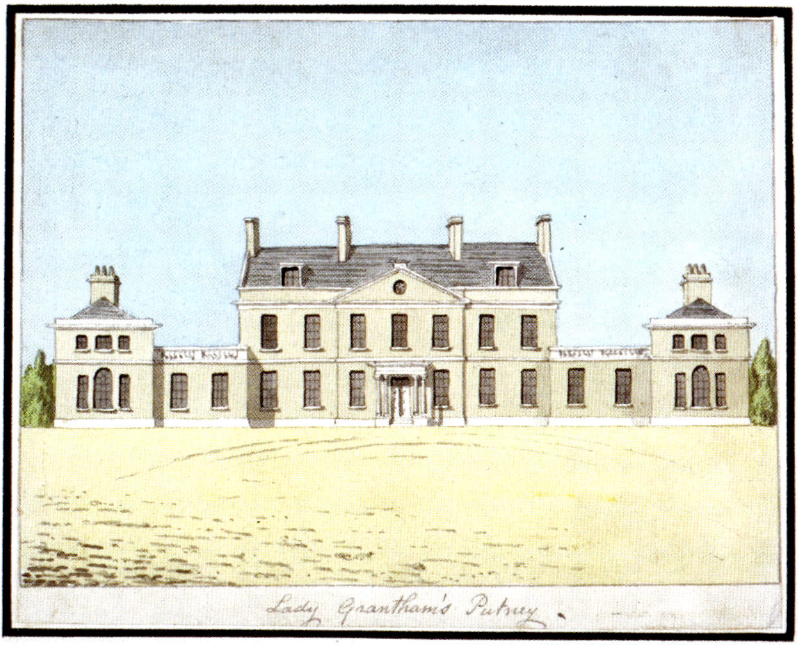

FIGURE 4.11 Unknown artist, *Lady Grantham's, Putney*, *c.* 1800, watercolour. Guildhall Library & Art Gallery/Heritage Images/Getty Images.

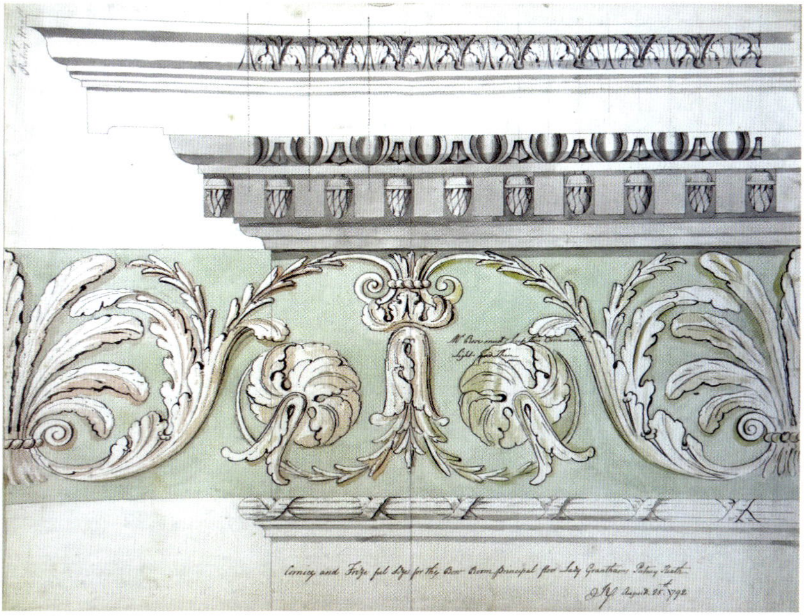

FIGURE 4.12 John Yenn, 'Cornice and Frieze full size for the Bow-Room principal floor Lady Granthams Putney Heath', 1792. Lambeth Archives, LP 26/188/GRAM6. By kind permission of London Borough of Lambeth, Archives Department.

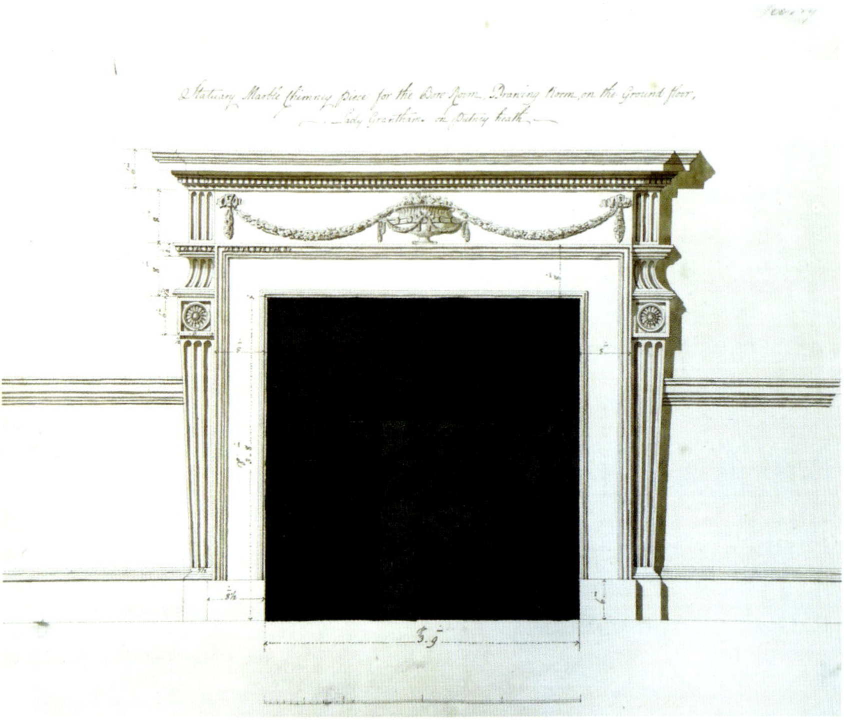

FIGURE 4.13 John Yenn, design for a chimney piece, 1792. Lambeth Archives, LP26/188/GRAM4. By kind permission of London Borough of Lambeth, Archives Department.

the highest specification. Surviving drawings of her Neo-Classical chimney pieces indicate that in every aspect her interiors were beautiful (Figure 4.13).

Once completed, both sisters enjoyed their villas until their deaths, whereupon Lady Grantham's was inherited by her eldest son Thomas, 3rd Baron Grantham, in 1830, and Lady Polwarth's was inherited by her nephew (Lady Grantham's second son), Frederick John Robinson, 1st Earl of Ripon, after which it became known as Ripon House.[43] This is a good example of how the creation of villas allowed women to participate in the provision of inheritance for their children, family members or friends. Although primogeniture dominated the laws of inheritance of the wealthy land-owning classes, women were still able to create tangible legacies (in the form of villa estates) separate from the patriarchal estate. This feature will be explored in greater depth later in this chapter, but it is certainly worth mentioning here.

Interestingly, just as the Yorke sisters were in the midst of building their Neo-Classical villas, their aunt, Agneta Yorke (1740–1820) (Figure 4.14), was just about to commission an entirely new villa to be built in Hamble,

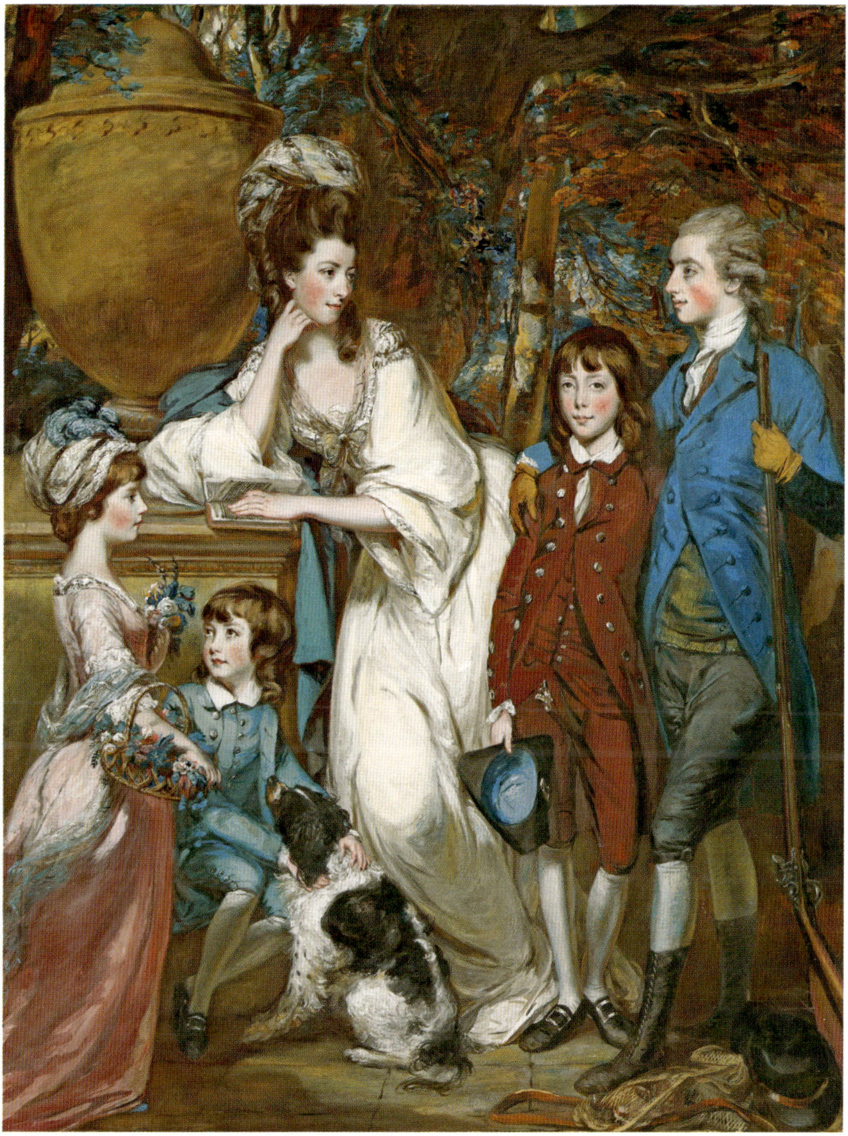

FIGURE 4.14 Daniel Gardner, *The Yorke Family*, *c*. 1775, pastel. National Gallery of Art, 2019.142.1. Courtesy National Gallery of Art, Washington.

near to Southampton. Agneta, the second daughter and co-heiress of Henry Johnson, had been widowed in 1770 with four young children under her care, the eldest of whom was her stepson, Philip Yorke, who became 3rd Earl of Hardwicke in 1790. Although Agneta had enjoyed living at her marital home, Tyttenhanger Park, for many years, by 1782 she had voiced her growing concerns about the financial viability of maintaining such a large house:

> My income now, will not support the magnificence of a Town & Country residence, especially a House of such consequence as this, were it a small mansion only sufficient to Lodge myself & Family, with a garden answerable to the size, I might then find great convenience in such a retreat. But the keeping up this garden properly and the number of servants necessary to take care of so large a House, requires more money than I can spare ... I must, to use a homely proverb, cut my Coat according to my cloth.[44]

Indeed, she soon vacated Tyttenhanger and relocated to the coast, purchasing a small villa called Sydney Farm, near Southampton. Part of her motivation for moving to the coast was so that she could better follow the naval career of her young teenage son, Joseph Sydney Yorke, who had entered the navy aged only eleven. Soon after taking up her new residence it became apparent that the villa was insufficient for her needs, so she commissioned John Soane to carry out some improvements, writing to her sister-in-law, Marchioness Grey, in 1787 that her villa was 'still in the midst of workmen and consequently great confusion'.[45] When completed, Agneta was still not satisfied, later complaining that Sydney Farm 'is so cramped for space that it is very inconvenient, and I can by no means get any more Land about me'.[46] By 1792 Agneta was fed up with trying to make Sydney Farm work and in a letter to her stepson she wrote that she was resolved to build a new house (Figures 4.15 & 4.16) on a parcel of land located a short distance away near the village of Hamble:

> Enclosed is a very rude sketch of a Farm I am just going to purchase. It is that beautiful space of ground at Hamble ... This will give you an idea of the extent and form of it. I have some thoughts of building a House upon it as it is certainly the most beautiful situation in the County, & the Fields already lie so well together only wanting to be laid down by the plow into Lawn or grass. Planting will be necessary, there being only one small coppice, besides the trees in the Hedgerows, of which there is no want. I have marked on the Plan, where the House should stand, tho there is not a single spot on the whole ground which does not afford a fine view. Where the Stable Yard and Garden should be, I must leave to one more conversant in such business to decide. The purpose of me troubling you with this, is to beg you would be so good as to speak to Mr Soane on the subject of building a small but convenient House for me, & to desire him to send me down some Plans.[47]

Agneta's tone suggests that she knew exactly what she wanted for her new home, and was particularly excited by the location, which promised beautiful

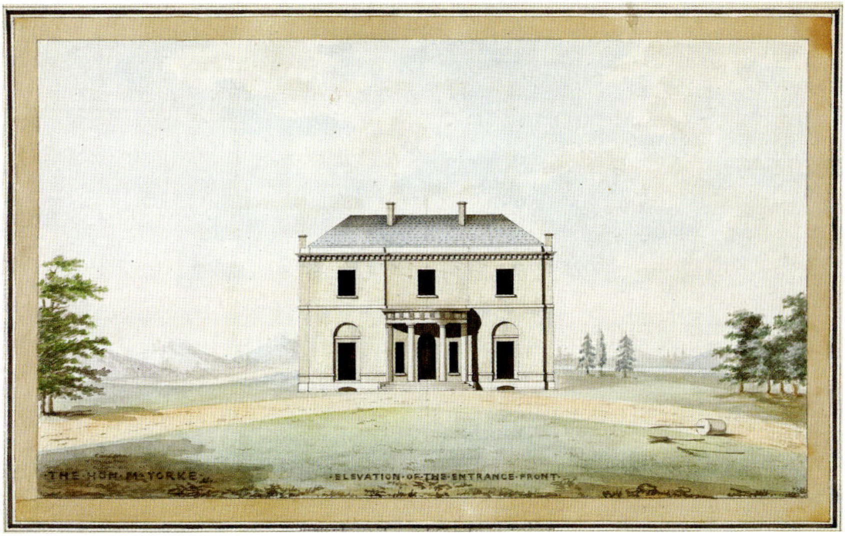

FIGURE 4.15 John McDonnell, presentation drawing of the entrance front of Sydney Lodge, 1793. SM Volume 59/39: © Sir John Soane's Museum, London. Photo: Ardon Bar-Hama.

views. Her desire for a small and convenient villa is emphasized, indicating that she wanted a house that was comfortable and affordable. Her chosen architect was Soane and as a discerning architectural patroness, Agneta also knew precisely what she wanted in terms of design and plan form:

> The sort of Plans I should like, would be a Square. The offices underneath & the Kitchen arched to prevent the smell of it in the upper stories. On the principal floor, two very good rooms (an Eating and drawing room) a Book Room & a Family apartment with all conveniences. In the attick or Roof some Bed rooms for company & maid servts. The mens sleeping room below in the offices (and the Butlers also). In this lower space I should wish all conveniences as Scullery, Larder, Hall, Butler & House Keepers Rooms & wine cellar &c. The Beer, coals and wood might be in the vaults in the area. You see my object is to have a low House, for I would have no Garrets over the Rooms I have specified. The windows of the Principal rooms should be down to the Floor and those of the Basement story only half way above Ground. The chimneys I should like to be almost level with the Roof & hardly visible. As I study use & convenience more than ornament or shew, I am very anxious for a Plan that should be perfectly comfortable with just elegance enough for pleasure.[48]

Agneta was a patroness with a very specific vision in mind and had carefully considered the architectural elements that she thought most important. Her

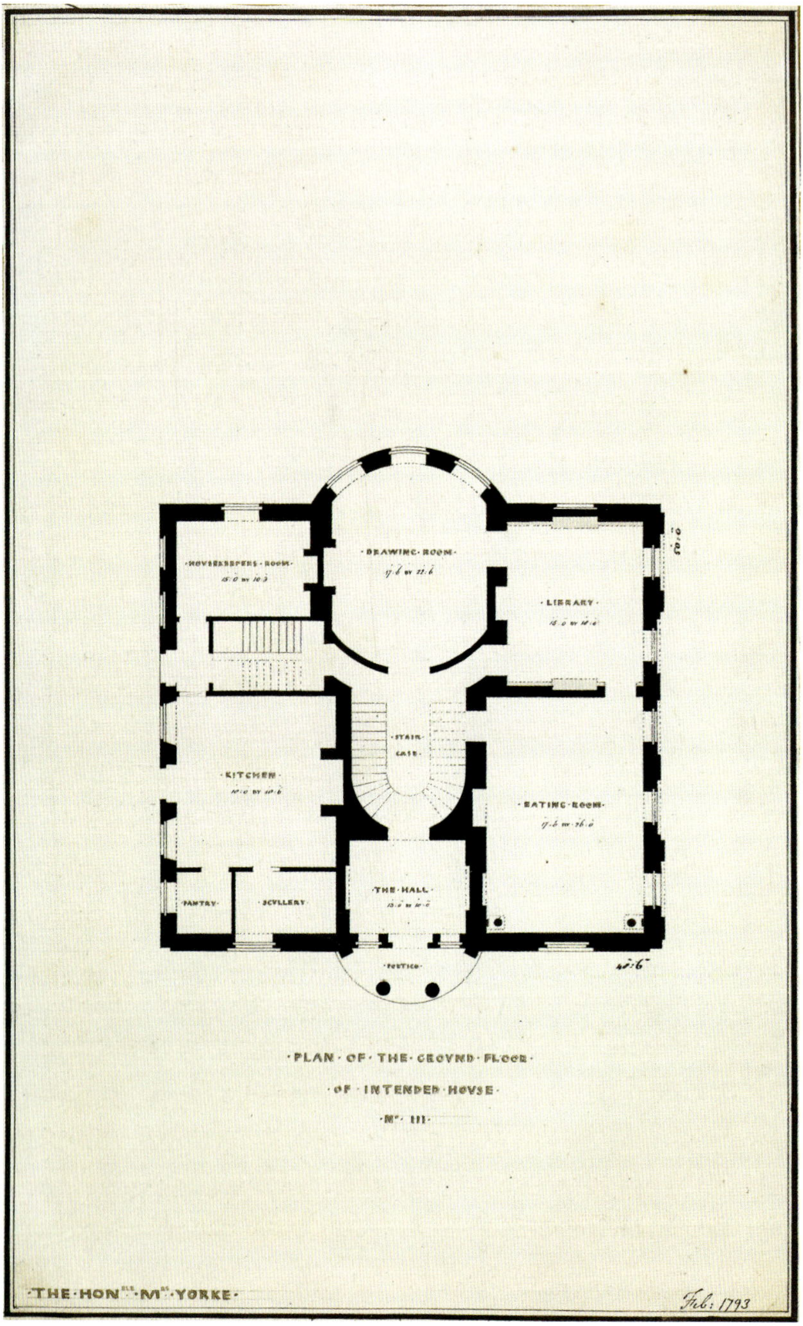

FIGURE 4.16 John McDonnell, ground-floor plan of Sydney Lodge, 1793. SM Volume 59/38: © Sir John Soane's Museum, London. Photo: Ardon Bar-Hama.

planning was extensive, having already decided that she wanted her house 'faced with white brick and slated', the slate was to be procured 'from the Western coast' and the stone 'from Swanage or Portland'; all of which was to be transported by water.[49] She also stipulated how much she wished to pay for such a villa: 'I should hope the whole might be done for 1500£'.[50]

Her stepson evidently obliged, because Soane soon sent 'six small variant plans and elevations' to Agneta for her consideration in 1792, followed by a visit with more plans sent in January 1793.[51] Eventually, Agneta was satisfied and building work commenced in the spring of 1793. She happily reported, that 'Mr. Soane is building I think a castle instead of a cottage which I originally designed and the foundation seems intended to rival that of the largest pyramid', which her son, 'Captain Yorke is not sorry for ... I dare say'.[52] Her mentioning of Captain Yorke is important here, because it was he that would inherit the villa upon her death. It is clear that she was building Sydney Lodge with him in mind, thereby emphasizing the important role that women played in the creation of architectural legacies in the eighteenth century.

Agneta was continuously concerned about the cost and the scale of the project, stating that 'I tremble at so great an undertaking, as making a place at my time of Life, in so alarming a period & with the Stocks tumbling down so fast every day'.[53] Yet, at the same time, the project also brought her great pride, and by October 1793 Agneta was delighted to report to Lady Grey, that:

> The Season on the whole, has been extremely favourable for Building, and my House has gone on as fast as I could possibly expect – I flatter myself it will do Mr Soane much credit, as certainly for its size, it is a very compleat mansion, and its appearance Elegant, but it is not a Palace.[54]

Indeed, in its final form, Sydney Lodge was an architectural endeavour that reflected well upon both patroness and architect.[55] Its refined use of Classical forms, together with its convenient plan, resulted in an elegant and sophisticated villa. To corroborate this sentiment, it was later featured in *The New Vitruvius Britannicus* (1808) with the accompanying description emphasizing its simple elegance: 'The building is of white bricks, with Portland stone-cornices and dressings; the whole plain and simple, convenience being the principal object'.[56] The interiors of Agneta's villa were fashionably Neo-Classical, with the ornamentation suitably refined and sophisticated.[57]

For Agneta, the smaller size of the villa and the lower costs associated with building and maintaining one, in comparison to a large country house, allowed her to realize her architectural vision by commissioning an entirely new build. She was able to choose every detail of her villa, including the precise location, the exact materials, as well as the design, plan form and interior decorative scheme. Once again, just as with her nieces' villas, the need for comfort was just as important as pursuing a fashionable Neo-Classical style.

Furthermore, the rural setting of Sydney Lodge was a significant attraction for Agneta, which she later enhanced with the assistance of William Emes, a prominent landscape gardener.[58] One of the final attractions of Agneta's villa building was that she was able to provide an inheritance for her younger son, to whom she left it upon her death in 1820. It later formed part of the 4th Earl of Hardwicke's estate and became the dower house of his widow, Susan, Countess of Hardwicke following his death in 1873.

Agneta was only able to build her villa due to the financial autotomy she gained from widowhood, which was also true for her nieces, Ladies Polwarth and Grantham. Elizabeth Armistead also had financial independence, gained from her career as a courtesan. But what about their married counterparts? Could married women build and create villas? As with town and country house building, it is much more difficult to decipher whether wives were responsible for building villas, due to the strictures of coverture and the fact that husbands usually paid for such projects. Nonetheless, there is an interesting category of married women who did build villas, which includes wives who were trapped in miserable, abusive marriages.

Villas as a means of escape

Not all women were as happily married as Elizabeth Armistead and for some, constructing a villa was vital in asserting their independence, especially when entangled in a terrible marriage. This was certainly true of Henrietta Howard (1689–1767), later Countess of Suffolk, who famously built Marble Hill House in Twickenham (Figure 4.17).[59] Henrietta was the daughter of Sir Henry Hobart of Blickling Hall in Norfolk and Elizabeth, daughter of Sir Joseph Maynard. Orphaned at twelve, she became the ward of Henry Howard, 5th Earl of Suffolk, marrying his youngest son, Charles Howard, in 1706. Howard was a cruel and violent man, who treated her appallingly throughout their marriage.[60] In 1717 she wrote of her tortured position, stating how Howard governed her 'with Tyranny; with Cruelty, my life in Danger, then am I not free? … Self preservation is ye first law of Nature, are Married Women then ye only part of human nature [that] must not follow it?.'[61]

Henrietta was the mistress of George II when Prince of Wales, and through this connection she was able to escape her husband, because in 1723 the Prince presented her with £11,500 of stock in trust, as well as all the furniture, furnishings and jewellery in her own and her servants' rooms at Leicester House and Richmond.[62] The liberating settlement stipulated that 'Charles Howard shall not have anything to doe or intermedle' with the gift and that Henrietta was to use the gift as she pleased 'as if she was sole and unmarryed'.[63] The Prince therefore provided his mistress with her financial freedom, finally severing the suffocating bond between herself and her tyrannical husband. This life-saving injection of capital, together with her salary as one of Princess Caroline's Women of the Bedchamber,

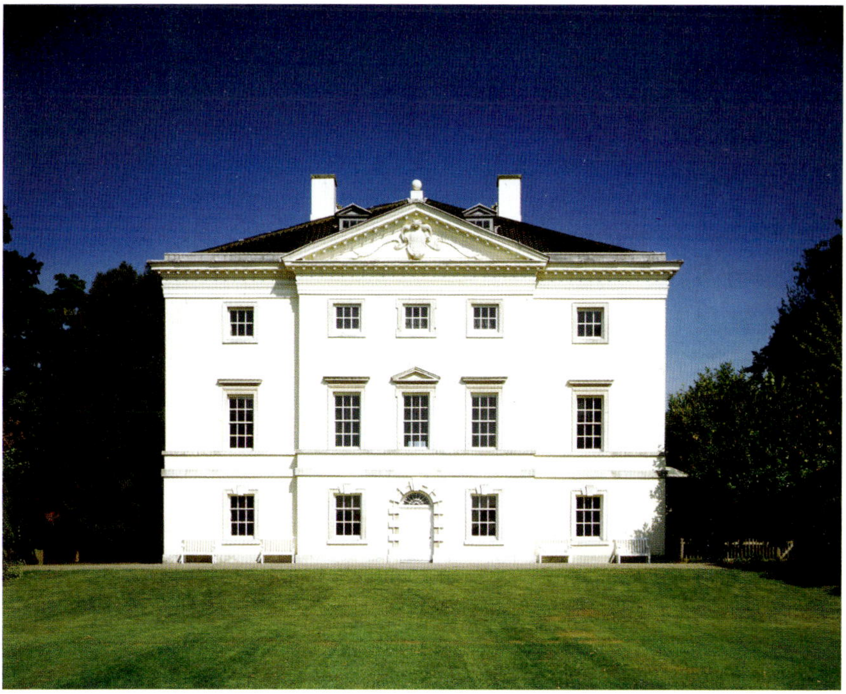

FIGURE 4.17 Marble Hill House, Twickenham. English Heritage/Heritage Images/ Getty Image.

enabled her to immediately set about planning and commissioning her Palladian Twickenham villa.

Henrietta enlisted the help of Lord Herbert, later 9th Earl of Pembroke, to oversee Colen Campbell's initial drawings of her house, and employed Roger Morris to assist in the building. She was passionately involved in Marble Hill's creation, and was a strong advocate for Palladianism, as indicated by her subscriptions to Campbell's *Vitruvius Britannicus* (1725) and William Kent's *Designs of Inigo Jones* (1727).[64] The completed villa was Henrietta's declaration to the world that she was free and independent. Her status as a lady of quality was solidified through her elegant and fashionable house and allowed her to live a happy and fulfilling life until her death in 1767. Her success was such that her architectural taste and judgement were respected, and her advice sought after. In 1729, for example, when her friend Lord Chesterfield was building a ballroom at his house in The Hague, he wrote to her asking whether the proposed proportions were correct, hoping that she and her architect would 'both be so good as to give me your Sentiments upon it'.[65]

A similar story of escape through architecture can be found in the architectural patronage of Elizabeth Herbert, Countess of Pembroke and Montgomery (Figure 4.18), described by Horace Walpole as the 'most beautiful woman in the world'.[66] Lady Pembroke was the long-suffering

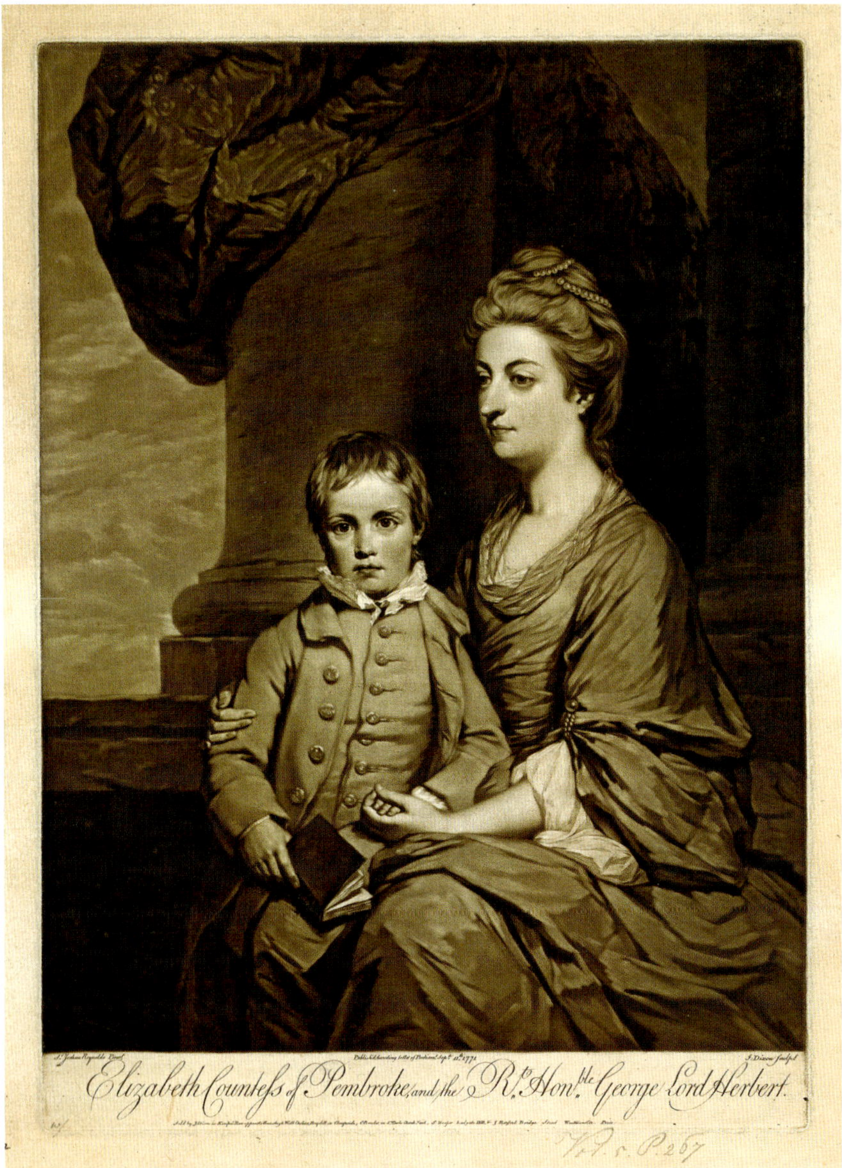

FIGURE 4.18 John Dixon, after Sir Joshua Reynolds, *Elizabeth, Countess of Pembroke, and the Rt. Honble. George, Lord Herbert*, 1771, mezzotint. Yale Center for British Art, Paul Mellon Collection, B1970.3.225. Courtesy of the Yale Center for British Art.

wife of the 10th Earl of Pembroke, the son of the architect earl who assisted Henrietta Howard at Marble Hill. As the daughter of Charles Spencer, 3rd Duke of Marlborough, Lady Pembroke's marriage had been a dynastic affair, linking the two noble families together in 1756. Although the Pembrokes were to have two children, George, Lord Herbert, and Lady Charlotte, their marriage was an unhappy one.

Lord Pembroke was an unpredictable, controlling and quarrelsome character, described by his son in 1784 as 'perhaps ... the most unaccountable of all human beings'.[67] He was notorious for his numerous affairs, his debauched escapades with the infamous Casanova and for his scandalous elopement in a packet-boat with the young and pretty Catherine 'Kitty' Hunter in 1762. This scandalous affair resulted in a son, Augustus Retnuh Reebkomp, whose unorthodox names are anagrams of Hunter and Pembroke respectively. Lady Pembroke was universally pitied; Elizabeth Montagu described her as 'one of the best and most beautiful women in the world' and Adam Smith, the Scottish political economist and moral philosopher, failed to understand Lord Pembroke's motivations: 'You know he is remarkable for having a very Handsome Wife, a Daughter of Marlborough, whom he never us'd well'.[68]

Remarkably, in March 1763 the Pembrokes were reconciled and lived together once again at Wilton House, their country seat near Salisbury, and Pembroke House in London.[69] However, from this point onwards they lived increasingly separate lives, especially as Lord Pembroke was posted abroad for prolonged periods in his capacity as Major-General during the Seven Years' War. Although these absences must have been a welcome respite for his wife, life became almost unbearable when they did have to share the same house. In an effort to escape the unpleasantness of London and her husband, Lady Pembroke constantly tried to organize small holidays, especially to Brighton, for her sickly daughter and herself. Her letters to her son offer a glimpse into her melancholy life in London:

> My Dr George,
>
> I have been so low & nervous of late, & my head so full of vexatious things, that I did not chuse to write to you ...
>
> Here I am *still*, nothing certain yet of where I am going, tired to death of being here, if it was not for Ld William's Lodge in the Grove in the Green Park where Charlotte & I go most days to tea, (*he* being still in Scotland) we shou'd die, but makes a sort of Villa. Whether I do or not go to Brighton is still a peut être que oui, peut être que non.[70]

Her depressed tone speaks volumes of her unhappiness and desperation to be free. Her lack of agency and independence is glaringly evident as she laments her virtual imprisonment in London, with her only solace being the rural retreat offered to her by a kind friend. In such instances, when a marriage was not convivial, a wife's lot could be a most tortuous thing, rendering her forever dependent and subordinate. Architecture, in an unequal marriage, remained the preserve of the wealthy male.

In 1780, fortune finally smiled upon Lady Pembroke, as George III and Queen Charlotte kindly granted her the use of Hill Lodge in Richmond Park:

> I am just now delighted with having leave to take some Lodgings at a Keeper's Lodge in Richmond Park; it is a leave they do not in general like to give, but the K. & Q. have said a thousand civil things at the same time they have given me leave. I pay for them myself but it is so cheap that I can afford it; there are rooms enough for Charlotte & I to go & lye there, for a night now & then, & often to breakfast; it is but nine miles, & just in the place I like. You know a Villa has always been my Hobby Horse. Sister Di has just taken a house at Richmond ... so that is quite comfortable.[71]

This property enabled her, for the first time, to live independently from her husband. Nonetheless, she was still very much married and her estranged husband, although not vocal in his objections about her quiet removal from his house, certainly resented his wife's actions. As he could not criticize the royal family, he instead sought to intimidate his wife by pacing around the boundary of her villa: 'He [Lord Pembroke] has been all round the Park wall backwards & forwards but has never enter'd it'.[72] Determined not to be bullied, Lady Pembroke threw herself into 'staking out where pales are to be put up to inclose ground of each side of me', which she had permission to do 'with my own money, so I shall be quite in rags soon, as I cannot possibly buy any more gowns'.[73] By establishing firm physical boundaries, she was able to further protect herself from her husband and create a safe, rural sanctuary for herself and her daughter.

In 1783, Lady Pembroke was made a Lady of the Bedchamber to Queen Charlotte, a position that she held until the Queen's death in 1818. This position not only provided her with a salary but also further protected her from her husband. Moreover, her close proximity to the king and queen allowed her to request permission to add stables to the Lodge, which was granted in March 1785:

> My dear Lady Pembroke,
>
> In order to convince you that I did not forget your commission I have the pleasure to acquaint you that the King not only grants your request, but does leave it to your judgement where abouts to place your Stables, being convinced of your good taste not to put it in any place where it can prove an Eye sore.[74]

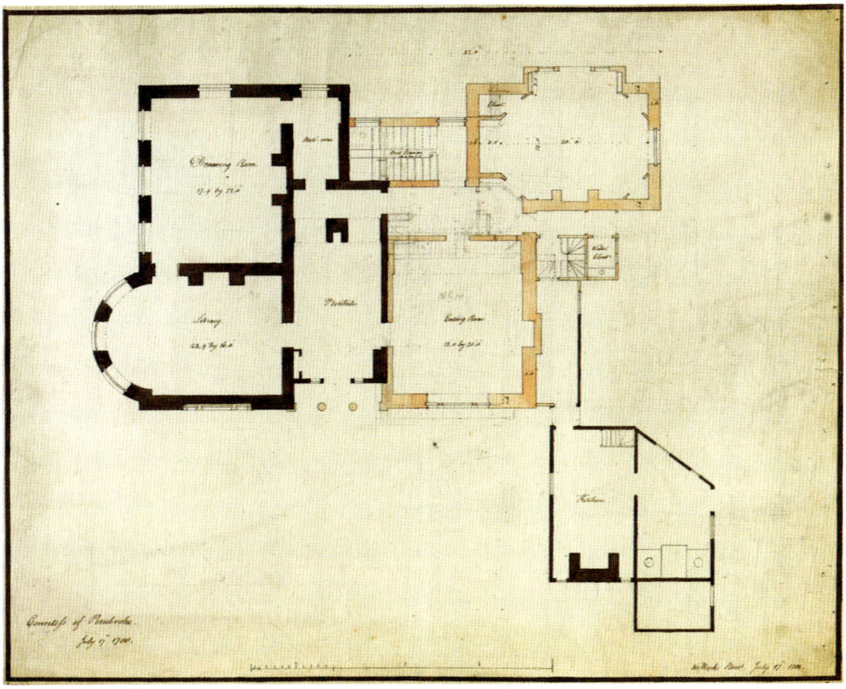

FIGURE 4.19 John Sanders (att.), presentation drawing showing proposed design for alterations and additions to the north-west of Pembroke Lodge, 1788. SM 29/3/8v: © Sir John Soane's Museum, London. Photo: Hugh Kelly.

Having been given the freedom to build the stable block, she soon commissioned John Soane to provide designs.[75] Then, a few years later she commissioned Soane to enlarge the villa, hiring him to build a new west wing, which included a new dining room and a new drawing room (Figure 4.19).[76]

The new drawing room was polygonal in design and featured unusual, coved alcoves in each corner. Two presentation drawings of the new drawing room illustrate the proposed decorative finishing, which features a design that seemingly resemble trellises or the wire of an aviary, complete with winding vines that reach up to the ceiling (Figure 4.20).[77] This unusual design was one that Soane later adapted and used elsewhere, including in his own breakfast parlour at No. 12 Lincoln's Inn Fields, which was executed by his favoured painter, John Crace, in *c.* 1794.[78] However, it is just as likely that Lady Pembroke was influenced by the decorative scheme of the Picnic Room (*c.* 1771) in Queen Charlotte's rustic cottage *orné* at Kew, which consisted of intertwining convolvulus and nasturtiums on the walls, ceiling and door mouldings.[79]

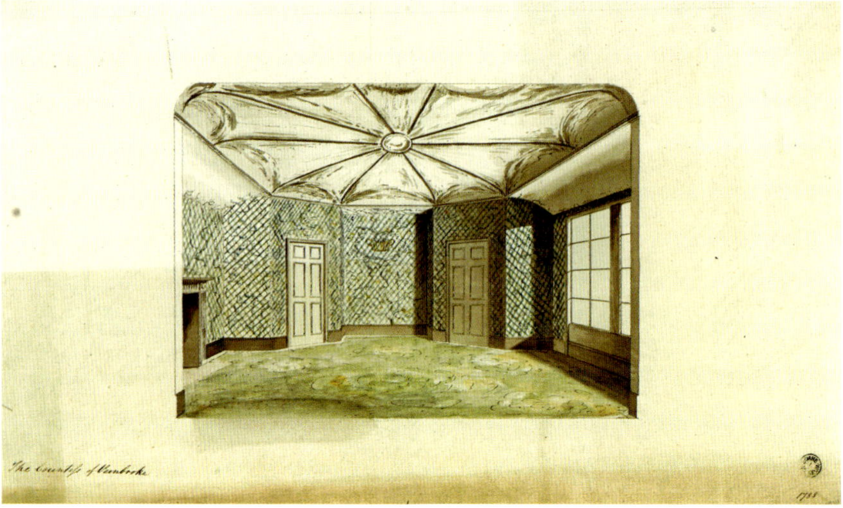

FIGURE 4.20 Soane Office hand, presentation drawing showing proposed interior decoration for the drawing room at Pembroke Lodge, *c.* 1788. SM 29/3/1: © Sir John Soane's Museum, London. Photo: Hugh Kelly.

This projected work was estimated at £800 (about £62,000 today), which according to Soane, 'was considerably more than she wished'.[80] A later estimate of £500 and Soane's proposals to include three additional bedchambers above the new wing were also rejected.[81] Soane's journal records numerous trips to Richmond and Whitehall (her town house), taking a plethora of different designs for Lady Pembroke's consideration, most of which were rejected. On 19 July 1788 Soane records that he 'called again on Lady Pembroke at Whitehall nothing settled – but order'd to call to mor[w]', which he did, recording that 'Ditto – called, wanted more estimates specifying particulars'.[82]

This reveals that although enthusiastic about remodelling her villa, Lady Pembroke was particular about what she wanted and how much she was willing to spend. It is apparent from a survey drawing completed in 1792 that, in the end, the north-west wing was the only major addition accepted by Lady Pembroke.[83] In December 1788 she also accepted Soane's designs for a pair of corner bedchamber chimneypieces, indicating that she may have modernized the bedchamber apartments too.[84] These small alterations were enough to allow her to live comfortably and fashionably and provided her with ample room to entertain her friends. In this way she was able to use architecture to create her perfect sanctuary, away from her husband, while also maintaining her respectability and dignity.

The sanctuary of the villa was also sought out by Lady Pembroke's sister, Lady Diana Beauclerk (1734–1808), who used her country villa to escape public humiliation following a tumultuous family affair. Before she was forced to hide from public view, she had initially taken a villa in Twickenham called Little Marble Hill and was therefore less than an hour's walk from her sister at Pembroke Lodge. Just like her sister, Lady Diana had also received her fair share of marital hardship, having been married to the notoriously unfaithful Lord 'Bully' Bolingbroke, whom she later deserted out of desperation. She then shocked society by engaging in an adulterous affair with Topham Beauclerk, which subsequently ended in her sensational divorce from Bolingbroke. Full of optimism, she married Beauclerk two days after the divorce was granted.

Unfortunately, her new husband later turned out to be unpleasant and possibly abusive towards the end of his life.[85] Plagued by ill health and addicted to laudanum, Beauclerk took little interest in personal hygiene and soon became infested with lice, which as Lady Louisa Stuart remarked, was 'beyond what one could have thought possible in anyone but a beggar or a gypsy'.[86] Thus, when Lady Di (as she was affectionately known) was finally widowed in 1780 and able to live independently in her small Twickenham villa, her friends were delighted for her, with Edmund Burke remarking:

> I am extremely glad ... to see her at last so well Housed; poor woman! ... I never, myself, so much enjoyed the sight of happiness in another as in that Woman when I first saw her after the Death of her Husband. It was really enlivening to behold her placed in that sweet House, released from all her cares, a thousand pounds a Year at her own disposal, *and* – her Husband was Dead! O it was pleasant, it was delightful, to see her enjoyment of her situation![87]

Lady Diana was a proficient artist and engaged in interior decoration by painting a trellis-like mural directly onto the wall, as Horace Walpole glowingly described:

> Lady Di Beauclerc is painting a room at her charming villa ... that I have christened *Spencer Grove*. It is nothing but a row of lilacs in festoons on green paper, but executed in as great a style as Michael Angelo would have done for a pope's villa; and without even making a sketch. You would know the *countenance of every* single flower, and call them by their names, but alas! those glorious wreaths ... are painted in water-colours, and will not last two summers. In each panel of the surbase she has painted a sprig or chaplet of geranium, or ivy, or periwinkle, and every one is a capital picture.[88]

This effect is reminiscent of the painted walls of Queen Charlotte's Cottage at Kew and predated the Mary Moser room at Frogmore House (*c.* 1792–5) in Windsor Home Park, both of which feature floral and botanical scenes and details. At Frogmore, Queen Charlotte commissioned Mary Moser (1744–1819), one of the founding members of the Royal Academy, to decorate the room with botanical works, some on canvas and some directly onto the walls, so that the room resembled a beautiful arbour. Similarly, in the Cross Gallery at Frogmore Princess Elizabeth, daughter of Queen Charlotte and George III, decorated the walls with garlands of flowers. Artistry was, therefore, an accepted method through which women could enhance the aesthetic of their interiors. For Lady Diana it was also an economical approach, saving money that would otherwise have gone to hired artisans, but this did not diminish the quality of the decoration. Indeed, Queen Charlotte reputedly paid Mary Moser over £900 (approximately £70,000 today) for her decorative scheme at Frogmore, thereby acknowledging the high level of skill required to execute such designs.[89]

In 1789, however, the story of the incestuous relationship of Lady Diana's son, the 3rd Viscount Bolingbroke, with his younger half-sister Mary Beauclerk, broke in the national newspapers.[90] Lady Diana was utterly unaware of the relationship and was devastated by it. The scandalous couple, who by this point had two sons with a third child on the way, ran away to the Continent to live there indefinitely. In an effort to escape the gossip and prying eyes of Twickenham, Lady Diana gave up her beloved villa and

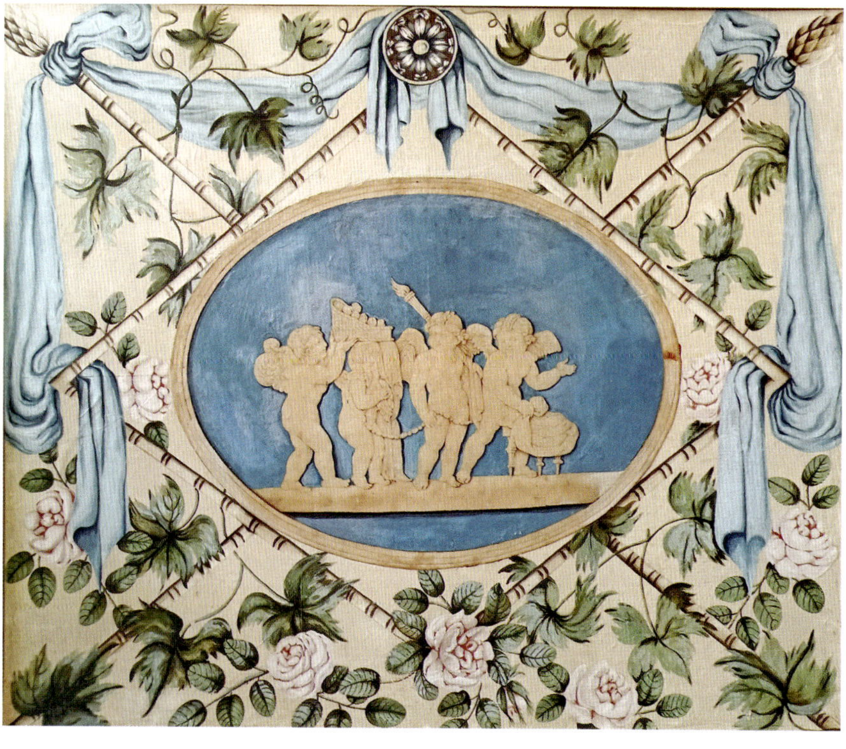

FIGURE 4.21 Detail of painted panel by Lady Diana Beauclerk. Courtesy of Lydiard Park, Wiltshire.

moved across the river to Petersham, where she leased a smaller and more isolated cottage. There she shut out the world by immersing herself in a new decorative project, painting 'six rectangular panels, each over twelve feet high by three feet wide, and three smaller ones, to go over doorways, totalling several hundred square feet of painted surfaces'.[91] Each of the panels (which survive at Lydiard Park) has a cornflower blue background with various floral and botanical details, some with baskets of flowers, others with cupids, but all interlinked with fantastically vivid flowers and ribbons (Figure 4.21).[92]

In the end, poor Lady Di's villas came to represent entirely different things. The first had represented freedom and independence from her disappointing husbands, a place where she could express herself artistically. The second, however, represented social isolation and exile; a place to hide from the cruel gossips of London.

Villas for status and business

Successful courtesans were just as likely as their more respectable counterparts to seek out villas to enjoy the benefits of the country air. For the extravagant Sophia Baddeley, the courtesan who used her Grafton Street residence in London to promote her desirability, the acquisition of a suburban villa was another means through which she could be fashionable, and thus she rented a 'ready furnished house at Hammersmith-hope'.[93] She and her companion Elizabeth Steele purchased the lease from Frances Abington (1737–1815), a fellow actress and style icon, and agreed to pay £250 (approximately £25,000 today) for her furniture. Sophia and Elizabeth were delighted with the villa, describing its situation near the river as 'delightful', and admiring its 'beauty, its neatness, and elegance', all of which they believed were qualities that 'Mrs. Abingdon possessed, and shewed us that she had equally as refined a taste in furnishing a house, as in making up a dress'.[94] The villa was not up to Sophia's standards however, so she quickly decided to make improvements, which she regularly supervised by riding out to Hammersmith:

> On arrival at Hammersmith-hope, we found the improvements going on, but not completed. A large bow-window was made in the front of the house, with a flat leaden roof and ballustrades, and a long room built over the kitchen for a laundry. We found twenty men at work, and made them happy by our ordering them a dinner at the public house.[95]

Sophia's improvements were both practical and aesthetic, costing about £80,000 in today's money. This was a significant sum for Sophia, and one that Elizabeth was exceedingly shocked by:

> [I] proposed settling with the builder, for the additions he had made to Hammersmith house, which Mrs Baddeley designed to pay. And when

> I looked over the bills, I was amazed; they came to seven hundred and fifty-nine pounds, eleven shillings, and eight-pence. My surprize at this, made me fly to her to tell her of it. She received the intelligence with great unconcern; said, we had a lease of it, and that it was now a good house, and I must set it down to the article of her extravagance.[96]

The extensive improvement Sophia made to her villa was another mark of her ostentatious display. In addition to enhancing her status, the villa also provided Sophia with an escape from the city and the demands of her lover and many admirers. With its distance from the city and its relative obscurity, Sophia was also able to use it as a clandestine rendezvous, away from scrutiny. On one occasion she secretly met the Duke of Northumberland, an avid admirer of hers, but at the very same time (as fate would have it) Lord Melbourne appeared at her London house expecting to see her. Luckily her good friend Elizabeth was quick to think up an excuse, saying that Sophia had gone to Hammersmith 'for a ride, and to give some directions about the house'.[97]

For Sophia, the possession of a villa was a status symbol that announced to the world that she was at the top of her game as the most popular courtesan about town. This in turn meant that she could still attract the wealthiest men, whose money allowed her to continue to live independently. Villas, therefore, could assist women in promoting their commercial ventures, whether that was the selling of their companionship, as with Sophia, or the selling of their goods, as we shall see with Eleanor Coade.

During the eighteenth century the seaside became a popular destination amongst the fashionable elite to holiday and seek health cures, which caused numerous coastal resorts to spring up along Britain's coastline.[98] New townhouses, villas, theatres, shops, assembly rooms, parks and promenades were built to attract and accommodate visitors. Brighton became one of the most famous resorts due to the patronage of the Prince Regent (future George IV), who made regular visits for his health from 1783, when he was just twenty-one.[99] In 1787 the Prince commissioned Henry Holland to remodel his rented lodgings into an elegant villa called the Marine Pavilion and in 1815 he hired John Nash to transform it into a magnificent oriental palace – the famous Royal Pavilion.[100]

This passion for the seaside was of course shared by women, some of whom also decided to build or improve marine villas of their own. We have already seen how Agneta Yorke chose to build her Neo-Classical villa near to Southampton, which boasted wonderful views over Southampton Water. Others also enjoyed the sea air, such as the intrepid businesswoman Mrs Eleanor Coade (1733–1821), who in 1784 was given Belmont, a maritime villa in Lyme Regis, by her uncle Samuel Coade. She subsequently remodelled it to suit her taste, using her own stone, Coade stone, to embellish the exteriors.

Born in Exeter Eleanor was the eldest daughter of George Coade, a wool merchant, and his wife Eleanor Enchmarch. Eleanor is renowned for devising a formula to mass-produce artificial stone, named initially as *Lythodipyra*, from the Greek meaning ‘twice-fired stone’, and then later confidently renamed to Coade stone.[101] She used this stone to create high-quality statuary and architectural embellishments, which proved to be highly durable and were consequently used by leading architects, including the Adam brothers, John Soane, James Wyatt and Jeffry Wyatville.

Eleanor was adept at marketing and exhibited at the Royal Academy, placed advertisements in the papers and produced a catalogue which contained 788 designs, entitled: ‘A Descriptive Catalogue of Coade’s Artificial Stone Manufactory, at King’s Arms Stairs, Narrow-Wall, Lambeth’ (1784) (Figure 4.22).[102] Her catalogue included fashionable designs for chimneypieces, statues, busts, friezes, fascia, coats of arms, balusters, pinnacles, medallions, paterae, mouldings, interior ornaments and furniture, all of which were made at her manufactory in London (Figure 4.23). Eleanor’s success was also partly due to the high calibre of sculptors that

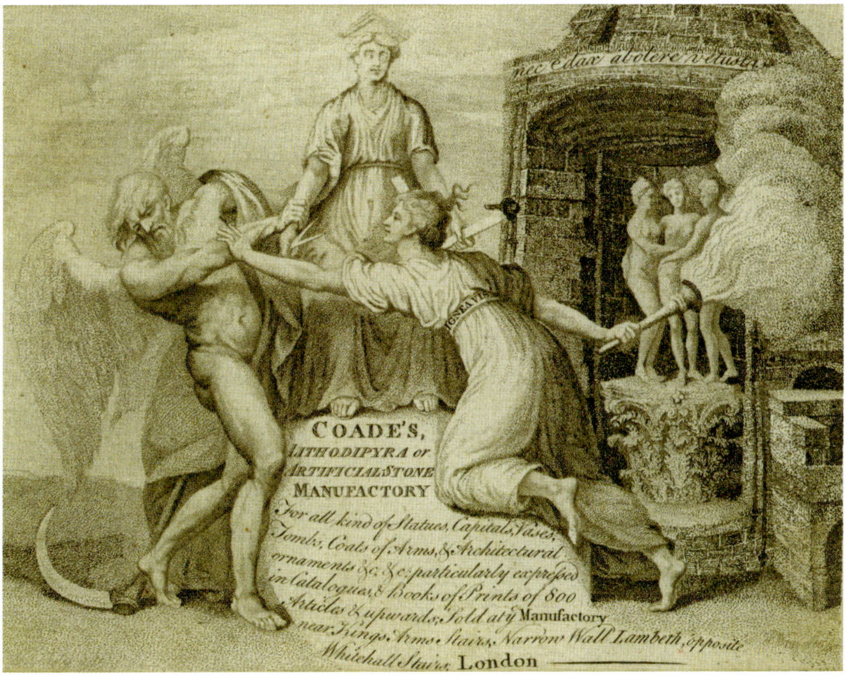

FIGURE 4.22 P. Wray, after Charles Reuben Ryley, ‘Coade’s Lithodipyra, or, Artificial Stone Manufactory’, *c.* 1784, engraved frontispiece to Coade’s 1784 Catalogue. Yale Center for British Art, Paul Mellon Collection. Courtesy of the Yale Center for British Art.

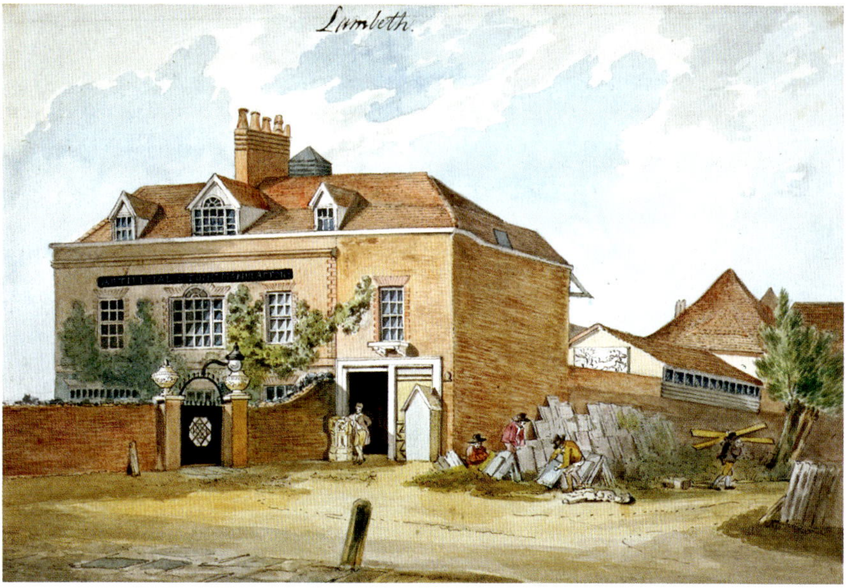

FIGURE 4.23 Unknown artist, *View of the Coade Stone Factory on Narrow Wall, Lambeth*, c. 1800, watercolour. Guildhall Library & Art Gallery/Heritage Images/Getty Images.

she employed, including John Bacon, John Flaxman, John Rossi, Thomas Banks and Joseph Panzetta. Her reputation and fame were such that the Coade manufactory held the royal appointment to both George III and his son George IV.

Belmont, therefore, provided Eleanor with another means by which she could display the versatility of her stone (Figure 4.24). She enlarged the villa and embellished the principal façade with examples of her trade, including the parapet urns (one of which was dated 1782), the frieze, the vermiculated quoins, the string course, the key stones above the windows decorated with the heads of Amphitrite (one of which is inscribed with 'J. Brabham fecit 1785'), and the large keystone above the entrance, decorated with the head of Neptune. These fashionable Classical elements advocated an appropriate nautical theme, with the presence of Neptune and his wife Amphitrite neatly reflecting its coastal location.

Eleanor not only created a comfortable and attractive villa for herself, but she also used it to further promote her product. Never one to miss a marketing opportunity, with the principal façade of Belmont facing a public road, Cobb Road, Eleanor was able to publicly demonstrate how attractive, fashionable and adaptable her stone was. Eleanor was an excellent businesswoman and was exceptional in her professional engagement in the architectural industry. Not only did she possess technical knowledge and expertise relating to artificial stone manufacture, she also successfully

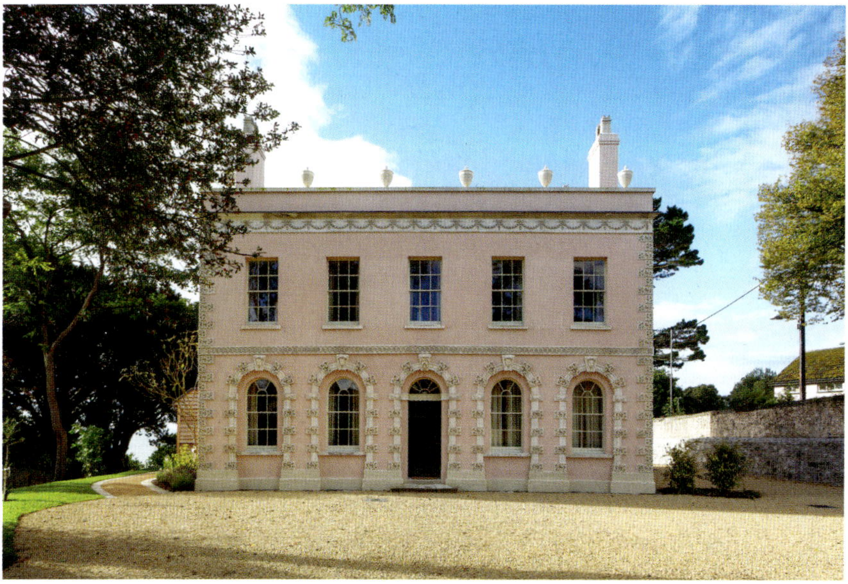

FIGURE 4.24 Belmont, Lyme Regis. Courtesy of John Miller/Landmark Trust, 2015.

marketed her product so that she was able to maintain her financial independence and thus never married. In so doing, a parallel can be drawn between her and Sophia Baddeley who made her fortune by advertising and selling her companionship. Both were entrepreneurial and utilized their villas to enhance their visibility for financial gain. This in turn allowed them both to continue their independent lives, free from the constraints of marriage and coverture.

Villas as legacy

This chapter has thus far explored how villas were created to establish comfortable, luxurious suburban retreats, or as places of escape and sanctuary from husbands or society, or to further some business venture. However, throughout these discussions a theme of legacy has often emerged, in which women acquired, embellished or built villas as a means of creating a tangible inheritance that could be bequeathed to a suitably deserving individual, such as a younger child, since such individuals were side-lined within the system of primogeniture.

Generally, wealthy widows were the ones who created such legacies, as they were rich enough to do so and often had children or relatives that they wanted to provide for. Sometimes widows sought to assist their less fortunate friends or companions, especially if they did not have children of their own. This was true of Lady Jane Coke (1706–61), who succeeded in enlarging and improving Sunbury Place (now Sunbury Court), her villa in Sudbury-upon-Thames.[103] Upon her death in 1761 she bequeathed it, along with the rest of her extensive estate, to her young companion Anna Maria Draycott (*c.* 1726–87), who used this substantial fortune to ascend the ranks of aristocracy and become the wife of the 2nd Earl of Pomfret (the terrible son of Lady Pomfret) in 1764.[104] By establishing a villa estate of her own, Lady Jane was able to circumvent the patriarchal inheritance system of the time, thereby allowing her to completely transform the fortunes of her female friend.

A contemporary of Lady Jane's, the wealthy, widowed Charlotte Digby (1707–78), also sought to provide an inheritance with the purchasing of a villa. Charlotte was born into a powerful Whig family – her father was Sir Stephen Fox and her two brothers were Stephen Fox-Strangways, 1st Earl of Ilchester and Henry Fox, 1st Baron Holland. In 1729 she married Edward Digby, son of the 5th Lord Digby, forging an important union between the two dynasties.

Twelve years after the death of her husband, in 1758, Charlotte took up residence at Fords Farm, a large villa located in Thames Ditton. She immediately set about enlarging it, a project that provided her with much enjoyment, as indicated in a letter from Lady Caroline Fox, her sister-in-law:

> [Charlotte] is surprisingly well when she is at that place of hers, more amused with and more eager about the works there, both in her house and garden, than I could ever imagine I should have seen her.[105]

Determined to establish herself permanently at her new suburban seat, in September 1763 she purchased the freehold of Fords for £7,000 (approximately £720,000 today) from George Tash and bought an additional twenty-three acres in October.[106] The following year she expanded her small estate further by purchasing an island in the river Thames, known as Ditton Hill.[107] Then, in 1771, she diverted the highway that ran from Thames Ditton to Kingston away from her house, so that she could extend her gardens even more.[108] Charlotte was systematically augmenting her estate so that it became one of the largest in the area. Her motivation for doing so was to create a legacy for one of her younger sons, since although her eldest son Edward was well provided for, having succeeded his grandfather as the 6th Baron Digby in 1752, her five younger sons had only received capital portions of £2,000 each from their father and a meagre allowance of £100 a year.[109] Thus, by establishing a respectably sized estate, Charlotte was ensuring that she could provide a suitable inheritance for at least one of her sons.

Upon her death in 1778, her estate at Fords passed to her fifth son, Colonel Stephen Digby. In 1782, Col. Digby leased Fords Farm to the recently widowed Charlotte Boyle Walsingham (1738–90), another widow of substantial means, who in 1781 had inherited the large sum of

£40,000 (approximately £3.5 million today) from her mother, Lady Frances Coningsby.[110] As befitted her rank, Charlotte (Figure 4.25) also had a 'splendid' London house in Stratford Place, which she had 'elegantly fitted up [with] her own Paintings & Drawings'.[111] Both Charlotte and her young daughter, also named Charlotte, were accomplished artists who enjoyed displaying their works of art.[112]

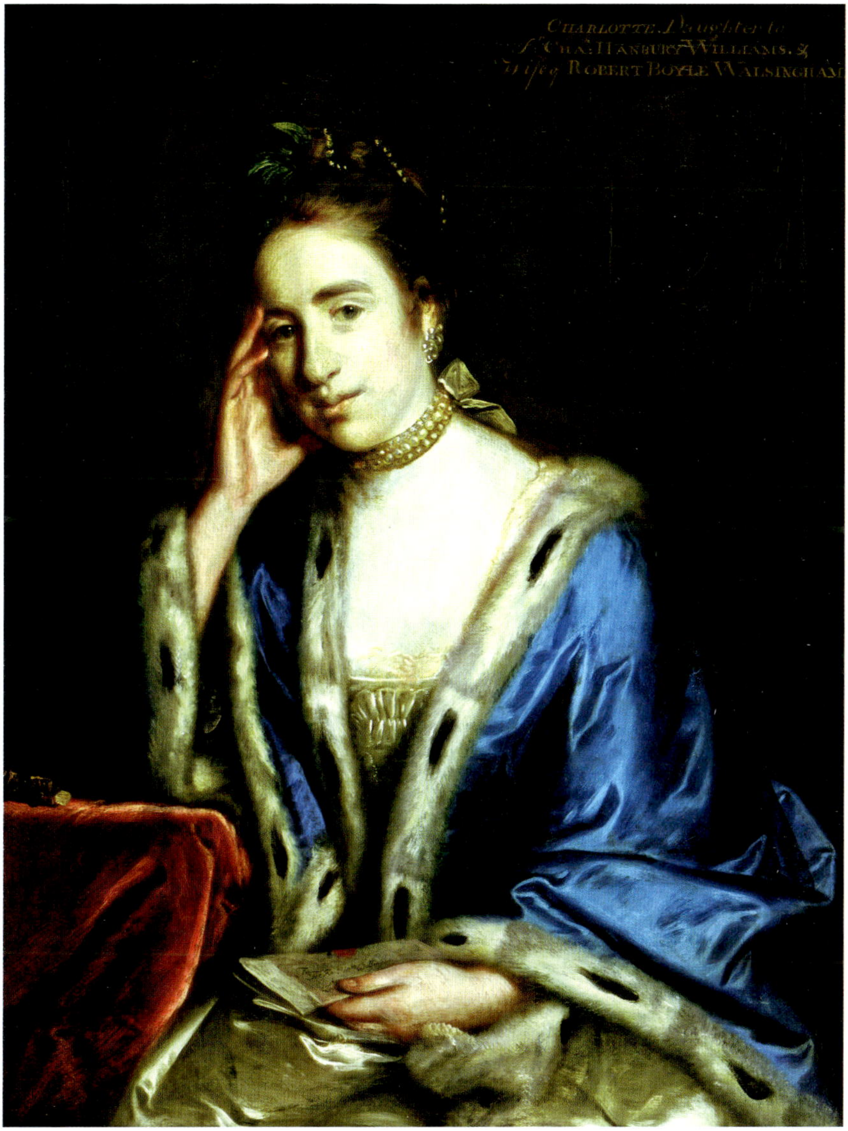

FIGURE 4.25 Sir Joshua Reynolds, *Charlotte Walsingham*, 1760, oil on canvas. Private collection. © Christie's Images/ Bridgeman Images.

Charlotte was a spirited and determined character and once she recovered from her grief, she set about cultivating a glittering social circle of beauties, intellectuals and wits. Although she had dearly loved her husband, Captain Boyle-Walsingham, he had certainly tested her patience with his affair with the courtesan Ann Sheldon. In fact, when rumours of their illicit relationship had reached Charlotte's ears, she concocted a plan to discover the truth. As Ann recounted in her memoirs, on one 'unsuspicious morning a gentlewoman [Charlotte] called upon me from … the milliner … with a suit of linen for me to look at'.[113] While in the process of leaving the suit of linen, the mystery woman complimented Ann on her appearance as well as the 'elegance of my furniture' and surmised that she must be 'protected by some person of first rank and fortune'.[114] Ann happily said that she was indebted to Captain Boyle-Walsingham, after which the woman complimented her again and then left. That same morning Ann was later visited by her lover, Boyle-Walsingham, who 'appeared to be under the impression of a very deep melancholy' and 'after moping for some time he asked me what visitors had been with me that morning', to which she mentioned the visit of the mystery woman.[115] The Captain then 'sighed as if his heart would burst; and, to my infinite astonishment, exclaimed *That woman is my wife* – and I am a ruined man'.[116] It turns out that after finding proof of her husband's betrayal Charlotte had issued him with an ultimatum: either Ann must leave the country or Ann must marry.

Given Charlotte's assertive mindset it is no surprise that as a widow she competently and confidently established herself in a suburban estate of her own. In 1783 she purchased the freehold of Fords Farm,[117] reputably paying £5,000 for '42 acres of land … House, Offices, Furniture &c.', enabling her to pursue her own architectural and aesthetic scheme.[118] Her plan for Fords Farm was more ambitious than that of her widowed predecessor; she demolished the existing villa and replaced it with a design of her own, advocating the Gothic Revival style for the exterior. An 1820 engraving of the south-west front depicts a villa of significant size (Figure 4.26), the whole stuccoed and surmounted with a crenelated parapet in the Gothic fashion.[119] The completion of her house in 1787 gave occasion for Charlotte to rename the villa as Boyle Farm, clearly denoting the degree of pride that she felt in her achievement.[120] The control that Charlotte was able to exert over her own finances and architectural schemes impressed her friends, especially the courtier, diarist and Bluestocking, Mary Hamilton, who wrote of it in her diary: 'Mrs. W is very much pleased with this place … here she is sole mistress, & every thing around her being her own property, it *interests* & amuses her'.[121]

Hamilton's remarks demonstrate just how passionate women could become in the creation of their suburban seats. As with their male counterparts, women often found great enjoyment in architecture, especially if they knew that their legacy would be continued by their children. Charlotte's daughter would eventually inherit Boyle Farm along with her

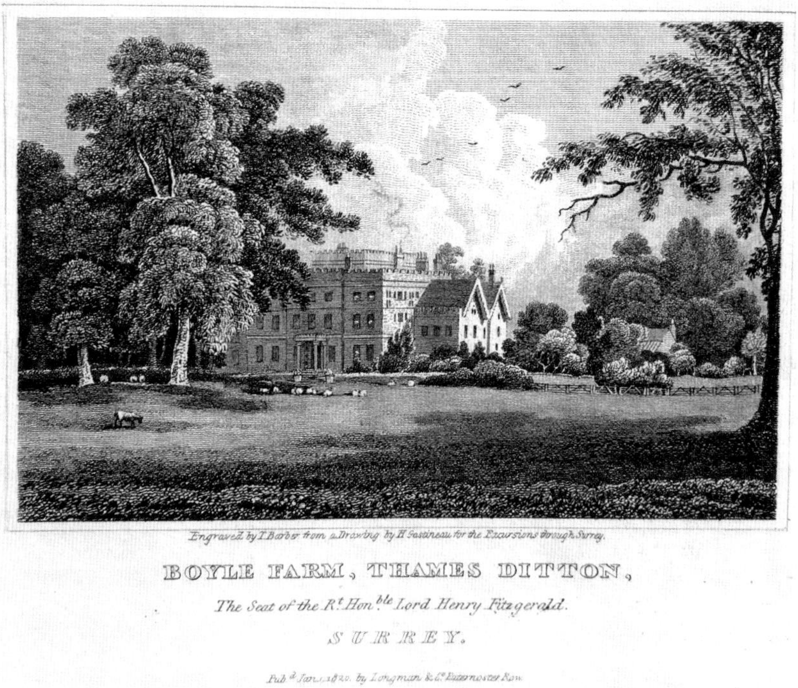

FIGURE 4.26 T. Barber, after Henry Gastineau, *Boyle Farm, Thames Ditton*, 1820, engraving. Photo: author's own.

mother's extensive fortune.[122] As such, Miss Boyle was instrumental in the execution of the villa's interior decoration, as remarked upon by another Bluestocking, Hannah More, to her sister in 1787:

> I never was so astonished as to see this large and very elegant house already completely furnished; all the beautiful purple and gold pilasters of the magnificent library, the chimney-pieces sculpture, as well as painting, both designed and executed by Miss Boyle. The doors are adorned with rich paintings copied from the Vatican; the panels pictures emblematic of the arts and sciences, from ... Herculaneum, all done by that young lady in the short space of a year![123]

Horace Walpole was also greatly impressed with the decorative talents of Miss Boyle:

> Miss Boyle, who has real genius, has carved three tablets in marble with boys, designed by herself. Those sculptures are for a chimney-piece and she is painting panels in grotesque for the library, with pilasters of glass in black and gold.[124]

Miss Boyle painted twenty-eight 'verre églomisé' pilasters which exist to this day; she signed one with 'C. BOYLE NOVEMBER 2D 1786'. These pilasters of black and gold feature dancing Classical figures, garlands and birds, and are surmounted by intricate anthemion capitals. More's reference to Herculaneum and the surviving details of Miss Boyle's work suggests that mother and daughter were pursuing a fashionable Neo-Classical scheme. The archaeological discoveries of Pompeii and Herculaneum that had inspired famous architects such as Robert Adam and James Stuart were just as eagerly embraced by Charlotte and her daughter at Boyle Farm.

The Bluestocking commentary of More, Hamilton and Burney regarding Charlotte's architectural endeavours signifies the mutual passion that this group of women had for architecture and the arts. Charlotte's villa not only stimulated architectural discourse but also provided an ideal setting for sophisticated gatherings. On 13 June 1788, for example, she held a fabulous ball, which Frances Boscawen described as 'charming, abounding with dancing men and with great ladies'.[125] Charlotte's villa was created with the knowledge that she was enhancing her daughter's inheritance; indeed, her daughter later married Lord Henry FitzGerald, fourth son of the 1st Duke and Duchess of Leinster of Carton House. They made Boyle Farm their marital home, where they raised their children, and had their extended family regularly to stay. In 1794 Lady Sarah Napier, aunt of Lord Henry, wrote of the beauty and tranquillity that she had found there:

> I passed a day with my sister [Duchess of] Leinster at Boyle Farm, which is now the seat of luxury, & beauty, & ingenuity; it would have taken me a week to see all the fine things in the house. The grounds are enlarged and improved by the growing of trees, & the pavilions opposite are improved by the addition of trees and buildings; otherwise the natural beauty of Thames Ditton can never alter. My dear sister & her girls enjoyed it so much this hot summer. It was a delight for me to see them there.[126]

Charlotte would no doubt have been gratified to know that her villa and gardens were so well liked and enjoyed even after her death. She could rest easy in the knowledge that she had succeeded in establishing a sizeable suburban estate for her daughter and grandchildren.

Although the bequeathing of property was generally limited to widows or unmarried women of fortune, there are some interesting examples of courtesans engaging in this process too. Courtesans could, under certain circumstances, use villas to provide for their children, ensuring that they would enjoy some standing in society through the possession of property. This was the dear hope of the beautiful actress and courtesan George Anne Bellamy (*c.* 1731–88), who spent large sums of her own money on Holwood Park in Kent because her lover had hinted that he would settle the estate upon her and their daughter, Caroline Elizabeth, when he died.

George Anne (Figure 4.27), whose name was apparently meant to be Georgiana or Georgianne, but was misheard at the Christening, was the illegitimate daughter of James O'Hara, 2nd Baron Tyrawley.[127] Although Lord Tyrawley educated and initially provided for his daughter, he later cut all financial ties with her when she decided to live with her mother (whom he despised). Driven by the need for money and as her mother had long been involved in the theatrical world,[128] it was not long before George Anne followed in her footsteps, aged 'just fourteen'.[129] Her professional debut was in November 1744 when she played the capital role of Monimia in Thomas Otway's *The Orphan* at Covent Garden Theatre.[130] George Anne's acting career soon took off; with her beauty, youth and talent she quickly became the talk of the town.[131] She particularly excelled in the roles of tragic heroines and sentimental ingenues and became a staunch favourite of the public. In fact, when Miss Wilford, a rival actress, was cast as Cordelia in *King Lear*, George Anne sneakily distributed pamphlets to the audience stating that the part had been unfairly taken from her and that should the audience prefer her, she would be honoured to step into the role.[132] As soon as the curtain went up there was 'a universal cry' for George Anne, and thus her humiliated rival was forced off the stage.[133]

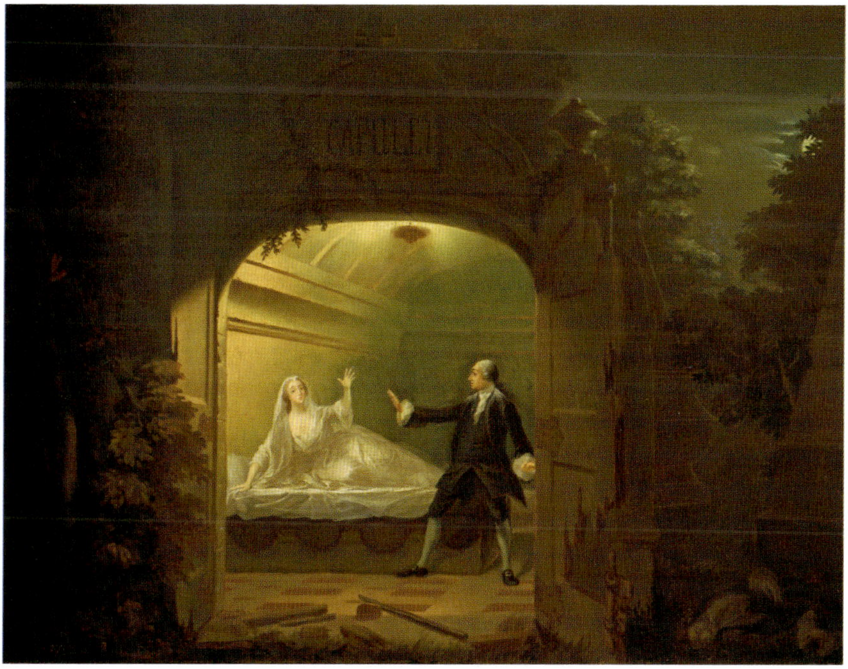

FIGURE 4.27 Benjamin Wilson, *David Garrick and George Anne Bellamy in "Romeo and Juliet", Act V, Scene iii*, 1753, oil on canvas. Yale Center for British Art, Paul Mellon Fund, B1975.5.29. Courtesy of Yale Center for British Art.

Given her spirited nature, together with her good looks, George Anne soon attracted the attention of wealthy admirers and rakes, and was at one point, according to her memoirs, dramatically abducted and carried off in a carriage by an unnamed earl at the behest of William, 5th Lord Byron (great-uncle of the famous poet), who sought to make George Anne his mistress.[134] Byron failed in his endeavour, and despite this sensational event George Anne recovered quickly, later becoming the mistress of Sir George Montgomery Metham in the latter 1740s. Within a few years however she became bored with him and instead took up with his friend John Calcraft.[135]

Calcraft was a successful army agent who had risen up under the patronage of Lord Granby and Henry Fox (to whom he was allegedly related) and through them gained a series of lucrative positions and commissions. George Anne became the 'domesticated wife' of Calcraft and moved into his house in Brewer Street where he agreed to pay 'one hundred guineas a quarter' for the housekeeping.[136] George Anne always believed that Calcraft intended to marry her, but unbeknown to her and society, Calcraft was actually already married to a woman called Bridget (surname unknown), from Grantham. Upon Calcraft's death in 1772 this shocking news came to light when Bridget made a successful claim for dower against his estate.[137]

By 1754 Calcraft's business was doing well enough for him to purchase the lease of a villa in Kent, called Holwood Park.[138] Upon Calcraft's insinuation that he would settle the house upon George Anne and their daughter,[139] she eagerly set about improving the property:

> During [his] fits [of gout] he used to say that he intended this seat for my daughter and myself; upon which account I spared no expence to clean and beautify it ... It not having been tenanted for four years, I found it required nearly as much cleaning as the Ægean [Augean] stable. For the house had as many inhabitants of the vermin kind, which were overrun with weeds, had of frogs, toads, and other reptiles. This made the task, which I had undertaken to see performed myself, not only troublesome but expensive.[140]

Such was her enthusiasm for the project that she both directed and paid for the work herself, describing her efforts 'as my Hurculean labour'.[141] She enlisted the assistance of various friends, including General Campbell who sent a gardener and 'supplied me with as many shrubs and exoticks from Combe-bank. He likewise favoured me with his advice how to lay out the ground, which consisted only of eleven acres'.[142] In addition, she also commissioned a series of garden buildings to increase the beauty and efficiency of her (potential) country seat, including 'a hot-house, a succession-house, a green-house, and an ice-house'.[143]

As a woman of precarious social standing and with an illegitimate daughter to provide for, coming into property would be a life-changing event for both. It would ensure that their status as elite women was maintained and would also provide them with some financial stability. At the end of the project George Anne claimed that she had 'expended six hundred pounds' in total (approximately £61,000 today), which suggests that George Anne truly believed that she was investing in her future.[144] Sadly, her great efforts were in vain however, because upon his death in 1772 Calcraft left George Anne absolutely nothing, much to her bitter disappointment. They had long since separated, with Calcraft bigamously marrying Elizabeth Bride, a younger actress in the 1760s. He left his estate to his eldest son by Bride but did provide a £5,000 portion to both his son and daughter by George Anne.[145]

Sharing a tragically similar fate to Sophia Baddeley and Teresa Cornelys, George Anne gradually fell into poverty. By 1767 she was already seeking aid from those she hoped would be kind, including Robert Clive, 1st Baron Clive, to whom she wrote three times with increasing desperation.[146] On the back of each letter either Clive or his secretary wrote the words 'no reply', indicating that her pleas for help were casually ignored. She was eventually forced to live under the 'Rules' of the King's Bench prison in Elliot's row, deserted and destitute.

In the end, George Anne's precarious social status, her inability to manage her finances and Calcraft's harsh treatment made it impossible for her to create a tangible legacy. Within this context it would seem that only widowed women of means or heiresses had the opportunity and financial stability to establish villa estates that could be bequeathed to relatives. For those women without status, wealth or stability, the hope of creating a legacy for their children was overshadowed by their own desperate struggle for existence.

* * *

Villas allowed women to establish their own suburban seats, creating a comfortable, convenient and attractive home in rural surroundings, in which they could entertain friends and family. Being a predominantly private space, women exerted great control over the design, plan form and ornamentation of their villas. This meticulous eye for detail also extended to the landscaped gardens associated with their properties. As we will see in the next chapter, the grounds in which country houses and villas were situated were as much an arena for display as the houses themselves.

5

The wider estate, garden design and ornamental buildings

Just as the country house revolved around the art of display, so too did the wider estate, parkland and garden. The country house sat at the epicentre of the estate, from which the landowning family's power radiated across the land to the furthest field and the most remote tenant. Self-respecting landowners of the eighteenth century strived to make their estates profitable, efficient and aesthetically pleasing. In fact, the estate itself was as much a part of conspicuous display as the country house, and an estate that boasted well-maintained lands, buildings, roads, boundaries, parkland and gardens immediately spoke of its owner's excellent management. Women, of course, also participated in the augmentation and beautification of estates. In addition to taking a hand in the more practical aspects of land management, they frequently undertook building projects on the estate, in which they were the dominant or sole patron.[1] Such building projects included public and domestic buildings used by the estate's workers and tenants, as well as ornamental garden structures to beautify the estate itself.

This chapter will firstly explore how women improved their own estates or those of their husbands through the commissioning of charitable buildings. Schools, almshouses and churches were either built or enhanced by women in a conscious effort to improve the standard of living of their tenants and workers, and as a public display of their feminine virtues, such as piety and benevolence. Under this guise women were able to freely engage in architectural patronage without straying outside of the stringent societal constraints of female propriety. These building schemes were often grand in their design and costly in their execution, indicating that they were also expressions of female architectural taste and ambition. The widowed Duchess of Marlborough, for example, built 'a hospital for distressed people of several sorts' in the Classical style (of course) in St Albans.[2] She did so with the intention of assisting the poor, whilst also reasserting her connection, and that of the late Duke, to St Albans – this she did with the prominent display of her marital coat of arms on the principal façade.

Secondly, the ways in which women were active in enhancing the pleasure grounds that surrounded their homes will be examined. Like architecture, landscape design was subject to its own trends and advancements, and prominent landscape designers were highly sought-after, much like fashionable architects. Women were as conscious of creating fashionable landscapes as their male peers and thus regularly sought out the most eminent landscape designers of the day, such as Charles Bridgeman and Lancelot 'Capability' Brown. Others enjoyed the act of beautifying their surroundings to such an extent that they directed the designs themselves and participated in the pleasurable minutiae of gardening. Sarah Churchill, of course, was no exception in seeking to create the very best gardens and commissioned royal gardeners to do her bidding. When building Marlborough House, she hired Henry Wise for which a detailed bill survives.[3] Later, when building Wimbledon House, the Duchess hired Charles Bridgeman, another royal gardener, to lay out the surrounding grounds.[4]

As well as carving out lakes, raising up hills and planting new woods, further embellishments in the form of ornamental garden buildings were added to the landscape. Due to their small and decorative nature, garden buildings and follies offered women the chance to experiment with the latest architectural and aesthetic trends. This subject will form the final section of this chapter, beginning with ornamental dairies, which were built in varying architectural styles and were especially popular in the second half of the eighteenth century. Similarly, grottoes were equally favoured at the beginning of the century, with many women executing innovative and creative schemes which they themselves had designed. Garden buildings, therefore, were built by women not only to enjoy the gardens in which they stood, but also to signal their taste, learning and creativity. As such, women were often pioneering in their commissions and were regularly at the forefront of the latest aesthetic fashion. This was also true of the Chinese pavilion or teahouse, a garden folly fashion that was forged by many architecturally ambitious women in the mid-eighteenth century.

All three sections of this chapter will amply illustrate the wide range of female patronage that took place across the estate at large. Through the creation of estate buildings, beautiful landscaped parks and pioneering garden follies, they were able to make a lasting mark upon the patriarchal estate.

Domestic and public structures on the estate

A large portion of the buildings on the estate were designed to benefit the lives of estate workers and tenants. These domestic and public structures were often built or embellished by women and provided a convenient architectural outlet, since these buildings were perceived to fall within the feminine sphere of influence. These buildings, such as schools, almshouses and churches, also allowed women to conform to the female ideals of benevolence, bountifulness and piety. Such projects, though charitable, represented an accessible avenue through which women could experiment with architectural styles, engage with their local communities and improve their estates. Indeed, this form of architectural patronage was so commonplace that following Frances Ingram, Viscountess Irwin's (1734–1807) marriage in 1758, one of her trustees, John Waple, wrote to her knowingly: 'if I hear of your building a church, erecting almshouses, charity schools etc. I shall not be surprised'.[5]

A woman celebrated for her feminine virtues and charitable works was Lady Elizabeth Hastings, the heiress of Ledston Hall whom we have previously met. She was a deeply religious and charitable woman who staunchly believed in educating the poor, and in 1721 built a girls' boarding school in Ledsham 'wherein twenty poor girls are to be wholly maintained with food, raiment, and learning'.[6] She also founded a number of other local schools including Aberford, Collingham, Thorp Arch and Ledsham, as well as financially supporting Mary Astell's girls' school at Chelsea. She generously bequeathed £1,000 towards the building of the Holy Trinity Church in Leeds,[7] together with an 'additional benefaction of 20*l* per annum to be settled upon the vicarage, if the town will do the like'.[8] In her will, she also bequeathed the manor of Wheldale to Queen's College, Oxford, for the support of five poor scholars drawn from twelve named schools in the north of England.

Lady Betty's charitable architectural patronage, which focused on and around her Yorkshire estate, not only enabled her to pursue her Christian and charitable duty, but also elevated the prominence and status of her family. This form of architectural patronage was commonplace and is one that we shall see again throughout this chapter.

Schools

The building of schools was a popular choice for female philanthropists, with many relishing the opportunity to manage building projects that were entirely of their own creation. Great care was taken over every decision, ranging from the site, size and design of the school, through to the syllabus and the appointment of the schoolteacher. Lavinia Spencer, Countess Spencer (1762–1831), daughter of Charles Bingham, 1st Earl of Lucan, and his wife, the portrait miniature painter Margaret Smyth, paid great attention to every feature of her girls' school at Althorp, Northamptonshire. It was designed as a pretty picturesque 'cottage ... thatched & dashed' with 'whitewashed [walls] and green Windows', located 'on a hill which looks all over Althorp Park & Nobothe Wood, & rich pastures covered over with sheep & flat open'.[9]

The schoolroom was '25 feet by 17, and 14 feet, high, with a very pretty Cottage-like bowwindow looking Southwards, & opening into a neat usefull little garden', behind which was a kitchen, pantry and a 'convenient good Shop of 12 feet sq^{m} where [the school mistress] is to dispose of the Articles made by the Girls'.[10] Similar consideration was given to the decoration of the schoolroom, described by Lady Spencer as having a floor 'whiter than snow' with 'the plinth ... painted green', and 'from the plinth upwards to the surbase I shall have dutch matting, nailed, which is of a pretty neat greenish colour & will give the room a look of great comfort'.[11] Above this the wall was to be covered with 'prints from the Bible & the subjects printed under them'.[12]

Lady Spencer's school, which was built in 1788, was designed not only to educate local girls, but also to create an attractive eyecatcher within Althorp Park. Her picturesque *cottage orné* style was highly fashionable and reflected the wider romantic cultural appreciation for the countryside and the desire to return to a more natural way of living. By teaching the local girls useful life skills like 'spinning, knitting, plain work & patching', Lady Spencer's school perfectly embodied the picturesque ideals of rustic simplicity and pastoral beauty.[13] Thus, by building her school, Lady Spencer was able to contribute positively to the lives of the local community while also enhancing the aesthetic of her husband's estate.

Almshouses

Female charitable commissions also extended to almshouses, designed to house elderly poor men and women under various stipulations. Women of all ages and marital statuses participated in this form of charitable architectural patronage. We have already seen that the widowed Duchess of Marlborough built an impressively large almshouse in St Albans. Her almshouse not only assisted the local poor, but also served as a permanent reminder of the Marlboroughs' ties to St Albans. In a similar vein, Margaret Coke, Countess of Leicester built almshouses on the Holkham estate (Figure 5.1) and recorded her involvement with two inscriptions, placed on the south gable ends of each range. Almshouses, much like schools, allowed women to increase their family's prominence within the local community and to act as a permanent legacy of their benevolence.

It is possible that Lady Leicester, at Holkham Hall, was induced to build her almshouses following the early death of her only surviving child, Edward, Viscount Coke, in 1753. Lord Coke had been a dissolute and disappointing son, more interested in gambling, drinking and partying than forging a career or assisting his parents in the management of Holkham. His marriage to Lady Mary Campbell, the daughter of the 2nd Duke of Argyll, had been a complete disaster, with Horace Walpole writing:

> Lord Coke has demolished himself very fast; I mean his character; ... he is always drunk, has lost immense sums at play, and seldom goes home to

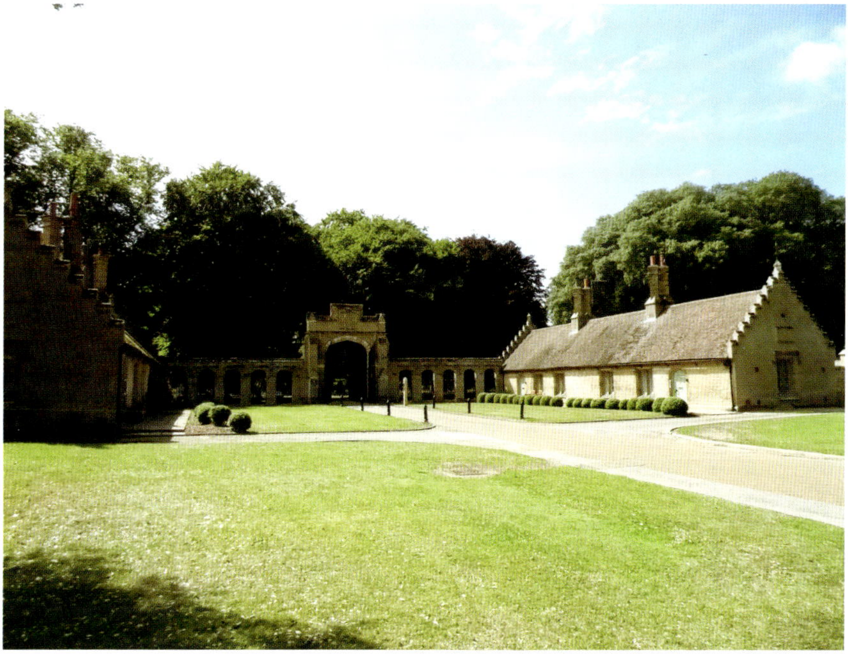

FIGURE 5.1 The Holkham Almshouses, Holkham, Norfolk. Photo: author's own.

> his wife till eight in the morning. The world is vehement on her side; and not only her family, but his own, give him up.[14]

Lady Mary later accused him of cruelty towards her and brought a very public, but ultimately unsuccessful, public action for divorce against him, and was later formally separated in 1750 – only five years after they had married.[15] The scandal, stress and heartbreak suffered by Lady Leicester during her son's lifetime were great, often forcing her to retire to Norfolk to recuperate. Lord Leicester despaired of his only son and heir, writing morosely of the situation in 1748:

> The unwillingness I have to come [to Town] is on account of Ly. Leicester. She cant bear as I can the evils her son has drawn on himself, and he has already almost broke her heart, wch. is the greatest grudge I bear him. Here she is quiet and recovers her spirits, I have kep't from her the knowledge his last most enormous behaviour, & I wd. for her sake ever confine myself for ever in the country, rather that she sd. undergo those griefs she has had for her ungrateful son, & whenever I come to town, she will certainly come to the knowledge of all.[16]

Despite his parents' best efforts to help him reform and recover, including a treatment of cold baths as prescribed by a Doctor Hepburn, Lord Coke died aged only thirty-four.[17] Following this sorrowful event Lord Leicester wrote but a few lines on their terrible grief: 'We had but too much preparation to fortify ourselves against the last [misfortune], yet it could not but be very shocking when it came, besides the great grief of my Wife, who has always behaved in so good and tender a manner to me, I own it gives me so great concern that I cannot think of recovering my spirits, till she does in some manner her's'.[18]

Without a son to inherit the Holkham estates and with the inevitable extinction of the hard-won Leicester earldom, Lady Leicester sought out other ways to leave a legacy. Only two years after the death of her son she drew up a settlement with her husband for the endowment of the Holkham almshouses. In consideration of £1250 (approximately £145,000 today) paid to Lord Leicester, he gave her the parcel of land to build the almshouses as well as the promise to 'Grant one Annuity or Yearly Rent Charge of fifty pounds to be ... payable for ever hereafter out of the Ffarm lands and parishes herein after mentioned'.[19] Together with the sum of £800 that Lady Leicester's father had bequeathed her for charitable purposes and the generous use of her own private capital, she independently directed the design and construction of the almshouses which were completed and inhabited in 1757.[20]

Lady Leicester's almshouses consisted of two one-storey ranges located at the north entrance to Holkham park, situated on either side of the road. Despite her husband's penchant for the Palladian style, Lady Leicester's almshouses are distinctly not Classical. They are cottage-like in appearance (Gothicized in the 1840s) and almost advocate the picturesque aesthetic, although this style was not to gain momentum for a few decades yet. Within the almshouses she housed three poor men and three poor women, each maintained with 'the sum of two shillings and six pense weekly' as well as 'one chauldren of coals for each of the said people'.[21] Additionally, every two years a 'Great Coat not exceeding the price or sum of twenty five shillings' was to be provided for the men and 'a Gown not exceeding the price or value of twenty shillings' was to be provided for the women, both of which should 'always be of a blue colour'.[22]

The establishment of the Holkham almshouses allowed Lady Leicester to discharge her benevolent duty as the lady of the manor, as well as to establish a tangible legacy on the Holkham estate. The inscriptions commemorating her munificence and the additional endowment that Lady Leicester settled in 1765 ensured that she would be remembered for posterity.[23] Indeed, poems celebrated her charity; a contemporary one published in 1758 admired her 'gen'rous Deeds' which 'Pours Joy, and gives neglected Worth to Bloom', and a later one published in 1839 likened her to an angel: 'She, like a guardian angel from on high, Supports their [the inhabitants] tottering footsteps till they die'.[24] Lady Leicester's architectural endeavour fitted neatly into the accepted realm of female action whilst enabling her to exert her architectural agency within the patriarchal estate.

Church restoration and embellishment

Another common estate improvement made by women was the embellishment or restoration of churches and chapels. Lady Leicester also participated in this form of female patronage, spending £1000 (approximately £90,000 today) of her own money in restoring and beautifying the church on the Holkham estate,[25] which she proudly commemorated in a stained-glass window:

In the years 1767 and 1768
This Church and Chancel were
repaired and beautified at the sole expence of
Margaret Baroness Clifford
Countess Dowager of Leicester

The inscription is emblazoned with her marital coat of arms, indicating that she wanted her achievement to be remembered (Figure 5.2). Similarly, in Dorset, the benevolence and patronage of Susanna Strangways Horner (1690–1758), the heiress of the Melbury estate, were commemorated with a plaque, placed in the chancel by the grateful parson of St Osmond church in Melbury Osmond.[26] Susanna completely rebuilt the church and adorned it with pews, a font, altarpiece and communion plate, which, according to the plaque, 'Shew only Part of [her] Piety and Munificence'.

To ensure that her charitable legacy was preserved, Susanna commissioned the renowned Huguenot silversmith Paul de Lamerie to make sets of communion plate for a number of her parish churches, engraved with her coat of arms.[27] In one of de Lamerie's accounts presented in September 1748, the total came to £130 4s. 7d. of which £6 18s. was for 'Engraving all the arms, glory etc. on the aforesaid plate'.[28] For another commission Susanna ordered the silver-gilt chalice, paten and flagon to be inscribed with 'The Gift of Mrs. Strangways Horner to ye Church of Stinsford in Dorsetshire in 1737'.[29] The inclusion of the inscriptions and coat of arms ensured that Susanna's generosity would not be forgotten, while also reasserting her presence (and that of her family's) within the local community.

As Susanna was the last surviving member of the Strangways family, whose pedigree stretched back into the middle ages, she clearly felt a keen sense of responsibility to reaffirm her family name and lineage. Indeed, in 1736 she caused a sensation when she married her thirteen-year-old daughter to the thirty-one-year-old Stephen Fox (Lord Hervey's lover and brother of the widowed Charlotte Digby) in a clandestine marriage without the knowledge or consent of the girl's father, Thomas Horner.[30] Her motivation for doing so was to secure a wealthy, pliable son-in-law whose own pedigree paled in comparison to her daughter's. This not only safeguarded the longevity of the Melbury estates, which were later inherited by Elizabeth and Stephen Fox, but later resulted in Fox changing his name to Fox-Strangways and adopting

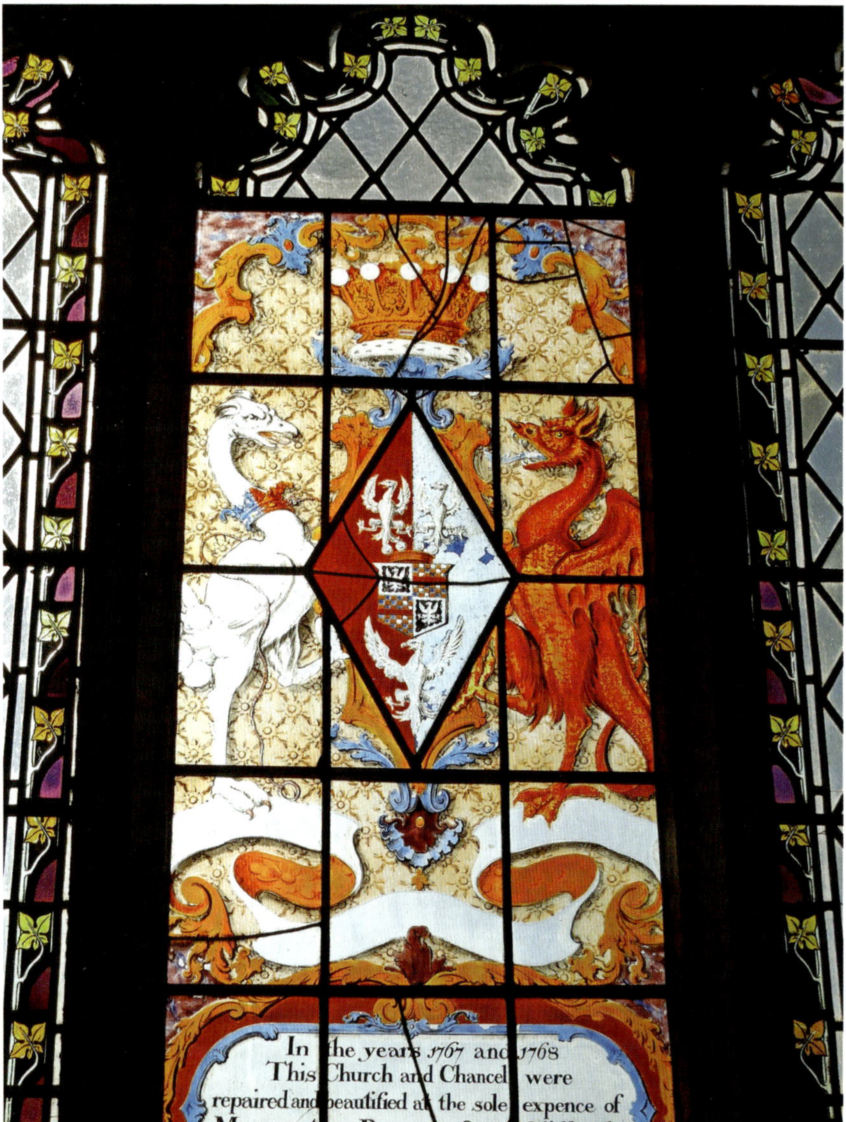

FIGURE 5.2 Lady Leicester's inscription and marital coat of arms on the church window inside St Withburga Church, Holkham. Photo: author's own.

the Strangways coat of arms.[31] This outcome would not have occurred had Elizabeth been married off to a man of greater rank, as the importance of her own pedigree would have been overshadowed by that of her husband.[32] In 1747 Fox was created Baron Ilchester and Stavordale of Redlynch and in 1756 he was created 1st Earl of Ilchester.

Given Susanna's shrewd dealings, it is unsurprising that she also utilized her architectural projects to display her taste. When she remodelled her private family church at Melbury Sampford she indulged her passion for the Rococo, much to the dismay of later generations:

> Mrs Horner ornamented the chancel of Melbury church with carved seats and a very fine red velvet cloth and reredos, richly decorated with gold lace and gilt carving. The whole is in a debased taste, but very handsome in its way. She probably took the idea from some of the Belgium churches she saw in her visit to Spa.[33]

To complete the aesthetic, Susanna had the family tombs cleaned, repaired and regilded, safeguarding their longevity and once more demonstrating her familial piety.

The opportunity to express one's architectural taste in the form of a religious building project was also used by Harriet Brocas (d. 1819), daughter of Henry Lannoy Hunter of Beech Hill, who commissioned John Soane in 1801 to design a new Gothic chapel for St James' Church in Bramley. The purpose of this new church was to house a monument to her late husband, Bernard Brocas of Beaurepaire Manor, who had died in 1777. Harriet had already worked with Soane previously, having commissioned him to make alterations to Wokefield Park in 1788, to design an entrance gate to Wokefield in 1789, and for work done 'at her house in town' in 1791.[34] At St James' Church Soane replaced the existing thirteenth-century chapel with his own Gothic creation, complete with a Coade stone tracery window.[35]

The large marble monument, which depicts a corpulent Bernard Brocas dying in the arms of his beautiful young wife, seems incongruous without other Brocas family tombs about him. Local legend has it that Brocas had a dispute with his neighbours, the Chute family of The Vyne, over the acquisition of a more prominent church pew at their shared parish church of St Andrew in Sherborne St. John, which so outraged him that he removed his family allegiances to St James' Church in Bramley.[36] If true, Harriet was publicly and boldly perpetuating her late husband's allegiance to their new church by building such a fine chapel and commissioning such a large monument.

While the majority of these patrons almost certainly felt a genuine desire to do good, it is clear that it was much easier for them to commission and control building projects by leveraging the perceived ideal of feminine humility, charity and virtue. Working within the constraints imposed upon them by society, these women managed to create an architectural legacy and improve the lives of those around them.

Garden design

Tastefully sculpted parklands and fashionably designed gardens were also an essential form of display in the eighteenth century. The garden was a place for aesthetic expression, where male and female patrons could showcase their knowledge of the latest horticultural, landscaping and architectural trends.

Commemorative paintings or conversation pieces can sometimes offer glimpses into female involvement in landscape design, particularly with regard to married women. At Carton House, Emily FitzGerald, Countess of Kildare's influence over the re-landscaping of the park was equal to that of her husband, an achievement commemorated in a double portrait by Arthur Devis in 1753 (Figure 5.3).[37] This painting depicts Lord and Lady

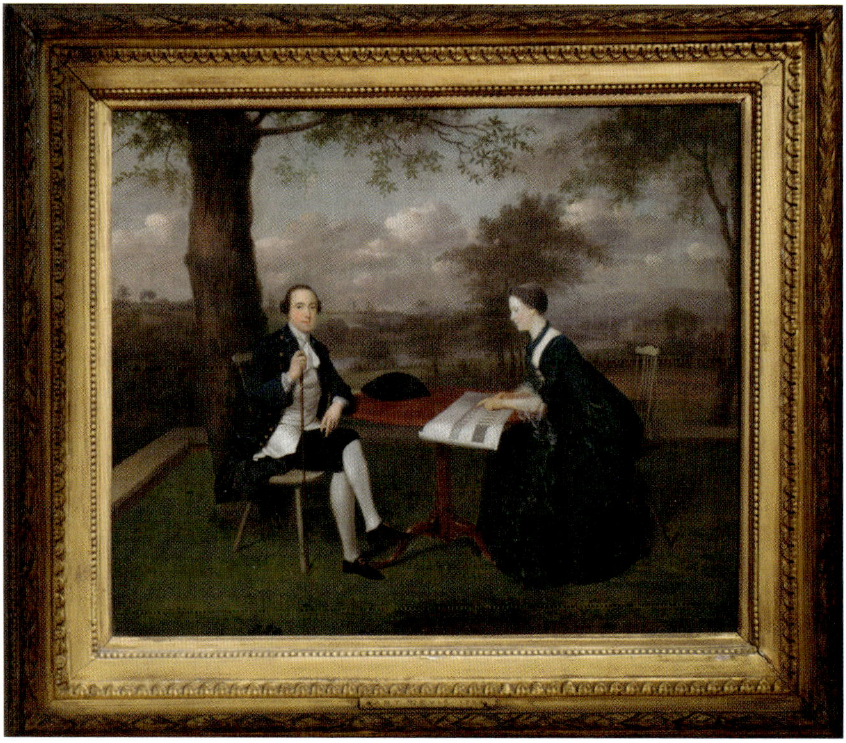

FIGURE 5.3 Arthur Devis, *Lord and Lady Kildare*, 1753, oil on canvas. Private collection. Malcolm Park editorial/Alamy Stock Photo.

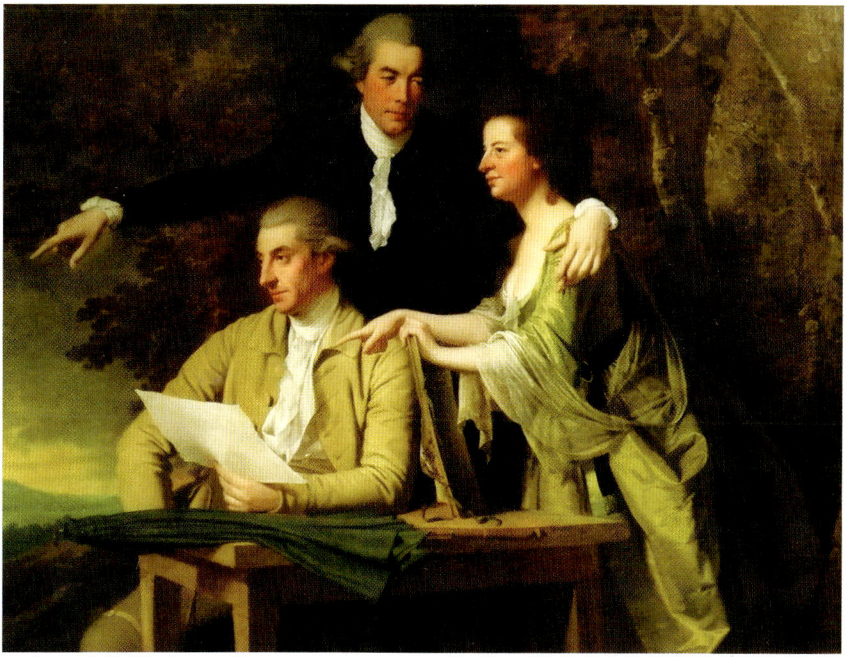

FIGURE 5.4 Joseph Wright, *D'Ewes Coke, His Wife Hannah and Daniel Parker Coke, MP*, 1780–2, oil on canvas. Derby City Art Gallery and Museum, 1965–676. The Picture Art Collection/Alamy Stock Photo.

Kildare seated at a table in their newly created naturalistic parkland, with Lady Kildare (and significantly not her husband) perusing the plans of a new bridge. Similarly, in a conversation piece dated to 1780–2, Joseph Wright of Derby depicts the Rev. D'Ewes Coke, his wife Hannah, and their kinsman Daniel Parker Coke, sitting in a landscape that possibly represents Brookhill Hall, the Rev. D'Ewes Coke's newly inherited property (Figure 5.4).[38] The Reverend affectionately embraces his wife as they consider one of her design sketches (held by Parker Coke) from her portfolio that she holds, thereby illustrating her direct involvement in the design process.

Just like their male peers, women of independent means regularly and enthusiastically embraced the challenge of creating beautiful landscaped gardens. To do so, they enlisted the best in the field, including Charles Bridgeman (1690–1738), who according to Horace Walpole in *The History of Modern Taste in Gardening* (1780), was 'the next fashionable designer of gardens' after Charles London and Henry Wise.[39] Bridgeman's work consciously moved away from the geometric shapes of formal Anglo-Dutch or French gardens of the late seventeenth and early eighteenth centuries and introduced new ideas of naturalistic landscape gardening. His designs included open spaces, 'cultivated fields, and even morsels of a forest appearance', as well as 'wilderness, and ... loose groves of oak', which according to Walpole, hailed 'the dawn of modern taste'.[40] Walpole also credited Bridgeman with the invention of the ha-ha:

> the capital stroke, the leading step to all that has followed, was (I believe the first thought was Bridgeman's) the destruction of walls for boundaries, and the invention of fossés [ditches] – an attempt then deemed so astonishing, that the common people called them Ha! Ha's! to express their surprize at finding a sudden unperceived check to their walk.[41]

Such an invention, or at least the introduction of the ha-ha to England (there were ha-has at the Grand Trianon at Versailles), served to harmonize the grounds of the garden with the sculpted park beyond.[42] Bridgeman worked on several significant garden projects, including Eastbury and Stowe, before he succeeded Henry Wise as royal gardener to George II and Queen Caroline in 1728. Queen Caroline had long supported and admired Bridgeman's work, having asked him to attend her gardening conference 'for the leading garden theorists and practitioners', in September 1719.[43]

Lady Betty Hastings of Ledston Hall was also an early supporter of Bridgeman, commissioning him to redesign her gardens in the 1720s. Having directed the remodelling of her ancestral home, she simultaneously re-landscaped her gardens, with the aim of making Ledston fashionable and relevant. In 1722 the antiquary Ralph Thoresby recorded in his diary that, 'we walked about the gardens ... then my Lady showed me what alterations were made, and what farther designed there'.[44] He also mentioned walking 'amongst the shady trees, in the new terrace walks, where were the statues'.[45] This account suggests that work began in 1722, which is corroborated by a contemporary account from a 'C. Fox', possibly the Hon. Charlotte Fox (later Digby), daughter of Sir Stephen Fox, who reported in June *c.* 1720 that 'My Lady is making good alterations in her garden. I believe it will be very pretty when it is done'.[46]

Three drawings of Ledston's new garden design survive, all attributed to Bridgeman. One located at Otterden Place (the home of Lady Betty's descendants) is inscribed with 'Lady Eliz Hastings at Ledstone Park', and depicts 'an asymmetrical layout, with a strong central axis, lawns, grass banking, and dense woodland containing walks, open groves, and irregular bosquets'.[47] This drawing shows the garden dwarfing the house in scale and illustrates the latest in landscape design with the eroding of rigid symmetrical layouts and the introduction of serpentine walks and hidden groves.[48] The two other drawings, dated to *c.* 1731 by Peter Willis, depict Ledston within its wider parkland, one of which shows the surrounding pastures and avenues.[49] This again demonstrates the latest in landscape design, with greater emphasis placed on the blurring of the boundary between the garden and its surrounding countryside. Bridgeman's work at Ledston would certainly have elevated its appearance, fashionableness and status, particularly once he was appointed as a royal gardener. To commemorate her endeavours at Ledston Lady Betty commissioned John Settrington to paint four landscape paintings of Ledston Hall in 1728.[50] These paintings originally graced her newly decorated dining room as overdoors, thereby allowing Lady Betty and her visitors to regularly admire all that she had accomplished at Ledston.[51]

When Lady Betty's contemporary, Henrietta Howard (later Countess of Suffolk), was building her Palladian villa in Twickenham, she also enlisted the services of Bridgeman, together with her friend and neighbour Alexander Pope, to design the gardens. In 1724 Bridgeman, Pope and Henrietta walked the grounds of Marble Hill and discussed ideas about how to best arrange the gardens. Shortly after, Bridgeman set to work on a design, writing to Pope that '[O]n Saturday morning I begun on the plann, & have not [lef]t from that time to this so long as I could see, nor shall [I] leave it till 'tis finish'd which I hope will be about tomorrow Noon'.[52] Although this design is now lost, a surviving plan of the pleasure grounds attributed to Pope of *c.* 1724 shows numerous progressive arcadian elements, including lawns and wildernesses, as well as some of the increasingly outdated formal features, such as the geometrically arranged avenues.[53] This proposal was presumably not arcadian enough for Marble Hill's discerning patroness, because a later plan (Figures 5.5–5.6), dating to about 1749, depicts a far more naturalistic landscape with sweeping lawns, densely planted thickets, wilderness areas, orchards and groves.[54] An accompanying key or legend indicates that the gardens also consisted of an Ice House, Green House, Flower Garden, Ninepin Alley and a Grotto.

Henrietta was as conscious as Lady Betty of creating a fashionable and progressive garden and thus her garden epitomizes the transitional phase from the formal gardens of the previous generation to the pastoral landscape gardens later championed by Lancelot 'Capability' Brown. Henrietta admired Bridgeman's work enough to recommend him to her good friend, Catherine (Kitty) Douglas, Duchess of Queensberry (1701–77). Catherine lived on the opposite side of the Thames at Douglas House in Petersham and was part of Henrietta's influential Marble Hill literary circle. The Duchess, born the daughter of Henry Hyde, 4th Earl of Clarendon, and his wife, Jane Leveson-Gower, was a renowned beauty and had served as a Lady of the Bedchamber to Queen Anne. In 1728 the Duchess was sensationally banished from Court by George II for continually petitioning for John Gay's (her dear friend) play *Polly*, the sequel to *The Beggar's Opera*, to be given a licence. Upon hearing the news of her banishment, she defiantly wrote to the king: 'That the Duchess of Queensbury is surprised and well pleased that the

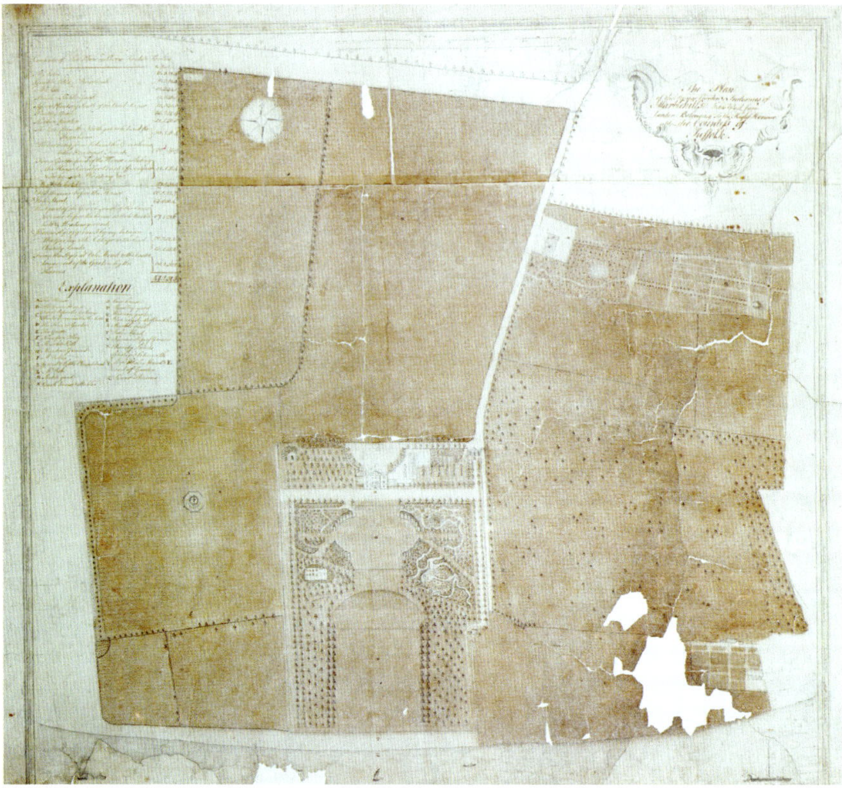

FIGURE 5.5 Unknown draughtsman, 'The Plan of the House Garden & Inclosures of Marblehill', *c.* 1749. Norfolk Record Office, MC184/10/1. Courtesy of Norfolk Record Office.

King hath given her so agreeable a command as to stay from Court, where she never came for diversion'.[55]

In 1730 the Duchess was intending to relandscape the gardens at Amesbury Abbey, her husband's Wiltshire country seat, so she and John Gay wrote to Henrietta asking after Bridgeman: 'if you chance to see him, pray tell him so [to contact her]'.[56] Henrietta obliged, but her role as go-between for the Duchess was rendered difficult by Bridgeman's busy schedule. In a letter to Gay in the summer of 1731 Henrietta wrote of her frustrations: 'I have never been more peevish in my life that I have been about this journey of Bridgeman's; I am sure I took true pains that it should be just as the duchess wished. I find upon strict inquiry, that he did not go as soon as I expected'.[57] Henrietta need not have worried because Bridgeman did eventually make the journey to Amesbury and was employed by the Duchess until 1738.

Women were thus instrumental in advocating Bridgeman's innovative style and were key players in garden design. This was true throughout the century, with many patronesses championing other landscape designers,

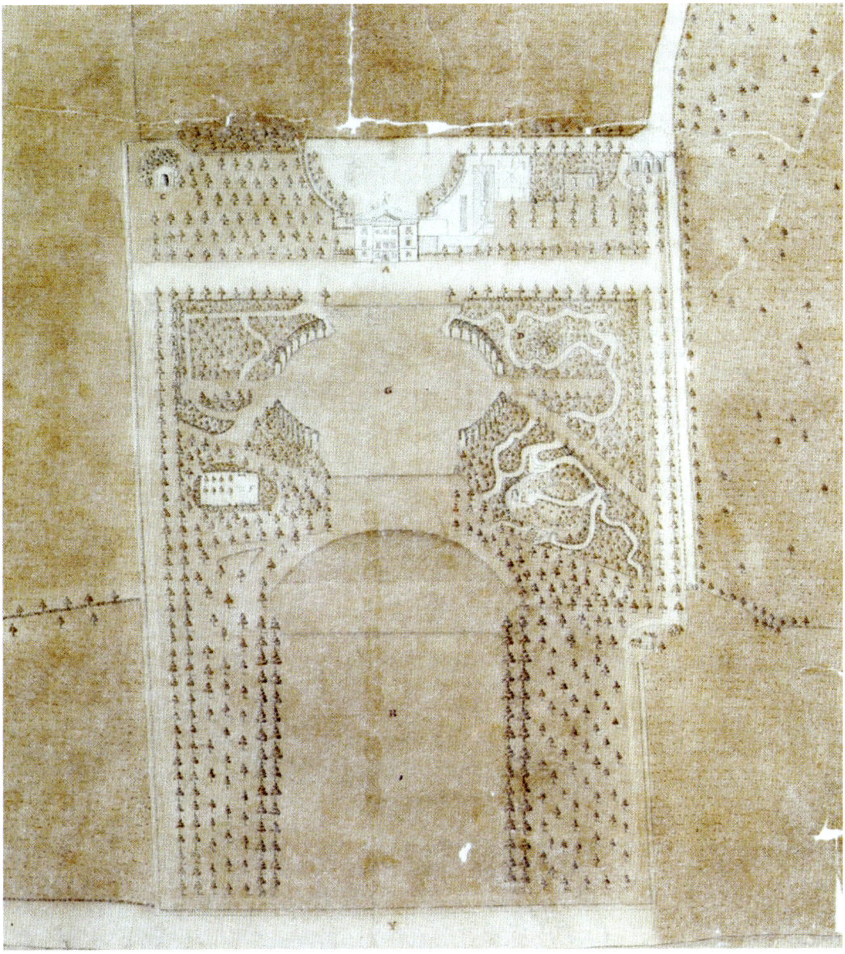

FIGURE 5.6 Detail of 'The Plan of the House Garden & Inclosures of Marblehill', *c*. 1749. Norfolk Record Office, MC184/10/1. Courtesy of Norfolk Record Office.

particularly Lancelot 'Capability' Brown, the successor of Bridgeman and William Kent. Such was Brown's success that he became one of the most influential, if not *the* most influential, landscape designers of the eighteenth century, and is associated with designing 250 parks. One of Brown's greatest patronesses was Jemima, Marchioness Grey, who struck a lasting friendship and commissioned him to re-landscape the grounds at both Wrest Park and Wimpole Hall.

From the moment Lady Grey and her husband, Philip Yorke, moved into Wrest Park in the 1740s, they were intent on updating the house and grounds. Wrest was renowned for its extensive formal gardens, having been created by the 11th Earl of Kent in the 1680s and 1690s, and continued by his son, the 1st Duke of Kent, throughout the early eighteenth century.[58] Consequently, the gardens consisted of a multitude of canals, terraces, avenues, as well as various ornamental buildings, including the Bowling Green House, Thomas Archer's baroque Pavilion (1707–11), and Cain Hill House (1717).[59]

In a similar vein to Lady Betty Hastings's modernization of the Ledston Hall gardens two decades previously, Lady Grey sought to create a garden at Wrest that reflected the latest tastes in landscape design. She quickly set about directing a series of alterations, which she personally supervised: 'I am called upon to visit my Workmen at the Serpentine Canal who are adding to its meanders & improving it very much. It is at present the great Object of my attention'.[60] Keen to keep up with the latest landscaping fashions, the Yorkes soon commissioned Brown to assist in their great project.[61] Having observed his work at Stowe in 1748 and at Moor Park, the home of the Ansons (her in-laws), in the mid-1750s, Lady Grey was inspired by his naturalistic style. In deference to her grandfather's garden layout, however, she commissioned Brown only to soften the lines of the formal canals, walks and terraces, with particular attention being given to the water:

> the whole when finished will appear one stream running in where the Brook now comes into the Garden, & winding on till it is lost among bushes &c, beyond the furthest Bank of what is now the Mill-pond; or Vice-Versa (which you please) coming out of those Bushes & running through the Garden till it goes out (where the Brook runs) into the Country.[62]

Relations between patroness and landscaper were so convivial that in 1760 Lady Grey erected a monument in his honour, commemorating his involvement at Wrest. The only other known patron's monument to Brown was erected by George Coventry, 6th Earl of Coventry, at Croome Park, Worcestershire, after Brown's death in 1797, commemorating his 'inimitable and creative genius'.

The inscription upon the plinth at Wrrest reads:

> These gardens originally laid out by Henry Duke of Kent, were altered by Philip Earl of Hardwicke and Jemima Lady Grey, with the professional assistance of Lancelot Brown Esq. in the years 1758, 1759, 1760.

This inscription not only hints at the pride that Lady Grey took in the project, but also places her contribution on equal terms with that of her grandfather and husband. It signifies that women were considered no less capable in the direction of landscaping and garden architecture than their male relatives. Lady Grey remained close friends with Brown and later invited him to re-landscape the grounds of Wimpole Hall, Cambridgeshire, following her husband's accession to the Earldom of Hardwicke in 1764. In

1769 Lady Grey wrote exhaustedly, but happily, of her two-hour walking consultation with Brown at Wimpole:

> Mr Brown has been leading me such a Fairy Circle & his Magic Wand has raised such landscapes to the Eye – not visionary for they were all there but his Touch has brought them out with the same Effect as a Painter's Pencil upon Canvass – that after having hobbled over rough Ground to Points that I had not seen before, for two Hours, I return half Tired, & Foot sore.[63]

Brown's work at Wimpole transformed the agricultural land north of the house into sweeping parkland, augmented with carefully placed clumps of trees. He also created picturesque serpentine lakes from two existing seventeenth-century fishponds, and freshly dug an entirely new lake. This new landscape was enclosed with a belt of woodland along the perimeter, through which a new carriage ride was constructed, devised with strategic vistas across the parkland. At the centre of this new landscape was the Gothic Tower (Figure 5.7), which had been devised decades earlier by Sanderson Miller. Agneta Yorke, Lady Grey's sister-in-law, wrote glowingly of her competence at directing these improvements in 1771: 'The Description you Ladyship gives of Wimple convinces me how much your taste and Mr Browns Capability have improved that place.'[64]

Lady Grey's successful working relationship with Brown was mirrored at Sandleford Priory, the country estate of the leading Bluestocking Elizabeth

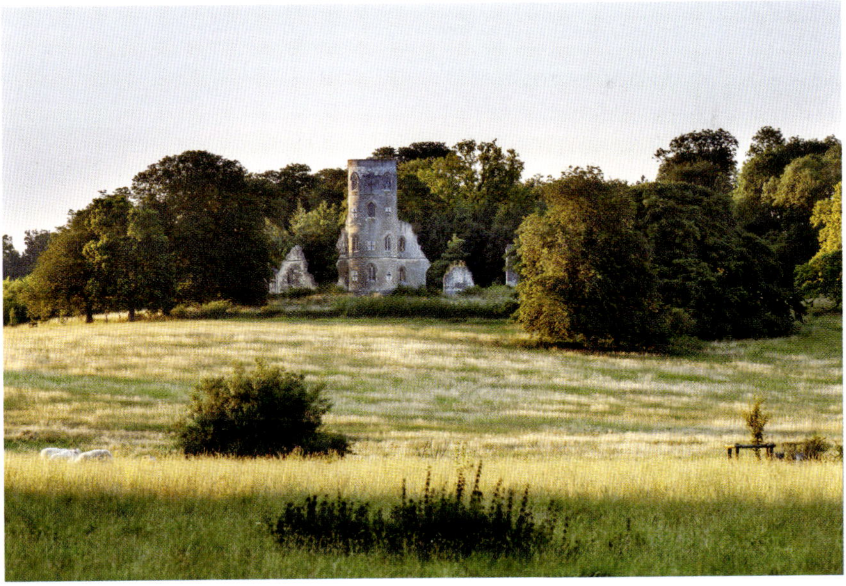

FIGURE 5.7 The Gothic Folly at Wimpole Hall, Cambridgeshire. National Trust Photo Library/Alamy Stock Photo.

Montagu. Elizabeth had inherited Sandleford following the death of her husband, Edward Montagu, in 1775, and during the 1780s she set about improving both the house and park. She hired James Wyatt to Gothicize the house and she brought Brown to Sandleford in July 1781 to reinvigorate the grounds.[65] When writing to Elizabeth Carter, a fellow Bluestocking, in 1782, Elizabeth expressed pride in her architectural and landscaping achievements at Sandleford and at Portman Square:

> by Fees to Lawyers, I laid out 36:000 in a purchase of Land ... and by ye help architects, Masons &c, I have built as good a house in Portman Square; and am now, by ye assistance of ye celebrated Messrs Brown & Wyatt, embellishing Sandleford within doors, & without as successfully, *as if I was Esquire instead of Madame*. All that I have mention'd has been effected in little more than 5 years, few Gentlemen in ye Neighbourhood have done more.[66]

Elizabeth's palpable delight in having achieved so much as a woman and her pride in having outdone her male peers clearly shows that such patronage was generally perceived to be the preserve of wealthy men. As an independent widow, Elizabeth did not have to operate through her male relatives and was able to fulfil her architectural and landscape ambitions, creating a 'lovely pastoral – a sweet Arcadian scene' at Sandleford. She was determined, however, that it would not appear excessive or ostentatious: 'We shall not erect temples to heathen gods, build proud bridges over humble rivulets, or do any of the marvellous things suggested by caprice, and indulged by the wantonness of wealth'.[67] Despite these claims of modesty and restraint, the scheme at Sandleford was vast, continuing beyond Brown's death (of 1783) into the 1790s. His work was continued on firstly by Samuel Lapidge, Brown's surveyor and draughtsman, and then by William Emes (1729–1803), another prominent landscape designer.

Designing a garden without a landscape designer

In contrast to the grand landscaping schemes enacted by Lady Betty Hastings, Henrietta Howard, Lady Grey and Elizabeth Montagu, other women of this period contented themselves with directing the improvements of their gardens themselves. Many craved the tranquillity of the garden and enjoyed spending hours working with their gardeners to achieve their landscaping ambitions, as exemplified by Caroline Fox, Baroness Holland's (1723–74) endeavours at Holland House in 1759: 'I have been mighty busy planting and making a very pretty alteration in my pleasure ground'.[68] Although the 64-acre park was designed by the Hollands' friend, Charles

Hamilton of Painshill Park, between 1750 and 1756, Lady Holland clearly enjoyed directing the improvements after this point. As the elder sister of Lady Kildare (later Duchess of Leinster) at Carton House and Lady Louisa Conolly at Castletown House, Lady Holland was in good company when it came to shaping her surroundings.

Henrietta Knight, Baroness Luxborough (1699–1756) (Figure 5.8), daughter of Henry St John, 1st Viscount St John, also enjoyed improving her

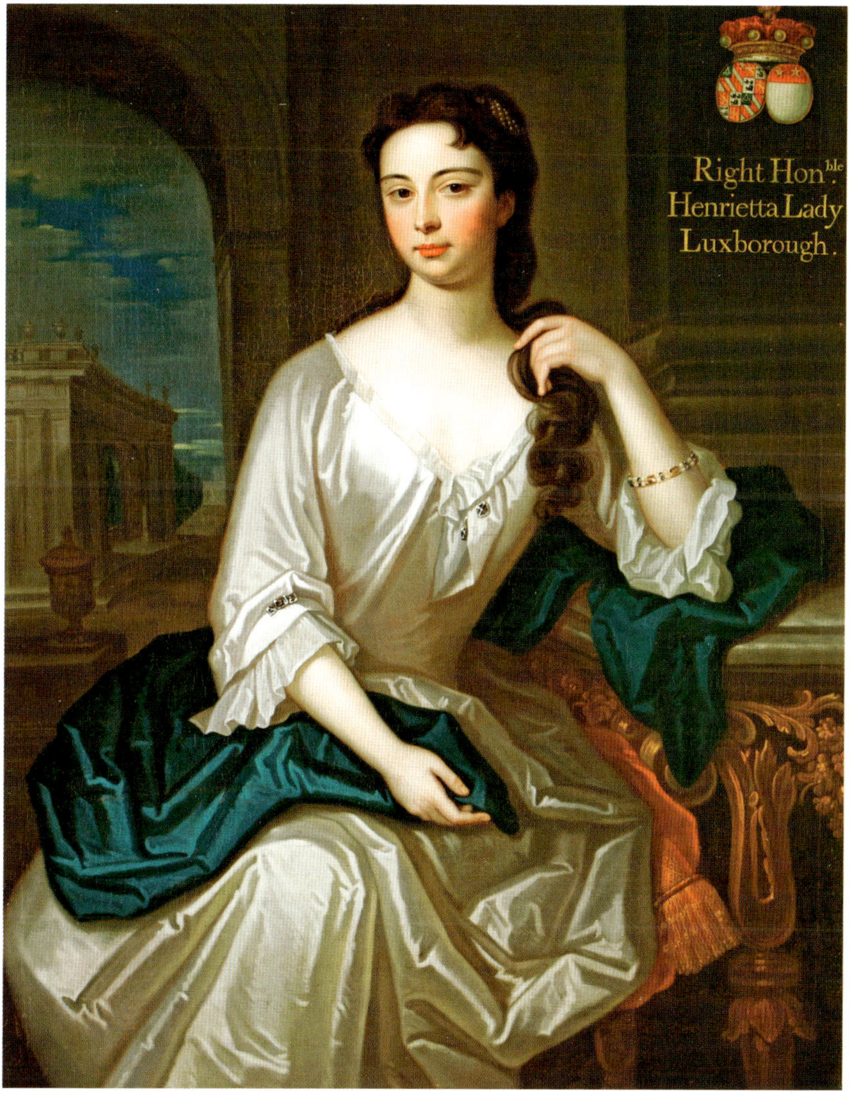

FIGURE 5.8 Maria Verelst (att.), *Henrietta St John, Lady Luxborough*, *c*. 1720, oil on canvas. Lydiard Park, Lyd 1993/057. Courtesy of the Friends of Lydiard Park.

gardens, but for her, it was one of the few joys she could find during her exile in the countryside. Lady Luxborough was publicly disgraced and forced to remove to Barrells Court, an old, run-down estate in Warwickshire, after her husband, Robert Knight, accused her of having multiple affairs.[69] Soon after her marriage in 1727 she was suspected of having an affair with her London physician, Dr Charles Peters, and then in the mid-1730s she was again accused by her jealous husband of having an affair with John Dalton, a tutor in the household of her friend Frances Seymour, Countess of Hertford.[70] Her husband's apparent evidence was a series of romantic letters from her to Dalton, which she claimed were simply 'a silly but Platonick passion'.[71] Although she begged for forgiveness, asking her husband to punish her in any way he pleased except banishment from his house, which she claimed would 'be the death of yr unfortunate wife', he remained unmoved and exiled her to the country for the rest of her life.[72]

It was decided by her half-brother, Henry St John, 1st Viscount Bolingbroke, and Knight that she should live in seclusion upon a meagre £500 per year (about £60,000 today).[73] Lady Luxborough's new geographical location 'confirmed her status as a woman in disgrace' which 'would insist on her shame'.[74] At the age of thirty-four, Lady Luxborough's social life was thus irrevocably over; she was banned from London and Bath and prohibited from ever seeing her children again. Forced to live in a property that was so derelict that it 'had not half the windows up, no doors to the house, and the roof uncovered', her future looked bleak.[75] Consequently, in an attempt to reconcile herself to her fate and in a desperate attempt to distract herself from her misery, Lady Luxborough embarked on the 'wholescale remodelling of the house and gardens at Barrells'.[76] During her twenty-year tenure, Lady Luxborough, 'being a person of great taste and judgement, made many improvements', which included numerous alterations and additions to the garden.[77]

Lady Luxborough constantly occupied herself with staking out ground for new paths, walks, trees and groves, and improving her picturesque vistas with carefully placed ornaments, such as an obelisk a piping fawn,[78] and a highly decorated urn (Figure 5.9).[79] Moreover, she regularly commissioned new buildings to enhance her fifty-acre garden including a summer house,[80] a pedimented pavilion,[81] and a thatched hermitage.[82] She took landscaping seriously, and also created a bowling green and a ha-ha.[83] Her demonstrable interest in architecture was enhanced by her study of the latest architectural treatises. In 1749, for example, she borrowed 'Gibb's book', referring to James Gibbs's *Book of Architecture* (1728), from her neighbour, the poet William Shenstone.[84] She promised Shenstone that she would take care of the book despite her apparent distaste for Gibbs's work: '[I] never yet could admire [Gibbs's] taste in Architecture ... His building at Cambridge I have seen, but never could like'.[85] A year previously she had lent Shenstone her copy of 'Inigo Jones's designs, as long as they can be of service to you'.[86]

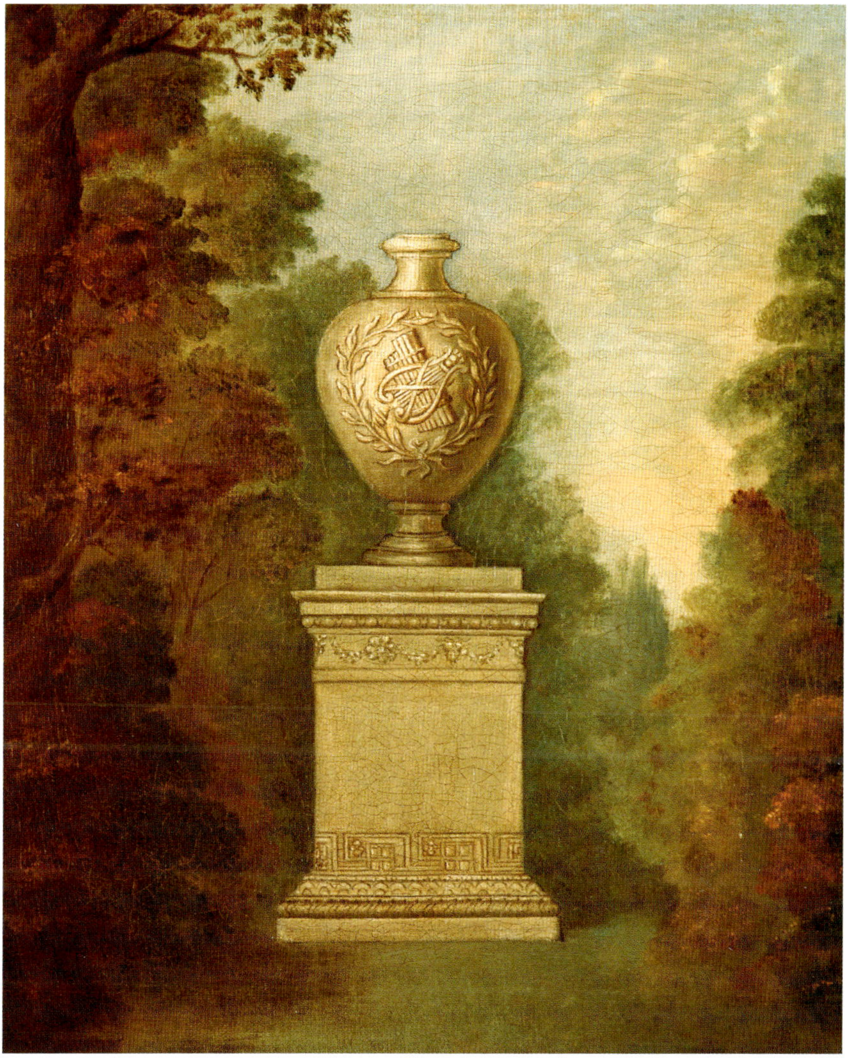

FIGURE 5.9 English School, *Urn to William Somerville in a garden landscape*, *c.* 1750s, oil on canvas. Lydiard Park, LYD 2001/24. Courtesy of the Friends of Lydiard Park.

Lady Luxborough's dedication to her garden was not only a distraction during her banishment, but also a method to repair her dire social status. The remodelling of Barrells and the improvements to her gardens enticed the fashionable world to visit her once again. In June 1749 she reported to Shenstone that 'the court has been honoured with Mrs. Kendall's coach and six, which found room sufficient', suggesting that she was at last deemed fit by society to visit.[87] Nonetheless, although visitors approved of her house and garden, her notoriety continued, because regardless of her design efforts 'her landscape signal[ed] a place of retired disgrace'.[88] Thus, society remained forever wary of Lady Luxborough, and despite her years of penitence, she was still regarded as a woman of questionable character.

Ornamental garden buildings

The landscaped and ornamental gardens of the eighteenth century were typically enhanced with the careful placing of ornamental garden buildings and follies. Contemporary pattern books such as Thomas Overton's *Original Designs of Temples and Other Buildings for Parks and Gardens* (1766) reveal the plethora of styles and designs available to patrons, indicating that the creation of such buildings was highly personalized.[89] Indeed, due to the smaller scale of the garden folly and because of its recreational purpose, patrons experimented freely with new and exciting decorative styles. Lady Luxborough, as we have seen, built a number of buildings in a variety of styles at Barrells. She did this to provide attractive places to sit within the gardens, whilst also expressing her refined taste in the latest architectural trends.

Women regularly commissioned garden buildings, usually taking particular care over their design and decoration. Ornamental dairies, for example, were a popular choice amongst women because they allowed for the demonstration of their feminine virtues.[90] Other popular garden follies included grottoes and Chinese pavilions, both of which allowed female patrons to experiment with design.

Ornamental dairies

The latter half of the eighteenth century saw the rise of the ornamental pleasure dairy, built in the grounds and gardens of country houses for wealthy women to partake in the pastoral industry of butter churning and cream making. The dairy's rise in popularity was a product of the wider trend that saw the landed classes strive for agricultural improvement and architectural refinement within the wider estate. As the dairy and its related activities were elevated to greater cultural prominence, they became the focus of increased architectural experimentation and display. Designed by society architects, they were created as spaces for industriousness as well as for pleasure. Many were built as part of the Model Farm complex, but a great number soon became ornamental features of their own, set within romanticized picturesque garden landscapes. As Prince Pückler-Muskau later observed in 1828:

> the dairy is one of the principal decorations of an English park and stands by itself, quite away from the cow-house. It is generally an elegant

> pavilion adorned with fountains, marble walls and rare and beautiful porcelain and its vessels large and small, filled with the most exquisite milk and its products in all their varieties.[91]

Dairies were objects of taste, thoughtfully placed as eye-catchers within the pleasure grounds. Many showcased the latest architectural fashions, such as the Chinese Dairy at Woburn Abbey, Bedfordshire, built by Henry Holland in 1786 for the 5th Duke of Bedford, or the Gothic Dairy at Cobham Hall, Kent, built by James Wyatt in the 1790s for the Earl of Darnley. Although built for both men and women as places for entertainment and retreat, the model dairy was often seen as a traditionally feminine space. Queen Mary II's dairy at Hampton Court Palace was completed in the early 1690s and is likely to have been the first in Britain, of which Daniel Defoe recorded that it had 'all its conveniences, in which her Majesty took great delight'.[92] Decorated with large blue and white Delft tiles, it was both a fashionable and functional space where the Queen could engage in honest, practical labour, thereby promoting her feminine purity, domesticity and virtue. A succession of royal women followed Mary II's example by commissioning dairies in the following century, including Queen Caroline at Richmond Gardens, her daughter Princess Amelia at Gunnersbury Park, and Queen Charlotte at Frogmore in Windsor Home Park.[93]

Queen Caroline's dairy was one of the first free-standing dairies to be placed within the landscaped garden in Britain and was described in 1736 as 'A neat but low Brick Building, with Venetian windows, the Walls covered with Stucco, within most amply furnished, the Utensils for the Milk being of the most beautiful China'.[94] The pastoral nature of the dairy allowed Caroline to 'maintain the appearance of adhering to culturally conceived gender boundaries'.[95] Thus, the dairy was often a tool through which women could flex their architectural muscles whilst appearing to remain within the approved feminine domain of domesticity and housewifery.

At Althorp in Northamptonshire Lavinia, Countess Spencer, was instrumental in the design of her dairy cottage, complete with a pyramid thatched roof (Figure 5.10). The interior was decorated with walls covered in fashionable Wedgewood tiles with a distinctive Ivy leaf pattern and was filled with bespoke Wedgewood dairy utensils. Built with the assistance of Henry Holland, in October 1787 Lady Spencer wrote to her husband of her impatience for it to be completed, 'My Cottage advances but so slowly!'.[96] Similarly, Elizabeth Armistead built a dairy at St Anne's Hill, which also boasted matching tiles and dairy ware: 'paved and lined with white tiles edged with green; the cream-pans, skimmers and ladles, of the same; the dressers and stands are of marble, supported by fluted green and white pillars'.[97]

Such dairies were usually designed with a room for entertainment and were handsomely decorated. For Elizabeth Smith-Stanley, Countess of Derby's (1753–97) dairy at Knowsley Park, Lancashire, the Robert Adam office

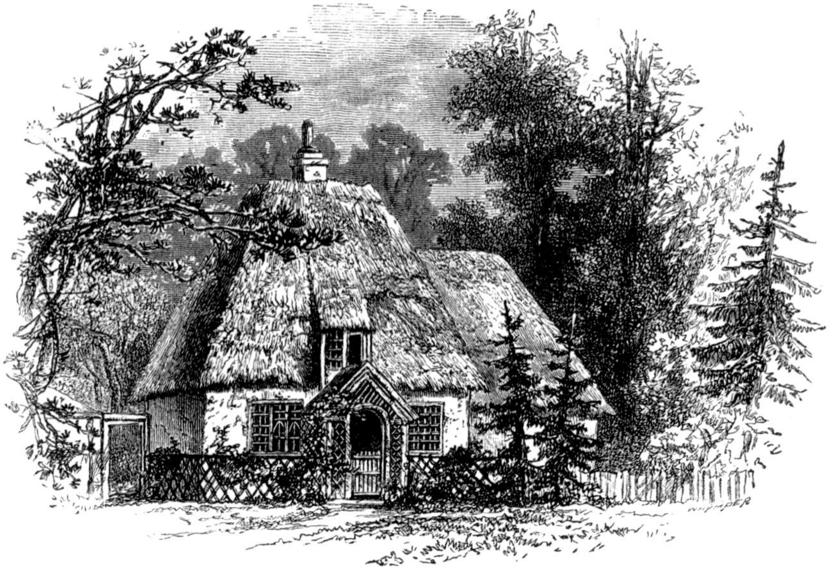

FIGURE 5.10 Edward Whymper, *The Dairy, Althorp*, nineteenth century. Timewatch Images/Alamy Stock Photo.

produced a beautiful preliminary design for a Neo-Classical chimneypiece to adorn her entertaining room, featuring an intricate central tablet of a tazza enclosed within an oval frame.[98] Similarly, in the collaborative dairy designs by John Soane and George Dance for Elizabeth Craven, Baroness Craven (1750–1828), both contained a tea room (Figure 5.11).[99] Although never built, the two designs showcase the fashionable primitive style and may have been a method by which Lady Craven was hoping to reemphasize her feminine virtues in a time when she was in the midst of public scandal, having recently separated from her husband. This may also have been true of the disgraced Lady Luxborough who built a dairy, presided over it herself and sent a range of dairy products to friends and family from whom she was isolated.[100]

Grottoes

In addition to dairies, naturalistic buildings such as rustic hermitages, grottoes and root houses were all popular features of the landscaped garden throughout the eighteenth century. Grottoes were a particular favourite, inspired by the natural and artificial subterranean grottoes and nymphaea of antiquity. The grottoes of the ancients were designed to provide tranquil, shaded retreats from the glaring sun and usually contained artificial springs and wells and were decorated beautifully with mosaics and statues. At

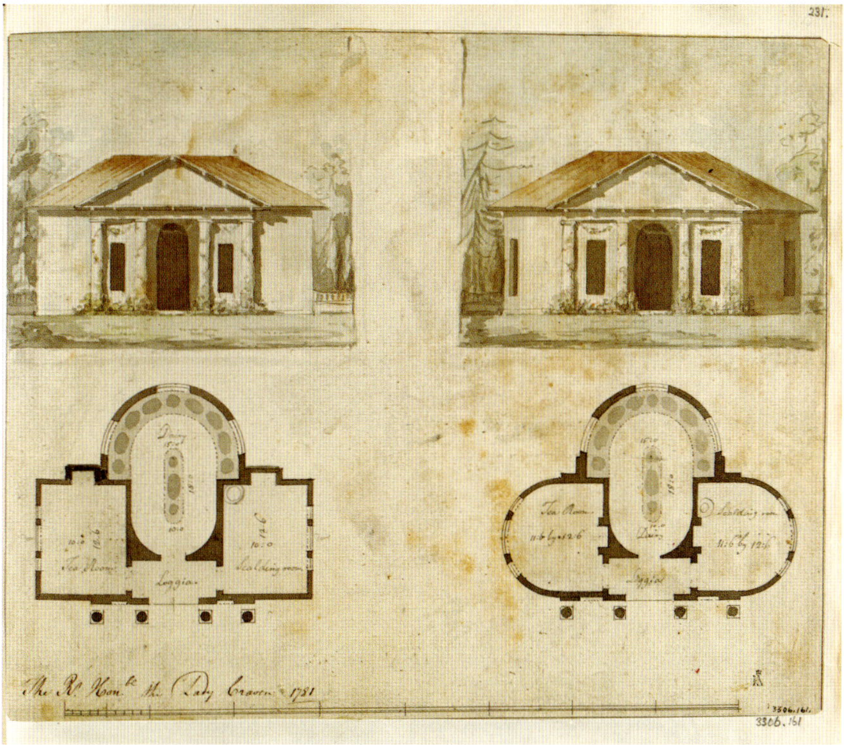

FIGURE 5.11 Sir John Soane, 'Dairy Design for Lady Craven', 1781, pen and ink with grey, green, brown and pink. Victoria and Albert Museum, 3306:161. Copyright of the Victoria and Albert Museum, London.

the House of the Mosaic of Neptune and Amphitrite in Herculaneum, for example, the walls of the nymphaeum garden triclinium (dining room) were decorated with pumice, shells and intricate polychromatic mosaics of the sea god and his wife.

Of course, the phenomenon of grotto building was not new in Britain. In the seventeenth century they had found great favour within the Stuart Court, with famous examples including James I's grotto in the undercroft of the Banqueting House, Whitehall, and the Earl of Pembroke's grotto at Wilton House, Wiltshire, both of which were filled with ingenious trick fountains designed by Isaac de Caus. During the English Civil War however, many grottoes and their complicated waterworks fell into disrepair, which resulted in their gradual removal. Thus, it was not until the early eighteenth century that the nation's enthusiasm for the grotto was renewed.

Women were at the forefront of this new fashion, with Mary Fane, Viscountess Fane (1686–1762) (served as Maid of Honour to Queen Anne), being one of the first to build a grotto during the 1720s. Her grotto was located close to the Thames within the park of her marital home, Basildon

Park, Berkshire. The grotto adjoined a 'New House' which was built by her husband for her use as a place of recreation and retirement. In 1747 Elizabeth Montagu visited:

> The Situation is, like most grottoes, placed where a grotto would not be looked for: it joins to the house ... The first room is fitted up entirely with shells, the sides and ceiling in beautiful mosaic, a rich cornice of flowers in baskets and cornucopias, and the little yellow sea snail is so disposed in shades as to resemble knots of ribbon which seem to tye up some of the bunches of flowers. There is a bed for a Hermit, which is composed of rich shells, and so shaded that the curtain seems folded and flowing ... The room adjoining it is the true and proper style for a grotto; it is composed of rough rock work in a very bold taste, the water falls down into a cold bath.[101]

Women took great care over the design of their grotto interiors, some of which were designed to look like natural caves, complete with flowing water features. Others featured elaborate and intricate designs of mosaics and shells, which were painstakingly planned and executed by the patronesses themselves. In 1739 Sarah Lennox, Duchess of Richmond (1705–51), and her daughters, the Ladies Caroline and Emily, began a seven-year project to decorate their remarkable shell-grotto at Goodwood, Sussex (Figure 5.12).[102] Together they spent hours sorting and arranging thousands of shells, many

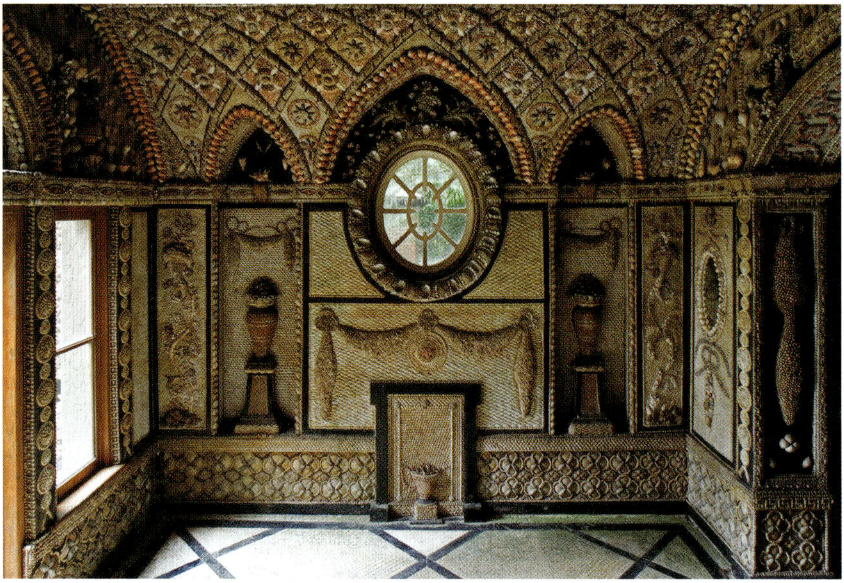

FIGURE 5.12 The Shell House at Goodwood, West Sussex. Photo: Clive Boursnell. By permission of the Trustees of the Goodwood Collection.

collected by Captain Knowles of HMS *Diamond*, into beautiful Rococo patterns used to ornament the walls and vaulted ceilings.[103] The shells were woven into exquisite flowers, bows, ropes and the initials 'EK' for Emily, Lady Kildare (later Duchess of Leinster), 'CF' for Lady Caroline Fox (later Baroness Holland) and 'CR' for their father the Duke.[104] Lady Emily went on to construct her own shell-grotto at her marital home in Ireland, Carton House, in the late 1740s, for which she combined the use of shells, mirrors, glass, bark, branches and fir cones to create intricate flowers and geometric patterns.[105] For the Lennox women the creation of their grotto at Goodwood was a form of motherly and sisterly bonding, which also allowed for creative expression.

The Lennox women's flair for shellwork, ornamentation and interior design was also shared by Jane (1764–1849) and Mary Parminter (1750–1811), the remarkable single cousins who created A La Ronde – a unique sixteen-sided house in Devon.[106] In 1795, following their prolonged Grand Tour of Europe, the unmarried pair set about building for themselves a modest folly-like house, which they decorated with elaborate ornamentation crafted from shells, feathers, mosaics and cut paper. Amongst their inventive creations is the amazing feather frieze in the drawing room, and the extraordinary octagonal Shell Gallery, where the walls are covered with intricate patterns of over 25,000 shells (Figure 5.13).

A shared passion for architectural design could therefore become the basis of lasting relationships and collaborations. Mary Delany's great friendship with Margaret Bentinck, Duchess of Portland (1715–85), led to their collaboration over the design and execution of the grotto at Busltrode, Buckinghamshire, the Duchess's marital home (Figure 5.14). The daughter of Henrietta, Countess of Oxford, of Welbeck Abbey, the Duchess shared her mother's passion for building, and, after having visited Catherine, Lady Walpole's (1682–1737) grotto in Chelsea in 1737, she was very clear about what she did not want in a grotto. She ruthlessly described it as a '*shellery*, (for *grotto* I will *not* call it,)' further stating, '*That regularity* is abominable; besides, all the red coral *is painted* – mine shall not be made after that model!'[107]

A key feature for some grottoes therefore was for them to look as cave-like as possible, decorated with natural objects, such as shells and stones. Mary was instrumental in sourcing appropriate shells to decorate the walls of the Bulstrode grotto and in 1771 she happily reported of the progress they had made:

> We took a tour yesterday to look at the plantations on the common, which thrive and have a very good effect; ended with the Cave, where the Duchess has desired a plantation of some trees on the right hand, which will be a great improvement. We also fixed upon a place in the Cave for the Ilam fossils, which are much admired, especially the great rock which is covered in coral, scientifically called *Madrepores*.[108]

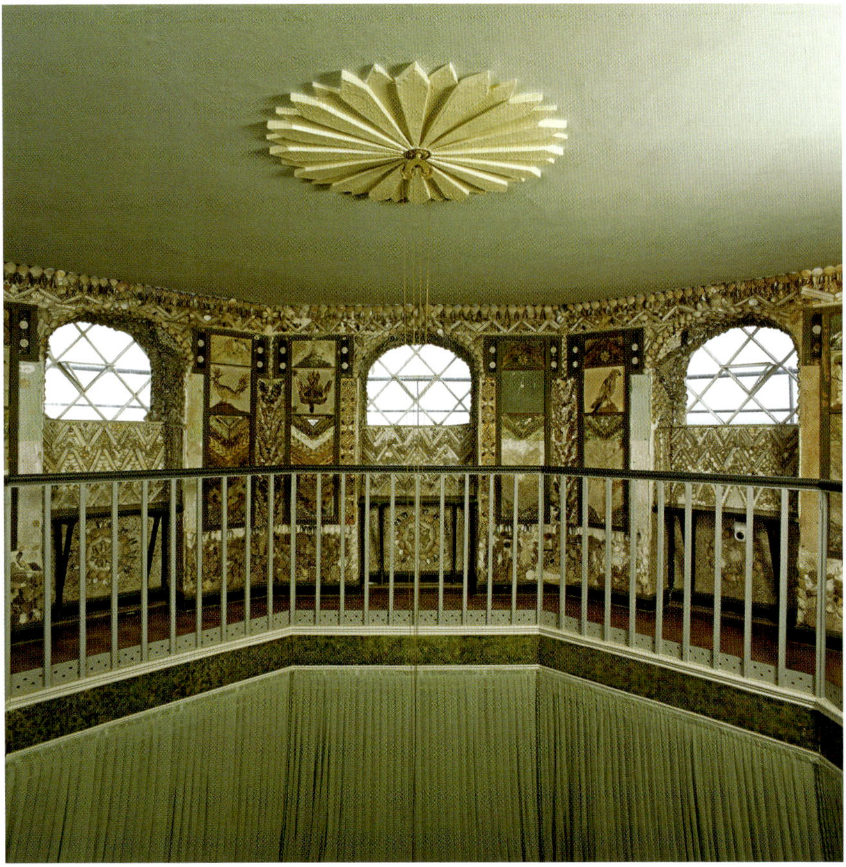

FIGURE 5.13 The Shell Gallery at A La Ronde, Devon. National Trust Photo Library/David Garner/Alamy Stock Photo.

The Duchess of Portland's grotto was not only a beautifully designed garden folly, it was also a space for her to display her intellectual interest in natural history. She was famed for her natural history collection, the largest in the country, which was curated by the naturalist John Lightfoot and the Swedish botanist Daniel Solander. It seems fitting then that she used her grotto to display some of her prized specimens, which no doubt enhanced its appearance and sparked scholarly discussion. The Duchess also populated her pleasure grounds with flower gardens and fishponds, botanical laboratories, a menagerie which boasted an Indian bull and a zebra, and a Chinese-fronted dairy.[109] The garden was a platform upon which she was able to express her varying tastes and interests. The Chinese-fronted dairy, for example, allowed her to experiment in the fashionable Chinoiserie aesthetic, while also conforming to the popular trend of feminine dairy-related activities.

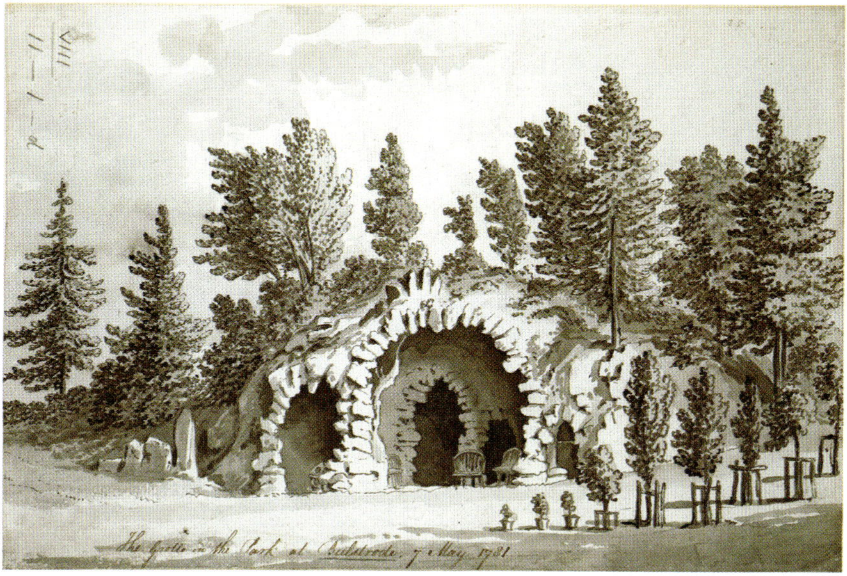

FIGURE 5.14 Samuel Hieronymus Grimm, *The Grotto in the Park at Bulstrode*, 1781, pen and ink drawing. Topographical Collection/Alamy Stock Photo.

Chinese garden buildings

Romantic notions about the exotic and distant Far East fuelled the demand for architectural experimentation within the eighteenth-century garden. Chinese-themed follies were being built as early as the 1740s and were popularized by later publications like William Halfpenny's *New Designs for Chinese Temples* (1750) and William Chambers' *Designs of Chinese Buildings* (1757). As we have already seen, the fashion for Chinoiserie interiors was often pioneered by women during this period and this also translated into the garden. Augusta, Dowager Princess of Wales, was one such patroness, who, as part of her extensive landscaping programme at Kew Gardens, commissioned William Chambers to build numerous exotic and oriental ornamental structures. In 1758 he built Alhambra, a folly which imitated the famous thirteenth-century Arab palace in Granada of the same name; in 1760 he built a Chinoiserie menagerie (Figure 5.15); in 1761 he built a Turkish Mosque, which consisted of a large dome with two smaller ones, two minarets and an Arabic inscription; and for Augusta's birthday he built the famous Chinese Pagoda (1761–2), which still survives, consisting of ten stories, decorated with eighty gilded dragons (Figure 5.16).

Another of Chambers' patrons was the energetic Catherine, Duchess of Queensbury, who commissioned him to alter and redecorate an existing Chinese summerhouse (dating from *c.* 1748) at Amesbury Abbey, Wiltshire,

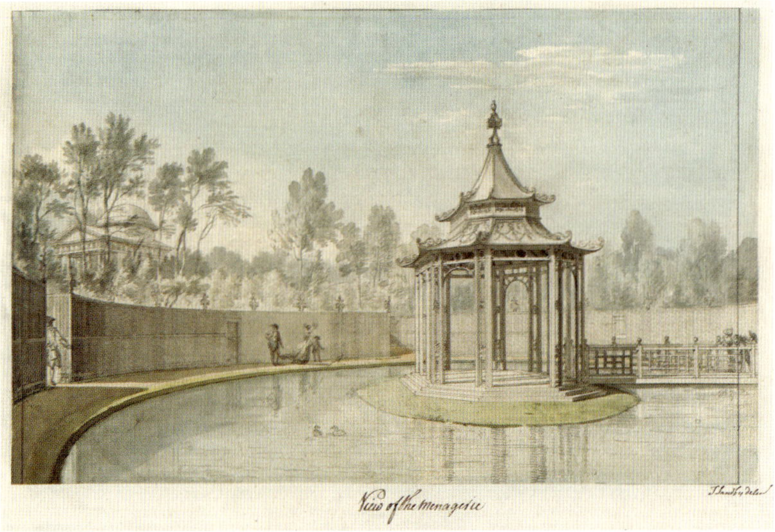

FIGURE 5.15 Thomas Sandby, *View of the Menagerie at Kew*, 1763, watercolour. The Metropolitan Museum of Art, NY, 25.19.40. Courtesy of The Metropolitan Museum of Art.

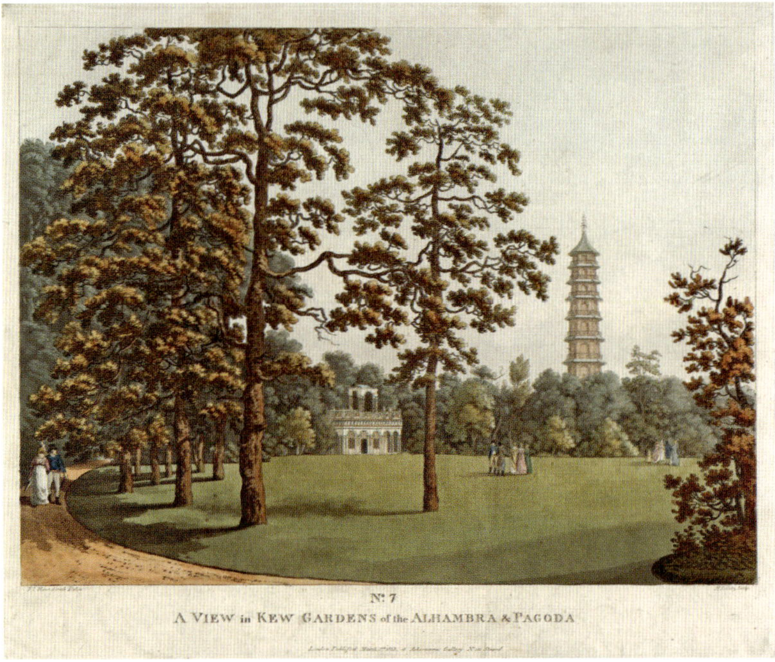

FIGURE 5.16 Heinrich Joseph Schütz, after Franz Joseph Manskirch, *A View in Kew Gardens of the Alhambra and the Pagoda*, 1813, aquatint with watercolour. The Metropolitan Museum of Art, NY, 63.617.28. Courtesy of The Metropolitan Museum of Art.

in *c.* 1772. The Duchess, who had been banished from Court in her youth, was also famed for storming the House of Lords with a group of ladies in 1739 to watch a debate. Having been denied their usual access to the viewing gallery, the Duchess and her friends 'raised their siege' outside the doors and stood there from nine in the morning to five in the afternoon 'without either sustenance or evacuation, every now and then playing vollies of thumps, kicks, and raps, against the door, with so much violence that the speakers in the House were scarce heard'.[110] When this proved unsuccessful the Duchess and the Duchess of Ancaster ordered 'a dead silence of half an hour', which tricked the Chancellor into thinking that they had given up, so when he opened the doors:

> they all rushed in ... and placed themselves in the front rows of the gallery. They stayed there till after eleven, when the House rose; and during the debate gave applause, and shewed marks of dislike, not only by smiles and winks (which have always been allowed in these cases), but by noisy laughs and apparent contempts.[111]

Now in her seventies, Catherine was still causing a sensation, this time through her relationship with Julius Soubise (1754–98).[112] Soubise was the son of an elnsaved Caribbean woman and at the age of ten was brought to the UK by Captain Stair Douglas of the Royal Navy and given to Catherine in 1764. She freed him, renamed him after the French duke, Charles de Rohan, Prince de Soubise, and gave him a privileged upbringing. He lived the life of a fashionable fop, became the Duchess's riding and fencing master, and was later rumoured to be her lover.

Ever conscious of fashion, it was during this time that the Duchess decided to update her Chinese House (Figure 5.17), writing to Chambers in 1772 and giving him very particular directions about the interior decoration:

> Sir William Chambers will remember most of the discourses (tho in great haste) held between him and the Ductchess of Queensbury relative to the by name Chinese house, she now puts him in mind that <u>Oake</u> leaves & Acorns were proposed instead of the Old Eggs & Anchors, she imagines Sir William will take care of the proportions as the acorn ought just to be large enough to be seen plainly & not big enough to disgust one, she thinks they should be painted the colour of an Acorn, & the cup a little carved & the <u>Oake</u> leaves double or <u>trible</u> in every cornet, enough to appear natural as if just gathered.[113]

With regard to '<u>embellishing Elegantifiing</u> the house in question' the Duchess of Queensbury wanted the interiors painted, and suggested Theodore de Bruyn (1730–1804), a Dutch painter known for his grisaille paintings of bas-relief sculpture as well as his landscape and topographical paintings. He had, according to her, been 'sent from abroad by the Dutchess of Norfolk' and

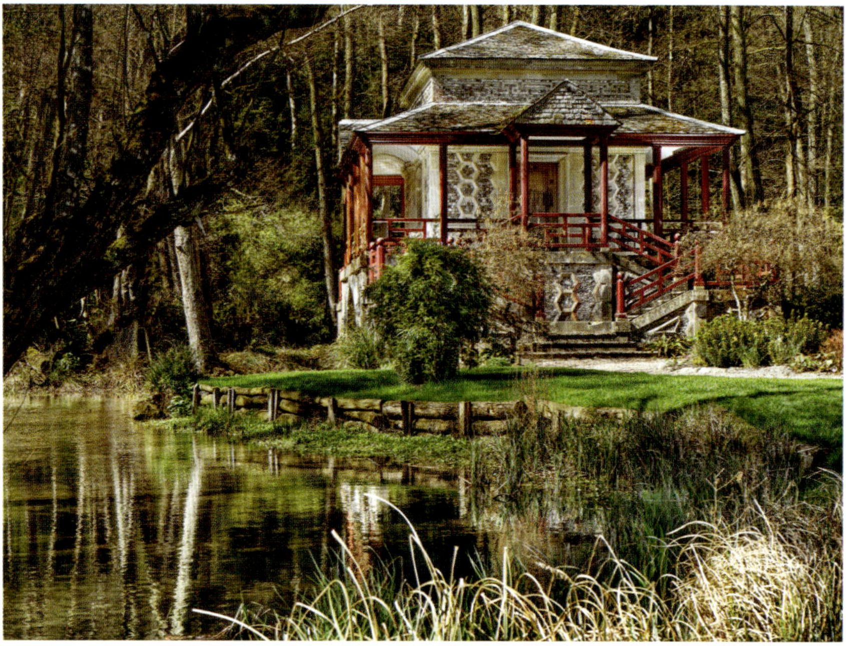

FIGURE 5.17 Chinese House or Temple in the grounds of Amesbury Abbey, Wiltshire. Courtesy of James O. Davies.

resided at 'little Castle Street Cavendish Square'.[114] Having apparently seen de Bruyn's work 'att Lord Radnors by Salisbury' (Longford Castle), the Duchess believed that Chambers 'might adapt something of that nature' for the Chinese Temple.[115] The paintings that she refers to have long since disappeared, but from her description they were from 'Designs of Montfaucon' and were:

> in two or three colours of this mans doing, but there was a parcell of Couleurs added by a painter towards the rough finishing, shocking to behold, as intollerably tawdry. Sr Wm knows that the assemblage & blending Coulerurs are great Principals of his own Masterfull Supream taste. [T]he Dutchess would have nothing done in black & white, but glowing & soft, not excluding the requisite light and shade.[116]

the Duchess's Chinese House survives and forms part of a bridge that spans a small tributary stream of the River Avon. The design is unusual, but one that certainly fulfils its objective as a playful, experimental garden folly. Her desire to hire de Bruyn suggests that she was not pursuing a typical Chinoiserie aesthetic for the interiors and may have intended to decorate it with grisaille paintings of classical and mythological scenes and motifs. This choice highlights the individualistic nature of the garden folly and indicates that such a building, precisely because of its informal nature, enabled women to engage in architectural and decorative experimentation within the garden.

* * *

The estate at large, as much as any building, was a canvas for architectural and aesthetic expression. Since the estate itself was inextricably linked to the concept of patriarchal display, so too was the discipline of landscape design. As a result, it was predominantly women with independent means who commissioned progressive landscape designers and when they did so, they competed on a national level, creating gardens that paved the way in stylistic design. The majority of women, however, lacked legal and financial independence and as such channelled their architectural ambition into the creation of estate buildings and ornamental garden architecture. It was easier for these female patrons to commission such projects, largely because it allowed them to reaffirm their feminine virtue. As ever, women shrewdly navigated the restrictive social context of the times to participate on the architectural stage and did so with great skill and innovation.

6

Conclusions

By the time that Sarah Churchill was in her seventies, she no longer had time for architects. When advising her granddaughter on the possibility of rebuilding Woburn Abbey, she stated:

> And if it [Woburn] must be pulled down, I fancy it may be built up again ... without the help of an architect, for I know of none that are not mad or ridiculous, and I really [think] that anybody that has sense with the best workmen of all sorts could make a better house without an architect, than any has been built these many years.[1]

With years of building experience behind her, together with the many quarrels that she had had with her architects, Sarah Churchill's exasperation was to be expected. After her tumultuous relationship with Vanbrugh, her mistrust of the Wrens and her frustrations with Lord Pembroke and Morris, she finally decided that architects were of no use at all. This conviction speaks volumes of the Duchess's authority and confidence in the realm of architectural patronage. By the time of her death in 1744, the Duchess of Marlborough had commissioned or directly influenced the building schemes and associated gardens of three country houses, one town house, one villa and a set of almshouses. She had hired the very best architects, craftsmen and landscape designers and had created an architectural legacy that was as impressive as any of her contemporaries, if not more so.

Although the Duchess was indeed an exceptional woman for her time, this book has shown that her passion for architecture was shared by many wealthy, educated women. Far from being the preserve of men, the sphere of architectural design and patronage was one in which women creatively participated. Working within the social restrictions of the time, they were passionate about building and were determined to leave their mark if the opportunity arose. They were ambitious in their building schemes, experimental in their design and aesthetic choices, and were always conscious of remaining at the height of fashion. They shaped country houses, built lavish town houses, commissioned stylish villas, built charitable almshouses and schools, embellished family churches, fashioned beautiful pleasure grounds and created tasteful garden follies.

This book began by demonstrating that elite women had a substantial impact on the country house, a building type traditionally associated exclusively with patriarchal power. Furthermore, their influence over the design and aesthetic of country houses was apparent regardless of marital status. For instance, unmarried women, if they were fortunate, could become the chatelaine of a country house for a male relative, which provided them with modest architectural opportunity. When married, collaboration between husbands and wives in the creation of their marital homes was a common occurrence amongst the landed classes, with wives occasionally even taking a dominant role in the design of a new patriarchal seat. When an ancestral seat was at risk of being lost due to the extinction of the male line, the strictures of primogeniture were skirted in order to bequeath it to a surviving female. In such cases, the desire to interact with familial dynasty and to shape the ancestral home took centre stage for many heiresses, and they ensured their contributions were immortalized. Finally, widowed women often possessed the greatest autonomy over country house design and patronage: they could be tasked with the completion of grand country houses that still remained unfinished after the death of their husbands, manage the patriarchal estates while the heir was still in his minority or dedicate themselves to the creation of their perfect dower house.

When it came to town house building, women were formidable in their quest to build the most lavish, fashionable and tasteful town houses in London. Without any of the patriarchal restrictions associated with the country house, women found it a liberating freedom to build houses as they saw fit. Just as with their male counterparts, women built town houses to make architectural statements, occasionally choosing bold and pioneering styles, such as the Gothic Revival. Furthermore, through the subtle arts of hospitality and hosting, women could use town houses to engage with political and intellectual matters of the day, influence those in power and cultivate powerful social networks. Similarly, the fascinating architectural exploits of the courtesans Sophia Baddeley and Teresa Cornelys highlight how town houses could be leveraged to gain and maintain a tenuous place amongst the social elite and to make one's fortune.

While the country house usually sat at the centre of patriarchal control and the town house sat at the centre of London's social scene, the suburban villa was predominantly employed as a refuge from the hustle and bustle of the city. Smaller in size, cheaper to build, remodel and maintain, and set within beautiful green surroundings, the villa was popular amongst women who wished to own a place of leisure and comfort in the countryside. The economic advantages and the rural location of the villa also enabled women to escape quite literally, either from abusive husbands or the ridiculing public. Although the trend for possessing both a town house and a suburban villa was apparent amongst wealthy women of the landed classes, the villa was also coveted by self-made women who used it as a status symbol or to further a business venture. A further financial motive for establishing a small villa estate was to create a sizable legacy for those disadvantaged by primogeniture, such as daughters and younger sons. By remodelling or building a fashionable villa, augmented with a small estate, women could effectively circumvent the patrilineal inheritance system, something that was not easily achieved with the patriarchal nature of country houses or the transitional nature of the London town houses.

Finally, as well exerting their architectural agency over country houses, town houses and villas, women also enjoyed influencing the aesthetic of the estate at large. The building of almshouses, schools and churches was considered to sit within the female sphere of action as it allowed women to express their benevolence, charity and piety. These charitable projects allowed married women to make a tangible impact upon their husbands' estates, by improving the lives of their tenants and workers, while also providing them with the opportunity to leave an architectural legacy. Correspondingly, just as women were interested in the improvement of the estate at large, so too were they interested in landscape and garden design and commissioned the most prominent landscape designers of the day, such as Charles Bridgeman and Lancelot 'Capability' Brown. Even when a landscape designer could not be afforded, women eagerly took to the designing and directing of their gardens themselves. Finally, to further elevate the appearance of the pleasure grounds and gardens, women often commissioned ornamental garden buildings, such as dairies, grottoes and Chinese summerhouses. These small, recreational buildings allowed women to experiment with architectural and decorative design.

In short, overwhelming historical evidence across the architectural spectrum demonstrates that as soon as women gained a measure of financial and legal independence, such as through an inheritance or widowhood, they leveraged their newfound freedom to realize their architectural ambitions. Women were adept at navigating the constraints of their era by commissioning projects and wielding influence in subtler ways: by working through their husbands and by veiling their architectural projects in the guise of feminine virtue. On occasion, however, they boldly disregarded society's censure and commissioned grand schemes in their own names to please nobody but themselves. Just as with their male peers, women built for a wide variety of purposes: to show off their learning, for self-gratification, for luxury and comfort, to gain social and political influence, to help those around them, to engage with the system of inheritance, to exalt their families or to make a permanent mark on the world.

Of course, these women were simply doing what had been done by many (now forgotten) women before them.[2] Women have always had an interest in architecture and a desire to mould their surroundings, and this of course continued after the eighteenth century into the Victorian era and through to the modern day.[3] During the nineteenth century in particular, architectural drawing was increasingly encouraged as an appropriate pastime for middle- and upper-class women, as 'it could not ... injure their health' because 'for them it would not be a matter of gain'.[4] 'By a little perseverance on their part', wrote the *Architectural Magazine* in 1836, 'attended with a degree of nicety and care, which very few ladies are without, architectural drawing could soon be accomplished; and this art ... would be an endless source of amusement to them'.[5] Herein lay the problem – architectural design was only acceptable, so far as it remained a female 'amusement'.

Due to the prevailing patriarchal opinion that women could not and should not enter the professional world of work, opportunities for women to practise architecture professionally continued to be limited. Nonetheless, the nineteenth century was a period of gradual change and the Women's Movement, which campaigned for equal rights and access to property, paid employment and the professions, slowly paved the way for women's entry into the architectural profession.[6] Despite this progress, however, most women continued to design exclusively for family and friends, operating within the confines of femininity and domesticity. For example, Violet Morris (1878–1958), daughter of the architect Joseph Morris, designed a number of buildings in the Reading and Wokingham areas for her family's practice, but they were predominantly domestic dwellings.[7]

Women were also excluded from the Royal Institute of British Architects (RIBA), which was founded in 1834 for the 'the general advancement of Architecture'. In the words of Thomas Leverton Donaldson, at the Institute's official opening in 1835, the aim of the architect-members was to 'To uphold in *ourselves*, the character of Architects, as Men of Taste, Men of Science, Men of Honour'.[8] The first woman, Ethel Mary Charles (1871–1962), would not be admitted into the Institute until 1898. Charles was a pioneering woman, as was her sister Bessie Ada, who in 1900 was the second woman member to be admitted into RIBA. In 1893, the sisters, after having completed a three-year tutorship under Ernest George and Harold Peto, sought to continue their training at the Architectural Association (AA), the oldest independent school of architecture in Britain, but were barred.[9] Women would not be admitted until 1917; the first of which were Ruth Gollancz (1898–1973), Winifred Ryle (1897–1987), Irene Graves and Gillian Cooke (1898–1974).

Charles went on to win the RIBA Silver Medal in 1905 and yet, although she expressed an interest in large-scale experimental work, she found herself largely confined to designing small, domestic buildings, usually for female clients.[10] Women's potential within the architectural profession was thus curtailed, with men such as Robert Atkinson, the head of the AA, expressing his hope that 'women would find a field for their abilities more particularly in decorative and domestic architecture rather than the planning of buildings 10 to 12 stories high'.[11]

Undaunted by this prejudice, women continued to strive, and in 1928 Elisabeth Whitworth Scott (1898–1972), a recent AA graduate, won the competition for the Shakespeare Memorial Theatre in Stratford-upon-Avon – the first major public building in Britain to be designed by a woman. Dame Jane Drew (1911–96), a successful Modernist architect, was another trailblazer. After she qualified in 1934, frustrated with the prejudice women faced with sexist hiring practises, she established a woman-only firm. She later relaxed this approach and in 1946 (formally created in 1950) set up practice with her second husband Maxwell Fry. Fry was recognized during his lifetime as a key figure in the development of the British Modern Movement and was awarded the RIBA Gold Medal in 1964. Drew, however, received no such recognition from her peers, despite receiving five separate Gold Medal nominations.

In fact, tales of her 'difficult personality' remain and 'often take precedence over her architecture'.[12] This, together with her lack of interest in the 'feminine' sphere of domesticity, resulted in Drew being seen as a 'divisive figure'.[13] Within the Fry-Drew duo, Fry was usually seen as the creative talent, the architectural genius, whilst 'Drew's "value" as a designer [was] often downplayed or dismissed entirely'.[14] Throughout her lifetime, Drew was often introduced as the wife of the great Maxwell Fry, with her own architectural achievements overlooked and ignored.[15] Her experience within the architectural world was, in many ways, very similar to that of her forebears, but she strove on to become the first woman to be elected onto the RIBA Council in 1964 and was elected the first woman to be president of the Architectural Association in 1969. However, it was not until 2009 when the first woman, Ruth Reed, was elected as president of RIBA and it took a further seven years for the first woman, Zaha Hadid, to be awarded the RIBA Gold Medal.

Progress has been undeniably slow within the professional world of architecture and there is still much more to be done in the striving for equality between men and women. However, in terms of architectural patronage, women are now free to commission whatever they wish without fear of censure or backlash. The proud eighteenth-century patrons of this book would no doubt be gratified to see this.

The vital contributions that women have made to the field of architectural history have been overlooked for far too long. The architectural landscape of eighteenth-century Britain was shaped not just by men, but also by the remarkable women of this era. By re-assessing the existing historical paradigm and by acknowledging women's achievements, we can move away from the notion that women are newcomers to the architectural stage. In doing so, it is the author's hope that contemporary female patrons and architects can lay claim to the architectural agency and equality for which women have strived throughout history.

NOTES

Chapter 1

1 G. E. Mingay, *English Landed Society in the Eighteenth Century* (London: Routledge and Paul, 1963), pp. 226–7.

2 Ibid.

3 Lady Hervey to Rev. Morris, London, 10 December 1747, in Lady Hervey, *Letters of Mary Lepel, Lady Hervey: With a Memoir and Illustrative Notes* (London: John Murray, 1821), p. 111.

4 See, Joanna Marschner, David Bindham and Lisa Ford (eds), *Enlightened Princesses: Caroline, Augusta, Charlotte, and the Shaping of the Modern World* (New Haven: Yale University Press and London: Historic Royal Palaces, 2017); Joanna Marschner, *Queen Caroline: Cultural Politics at the Early Eighteenth-Century Court* (New Haven and London: Yale University Press, 2014); James Anderson Winn, *Queen Anne: Patroness of Arts* (Oxford: Oxford University Press, 2014); Clarissa Campbell Orr, *Queenship in Britain, 1660–1815: Royal Patronage, Court Culture and Dynastic Politics* (Manchester: Manchester University Press, 2002).

5 For an insightful discussion about the difficulty in identifying seventeenth-century female patrons, see Anne Laurence, 'Women Using Building in Seventeenth-Century England: A Question of Sources?', *Transactions of the Royal Historical Society*, vol. 13 (2003), pp. 293–303.

6 See, for example, Amy Boyington, 'Maids, Wives and Widows: Female Architectural Patronage in Eighteenth-Century Britain' (PhD thesis, University of Cambridge, 2017); *Idem*, 'The Countess of Leicester and her Contribution to Holkham Hall', *Georgian Group Journal*, vol. 22 (2014), pp. 53–66, Frances Sands, 'Robert Adam's Female Patrons', *Georgian Group Journal*, vol. 30, pp. 91–124; Terence Dooley, Maeve O'Riordan and Christopher Ridgway (eds), *Women and the Country House in Ireland and Britain* (Dublin: Four Courts Press, 2018); Ruth Thorpe, *Women, Architecture and the Building in the East of Ireland, c.1790–1840* (Dublin: Four Courts Press, 2013); Finola O'Kane, '"Obliges Me to Dip My Hands in Mortar": Catherine O'Brien's Influence at Dromoland', *Irish Architectural and Decorative Studies*, vol. 7 (2007), pp. 80–105; Freya Gowrley, *Domestic Space in Britain, 1750–1840: Materiality, Sociability and Emotion* (London: Bloomsbury, 2022); Briony McDonagh, *Elite Women and the Agricultural Landscape, 1700–1830* (Abingdon: Routledge, 2018); Emma Purcell, *Women's Agency within the Montagu Property Network, c.1709–1827* (PhD thesis, University of Leicester, 2018); Rosemary Baird, *Mistress of the House: Great Ladies and Grand*

Houses 1670–1830 (London: Weidenfeld & Nicolson, 2003); Trevor Lummis and Jan Marsh, *The Woman's Domain: Women and the English Country House* (London: Penguin Books Ltd., 1993); Joanna Martin, *Wives and Daughters: Women and Children in the English Country House* (Hambledon and London: Continuum, 2004); Ruth Larsen (ed.), *Maids and Mistresses: Celebrating 300 Years of Women and the Country House* (York: Yorkshire Country House Partnership, 2004); Amanda Vickery, *Behind Closed Doors: At Home in Georgian England* (New Haven and London: Yale University Press, 2009); Amanda Vickery, *The Gentleman's Daughter: Women's Lives in Georgian England* (New Haven and London: Yale University Press, 1998); Dana Arnold, 'Defining Femininity: Women and the Country House', in Dana Arnold (ed.), *The Georgian Country House: Architecture, Landscape and Society* (Stroud: Sutton Publishing, 1998), pp. 79–99; Lucy Worsley, 'Female Architectural Patronage in the Eighteenth Century and the Case of Henrietta Cavendish Holles Harley', *Architectural History*, vol. 48 (2005), pp. 139–62; Judith S. Lewis, 'When a House Is Not a Home: Elite English Women and the Eighteenth-Century Country House', *Journal of British Studies*, vol. 48, no. 2 (2009), pp. 336–63.

7 Juliet Learmouth, 'Elite Women and the West End Town House: Creating, Maintaining and Inhabiting a Residence in London, *c.*1710–*c.*1750' (PhD thesis, Birkbeck, University of London, 2021); *idem*, 'The London Town House of Lady Isabella Finch', *The Georgian Group Journal*, vol. 25 (2017), pp. 73–94; Kerry Bristol, '22 Portman Square: Mrs Montagu and Her "Palais De La Vieillesse"', *British Art Journal*, vol. 2, no. 3 (2001), pp. 72–85.

8 For example, see John Harris, 'William Kent's 44 Berkeley Square', *Apollo*, vol. 126, no. 306 (August 1987), pp. 100–4; Clifford Musgrave, 'A London Palazzo: 44 Berkeley Square', *Connoisseur* (June 1964) pp. 74–80; Eileen Harris, 'Home House: Adam versus Wyatt', *The Burlington Magazine*, vol. 139, no. 1130 (May 1997), pp. 308–21.

9 Amy Louise Erickson, *Woman and Property* (London: Routledge, 1995), p. 24; *idem*, 'Common Law vs. Common Practice: The Use of Marriage Settlements in Early Modern England', *Economic History Review*, 2nd ser., vol. 43, no. 1 (1990), p. 24.

10 Erickson, *Women and Property*, pp. 102–51.

11 Ibid., p. 102.

12 For biographies of famous eighteenth-century courtesans, see Katie Hickman, *Courtesans* (London: HarperCollins, 2004); Barbara White, *Queen of the Courtesans: Fanny Murray* (Stroud: The History Press, 2014); Julie Peakman, *Peg Plunkett: Memoirs of a Whore* (London: Quercus Publishing Ltd., 2015).

13 See, Ann Bermingham, *Learning to Draw: Studies in the Cultural History of a Polite and Useful Art* (New Haven: Published for the Paul Mellon Centre for Studies in British Art by Yale University Press, 2000), pp. 183–227; Martin Postle, 'Arthur Pond, Doddington and the Patronage of the Delavals', in Martin Postle (ed.), *Art and the Country House* (Online Publication: Paul Mellon Centre, 2020).

14 The National Gallery of Art, Washington, DC, Andrew W. Mellon Collection, 1937.1.111, John Hoppner, *The Frankland Sisters*, 1795, oil on canvass.

15 Worcester Art Museum, Worcester, 1917.181, Thomas Gainsborough, *Portrait of an Artists Daughters*, 1763–4, oil on canvas, 127.3 × 101.7 cm.

16 For a discussion on female professional painters in the eighteenth century, see, for example, Paris Spies-Gans, *A Revolution on Canvas: The Rise of Women Artists in Britain and France, 1760–1830* (London: Paul Mellon Centre, 2022); Caroline Chapman, *Eighteenth-Century Women Artists: Their Trials, Tribulations and Triumphs* (London: Unicorn Publishing Group LLP, 2017); Wendy Wassyng Roworth (ed.), *Angelica Kauffman: A Continental Artist in Georgian England* (London: Reaktion Books, 1992).

17 Royal Collection Trust, RCIN 400747, Johan Zoffany, *The Academicians of the Royal Academy*, 1771–2, oil on canvas, 101.1 × 147.5 cm.

18 Amanda Vickery, 'Hidden from History: The Royal Academy's Female Founders', *RA Magazine* (June 2016), https://www.royalacademy.org.uk/article/ra-magazine-summer-2016-hidden-from-history#related-articles.

19 Ibid.

20 Kim Sloan, 'Alexander Cozens and Amateurs Drawn to Etch', *Print Quarterly*, vol. 28, no. 4 (December 2011), pp. 405–7; for surviving examples of Lady Amabel's work, see British Museum, London, inv. 1208.2603, 2604, 2606, 2608, reproduced in, Kim Sloan, *Alexander and John Robert Cozens: The Poetry of Landscape* (New Haven and London: Yale University Press, 1986), pp. 40–8, fig. 58.

21 David Adshead, 'Wedgwood, Wimpole and Wrest: The Landscape Drawings of Lady Amabel Polwarth', *Apollo* (April 1996), pp. 31–7.

22 For example, see, The Hermitage Museum, St Petersburg, ГЧ-9044, *Dessert Plate Ornamented with a View in Wrest Garden*, 1773–4, faience with overglaze painting; ГЧ-9152, *Dessert Plate Ornamented with a View of a Ruin at Wimpole, Cambridgeshire*, 1773–4, faience with overglaze painting.

23 Private collection of Leslie B. Durst, Margaret Eiston, *Scottish Sampler of Dalquharran Castle*, 1810, silk on linen.

24 Adam's designs were reproduced in Alistair Rowan, *Designs for Castles and Country Villas by Robert & James Adam* (Oxford: Rizzoli Publishing, 1985), plates 51 and 52.

25 Clarissa Campbell Orr, 'Conversations, Knowledge, and Influence', in Joanna Marschner, David Bindham and Lisa Ford (eds), *Enlightened Princesses: Caroline, Augusta, Charlotte, and the Shaping of the Modern World* (New Haven: Yale University Press and London: Historic Royal Palaces, 2017), p. 283.

26 Joshua Kirby, *Dr. Brook Taylor's Method of Perspective Made Easy; Both in Theory and Practice: In Two Books. Being an Attempt to Make the Art of Perspective Easy and Familiar; to Adapt It Entirely to the Arts of Design; and to Make It an Entertaining Study to Any Gentleman Who Shall Chuse so Polite an Amusement* … (London, 1768).

27 Museum of the History of Science, University of Oxford, inventory no. 23312.

28 Bedford and Luton Archive and Record Services (hereafter BLARS), L30/9/111/22, Mary Yorke to Marchioness Grey, 20 October 1779.

29 Lucy Rumble, '"Of Good Use or Serious Pleasure": *Vitruvius Britannicus* and Early Eighteenth Century Architectural Discourse' (PhD thesis, University of Leeds, 2001), p. 62.

30 For a discussion on Queen Caroline's library, see Emma Jay, 'Queen Caroline's Library and Its European Contexts', *Book History*, vol. 9 (2006), pp. 31–55.

31 James Stuart and Nicholas Revett, *The Antiquities of Athens* (London: John Haberkorn, 1762).

32 Abraham Rees, *The Cyclopaedia; or, Universal Dictionary of Arts, Sciences, and Literature* (London: Longman et al., 1803), unpaginated.

33 Anne Laurence, 'Women Using Building in Seventeenth-Century England: A Question of Sources?', *Transactions of the Royal Historical Society*, vol. 13 (2003), pp. 295–6; John Harris, 'Some Thoughts on the Amateur Invention in English Architecture', in *A Passion for Building: The Amateur Architect in England 1650–1850* an exhibition curated by John Harris and Robert Hradsky (London: Sir John Soane's Museum, 2007), p. 7.

34 Weston Park, Library, acc. no. 118.0539, Godfrey Richards, *The First Book of Architecture by Andrea Palladio* (1663).

35 Richard Hewlings, 'The Architect of Weston Park, Staffordshire', *Georgian Group Journal*, vol. 20 (2012), p. 22.

36 Ibid.

37 Harris, 'Some Thoughts', p. 8.

38 Gareth Williams, *Weston Park: The House, the Families and the Influence* (Woodbridge: Boydell & Brewer, 2002), pp. 15–35; Hewlings, 'The Architect of Weston Park', p. 23; Laurence, 'Women Using Building in Seventeenth-Century England', p. 295.

39 See, Judith Hill, 'Catherine Maria Bury of Charleville Castle, Co. Offaly, and the design of the country house, 1800–12', in Dooley, O'Riordan and Ridgway (eds), *Women and the Country House*, pp. 116–38.

40 As quoted in Gerald O'Carroll (ed.), *Robert Day: The Diaries and the Addresses to Grand Juries, 1793–1829* (Tralee: Polymath, 2004), pp. 224–5.

41 See, for example, Irish Architectural Archive, Charleville Forest Drawings Collection, 86/24/17, Charles William Bury, 1st Earl of Charleville (attr.), 'Perspective sketch of proposed castle at Charleville', *c.* 1800, ink and watercolour.

42 Hill, 'Catherine Maria Bury of Charleville Castle', p. 117.

43 British Museum, London, C,1.631–3, folded sheet of three visiting cards belonging to the Countess Charleville, with view of Charleville Castle, *c.* 1802–6, etching, 8 × 11.5 cm.

44 Recognized in the Dictionary of Irish Architects 1720–1940.

45 Ruth Thorpe, *Women, Architecture and Building in the East of Ireland, c.1790–1840* (Dublin: Four Courts Press, 2013), p. 14.

46 The plans of the principal and bed chamber floors are reproduced in Thorpe, *Women, Architecture and the Building in the East of Ireland*, p. 15, figs 5–6.

47 Reproduced in Thorpe, *Women, Architecture and Building in the East of Ireland*, p. 17, figs 7–8. The sketchbooks are in the possession of Eileen, Countess of Mount Charles.

48 Kent History and Library Centre, R/U774/P3, Mary Townley, small plan showing Farley House, a cottage and part of Queen Street, n.d., *c.* 1820.

49 Geraint Franklin, Nick Dermott and Allan Brodie, *Ramsgate: The Town and Its Seaside Heritage* (Swindon: Historic England, 2020), p. 47.

50 Ibid., pp. 47–9.

51 Ibid.

52 *The Repertory of Arts, Manufactures, and Agriculture*, vol. 17 (London: John Nichols & Son, 1810), p. 191.

53 For example, see 'Ladies Amusements', in John Fowler and John Cornforth, *English Decoration in the 18th Century* (London: Barrie and Jenkins, 1974), pp. 248–53; Katherine Sharpe, 'Women's Creativity and Display in the Eighteenth-Century British Interior', in Susie McKellar and Penny Sparke (eds), *Interior Design and Identity* (Manchester: Manchester University Press, 2004), pp. 10–26; Gowrley, *Domestic Space in Britain.*

54 For biographies, see Ophelia Field, *The Favourite: Sarah, Duchess of Marlborough* (London: Hodder and Stoughton, 2002); Frances Harris, *A Passion for Government: The Life of Sarah, Duchess of Marlborough* (Oxford: Clarendon Press, 1991) and David Green, *Sarah, Duchess of Marlborough* (London: Collins, 1967).

55 Field, *The Favourite*, p. 2.

56 Ibid., p. 3.

57 For discussions on Sarah's architectural patronage, for example, see Kathleen Szpila, 'Sarah Jenyns Churchill at Blenheim Palace – Setting the Record Straight: A Re-evaluation of the Activity of the First Duchess of Marlborough as Patron of the Arts' (PhD thesis, Temple University USA, 1997); *idem*, 'An Eighteenth-Century Artemisia: Sarah Churchill and the Invention of the Blenheim Memorials', in Cynthia Lawrence (ed.), *Women and Art in Early Modern Europe: Patrons, Collectors, and Connoisseurs* (Pennsylvania: State University Press, 1997), pp. 189–206; Marie P. G. Draper, 'When Marlborough's Duchess Built', *Country Life* (2 August 1962), pp. 248–50; Ruth Smith, 'Sarah, Duchess of Marlborough: An Analysis of Her Relationship with Architecture' (MA dissertation, Courtauld Institute of Art, University of London, 1998); Hilary Shepherd Webb, 'The Architectural Activity of Sarah Churchill, Duchess of Marlborough' (MA dissertation, Courtauld Institute of Art, University of London, 2011).

Chapter 2

1 See, for example, Mark Girouard, *Life in the English Country House: A Social and Architectural History* (London and New Haven: Yale University Press, 1978); T. C. W. Blanning, *The Culture of Power and the Power of Culture: Old Regime Europe 1660–1789* (Oxford: Oxford University Press, 2002); Peter

Mandler, *The Fall and Rise of the Stately Home* (New Haven: Yale University Press, 1997); Richard Wilson and Alan Mackley, *Creating Paradise: The Building of the English Country House* (London: Hambledon, 2000); Jeremy Musson and David Cannadine (eds), *The Country House: Past, Present, Future: Great Houses of The British Isles* (New York: Rizzoli, 2018).

2 Ingrid Tague, *Women of Quality: Accepting and Contesting Ideals of Femininity in England, 1690–1760* (Woodbridge: The Boydell Press, 2002), p. 98.

3 For an excellent discussion on Blenheim's iconographical programme, see James A. Legard, 'Vanbrugh, Blenheim Palace, and the Meanings of Baroque Architecture' (PhD thesis, University of York, 2013).

4 For details of Sarah's turbulent relationship with Vanbrugh, see Samuel J. Rogal, 'John Vanbrugh and the Blenheim Palace Controversy', *Journal of the Society of Architectural Historians*, vol. 33, no. 4 (1974), pp. 293–303.

5 Duke of Marlborough to Duchess of Marlborough, Meldert, 16/27 July 1707, in H. L. Snyder (ed.), *The Marlborough-Godolphin Correspondence* (Oxford: Oxford University Press, 1975) (henceforth MGC), vol. 2, p. 851.

6 Marlborough to Duchess of Marlborough, Meldert, 17/28 July 1707, in Snyder (ed.), *MGC*, vol. 2, p. 853.

7 Harris, *Passion for Government*, p. 211.

8 Duchess of Marlborough to Mrs Clayton, n.d., *c.* 1716, quoted in William Coxe, *Memoirs of John, Duke of Marlborough* (London: Longman et al., 1820), vol. 6, p. 372.

9 John Vanbrugh to Duchess of Marlborough, 8 November 1716, in Bonamy Dobrée and Geoffrey Webb (eds), *The Complete Works of Sir John Vanbrugh* (London: Nonsuch Press, 1927–8), vol. 4, p. 85.

10 The British Library (hereafter BL), Evelyn Papers, Add MS 78530, f. 12, Duchess of Marlborough to Mrs Jael Boscawen, 20 September 1718.

11 John Vanbrugh to Jacob Tonson, 18 June 1722, in Dobrée and Webb (eds), *The Complete Works*, vol. 4, p. 146.

12 Field, *The Favourite*, p. 455.

13 In 1713, Cassandra married as his second wife James Brydges, who was later created Earl of Carnarvon in 1714 and Duke of Chandos in 1719. For biographies of her life, see Joan Johnson, *Excellent Cassandra. The Life and Times of the Duchess of Chandos* (Gloucester: Sutton, 1981); Rosemary O'Day (ed.), *Cassandra Brydges, Duchess of Chandos, 1670–1735: Life and Letters* (Woodbridge: Boydell Press, 2007).

14 A. C. Wood (ed.), *The Continuation of the History of the Willoughby Family, by Cassandra, Duchess of Chandos* (Eton, Windsor: Shakespeare Head Press for University of Nottingham, 1958), p. 125.

15 Sir Francis Willoughby died in 1688 aged twenty years old; Elizabeth Hagglund, 'Cassandra Willoughby's Visits to Country Houses', *The Georgian Group Journal*, vol. 11 (2001), p. 186.

16 Elizabeth Hagglund, 'Willoughby, Cassandra [married name Cassandra Brydges, duchess of Chandos] (1670–1735)', in *Oxford Dictionary of National Biography Online (hereafter ODNB)* (Oxford: Oxford University Press, 2004).

17 For particular investigations into the architectural and art patronage of Theresa, see Lummis and Marsh, *The Woman's Domain*, pp. 63–76; Baird, *Mistress of the House*, pp. 220–36; Kate Retford, 'Reynolds's Portrait of Mrs Theresa Parker: A Case Study in Context', *British Art Journal*, vol. 4, no. 3 (2003), pp. 80–6.

18 Plymouth and West Devon Record Office (hereafter PWDRO), 1259/1/74, Anne Robinson to Frederick Robinson, Saltram, 16 July 1791.

19 PWDRO, 1259/2/309, Anne Robinson to Mrs Catherine Robinson, Saltram, 14 December 1796.

20 Ibid.

21 See, for example, Amanda Vickery's discussion of how the heroines in Jane Austen's novels have a penchant for interior design, Vickery, *Behind Closed Doors*, pp. 83–8; See also Sharpe, 'Women's Creativity and Display in the Eighteenth-century British Interior', in McKellar and Sparke (eds), *Interior Design and Identity*, pp. 10–26.

22 North Yorkshire County Records Office, Zetland Papers, KNK X1/2/18, Lawrence Dundas to Margaret Dundas, 18 November 1762, as quoted in Christopher Warleigh-Lack, 'John Carr of York and Hidden Architectural Histories' (PhD thesis, Middlesex University, 2013), p. 166.

23 Mary Delany to Anne Dewes, Delville, 26 July 1744, in Lady Llanover (ed.), *Autobiography and Correspondence of Mary Granville, Mrs. Delany*, 1st ser. (London, 1861), vol. 2, p. 319.

24 Mary Delany to Anne Dewes, Delville, 23 September 1744, in Llanover (ed.), *Autobiography*, 1st ser., vol. 2, p. 330.

25 Ibid.

26 Mary Delany to Anne Dewes, Delville, 15 September 1759, in Llanover (ed.), *Autobiography*, 1st ser., vol. 3, pp. 564–5.

27 Lady Kildare to Lord Kildare, 7 July 1757, in Brian Fitzgerald (ed.), *Correspondence of Emily, Duchess of Leinster, 1731–1814* (Dublin: Stationery Office, 1949), vol. 1, p. 59.

28 Lady Kildare to Lord Kildare, 10 May 1759, in Fitzgerald (ed.), *Correspondence*, vol. 1, p. 80.

29 Joanna Banham (ed.), *Encyclopaedia of Interior Design* (London and Chicago: Fitzroy Dearborn Publishers, 1997), p. 616.

30 For discussions on Chinoiserie, see Stacey Sloboda, *Chinoiserie: Commerce and Critical Ornament in Eighteenth-Century Britain* (Manchester: Manchester University Press, 2014); David Porter, *The Chinese Taste in Eighteenth-Century England* (Cambridge: Cambridge University Press, 2010).

31 Ibid.

32 Gillian Byrne, 'The Redecoration and Alteration of Castletown House by Lady Louisa Conolly 1759–76' (PhD thesis, Maynooth University, 1997), p. 28.

33 Ibid., pp. 37–9.

34 Ibid., p. 41.

35 Ibid., p. 43.

36 Banham, *Encyclopaedia*, p. 616.

37 Castletown House letters, Lady Louisa Connolly to Lady Sarah Lennox, 25 May 1768, as quoted in Byrne, 'Alteration of Castletown House', p. 49.

38 Lady Louisa Conolly to the Duchess of Leinster, 21 January 1773, as quoted in Byrne, 'Alteration of Castletown House', p. 76.

39 Castletown House Letters, Lady Louisa Conolly to Lady Sarah Bunbury, 2 November 1774, as quoted in Byrne, 'Alteration of Castletown House', p. 78.

40 Lady Louisa Conolly to the Duchess of Leinster, 25 June 1775, in Fitzgerald (ed.), *Correspondence*, vol. 3, p. 141.

41 Ibid.

42 Marquess of Kildare to the Duchess of Leinster, 24 February 1767, Naples, in Fitzgerald (ed.), *Correspondence*, vol. 3, p. 459.

43 Castletown House Letters, Lady Louisa Conolly to Lady Sarah Bunbury, 17 August 1776, as quoted in Byrne, 'Alteration of Castletown House', p. 82.

44 The Soane Museum (hereafter 'SM'), Journal No. 5, 17 June 1809, p. 126.

45 SM, Journal No. 6, 18 September 1813, p. 64.

46 Edward Boscawen to Frances Boscawen, *Invincible*, 17 May 1756, in Peter Kemp (ed.), 'Boscawen's Letters to His Wife, 1755–1756', in Christopher Lloyd (ed.), *The Naval Miscellany* (London: Navy Records Society, 1952), vol. 4, pp. 209–10.

47 Edward Boscawen to Frances Boscawen, Whitehall 6 June 1756, in Kemp (ed.), 'Boscawen's Letters', p. 219.

48 Frances Boscawen to Edward Boscawen, Level's Grove, 21 September 1757, in Cecil Aspinall-Oglander (ed.), *Admiral's Wife, Being the Life and Times of the Hon. Mrs Edward Boscawen from 1719 to 1761* (London: Longmans, Green & Co., 1940), p. 256.

49 Edward Boscawen to Frances Boscawen, *Royal George?*, 18 August 1756, in Kemp (ed.), 'Boscawen's Letters', p. 246.

50 For discussions of the Bluestocking society, see Elizabeth Eger, *Bluestockings: Women of Reason from the Enlightenment to Romanticism* (Basingstoke: Palgrave Macmillan, 2010); Elizabeth Eger (ed.), *Bluestockings Displayed: Portraiture, Performance and Patronage, 1730–1830* (Cambridge: Cambridge University Press, 2013); Elizabeth Eger and Lucy Peltz, *Brilliant Women: 18th-Century Bluestockings* (New Haven: Yale University Press, 2008); Sylvia Harcstark Myers, *The Bluestocking Circle: Women, Friendship, and the Life of the Mind in Eighteenth-Century England* (Oxford: Clarendon Press, 1990); Vivien Jones (ed.), *Women in the Eighteenth Century: Constructions of Femininity* (London and New York: Routledge, 1990); Gary Kelly (ed.), *Bluestocking Feminism: Writings of the Bluestocking Circle, 1738–1785*, 6 vols (London: Pickering & Chatto, 1999); Karen O'Brien, *Women and Enlightenment in Eighteenth-Century Britain* (Cambridge: Cambridge University Press, 2009).

51 National Portrait Gallery, NPG 4905, Richard Samuel, *Portraits in the Characters of the Muses in the Temple of Apollo*, 1778, oil and canvas, 132.1 × 154.9 cm.

52 Eger, *Bluestockings*, p. 1.

53 For a discussion on female learning, see Jacqueline Pearson, *Women's Reading in Britain, 1750–1835: A Dangerous Recreation* (Cambridge: Cambridge University Press, 1999).

54 William Napier to Mary Hamilton, August 1772, in Elizabeth and Florence Anson (eds), *Mary Hamilton: Afterwards Mrs. John Dickenson, at Court and at Home. From Letters and Diaries, 1756 to 1816* (London: John Murray, Albemarle Street, 1925), p. 17.

55 Quoted in Joseph Rykwert and Anne Rykwert, *Robert and James Adam: The Men and the Style (Architectural Documents)* (New York: Electa/Rizzoli, 1985), p. 53.

56 Lydia Greeves, *Houses of the National Trust* (London: National Trust Books, 2008), p. 164.

57 SM, Adam volume 11/3, [7] 'Ceiling for Admiral Boscawens Drawing Room', now the library, as executed, 1759.

58 Boyington, 'Maids, Wives and Widows', pp. 133–4.

59 See, Peter Sherlock, 'Monuments and Memory', in Patricia Phillippy (ed.), *A History of Early Modern Women's Writing* (Cambridge: Cambridge University Press, 2018), pp. 292–311.

60 Szpila, 'An Eighteenth-Century Artemisia', p. 196.

61 SM, Adam volume 54/2/20 [1] and 54/2/17 [2] belong to scheme one; 54/2/25 [3], 54/2/24 [4], 54/2/28 [5] and 19/23 [6] belong to scheme two; 54/2/32 [7] and 19/5 [8] belong to scheme three; 54/2/31 [9], 19/4 [10] and 19/3 [11] belong to scheme four; 54/2/18 [12], 54/2/29 [13] and 19/2 [14] belong to scheme five.

62 SM, Adam volume 19/1 [15], 'Design for a Monument for the Right Honble Admiral Boscawen', as executed, 1761.

63 Corinne Miller and Sylvia Thomas (eds), *Drawing from the Past: William Weddell and the Transformation of Newby Hall* (Leeds: Leeds Museums and Galleries, 2004), p. 27.

64 BLARS, L30/11/240/4, Lady Grantham to Lady Polwarth, Newby Park, 3 October 1780.

65 BLARS, L30/11/240/1, Lady Grantham to Lady Polwarth, Newby Park, 29 August 1780.

66 BLARS, L30/11/240/4, Lady Grantham to Lady Polwarth, Newby Park, 3 October 1780.

67 BLARS, L30/11/240/18, Lady Grantham to Lady Polwarth, Newby Park, 10 August 1781.

68 Ibid.

69 BLARS, L30/9/81/52, Lady Grantham to Lady Grey, Newby Park, 14 June 1783.

70 Sir George Lyttelton to Sanderson Miller, June 1752, Tunbridge, quoted in Lillian Dickins and Mary Stanton, *An Eighteenth-Century Correspondence* (London: John Murray, 1910), p. 285.

71 Nikolaus Pevsner, rev. by Alan Brooks, *Worcestershire* [rev. and expanded edn] (New Haven, CT and London: Yale University Press, 2007), p. 335.

72 Quoted in Dickins and Stanton, *Correspondence,* p. 284; Numerous surviving plans and drawings by Chute are located at The Lewis Walpole Library, Folio 49 3490, 'Slight sketches of architecture' by John Chute, Esq., of the Vine in Hampshire, 1753.

73 For the building of Hagley Hall, see Michael McCarthy, 'The Building of Hagley Hall, Worcestershire', *The Burlington Magazine*, vol. 118, no. 877 (1976), pp. 214–25; Michael Cousins, 'Hagley Park, Worcestershire', *Garden History*, vol. 35 (2007), pp. iii–iv, vi–xii, and 1–152.

74 Quoted in Dickins and Stanton, *Correspondence*, p. 283.

75 Sir George Lyttelton to Sanderson Miller, June 1754, quoted in Dickins and Stanton, *Correspondence,* p. 287.

76 Saltram House, NT 871169, presentation drawing of a proposed elevation for a house, *c.* 1740s, pen and coloured wash.

77 Lady Lyttelton to Sanderson Miller, May 1753, quoted in Dickins and Stanton, *Correspondence,* pp. 286–7.

78 Helen Berry, *The Castrato and His Wife* (Oxford: Oxford University Press, 2011), pp. 54–7.

79 Mary Delany to Bernard Granville (her brother), Mount Panther, 29 August 1763, in Llanover (ed.), *Correspondence,* 2nd ser., vol. 1, p. 21.

80 Patricia U. Bonomi, 'Lord Cornbury Redressed: The Governor and the Problem Portrait', *The William and Mary Quarterly*, vol. 51, no. 1 (January 1994), pp. 106–18.

81 Public Records Office of Northern Ireland, Tighe Papers, D/2685/14/1, typescript family history entitled 'The Tighe Story' by Rear-Admiral W. G. S. Tighe, p. 21.

82 A. P. W. Malcomson, *The Pursuit of an Heiress: Aristocratic Marriage in Ireland 1740–1840* (Belfast: Ulster Historic Foundation, 2006), p. 237.

83 Countess of Moira to Countess Thun?, *c.* 1796, as quoted in Anthony Malcomson, 'A Woman Scorned? Theodosia, Countess of Clanwilliam (1743–1817)', *Familia: Ulster Genealogical Review*, vol. 2, no. 15 (1999), p. 16.

84 S. J. Connolly, 'A Woman's Life in Mid Eighteenth-Century Ireland: The Case of Letitia Bushe', *The Historical Journal*, vol. 43, no. 2 (June 2000), pp. 433–51.

85 For a short biography of Marchioness Grey, see Joyce Godber, 'Marchioness Grey of Wrest Park', *Bedfordshire Historical Society*, vol. 47 (1968), entire volume. Although a good introduction to Marchioness Grey and her circle, the work neglects her architectural involvement; see also ODNB online, 'Yorke, Jemima, suo jure Marchioness Grey (1722–1797)'.

86 BL, 17th–18th Century Burney Collection Newspapers, *London Gazette*, Issue 7914, 27–31 May 1740.

87 The primary discussion on the history of the old Wrest Park from 1700 onwards is to be found in James Collett-White, 'The Old House at Wrest – Part II', *The Bedfordshire Magazine*, vol. 23, no. 177 (summer 1991), pp. 4–12. This only briefly touches upon Marchioness Grey's involvement and is repeated in James Collett-White (ed.), 'Inventories of Bedfordshire Country Houses, 1714–1830', *Bedfordshire Historical Record Society*, vol. 74 (1995), pp. 243–51.

88 BLARS, L31/230-41, building accounts, *c.* 1676; briefly discussed in James Collett-White (ed.), 'Inventories', pp. 244–5.

89 BLARS, L30/9a/2/32, Lady Grey to Lady Mary Gregory, Wrest, 14 May 1749.

90 BLARS, L31/260, John Smith to Philip Yorke, Kensington Palace, 13 October 1763.

91 BLARS, L31/263 for the final presentation drawing; L31/266, 'Estimate for building the Drawing room &c at Wrest', John Smith, n.d., *c.* 1763.

92 BLARS, L31/273, Bill for hanging Indian paper, n.d., *c.* 1760s.

93 BLARS, L31/277, Estimate for the alterations at Wrest Park, 1791.

94 See, Boyington, 'The Architectural Endeavours of the Widowed Jemima Yorke, Marchioness Grey', in Dooley, O'Riordan and Ridgway (eds), *Women and the Country House*, pp. 15–32.

95 For a detailed discussion on Lady Oxford's architectural endeavours at Welbeck, see Worsley, 'Female Architectural Patronage', pp. 139–62; Peter Smith, 'Lady Oxford's Alterations at Welbeck Abbey 1741–55', *Georgian Group Journal*, vol. 11 (2001), pp. 133–68.

96 For a discussion on ancestral reverence in country houses, see Jonny Yarker, 'Continuity and the Country House: Preservation as a Strategy of Display from 1688 to 1950', in Martin Postle (ed.), *Art and the Country House* (Online Publication: Paul Mellon Centre, 2020).

97 Bess has received considerable academic attention, for example, see Kate Hubbard, *Devices and Desires: Bess of Hardwick and the Building of Elizabethan England* (London: Chatto & Windus, 2018); Sara French, 'A Widow Building in Elizabethan England: Bess of Hardwick at Hardwick Hall', in Allison Levy (ed.), *Widowhood and Visual Culture in Early Modern Europe* (London: Routledge, 2003), pp. 161–76.

98 For a discussion of Hardwick Hall, see David Adshead and David A. H. B. Taylor (eds), *Hardwick Hall: A Great Old Castle of Romance* (New Haven: Yale University Press, 2016).

99 BL, Portland Papers, Add. MS 70432, Misc 13a, Draft letter, Lady Oxford to Lady Mary Wortley Montagu, Dover Street, 7 June 1744.

100 BL, Portland Papers, Add. MS 70432, Misc. 13a, Draft letter, Lady Oxford to Lady Mary Wortley Montagu, Dover Street, 7 June 1740.

101 BL, Portland Papers, Add. MS 70432, Misc 13b, Draft letter, Lady Oxford to Lady Mary Wortley Montagu, Welbeck, 17 October 1747.

102 Lady Mary Wortley Montagu to Lady Oxford, Avignon, 2 July 1744 in Robert Halsband (ed.), *The Complete Letters of Lady Mary Wortley Montagu, 1721–1751* (Oxford: Oxford University Press, 1966), vol. 2, p. 332.

103 Worsley, 'Female Architectural Patronage', pp. 155–6.

104 Nottinghamshire Archives, DDP5.6/26/19 and 14, 1750, cited in Worsley, 'Female Architectural Patronage', p. 145.

105 BL, Portland Papers, Add. MS 70432, Misc 13a, Draft letter, Lady Oxford to Lady Mary Wortley Montagu, Dover Street, 7 June 1744.

106 Ibid.

107 See, Kate Retford, 'Patrilineal Portraiture? Gender and Genealogy in the Eighteenth-Century Country House', in J. Styles and A. Vickery (eds), *Gender, Taste, and Material Culture in Britain and North America, 1700–1830* (New Haven: Yale Centre for British Art, 2006), p. 329.

108 A comprehensive biography can be found in Beatrice Scott, 'Lady Elizabeth Hastings', *The Yorkshire Archaeological Journal*, vol. 55 (1983), pp. 109–12.

109 For discussions on Lady Betty's finances and investing activity, see Anne Laurence, 'Lady Betty Hastings (1682–1739): Godly Patron', *Women's History Review*, vol. 19, no. 2 (2010), pp. 201–13; Anne Laurence, 'Women Investors, "That Nasty South Sea Affair" and the Rage to Speculate in Early Eighteenth-Century England', *Accounting, Business and Financial History*, vol. 16, no. 2 (2006), pp. 245–64; Anne Laurence, 'Lady Betty Hastings, Her Half-Sisters and the South Sea Bubble: Family Fortunes and Strategies', *Women's History Review*, vol. 15, no. 4 (2006), pp. 533–40.

110 Diary entry of Ralph Thoresby, 14 February 1721, in Rev. John Hunter (ed.), *The Diary of Ralph Thoresby, F. R. S., Author of the Topography of Leeds (1677–1724)* (London: Henry Colburn and Richard Bentley, 1830), vol. 2, p. 313.

111 Reuben and Sholto Percy, *The Percy Anecdotes: Women* (London: T. Boys, 1822), p. 132.

112 Howard Colvin, *A Biographical Dictionary of British Architects 1600–1840*, 3rd edn (New Haven, CT and London: Yale University Press, 1995), p. 122.

113 Colvin, *Dictionary of British Architects*, p. 978; Linstrum, *West Yorkshire: Architects*, p. 61.

114 Rebecca Burrows on behalf of Purcell, 'Ledston Hall Heritage Statement' (2014), pp. 42–3.

115 BL, Coke Papers, Add. MS 69965, ff. 45–6, plasterers bill, n.d.

116 BL, Coke Papers, Add. MS 69965, f. 53, rough plan of chapel floor, n.d.

117 BL, Coke Papers, Add. MS 69965, f. 47, note relating to the paving of the chapel floor, n.d.

118 BL, Coke Papers, Add. MS 69965, f. 48, rough armorial sketch, n.d.

119 BL, Coke Papers, Add. MS 69965, f. 49, sketch of the chapel wall, n.d.

120 For a detailed discussion on Lady Leicester's involvement at Holkham, see Amy Boyington, 'Margaret Coke, Countess of Leicester: A Re-evaluation of Her Contributions to Holkham' (Master's dissertation, University of Cambridge, 2013); Boyington, 'The Countess of Leicester and Her Contribution to Holkham Hall', pp. 53–66.

121 Holkham Hall Archives (hereafter HHA), DD/FD 56B (1), Office Copy of the Will and Codicil of Thomas Earl of Leicester, 1759.

122 HHA, H/Inv 7, Lady Leicester's inventory annotated as 'an exact account of the furniture in Holkham House bought by Lady Leicester to compleat the apartments, and what she bought from Russell Street, and also the furniture she has removed to different rooms', with records of purchases from May 1759 to November 1765; H/Inv1, Lady Leicester's inventory which contains an accumulative total of £3096 05s. 08d. that she spent on furnishing Holkham from 1752 to 1771.

123 HHA, E/A/44, 'An account made by Ralph Cauldwell of all money paid by him for carrying on the buildings at Holkham as directed by the will of the late Right Honble Thomas Earl of Leicester', 1760–66, f. 40, 1764; Boyington, 'Countess of Leicester: A Re-evaluation', p. 55.

124 John Chambers, *A General History of the County of Norfolk, Intended to Convey All the Information of a Norfolk Tour* (Norwich: John Stacy, 1829), vol. 2, p. 598.

125 Matthew Brettingham [sr.], *The Plans, Elevations and Sections of Holkham in Norfolk* (London: Haberkorn, 1761), plates 14–15.

126 Matthew Brettingham [jr], *The Plans, Elevations and Sections of Holkham in Norfolk, The Seat of the late Earl of Leicester, to Which Are Added, The Ceilings and Chimney Pieces; and also, A Descriptive Account of the Statues, Pictures, and Drawings; Not in the Former Edition* (London, 1773), p. 15.

127 For a detailed discussion, see Boyington, 'Countess of Leicester: A Re-evaluation', pp. 43–7.

128 HHA, E/A/44, f. 47, Account Book 1760–6, 16 November 1765.

129 PWDRO, 1259/1/214, Lady Grantham to Frederick Robinson, Putney Heath, 30 July 1790.

130 For more detail upon the provenance and movement of the furniture, see Judith Goodison, 'A Puzzle Solved: Furniture at Newby Hall, Yorkshire', *The Burlington Magazine*, vol. 151, no. 1270 (January 2009), pp. 28–31.

131 PWDRO, 1259/1/218, Lady Grantham to Frederick Robinson, Wrest Park, 18 August 1790.

132 For discussions on the architectural history of Newby Hall, see Corinne Miller and Sylvia Thomas (eds), *Drawing from the Past: William Weddell and the Transformation of Newby Hall* (Leeds: Leeds Museums and Galleries, 2004); Jill Low, 'Newby Hall: Two Late Eighteenth-Century Inventories', *Furniture History*, vol. 22 (1986), pp. 135–75.

133 BLARS, L30/11/240/66, Lady Grantham to Lady Polwarth, Newby Hall, 3 August 1797.

134 He is referred to two years later in 1799, in PWDRO, 1259/2/480, Lady Grantham to Mrs Catherine Robinson, Putney Heath, 21 November 1799.

135 PWDRO, 1259/2/458, Lady Grantham to Mrs Catherine Robinson, Newby Hall, 12 September 1799.

136 BLARS, L30/11/240/100, Lady Grantham to Lady Polwarth, Newby Hall, 22 July 1800.

137 PWDRO, 1259/2/480, Lady Grantham to Mrs Catherine Robinson, Putney Heath, 21 November 1799.

138 The complex building programme of the new Peper Harow house has previously been discussed, see Michael Snodin (ed.), *Sir William Chambers* (London: V&A Publications, 1996), p. 158; John Harris, *Sir William Chambers: Knight of the Polar Star* (London: A. Zwemmer Ltd., 1970), pp. 240–1.

139 Surrey History Centre (hereafter SHC), 1567/1&2, Brown's plans of the ground and first floors, n.d.; G145/92/86, Brown's plan of the second floor, n.d.; 1567/3, plan showing 'Elevation of South-West Front with Bow Window in Center', 1752.

140 SHC, G145/91/4&5, John Vardy's plans, 1753; G145/92/46-47, for 'Mr Flitcroft's Plans', n.d.

141 John Harris and Michael Snodin (eds), *Sir William Chambers: Architect to George III* (New Haven and London: Yale University Press, 1996), p. 85.

142 SHC, G145/Box64/8, f. 6 r., account book covering 3rd Lord Midleton's minority, 29 September 1767.

143 Ibid.

144 SHC, G145/Box64/8, account book covering 3rd Lord Midleton's minority, 1765–76.

145 SHC, G145/Box64/8, f. 6 r., account book covering 3rd Lord Midleton's minority, 29 September 1767.

146 SHC, G145/Box44, f. 1 r., 28 October 1765; f. 40 r., 8 February 1768 and 4 March 1768.

147 SHC, G145/Box44, f. 9 v., 20 February 1766.

148 SHC, G145/Box44, f. 23 v., 7 March 1767; G145/Box44, f. 33 v., 8 February 1768.

149 SHC, G145/Box44, f. 36 v., 8 February 1768.

150 Vickery, *Behind Closed Doors*, pp. 94–5.

151 Hannah More to her sister, Holywell House, March 1784, in William Roberts (ed.), *Memoirs of the Life and Correspondence of Mrs. Hannah More* (New York: Harper and Brothers, 1834), vol. 1, p. 179.

152 For a discussion on this transformation, see Frances Harris, 'Holywell House: A Gothic Villa at St Albans', *British Library Journal* (1986), pp. 176–83.

153 BL, Althorp Papers, Add. MS 75623, Lady Spencer to Mrs Howe, 5 May 1784.

154 Ibid.

155 BL, Althorp Papers. Add. MS 75684, Lord Harcourt to Lady Spencer, 29 April 1784.

156 Ibid.

157 Ibid.

158 Ibid.

159 BL, Althorp Papers, Add. MS 75684, Lord Harcourt to Lady Spencer, Nuneham, 15 June 1784.

160 BL, Althorp Papers, Add. MS 75622, Lady Spencer to Mrs Howe, 6 April 1784.

161 BL, Althorp Papers, Add. MS 75622, Mrs Howe to Lady Spencer, 8 April 1784.

162 BL, Althorp Papers, Add. MS 75622, Lady Spencer to Mrs Howe, 15 April 1784; BL, Althorp Papers, Add. MS 75622, Lady Spencer to Mrs Howe, 26 April 1784.

163 BL, Althorp Papers, Add. MS 75627, Lady Spencer to Mrs Howe, 22 June 1785.

164 For Stoke's architectural and archaeological histories, see Kirsty Rodwell, 'The Dower House, Stoke Park, Bristol: A Study in Structural Archaeology', *Post-Medieval Archaeology*, vol. 42, no. 1 (2008), pp. 1–48; David Lambert and Stewart Harding, 'Thomas Wright at Stoke Park', *Garden History*, vol. 17, no. 1 (1989), pp. 68–82.

165 Neil Jeffares, 'Two English Portraits by Liotard: Lady Anne Somerset and Catherine, Lady Hawke', *British Art Journal*, vol. 15, no. 3 (Spring 2015), p. 6.

166 See William Evans, 'Paradise on a Limited Budget: How Norborne Berkeley Funded His Improvements at Stoke Park', *Trans. Bristol & Gloucestershire Archaeological Society*, vol. 12, no. 6 (2008), pp. 157–65.

167 Gloucester Archives (hereafter 'GA'), D2700/QP4/6/4, letters to the Dowager Duchess of Beaufort from Silas and Jonas Blandford enclosing accounts, 1771–87.

168 GA, 2700/QP4/6/4, Silas Blandford to the Dowager Duchess of Beaufort, Stoke, 17 July 1776.

169 GA, 2700/QP4/6/4, Dowager Duchess of Beaufort to Silas Blandford, 17 April 1777.

170 'M' in Geoffrey Beard and Christopher Gilbert (eds), *Dictionary of English Furniture Makers 1660–1840* (Leeds: Furniture History Society, 1986), pp. 563–638; *British History Online*, http://www.british-history.ac.uk/no-series/dict-english-furniture-makers/m [accessed 19 June 2020]; Badminton Muniments, D2700/RE2/1/1, 2, 3, 4 John Capper's account of household expenses, countersigned by the Duchess, including Ince and Mayhew, 1789, 1790–2, 1793–5, 1796–8.

171 For example, see D2700/RE2/1/3, John Capper's account of household expenses; countersigned by the Duchess, 1792–1795.

172 GA, D2700/QP4/6/1, Charles Evans to the Dowager Duchess of Beaufort, London 3 August 1782; GA, D2700/QP4/6/1, Charles Evans to the Dowager Duchess of Beaufort, 1789.

173 GA, D2700/QP4/6/1, Charles Evans to the Dowager Duchess of Beaufort, London 3 August 1782.

174 GA, D2700/QP4/6/4, Silas Blandford to the Dowager Duchess of Beaufort, Stoke, 5 July 1777.

175 GA, D2700/QP3/4/8, part 1, f.143 r, 2 February 1791; GA, 2700/QP3/4/8, part 1, f.161 r, 20 April 1791.

176 GA, D2700/QP3/1/6, f. 97 r, 'Stoke Rental One Year Michs 1796 & Disbursements Ending May 12th 1797'.

Chapter 3

1 Rachel Stewart, *The Town House in Georgian London* (London: Yale University Press, 2009), p. 28.

2 Ibid., p. 29.

3 'Grosvenor Square: Introduction', in F. H. W. Sheppard (ed.), *Survey of London: Volume 40, the Grosvenor Estate in Mayfair, Part 2 (The Buildings)* (London: London County Council, 1980), pp. 112–17. *British History Online*, http://www.british-history.ac.uk/survey-london/vol40/pt2/pp112-117 [accessed 20 April 2021].

4 Ibid.

5 Ibid.

6 See Andrew Carrington Shelton, 'Storming the Acropolis: Gender, Class and Classicism in Eighteenth-Century England', in Elise Goodman (ed.), *Art and Culture in the Eighteenth Century: New Dimensions and Multiple Perspectives* (Newark: University of Delaware Press, 2001), pp. 125–41; Stanley Harris, *A Letter Written by Sarah Clayton of Liverpool from Bath in 1749, with Some Notes on the Writer and on John Wood the Elder, Architect* (1948).

7 Rachel Stewart, 'Choice and Reasoning in the Eighteenth-Century London House', *Revue belge de Philologie et d'Histoire*, vol. 94, no. 2 (2016), pp. 371–2.

8 'Grosvenor Square: Introduction' in *Survey of London*, pp. 112–17. *British History Online*, http://www.british-history.ac.uk/survey-london/vol40/pt2/pp112-117 [accessed 20 April 2021].

9 See Kate Retford and Susanna Avery-Quash (eds), *The Georgian London Town House Building: Collecting and Display* (London; New York: Bloomsbury Visual Arts, 2019).

10 Stewart, *The Georgian Town House*, p. 38.

11 Anon., 'Beware the Ides of January, or Advice to the FAIR, on Their Return to London', *Gentleman's Magazine*, viii (January 1738), p. 30.

12 Julie Schlarman, 'The Social Geography of Grosvenor Square: Mapping Gender and Politics, 1720–1760', *The London Journal*, vol. 28, no. 1 (2003), pp. 18.

13 Ibid.

14 Anna Clark, 'Women in Eighteenth-Century British Politics', in S. Knott and B. Taylor (eds), *Women, Gender and Enlightenment* (London: Palgrave Macmillan, 2005), pp. 570–86.

15 Robert Scott-Moncrieff (ed.), *The Household Book of Lady Grisel Baille 1692–1733*, 2nd ser. (Edinburgh: Scottish History Society, 1911), vol. 1, p. xxxiv.

16 21 June 1715, London, in Scott-Moncrieff (ed.), *Household Book*, p. 34.

17 24 June 1715, London, in Scott-Moncrieff (ed.), *Household Book*, p. 35.

18 30 July 1715, London, in Scott-Moncrieff (ed.), *Household Book*, p. 35; 7 Aug 1715, London, in Scott-Moncrieff (ed.), *Household Book*, p. 35.

19 26 Aug 1715, London, in Scott-Moncrieff (ed.), *Household Book*, p. 181; 16 November 1715, London, in Scott-Moncrieff (ed.), *Household Book*, p. 188.

20 26 August 1715, in Scott-Moncrieff (ed.), *Household Book*, p. 181; 18 September 1715, in Scott-Moncrieff (ed.), *Household Book*, p. 183.

21 16 November 1715, London, in Scott-Moncrieff (ed.), *Household Book*, p. 187.

22 Sir Lawrence Dundas to Lady Dundas, 3 March 1766, as quoted in Arthur T. Bolton, *The Architecture of Robert and James Adam, 1758–1794* (London: Country Life; Southampton: George Newnes, 1922), vol. 2, p. 354.

23 For a discussion on the Duchess's patronage, see Baird, *Mistress of the House*, pp. 132–54; Clare Haynes, 'Of Her Making: The Cultural Practice of Mary, 9th Duchess of Norfolk', *Tulsa Studies in Women's Literature*, vol. 31, no. 1/2 (2012), pp. 77–98. For a recent discussion on Norfolk House, see Jeremy Howard, '"You never saw such a scene of magnificence and taste": Norfolk House after Its Grand Reopening in 1756', in Avery-Quash and Retford (eds), *The Georgian London Town House*, pp. 49–70.

24 As quoted in Baird, *Mistress of the House*, p. 138.

25 Horace Walpole to Henry Seymour Conway, Arlington Street, 12 February 1756, in W. S. Lewis (ed.), *The Yale Edition of Horace Walpole's Correspondence*, 48 vols (New Haven: Yale University Press, 1937–83), vol. 37, p. 438.

26 Duke of Marlborough to the Duchess of Marlborough, 3/14 June 1708?, in Snyder (ed.), *MGC*, vol. 2, p. 1003.

27 Quoted in Green, *Blenheim Palace*, p. 106.

28 Howard Colvin (ed.), *The History of the King's Works* (London: HMSO, 1976), vol. 5, p. 471.

29 Ibid., p. 1090.

30 Quoted in Green, *Blenheim Palace*, p. 106.

31 BL, Blenheim Papers, Add. MS 61357, ff. 8–9, Christopher Wren [jr] to the Duchess of Marlborough, Whitehall, 8 March 1710/19 March 1711.

32 Quoted in Green, *Blenheim Palace*, p. 106.

33 For a discussion on Laguerre's murals, see Lydia Hamlett, 'Rupture through Realism: Sarah Churchill and Louis Laguerre's Murals at Marlborough House', in Mark Hallett, Martin Myrone and Nigel Llewellyn (eds), *Court, Country, City: British Art and Architecture, 1660–1735* (New Haven and London: Yale Center for British Art: The Paul Mellon Centre for Studies in British Art, 2016); Lydia Hamlett, *Mural Painting in Britain 1630–1730: Experiencing Histories* (London: Abingdon, 2020), pp. 116–20.

34 Lady Hervey to Rev. Morris, London, 10 December 1747, in Lady Hervey, *Letters of Mary Lepel, Lady Hervey: With a Memoir and Illustrative Notes* (London: John Murray, 1821), p. 111.

35 Lady Hervey to Rev. Morris, Ickworth Park, 25 January 1748, in Hervey, *Letters of Mary Lepel*, p. 117.

36 Lucy Moore, *Amphibious Thing: The Life of Lord Hervey* (London: Penguin Group, 2000), p. 218.

37 For references to the fraught relationship between Lady Hervey and Lady Bristol, see Moore, *Amphibious Thing*, pp. 18–19, 54, 98.

38 Lord Chesterfield to his son Philip Stanhope, London, 22 October 1750, in Lord Chesterfield, *The Works of Lord Chesterfield* (New York: Harper & Brothers, 1860), p. 355.

39 For example, see National Trust, Ickworth, NT 3095099: François-Marie-Arouet Voltaire, *Voltaire Oeuvres de Mr. de Voltaire*, vols 1–4 (Amsterdam: Etienne Ledet & Company, 1738–9).

40 On Chesterfield House, see for example, Roger White, 'Isaac Ware and Chesterfield House', in Charles Hind (ed.), *The Rococo in England: A Symposium* (London: Victoria and Albert Museum, 1986), pp. 175–92; Diana Cheng, 'Lord Chesterfields Boudoir: A Room without the Sulks', in Christina Smylitopoulos (ed.), *Agents of Space: Eighteenth-Century Art, Architecture, and Visual Culture* (Newcastle: Cambridge Scholars, 2016), pp. 154–73.

41 Lady Hervey to Rev. Morris, London, 14 November 1748, in Hervey, *Letters of Mary Lepel*, pp. 138–9.

42 Ibid., p. 139.

43 Quoted in Dorothy M. Stuart, *Molly Lepell, Lady Hervey* (London: George G. Harrap & Co. Ltd., 1936), p. 119.

44 Frances Russell to Lieutenant-Colonel Charles Russell, 26 August 1743, published in HMC Russell-Astley, *Report on the Manuscripts of Mrs. Frankland-Russell-Astley, of Chequers Court, Bucks* (London: Her Majesty's Stationery Office, 1900), p. 285.

45 Moore, *Amphibious Thing*, p. 91.

46 William Pulteney, '*A Proper Reply to a Late Scurrilous Libel; Intitled, Sedition and Defamation Display'd (1731)*', in H. T. Dickinson (ed.), *British Ideas and Issues, 1660–1820*, 2 (New York: AMS Press, 1723; 1998), pp. xxi and 46.

47 For discussions of Lord Hervey's life and relationships, see Moore, *Amphibious Thing*; Robert Halsband, *Lord Hervey: Eighteenth-Century Courtier* (Oxford: Clarendon Press, 1973); Rictor Norton (ed.), 'The Gay Love Letters of John, Lord Hervey to Stephen Fox', in *idem*, *My Dear Boy: Gay Love Letters through the Centuries* (San Francisco: Leyland Publications, 1998), pp. 87–92.

48 For Hervey's relationship with Anne Vane, see Moore, *Amphibious Thing*, pp. 95–7, 137–45; Halsband, *Lord Hervey*, pp. 128–9, 135–9.

49 Moore, *Amphibious Thing*, p. 91; Halsband, *Lord Hervey*, p. 104.

50 Lady Hervey to Rev. Morris, Ickworth Park, 2 April 1748, in Hervey, *Letters of Mary Lepel*, p. 125.

51 Lady Louisa Stuart to Louisa Cinton, January 1822, in Hon. James A. Home (ed.), *Letters of Lady Louisa Stuart to Miss Louisa Clinton* (Edinburgh: David Douglas, 1901), vol. 1, p. 225.

52 Edith A. Standen, 'Country Children: Some Enfants De Boucher in Gobelins Tapestry', *Metropolitan Museum Journal*, vol. 29 (1994), p. 111.

53 The Metropolitan Museum, New York, 14.58.193, Nutmeg or spice box with arms of Mary, Lady Hervey of Ickworth, 1743–68, silver, maker unknown.

54 National Trust, Ickworth, NT 851727, Hubert Gravelot, with Jean-Etienne Liotard and possibly Francis Hayman, *The Hon. Mrs Constantine Phipps Being Led to Greet Her Brother, Captain the Hon. Augustus Hervey, Later 3rd Earl of Bristol, with Molly, Lady Hervey Seated*, 1750, oil on canvas, 99.1 × 124.5 cm.

55 Lady Hervey to Rev. Morris, Ickworth Park, 5 April 1750, in Hervey, *Letters of Mary Lepel*, p. 177.

56 Lord March to George Selwyn, Seymour Place, 20 October 1762, in John Robert Robinson, *'Old Q'; A Memoir of William Douglas, Fourth Duke of Queensberry, K.T., One of 'the Fathers of the turf,' with a Full Account of His Celebrated Matches and Wagers, Etc*, 2nd edn (London: S. Low, Marston and Company Ltd., 1895), p. 274.

57 Edward Gibbon to his father, New Bond Street, 30 December 1758, in Edward Gibbon, *Private Correspondence of Edward Gibbon, (1753–1794)* ed. Rowland E. Prothero, 2 vols (London: John Murray, 1896), vol. 1, p. 21.

58 Edward Gibbon, *The Autobiographies of Edward Gibbon*, ed. J. Murray (London: John Murray, 1896), pp. 245–6 (from draft 'C').

59 This house, demolished in 1934, has been discussed previously, for example, see Sarah Freeman, 'An Englishwoman's Home Is Her Castle: Lady Pomfret's House at 18 Arlington Street', *The Georgian Group Journal*, vol. 20 (2012), pp. 87–102; Peter Lindfield, 'The Countess of Pomfret's Gothic Revival Furniture', *The Georgian Group Journal*, vol. 22 (2014), pp. 77–94; Will Hawkes, 'Walpole Right or Wrong? More on No. 18 Arlington Street', *The Georgian Group Journal*, vol. 21 (2013), pp. 204–11; Simon Houfe, 'A Taste for the Gothick: Diaries of the Countess of Pomfret I', *Country Life*, 161 (24 March 1977), pp. 728–30; Simon Houfe, 'Antiquarian Inclinations: Diaries of the Countess of Pomfret II', *Country Life*, 161 (31 March 1977), pp. 800–2.

60 Lady Pomfret to Lady Hertford, Florence, 30 July 1740, in T. Gillet (ed.), *Correspondence between Frances, Countess of Hartford, (Afterwards Duchess of Somerset), and Henrietta Louisa, Countess of Pomfret between the Years 1738 and 1741* (London: Richard Phillips, 1805), vol. 2, pp. 30–1.

61 Gillet (ed.), *Correspondence*, vol. 1, pp. xxi–xxiii.

62 For discussions on Lady Pomfret's bequest, see Dennine Lynette Dudley, 'Henrietta Louisa Jeffreys, Oxford University and the Pomfret Benefaction of 1755: Vertu made Visible' (PhD thesis, University of Victoria, 2004).

63 Ibid., pp. 41, 43–5.

64 The National Archives (hereafter TNA), PROB 11/803/199, Will of The Right Honorable Thomas Earl of Pomfret and Baron of Lempster, 20 July 1753. For a discussion on Lord Pomfret's rewritten will, see Dudley, 'Oxford University and the Pomfret Benefaction of 1755', pp. 119–23.

65 Horace Walpole to Horace Mann, Strawberry Hill, 21 July 1753, in Lewis (ed.), *Horace Walpole's Correspondence*, vol. 20, p. 390.

66 Joanna Marschner, 'Michael Rysbrack's Sculpture Series for Queen Caroline's Library at St James's Palace', in Diana Dethloff, Tessa Murdoch, Kim Sloan and Caroline Elam (eds), *Burning Bright: Essays in Honour of David Bindman* (London: University College London Press, 2015), pp. 27–8.

67 The Lewis Walpole Library, Yale University, Quarto 498 P77 Ms, Pedigree showing descent of Lord and Lady Pomfret from King Edward I, *c.* 1750.

68 Lady Pomfret to Sir Roger Newdigate, 17 July 1755, in Freeman, 'An Englishwoman's Home Is Her Castle', p. 101.

69 'This Day my Ld Granville & I sign'd the agreement for the ground next to his House in Arlington Street', Lady Pomfret's Diary entry dated 18 February 1757, as quoted in Dudley, 'Oxford University and the Pomfret Benefaction', p. 125, n. 84.

70 Lady Pomfret's Diary entry dated summer 1757, as quoted in Houfe, 'Antiquarian Inclinations', p. 801. For three of Biggs' plans, see SM, 43/5/5, Design for the courtyard front, inscribed on verso with Sketch of a Gothic Building, February 1757; SM 43/5/8, Copy of a design for the park front, hand of Richard Biggs, n.d.; SM 43/5/9, Copy of the Park Front design, slightly different, hand of Richard Biggs, n.d.

71 Freeman, 'An Englishwoman's Home Is Her Castle', pp. 91–4.

72 Ibid., pp. 96–8.

73 Lindfield, 'The Countess of Pomfret's Gothic Revival Furniture', pp. 87–9; Houfe, 'Antiquarian Inclinations', p. 802.

74 Dudley, 'Oxford University and the Pomfret Benefaction of 1755', pp. 211–15.

75 Vickery, *Behind Closed Doors*, p. 258.

76 Explored further in Matthew M. Reeve, 'Gothic Architecture, Sexuality, and License at Horace Walpole's Strawberry Hill', *Art Bulletin*, vol. 95, no. 3 (2013b), pp. 411–39.

77 For discussions on women's socio-political involvement in eighteenth-century Britain, see for example, Elaine Chalus, *Elite Women in English Political Life c.1754–1790* (Oxford: Clarendon Press, 2005); *idem*, 'Elite Women, Social Politics, and the Political World of Late Eighteenth-Century England', *The Historical Journal*, vol. 43, no. 3 (September 2000), pp. 669–97; Judith S. Lewis, *Sacred to Female Patriotism: Gender, Class, and Politics in Late Georgian Britain* (New York and London: Routledge, 2003); Anna Clark, *Scandal: The Sexual Politics of the British Constitution* (Princeton: Princeton University Press, 2004); *idem*, 'Women in Eighteenth-Century Politics', in Sarah Knott and Barbara Taylor (eds), *Women, Gender and Enlightenment* (Basingstoke: Palgrave Macmillan, 2005), pp. 570–86; Amanda Vickery (ed.), *Women, Privilege, and Power: British Politics, 1750 to the Present* (Stanford: Stanford University Press, 2001).

78 Juliet Learmouth, 'The London Town House of Lady Isabella Finch', *The Georgian Group Journal*, vol. 25 (2017), p. 78.

79 David Watkin, 'Town Houses', in Susan Weber (ed.), *William Kent: Designing Georgian Britain* (New Haven and London: Yale University Press, 2013), p. 173.

80 See ODNB online, Elaine Chalus, 'Finch, Lady (Cecilia) Isabella (1700–1771)' (2004).

81 BL, Add. MS 32919, f. 122, Lady Bell Finch to the Duke of Newcastle, Berkeley Square, 19 February 1761, as quoted in Chalus, *Elite Women in English Political Life*, p. 119, n. 33.

82 For architectural histories of No 44, see Learmouth, 'The London Town House', pp. 73–94; Watkin, 'Town Houses', in Weber (ed.), *William Kent*, pp. 173–7; Mark Girouard, '44, Berkeley Square, London', *Country Life*, 132 (27 December 1962), pp. 1648–51; John Harris, 'William Kent's 44 Berkeley Square', *Apollo*, vol. 126, no. 306 (August 1987), pp. 100–4; Musgrave, 'A London palazzo'.

83 Watkin, 'Town Houses', p. 75.

84 SM, Building Accounts 39B, as cited in Watkin, 'Town Houses', p. 174.

85 Walpole, *Anecdotes of Painting in England*, 3rd edn, vol. 4, pp. 242–3.

86 Royal Institute of British Architects (hereafter RIBA) Architectural Library, SD92/7, measured drawing, plan and two sections of the staircase at No. 44 Berkeley Square, with scale, attributed to Stephen Wright, *c.* 1743.

87 Watkin, 'Town Houses', p. 177.

88 RIBA Architectural Library, SC50/2, design for the coffered ceiling of the saloon at 44 Berkeley Square, designed by William Kent, drafted by Stephen Wright, *c.* 1742–4.

89 Learmouth, 'The London Town House', p. 86.

90 TNA, PROB, 11/761, Will of William Kent, made 13 October 1743, codicil 10 April 1748, proved 18 June 1748, as quoted in Watkin, 'Town Houses', p. 172.

91 Catherine Arbuthnott, 'Kent and Italy', in Weber (ed.), *William Kent*, p. 79.

92 Learmouth, 'The London Town House', p. 91.

93 Northamptonshire Record Office (hereafter NRO), Finch Hatton Papers, FH 4208, undated version of Lady Bell's will in which she bequeathed 'all the Latin books I die possessed of' to her nephew, John Emilius Daniel Finch, as quoted in Learmouth, 'The London Town House', p. 86.

94 Patricia L. Hamilton, 'In Search of Lady Isabella's Library; or, a Question of Access', *ABO: Interactive Journal for Women in the Arts, 1640–1830*, vol. 2, no. 1 (2012), p. 5.

95 Lady Mary Wortley Montagu to Lady Bute, 1 March 1752, in Halsband (ed.), *The Complete Letters*, vol. 3, p. 8.

96 Jay, 'Queen Caroline's Library', pp. 31–55; Marschner, *Queen Caroline*, pp. 121–47.

97 Sheffield Archives, Wentworth Woodhouse Muniments, M2/220, Lady Bell Finch to Lord Malton (later Rockingham), 5 September 1745, as quoted in Learmouth, 'The London Town House', p. 89.

98 BL, Add MS 32955, f. 56, Lady Isabella Finch to the Duke of Newcastle, 4 January 1764.

99 Royal governess to the children of George III and Queen Charlotte, 1762–93.

100 Horace Walpole to Horace Mann, 10 April 1747, Arlington Street, in Lewis (ed.), *Horace Walpole's Correspondence*, vol. 19, p. 389.

101 Ibid., p. 390.

102 NRO, Finch Hatton Papers, FH 4208, as quoted in Stewart, *The Town House*, p. 49.

103 See Colin Thom, 'Robert Adam's First Marylebone House: The Story of General Robert Clerk, the Countess of Warwick and Their Mansion in Mansfield Street', *The Georgian Group Journal*, vol. 23 (2015), pp. 125–46.

104 Ibid., p. 130.

105 BL, Hamilton and Greville Papers, Add. MS 40714, f. 116 r., 'Major General Clerk and The Right Hon'ble The Countess Dowager of Warwick in Acc[t] with Robert & James Adam', n.d.

106 Ibid.

107 The John Rylands Library, University of Manchester, Mary Hamilton Papers, GB 133 HAM/1/5/4/1, architectural plan of Lady Warwick's house in Mansfield Street, London, 1775. A note on the plan states that the whole building is designed with arches and 'is the first & only one so built in London this year'.

108 Ibid.

109 SM, Adam vol. 23/160, Adam office drawing based on pencil drawing by Robert Adam, 'Chimney piece for the Drawing room at General Clerks', June 1779; Adam vol. 14/58, Adam office, 'Design of a Ceiling for the Drawing Room at Genrl Clerks', June 1779; Adam vol. 23/280-4, designs for window shutter panels for Clerk House, June 1779.

110 T. F. Henderson, revised by Stuart Handley, 'Home, William, Eighth Earl of Home, (d. 1761)', *Oxford Dictionary of National Biography* (online ed.), Oxford University Press, 2004.

111 'Elizabeth Home Countess of Home, Formerly Lawes (née Gibbons)', *Legacies of British Slave-Ownership Database*, http://wwwdepts-live.ucl.ac.uk/lbs/person/view/2146649547 [accessed 21 April 2021].

112 Ibid.

113 See Hannah Young, 'Gender and Absentee Slave-Ownership in Late Eighteenth and Early Nineteenth-Century Britain' (PhD thesis, University College London, forthcoming); *idem*, 'Negotiating Female Property- and Slave-Ownership in the Aristocratic World', *The Historical Journal*, vol. 63, no. 3 (2020), pp. 581–602.

114 For a discussion on Anna Eliza Elletson's slave ownership, see Hannah Young, 'Forgotten Woman: Anna Eliza Elletson and Absentee Slave Ownership' in Katie Donington, Ryan Hanley and Jessica Moody (eds), *Britain's History and Memory of Transatlantic Slavery: Local Nuances of a 'National Sin'* (Liverpool: Liverpool University Press, 2016), pp. 83–101; Linda L. Sturtz, 'The "Dimduke" and the Duchess of Chandos: Gender and Power in Jamaican Plantation Management – A Case Study or, a Different Story of "A Man [and his wife] from a Place Called Hope"', *Revista/Review Interamericana*, vol. 29 (1999), pp. 1–15.

115 See, for example, Madge Dresser and Andrew Hann (eds), *Slavery and the British Country House* (London: English Heritage, 2013); Sally-Anne Huxtable, Corinne Fowler, Christo Kefalas, and Emma Slocombe (eds),

'Interim Report on the Connections between Colonialism and Properties now in the Care of the National Trust, Including Links with Historic Slavery' (Swindon: National Trust, 2020); Madge Dresser, 'Legacies of British Slave Ownership: Facing a Difficult Past' in David Cannadine and Jeremy Musson (eds), *The Country House, Past, Present, Future* (New York: Rizzoli International Publications, 2018).

116 Joan Coutu, *Persuasion and Propaganda: Monuments and the Eighteenth-Century British Empire* (Montreal: McGill-Queen's University Press, 2006), pp. 43–5.

117 For architectural histories, see for example, Margaret Whinney, *Home House: No. 20 Portman Square* (London: Country Life Publications, 1969); Eileen Harris, 'Home House: Adam versus Wyatt', *The Burlington Magazine*, vol. 139, no. 1130 (May 1997), pp. 308–21; Lesley Lewis, 'Elizabeth, Countess of Home, and Her House in Portman Square', *The Burlington Magazine*, vol. 109, no. 773 (August 1967), pp. 443–53.

118 Lewis, 'Elizabeth, Countess of Home', p. 450.

119 Ibid., p. 449.

120 Five ceiling designs by James Wyatt, dated *c.* 1773, are located in the National Library of Ireland, Penrose-Wyatt Collection. These were reproduced in, Harris, 'Home House: Adam versus Wyatt', figs. 17, 19, 28, 29, 33.

121 Harris, 'Home House: Adam versus Wyatt', p. 309.

122 BL, RP 3031/1, Lady Home to Robert Adam, 24 February 1775.

123 Harris, 'Home House: Adam versus Wyatt', p. 310.

124 For Adam's drawings relating to the staircase, see the SM, Adam vol. 14/116, Robert Adam, 'Lady Home's Staircase', *c.* 1775; Adam vol. 52/3, Robert Adam, 'Iron Ballustrade for Lady Houme', *c.* 1775.

125 William Beckford, 1782, as quoted in John W. Oliver, *The Life of William Beckford* (London: Oxford University Press, 1932), pp. 106–7.

126 Coutu, *Persuasion and Propaganda*, p. 38.

127 Adam's designs for the Music Room, completed on 27 January 1775, include: SM, Adam vol. 50/33–36; Adam vol. 12/164.

128 SM, vol. 25/15, Robert Adam, 'Organ Case for Lady Home' including 'Plan of the Organ', June 1775.

129 Harris, 'Home House: Adam versus Wyatt', pp. 314–15; Lewis, 'Elizabeth, Countess of Home', p. 448.

130 TNA, PROB 11/1112/304, 'Will of The Right Honourable Elizabeth Countess of Home, Dowager, Widow of Portman Square, Middlesex', 24 January 1784.

131 SM, Adam vol. 20/162, Robert Adam, 'Frame for the Duke of Cumberland's Picture for the Countess of Home', May 1777.

132 Hoare's Bank, London, vol. 95, fol. 1, a building account book was opened for Lady Home at Hoare's Bank on 7 November 1775 and closed on 11 March 1779, as mentioned in Harris, 'Home House: Adam versus Wyatt', p, 308, n. 10.

133 TNA, PROB 11/1112/304.

134 The Royal Collection, RCIN 405937, Thomas Gainsborough, *Anne, Duchess of Cumberland*, *c.* 1773–7, oil on canvas, 241.7 x 142.6 cm; RCIN 405936, Thomas Gainsborough, *Henry Frederick, Duke of Cumberland*, *c.* 1773–7, oil on canvas, 240.3 x 143.0 cm.

135 See, J. V. Beckett, 'Elizabeth Montagu: Bluestocking Turned Landlady', *Huntington Library Quarterly*, vol. 49, no. 2 (Spring 1986), pp. 149–64.

136 For discussions on Elizabeth's commercial activities, see Les Turnbull, 'Elizabeth Montagu: "A Critick, a Coal Owner, a Land Steward, a Sociable Creature"', *Huntington Library Quarterly*, vol. 81, no. 4 (2018), pp. 657–86; Elizabeth Child, 'Elizabeth Montagu, Bluestocking Businesswoman', *Huntington Library Quarterly*, vol. 65, no. 1/2 (2002), pp. 153–73.

137 For discussions on the construction of Montagu House, see Kerry Bristol, '22 Portman Square: Mrs Montagu and Her "Palais De La Vieillesse"', *British Art Journal*, vol. 2, no. 3 (2001), pp. 72–85; Baird, *Mistress of the House*, pp. 188–219.

138 Huntington Library, California (hereafter HO), MO 6005, Elizabeth Montagu to Sarah Scott, 6 July 1777, as quoted in Baird, *Mistress of the House*, pp. 203–4.

139 Clarissa Campbell Orr, 'The Queen of the Blues, the Bluestocking Queen and Bluestocking Masculinity', in Eger (ed.), *Bluestockings Displayed*, pp. 233–53.

140 Sloboda, 'Fashioning Bluestocking Conversation', pp. 137–8.

141 C. Barrett and A. Dobson (eds), *The Diary and Letters of Madame d'Arblay* (London, 1904), vol. 1, pp. 460–1, as quoted in Eger and Peltz (eds), *Brilliant Women*, p. 26.

142 Sloboda, 'Fashioning Bluestocking Conversation', p. 132.

143 Ibid., p. 129. For discussions on Elizabeth's Hill House commission, see David Pullins, 'Robert Adam's Neoclassical Chinoiserie', *West 86th: A Journal of Decorative Arts, Design History, and Material Culture*, vol. 24, no. 2 (Sep., 2017), pp. 177–200; Rosemary Baird, '"The Queen of the Bluestockings": Elizabeth Montagu's House at 23 Hill Street Rediscovered', *Apollo*, vol. 157 (August 2003), pp. 43–9; and *idem*: *Mistress of the House*, pp. 177–82; Kerry Bristol, 'The Painted Rooms of Athenian Stuart', *The Georgian Group Journal*, vol. 10 (2000), pp. 167–79; David Pullins, 'Reassessing Elizabeth Montagu's Architectural Patronage at 23 Hill Street, London', *The Burlington Magazine*, vol. 150, no. 1263 (2008), pp. 400–4.

144 Elizabeth Montagu to Sarah Scott, 3 January 1750, in Emily J. Climenson (ed.), *Elizabeth Montagu: The Queen of the Bluestockings, Her Correspondence from 1720 to 1761*, 2 vols (London, 1906), vol. 1, p. 271.

145 HO, MO 5705, Elizabeth Montagu to Sarah Scott, 30 October 1748, as quoted in Sloboda, 'Fashioning Bluestocking Conversation', p. 136.

146 Helena Hayward and Pat Kirkham, *William and John Linnell, Eighteenth Century London Furniture Makers*, 2 vols (London: Rizolli with Christie's, 1980), vol. 1, pp. 74–5.

147 Sloboda, 'Fashioning Bluestocking Conversation', pp. 141–2.

148 HO, MO 6686, Gilbert West to Elizabeth Montagu, 25 May 1752, MO 6634; Gilbert West to Elizabeth Montagu, 30 May 1752, MO 6635; Gilbert West to Elizabeth Montagu, 19 June 1752, as referenced in Sloboda, 'Fashioning Bluestocking Conversation', p. 139.

149 Sloboda, 'Fashioning Bluestocking Conversation', p. 142.

150 Birmingham Central Library, Matthew Boulton and Family Papers, MS 3782/12/93/17, Elizabeth Montagu to Matthew Boulton, Sandleford, 20 August 1780.

151 Stuart and Revett, *The Antiquities of Athens.*

152 HO, MO 5026, Mrs Montagu to Leonard Smelt, Bath, 26 April 1780, as cited in Bristol, '22 Portman Square', p. 80.

153 Horace Walpole to William Mason, Berkeley Square, 14 February 1782, in Lewis (ed.), *Horace Walpole's Correspondence,* vol. 29, p. 184.

154 Ibid.

155 HO, MO 1133, James Harris to Mrs Montagu, 4 November 1780, as quoted in Baird, *Mistress of the House*, p. 208.

156 Bristol, '22 Portman Square', p. 82.

157 *St. James's Chronicle or the British Evening Post*, London, 11–14 June 1791.

158 RIBA Library Drawings Collection, DR127/2, Joseph Bonomi, interior perspective of the Great Drawing Room, 1790; SA5/3(4), Joseph Bonomi, plan for the carpet for the Great Room, 1790.

159 *St. James's Chronicle*, London, 11–14 June 1791, as quoted in Bristol, '22 Portman Square', p. 83.

160 George L. Phillips, 'Mrs. Montagu and the Climbing-Boys', *The Review of English Studies*, vol. 25, no. 99 (1949), pp. 237–44.

161 'Grosvenor Square: Individual Houses Built before 1926', in F. H. W. Sheppard (ed.), *Survey of London: Volume 40, the Grosvenor Estate in Mayfair, Part 2 (The Buildings)*, pp. 117–66. *British History Online,* http://www.british-history.ac.uk/survey-london/vol40/pt2/pp117-166 [accessed 23 April 2019]. A series of drawings relating to these alterations survive in the Soane Museum, for example see, SM 39/1/50, George Mansfield, 'Plan of the One Pair Floor and Plan of the One Pair Floor with the Proposed Alterations', March 24 1798; 81/1/34, attributed to George Mansfield, Designs for four chimney-pieces, *c.* 1798.

162 Lincolnshire Archives, 2 ANC 12/D/D/36, p. 1, Lady Heathcote's Thomas Chippendale bill, 1800.

163 For a discussion on the eighteenth-century sex industry, see Fergus Linnane, *Madams: Bawds & Brothel-Keepers of London* (Stroud: The History Press, 2011); Mike Rendell, *In Bed with the Georgians: Sex, Scandal and Satire in the 18th Century* (Barnsley: Pen & Sword History, 2016); Dan Cruickshank, *The Secret History of Georgian London: How the Wages of Sin Shaped the Capital* (London: Windmill, 2010).

164 Johann Wilhelm von Archenholz, *A Picture of England: Containing a Descriptions of the Laws, Customs, and Manners of England*, translated from French (Dublin: P. Byrne, 1790), p. 193.

165 Ibid. p. 194.

166 Frederic George Stephens et al., *Catalogue of Prints and Drawings in the British Museum: Division I. Political and Personal Satires (No. 2061 to No. 4838)*, vol. 3, part. 1 (London, 1877), p. 306.

167 *The Covent Garden Magazine or the Amorous Repository, Calculated Solely for the Entertainment of the Polite World, and the Finishing of a Young Man's Education* (London: G. Allen, 1773), vol. 2, p. 384.

168 Ibid.

169 Anon., *Memoirs of the celebrated Miss Fanny M[urray]*, 2nd edn (London, 1759), p. 147.

170 Ibid., p. 200.

171 White, *Queen of the Courtesans: Fanny Murray*, p. 105.

172 The Colonial Williamsburg Foundation, 2009–22: *A St James's Beauty*, black and white mezzotint engraving with period hand colour, 1784, printed and published by Carington Bowles.

173 Elizabeth Steele, *The Memoirs of Mrs. Sophia Baddeley, Late of Drury Lane Theatre*, 6 vols (London, 1787), vol. 1, p. 23.

174 Ibid., p. 26.

175 Ibid., p. 28.

176 Ibid., pp. 28–31.

177 Ibid., pp. 32–3.

178 Ibid., p. 34.

179 Ibid., vol. 6, p. 157.

180 Ibid., vol. 1, pp. 62–4; ibid., vol. 4, pp. 38–9.

181 Ibid., vol. 1, pp. 75, 78–9.

182 Ibid., pp. 83–4.

183 Ibid., vol. 1, p. 119.

184 Ibid., vol. 2, p. 149.

185 Ibid., p. 161.

186 Ibid., p. 33.

187 Ibid., vol. 1, p. 185.

188 Ibid.

189 Ibid., vol. 2, p. 151.

190 Ibid., pp. 197–8.

191 Ibid., vol. 6, p. 57.

192 Amy Culley, 'The Sentimental Satire of Sophia Baddeley', *Studies in English Literature, 1500–1900*, vol. 48, no. 3 (2008), p. 687.

193 For a biography of Teresa, see Judith Summers, *Empress of Pleasure* (London: Penguin Book Group, 2004). For an excellent overview of Teresa's activities at Carlisle House see F. H. W. Sheppard (ed.), 'Soho Square Area: Portland Estate, Carlisle House, Soho Square', in *Survey of London: Volumes 33 and*

34, St Anne Soho (hereafter SoL) (London: London County Council, 1966), pp. 73–9, accessed via *British History Online*; see also Cruickshank, *The Secret History of Georgian London*, pp. 193–202.

194 Teresa had worked in London for a few months in the mid-1740s as an opera singer, with no success.

195 von Archenholz, *A Picture of England*, pp. 246–7

196 Horace Walpole to Sir Horace Mann, 22 February 1771, in Lewis (ed.), *Horace Walpole's Correspondence*, vol. 23, p. 271.

197 Summers, *Empress of Pleasure*, pp. 106–7.

198 TNA, C 12/1471/1, *Cornelys v Fermor* (1763, amended 1764); C 12/1585/16, *Fermor v Cornelys* (1763); Sheppard (ed.), 'Soho Square Area', pp. 193–202; Summers, *Empress of Pleasure*, pp. 107–8.

199 BL, 17th–18th Century Burney Collection Newspapers, *Public Advertiser*, Issue 8128, 22 November 1760.

200 Sheppard (ed.), 'Soho Square Area', pp. 193–202.

201 Details of Samuel Norman's involvement can be traced through the various court cases involving Teresa during the 1760s: TNA, C 107/149, *Cornelys v Fermor* (1760–1); C 12/1289/16, *Cornelys v Bodycoate* (1762); C 12/1585/16, *Fermor v Cornelys* (1763), C 12/1471/1 1763–4) *Cornelys v Fermor*. Later additional cases involving Teresa can be found at TNA, C 12/1518/16, *Fermor v Chamberlain* (1772); C 12/392/28, *Cornelys v Burger* (1772).

202 TNA, C 12/1289/16, *Cornelys v Bodycoate* (1762), 'The further Several Answer of Samuel Norman one of the Defendants to the Bill of Complaint of Teresa Cornelys, 4 February 1763'.

203 TNA, C 12/1289/16, *Cornelys v Bodycoate* (1762), 'The Third Schedule …'.

204 Ibid.

205 Ibid.

206 Sheppard (ed.), 'Soho Square Area', pp. 193–202.

207 Ibid.

208 TNA, C 12/1289/16, *Cornelys v Bodycoate* (1762), 'The Third Schedule …'; Summers, *Empress of Pleasure*, p. 120.

209 Sheppard (ed.), 'Soho Square Area', pp. 193–202.

210 Count Friedrich von Kielmansegge, *Diary of a Journey to England the Years 1761–1762*, trans. by Countess Kielmansegge (London: Longmans & Co., 1902), p. 196.

211 Horace Walpole to Lord Hertford, Arlington Street, 22 January 1764 (but partly written on Wednesday 25th), in Lewis (ed.), *Horace Walpole's Correspondence*, vol. 38, p. 291.

212 von Archenholz, *A Picture of England*, p. 247.

213 Ibid.

214 BL, 17th–18th Century Burney Collection Newspapers, *Public Advertiser*, Issue 9341, 10 October 1764.

215 Horace Walpole to George Montagu, Arlington Street, 16 December 1764, in Lewis (ed.), *Horace Walpole's Correspondence*, vol. 10, p. 138.

216 BL, 17th–18th Century Burney Collection Newspapers, *London Chronicle*, Issue 1381, 24–26 October 1765.

217 Ibid., *London Chronicle*, Issue 1393, 21–23 November 1765.

218 Ibid., *Public Advertiser*, 26 November 1765, Issue 9694; *Public Advertiser*, Issue 9702, 5 December 1765.

219 Ibid., *Public Advertiser*, Issue 9694, 26 November 1765.

220 Ibid., *London Chronicle*, Issue 1437, 4–6 March 1766.

221 Sheppard (ed.), 'Soho Square Area', pp. 42–51.

222 Ibid.

223 George A. Ward (ed.), *Journal and Letters of the Late Samuel Curwen, Judge of Admiralty, etc., An American Refugee in England from 1775–1784* (New York: C. S. Francis, 1842), pp. 289–90.

224 Summers, *Empress of Pleasure*, p. 147.

225 Steele, *The Memoirs*, vol. 5, pp. 149–50.

226 British Museum, 1850,1109.50, James Cole, *The World in Masquerade*, n.d., *c.* 1770s, print, 25.4 × 40.6 cm.

227 For a discussion on the architectural history of the Pantheon see Sheppard (ed.), 'The Pantheon', in *Survey of London: Vols 31–2, St James Westminster, Part 2* (London, 1963), pp. 268–83, accessed via *British History Online*.

228 Horace Walpole to the Rev. William Mason, Strawberry Hill, 29 July 1773, in Lewis (ed.), *Horace Walpole's Correspondence*, vol. 28, p. 102.

229 BL, 17th–18th Century Burney Collection Newspapers, *London Evening Post*, Issue 6900, 26–28 March 1772.

230 Ibid., *London Evening Post*, Issue 6898, 21–24 March 1772.

231 Ibid., *Gazetteer and London Daily Advertiser*, Issue 136533, December 1772.

232 Summers, *Empress of Pleasure*, pp. 243–4.

233 Ibid., p. 282.

Chapter 4

1 Duchess of Marlborough to the Duchess of Bedford, Marlborough House, 5 August 1734, in Gladys Scott Thomson (ed.), *Letters of a Grandmother. 1732 – 1735. Being the Correspondence of Sarah Duchess of Marlborough with Her Granddaughter Diana Duchess of Bedford* (London: Jonathan Cape, 1943), p. 142.

2 For discussions on Wimbledon House, see '"The Best Workmen of All Sorts" The Building of Wimbledon House, 1730–1742', *The Georgian Group Journal*, vol. 2 (1992), pp. 87–90; Caroline Knight, *London's Country Houses* (Andover: Phillimore, 2010), pp. 331–2.

3 Duchess of Marlborough to Duchess of Bedford, July 1732, in Thomson (ed.), *Letters of a Grandmother*, p. 52.

4 As quoted in Harris, 'The Best Workmen of All Sorts', p. 87.

5 Draper, 'When Marlborough's Duchess Built', pp. 248–50.

6 Lady Mary Wortley Montagu to the Countess of Bute, Venice, 22 May 1759, in Halsband (ed.), *The Complete Letters*, vol. 3, p. 211.

7 Duchess of Marlborough to the Duchess of Bedford, 5 August 1734, in Thomson (ed.), *Letters of a Grandmother*, p. 142.

8 Wiltshire and Swindon Archives, Wilton House and Estate Papers, 2057/F6/15, annotated plan of Wimbledon House, n.d., *c.* 1730s.

9 Ibid.

10 Harris, 'The Best Workmen of All Sorts', p. 88.

11 William King (ed.), *Memoirs of Sarah, Duchess of Marlborough* (New York: Dutton, 1930), p. 315.

12 Mantha Zarmakoupi, *Designing for Luxury on the Bay of Naples: Villas and Landscapes (c. 100 BCE-79 CE)* (Oxford: Oxford University Press, 2014), p. 5; Kim Williams, *The Villas of Palladio* (New York: Princeton Architectural Press, 2003).

13 Anthony Beckles Willson, 'Alexander Pope's Grotto in Twickenham', *Garden History*, vol. 26, no. 1 (1998), pp. 31–59.

14 Lady Hertford to Lady Pomfret, Richkings, 14 May 1741, in Gillet (ed.), *Correspondence*, vol. 1, pp. 279–80.

15 For a biography of Elizabeth see Hickman, *Courtesans*, pp. 83–147.

16 'Histories of the Tête-à-tête Annexed, or Memoirs of ... the Celebrated Mrs. A—mst—d', in *The Town and Country Magazine, or, Universal Repository of Knowledge, Instruction, and Entertainment.* vol. 11 (1779), p. 124.

17 Hickman, *Courtesans*, p. 98.

18 *The Town and Country Magazine*, vol. 11 (1779), p. 124.

19 Hickman, *Courtesans*, pp. 99–101.

20 Derek Sumeray and John Sheppard, *London Plaques* (Bloomsbury: Shire Publications, 2011), p. 60; Hickman, *Courtesans*, p. 101.

21 SHC, 350/2/2, Copy of Court Roll, 6 September 1785.

22 BL, Add MS 61811, f. 26, Survey of the St Anne's Hill estate, n.d., mid-nineteenth century.

23 Samuel Rogers, *Recollections*, ed. W. Sharpe, 2nd edn (London, 1859), pp. 28–9.

24 The Tate, D27687, J. M. W. Turner, vignette of *St. Anne's Hill*, I, for Rogers's *Poems*, *c.* 1830–2, graphite and watercolour on paper, support: 23.5 × 30.7 cm.

25 BL, Add MS 61811, f. 27, 'Ground Floor Plan of St Anne's Hill, Chertsey, Proposed Alterations', n.d., mid-nineteenth century.

26 Rogers, *Recollections*, pp. 28–9.

27 Charles James Fox to Lord Holland, St Ann's Hill, 25 April 1794, in Lord John Russell (ed.), *Memorials and Correspondence of Charles James Fox*, 4 vols (London: Richard Bentley, 1853–7), vol. 3, p. 71.

28 Charles James Fox to Lord Holland, 12 April 1795, in Russell (ed.), *Charles James Fox*, vol. 3, p. 106.

29 Georgiana Chatterton, *Home Sketches and Foreign Recollections*, 3. vols (London: Saunders and Otley, 1841), vol. 1, p. 235.

30 Charles James Fox to Lord Holland, 6 March 1795, in Russell (ed.), *Charles James Fox*, vol. 3, p. 100.

31 'Funeral of the Late Hon. Mrs. Fox', in *Windsor and Eton Express*, 16 July 1842, p. 4.

32 West Yorkshire Archive Service (hereafter WYAS), Leeds, WYL150/7/6/9/063, Diaries of Lady Amabel Yorke [Lady Polwarth], vol. 9, 23–26 November 1786.

33 For an account of Lady Polwarth's association with 49 Upper Brook Street, see Anthea Jones, 'Letters from Mary Yorke, the Wife of the Bishop of Ely 1781–1808', *PCAS*, vol. 94 (2005), pp. 150–3.

34 BLARS, L31/284/7, 'Receipt of Mr Yenn, Architect, £200 on Account Aug. 17th 1791'.

35 BLARS, L30/11/240/49, Lady Grantham to Lady Polwarth, Whitehall, 14 December 1791.

36 WYAS, Leeds, WYL150/7/6/13/256, Diaries of Lady Amabel Yorke, vol. 13, 17 December 1792.

37 The Royal Academy of Arts, London, 09/440, John Yenn, Floor plan and south elevation of Lady Polwarth's villa, *c.* 1780, pencil, pen with black ink and coloured washes, 45.2 × 35.6 cm.

38 Lambeth Archives, London (henceforth 'LA'), LP26/188/POL7, John Yenn, 'Chimney Piece Details for Lady Polwarths Bed Chamber', 1 May 1792; LP26/188/POL6, John Yenn, Chimney Piece Details for Lady Polwarth's Dressing Room, 1 May 1792; LP26/188/POL5, John Yenn, Chimney Piece Details for Lady Polwarth's Library, 1 May 1792.

39 WYAS, Leeds, WYL150/7/6/13/077, Diaries of Lady Amabel Yorke, vol. 13, 20 March 1792.

40 WYAS, Leeds, WYL150/7/6/14/210, Diaries of Lady Amabel Yorke, vol. 14, 12 December 1793.

41 LA, LP26/188/GRAM7, John Yenn, 'Cornice Ful Size for the Dressing Room One Pair of Stairs Floor and Ground Floor', 25 August 1792; LP26/188/GRAM10, John Yenn, 'Cornice ful Size for the Hall in the South Front, Lady Granthams House on Putney Heath', 1 October 1792; LP26/188/GRAM3, John Yenn, 'Statuary Marble Chimney Piece for the Bow Room on the Ground Floor', 3 September 1792; LP26/188/GRAM4, John Yenn, 'Statuary Marble Chimney Piece for the Bow Room, Drawing Room, on the Ground floor, Lady Granthams in Putney Heath', *c.* 1792; LP26/188/GRAM5, John Yenn, 'Frieze Ful Size for the Bow Room Chimney Piece Lady Grantham Putney Heath', 3 September 1792.

42 LA, LP26/188/GRAM6, John Yenn, 'Cornice and Frieze Full Size for the Bow-Room principal Floor Lady Granthams Putney Heath', 25 August 1792.

43 Dorian Gerhold, *Villas and Mansions of Roehampton and Putney Heath* (London: Wandsworth Historical Society, 1997), pp. 44–5.

44 BL, Hardwicke Papers, Add. MS 35386, f. 371, Agneta Yorke to Philip Yorke, Tyttenhanger, 2 October 1782.

45 BLARS, L30/9/97/114, Agneta Yorke to Marchioness Grey, Sydney Farm, 17 July 1787.

46 BL, Hardwicke Papers, Add. MS 35386, f. 499, Agneta Yorke to Philip Yorke, Sydney Farm, 4 November 1792.

47 Ibid.

48 BL, Hardwicke Papers, Add. MS 35386, ff. 499–500, Agneta Yorke to Philip Yorke, Sydney Farm, 4 November 1792.

49 Ibid.

50 Ibid.

51 SM, Journal No 2, 1 December 1792, p. 305.

52 BLARS, L30/9/97/129, Agneta Yorke to Marchioness Grey, Sydney Farm, 13 June 1793.

53 BL, Hardwicke Papers, Add. MS 35386, f. 504, Agneta Yorke to Philip Yorke, Sydney Farm, n.d., *c.* 1792.

54 BLARS, L30/9/97/130, Agneta Yorke to Marchioness Grey, Sydney Farm, 1 October 1793.

55 SM, (2) volume 59/39, 'Elevation of the Entrance Front' (to the west) set in a landscape, 1793; (3) 46/3/16, 'Elevation of the Lawn Front' (to the east), 1793.

56 George Richardson, *The New Vitruvius Britannicus* (London, 1808), vol. 1, p. 5 and plate X.

57 SM, (8) 80/1/58 recto and verso, for the Drawing Room, 1794; (9) 80/1/59 recto and verso, for the Eating Room, 1794; 10) 81/2/82, 'M[rs] Yorke's Chamber', 1794–5; (11) 81/2/45, working drawing of chimneypiece, 1794–5.

58 BLARS, L30/9/97/129, Agneta Yorke to Marchioness Grey, Sydney Farm, 13 June 1793.

59 For a discussion on the villa, see Megan Leyland and Emily Parker, *Marble Hill* (London: English Heritage, 2022).

60 See Tracy Borman, *King's Mistress, Queen's Servant: The Life and Times of Henrietta Howard* (London: Vintage, 2010), pp. 14–27.

61 Quoted in Bryant, *Marble Hill*, p. 32.

62 Ibid., p. 33.

63 Norfolk Record Office, NRS 22955, Z76, Settlement in Trust for Henrietta Howard on separation from Charles Howard, as quoted in Borman, *King's Mistress, Queen's Servant*, p. 129.

64 William Kent, *Designs of Inigo Jones Consisting of Plans and Elevations for Public and Private Buildings* (London, 1727).

65 BL, Add. MS 22626, vol. II. 9, f. 92, Lord Chesterfield to Henrietta Howard, n.d., *c.* 1729.

66 Horace Walpole to George Montagu, 22 February 1762, Arlington Street, in Lewis (ed.), *Horace Walpole's Correspondence*, vol. 10, p. 14.

67 Lord Herbert to Rev. William Coxe, Bath, 11 September 1784, in Lord Herbert (ed.), *The Pembroke Papers (1780–94): Letters and Diaries of Henry, Tenth Earl of Pembroke and His Circle* (London, 1950), vol. 2, p. 260.

68 Elizabeth Montagu to Mrs W. Robinson, February 1762, in Blunt (ed.), *Mrs Montagu 'Queen of the Blues'* , vol. 1, p. 15; Hon. Thomas Fitzmaurice to Adam Smith, St. Mary Hall, Oxford, 26 February 1762, in Ernest Campbell Mossner and Ian Simpson Ross (eds), *The Glasgow Edition of the Works and Correspondence of Adam Smith* (Oxford: Oxford University Press, 1987), vol. 6, p. 83.

69 Horace Walpole to George Montagu, Arlington Street, 25 March 1763, in Lewis (ed.), *Horace Walpole's Correspondence*, vol. 10, p. 52.

70 Lady Pembroke to Lord Herbert, London, 31 August 1779, in Herbert (ed.), *The Pembroke Papers*, vol. 1, pp. 234–5.

71 Lady Pembroke to Lord Herbert, April 1780, in Herbert (ed.), *The Pembroke Papers,* vol. 1, p. 464.

72 Lady Pembroke to Lord Herbert, Richmond Park, 21 August 1780, in Herbert (ed.), *The Pembroke Papers,* vol. 2, p. 34.

73 Ibid., p. 35.

74 Queen Charlotte to Lady Pembroke, Queen's House, 26 March 1785, in Herbert (ed.), *The Pembroke Papers,* vol. 2, p. 269.

75 SM, (1) volume 41/54, John Sanders (att.), Copy a presentation drawing for a stables and coach house, May 1785.

76 SM, (3) 29/3/5, Soane office and Soane, 'The Countess of Pembroke, Plan of Cottage in Richmond Park', 1788; (8) 29/3/1 and (9) 29/3/2, Soane office, Presentation drawings for the new drawing room, *c.* 1788.

77 SM, (8) 29/3/1 and (9) 29/3/2.

78 Gillian Darley, *John Soane: An Accidental Romantic* (New Haven and London: Yale University Press, 1999), p. 100.

79 Ray Desmond, *Kew: The History of the Royal Botanic Gardens* (London: Harvill with the Royal Botanic Gardens, Kew, 1998), p. 78.

80 SM, Journal No 1, 18 July 1788, p. 63.

81 SM, (6) 29/3/8, John McDonnell and Robert Woodgate, 'Bedchamber Floor', 23 July 1788.

82 SM, Journal No 1, 19 and 20 July 1788, p. 64.

83 SM, (13) 29/3/10, Frederick Meyer, 'The Countess of Pembroke, Plan of the Ground Floor', 9 December 1793.

84 SM, (7) 81/2/49, Soane (att.), 'Countess of Pembroke, Richmond Chimney Pieces for 2 Angle Chimneys, One Pair', 1788.

85 See Carola Hicks, *Improper Pursuits: The Scandalous Life of Lady Di Beauclerk* (London: Macmillan, 2001), pp. 253–7.

86 W. S. Lewis (ed.), *Notes by Lady Louisa Stuart on George Selwyn and His Contemporaries by John Heneage Jesse* (New York and London: Oxford University Press and H. Milford, 1928), pp. 22–3.

87 Fanny Burney recalled Burke's remarks in her letter to Susanna Burney Phillips, St Martin's Street, 9 July 1782, in Lars Troide and Stewart Cooke (eds), *The Early Journals and Letters of Fanny Burney, Vol. 5: 1782–1783* (Oxford: Oxford University Press and McGill-Queen's University Press, 1994), pp. 70–1.

88 Horace Walpole to William Mason, Strawberry Hill, 4 August 1782, in Lewis (ed.), *Horace Walpole's Correspondence*, vol. 29, p. 272.

89 Marcia Pointon, *Strategies for Showing: Women, Possession, and Representation in English Visual Culture, 1665–1800* (Oxford: Oxford University Press, 1997), p. 160.

90 For an account of this affair, see Hicks, *Improper Pursuits*, pp. 302–8.

91 Hicks, *Improper Pursuits*, p. 310.

92 Lydiard Park, Lyd 1992/32 A-I, painted panels in gouache and water colour on paper over canvas by Lady Diana Beauclerk.

93 Steele, *The Memoirs*, vol. 1, p. 154.

94 Ibid., pp. 154–5.

95 Ibid., vol. 2, p. 117.

96 Ibid., pp. 188–9.

97 Ibid., vol. 3, pp. 80–1.

98 For example, see John Walton, *The English Seaside Resort: A Social History 1750–1914* (Leicester: Leicester University Press, 1983).

99 For a discussion on Georgian Brighton, see Sue Farrant, *Georgian Brighton 1750–1820* (Brighton: University of Sussex, 1980).

100 For a comprehensive discussion on the Pavilion, see John Morley, *The Making of the Royal Pavilion, Brighton: Design and Drawings* (London: Philip Wilson for Sotheby Publications, 1984).

101 Caroline Stanford, 'Revisiting the Origins of Coade Stone', *The Georgian Group Journal*, vol. 14 (2016), p. 110.

102 Ibid.

103 The London Metropolitan Archives, ACC/2552/001, Private Act of Parliament for vesting estate in manor of Kempton in trustees for sale to Lady Jane Coke, 1755.

104 TNA, PROB 11/862/216, Will of The Right Honorable, Lady Jane Coke, Widow of Longford, Derbyshire, 19 January 1761.

105 Lady Caroline Fox to Lady Kildare, 15 June 1759, in Fitzgerald (ed.), *Correspondence*, vol. 1, p. 225.

106 SHC, 188/4, Copy of court roll, manor of West Molesey: attested copy of surrender of John Johnston esq and admission of Hon Charlotte Digby, 17 October 1763.

107 SHC, 188/5, Copy of court roll (attested copy), manor of Hampton Court: admission of Hon Charlotte Digby, 17 May 1764.

108 TNA, C 202/159/18, Charlotte Digby's enclosure of the highway in Thames Ditton, 11 January 1771.

109 Martin, *Wives and Daughters*, p. 394.

110 Elizabeth Montagu to Elizabeth Carter, Hill Street, 1781, in Blunt (ed.), *Mrs Montagu 'Queen of the Blues'*, vol. 2, p, 113.

111 Fanny Burney's journal entry, 15 December 1782, in Lars E. Troide and Stewart J. Cooke (eds), *The Early Journals and Letters of Fanny Burney: 1782–1783* (Kingston, ON: McGill-Queen's Press, 1988), vol. 5, p. 204.

112 Fanny Burney's journal entry, 23 December 1782, Toide and Cooke (eds), *The Early Journals*, vol. 5, pp. 216–17.

113 Ann Sheldon, *The Authentic and Interesting Memoirs of Miss Ann Sheldon; (Now Mrs Archer:) A Lady Who Figures, during Several Years, in the Biggest Line of Public Life, and in Whose History Will Be Found, All Vicissitudes, Which So Constantly Attend on Women of Her Description. Written by Herself*, 4 vols (London, 1788), vol. 3, p. 144.

114 Ibid., p. 145.

115 Ibid., pp. 145–6.

116 Ibid., p. 146.

117 SHC, 188/11–12, lease and release with covenant to surrender copyhold and assignment of fixtures and fittings for Fords Farm between 1) Hon. Stephen Digby 2) Hon. Charlotte Boyle Walsingham, 24–25 March 1783; 188/13, covenant to produce deeds for capital messuage or mansion called Fords in Thames Ditton between 1) Hon Stephen Digby 2) Hon Charlotte Boyle Walsingham, 25 March 1783.

118 Mary Hamilton's journal entry, 4 July 1783, in Elizabeth and Florence Anson (eds), *Mary Hamilton: Letters and Diaries 1756–1816* (London: John Murray, 1925), p. 141.

119 T. Barber after Henry Gastineau, 'Boyle Farm, Thames Ditton, Seat of Lord Henry Fitzgerald', for *Excursions through Surrey* (London: Longman & Co., 1820), engraving.

120 Horace Walpole to the Earl of Strafford, Strawberry Hill, 28 July 1787, in Lewis (ed.), *Horace Walpole's Correspondence*, vol. 35, p. 390.

121 Mary Hamilton's journal, in Anson (eds), *Mary Hamilton: Letters and Diaries 1756–1816*, p. 138.

122 Charlotte Boyle married Lord Henry FitzGerald, younger brother of the Duke of Leinster, in 1791 and was created Baroness de Ros in 1806.

123 Hannah More to her sister, Boyle Farm, 1787, in Roberts (ed.), *Life and Correspondence of Mrs. Hannah More*, vol. 1, p. 279.

124 Horace Walpole to the Earl of Strafford, Strawberry Hill, 28 July 1787, in Lewis (ed.), *Horace Walpole's Correspondence*, vol. 35, p. 390.

125 Frances Boscawen to her cousin, Rosedale, 13 June 1788, in Aspinall-Oglander (ed.), *Admiral's Widow*, pp. 131–2.

126 Lady Sarah Napier to Lady Sarah O'Brien, Park Gate, 9 September 1794, in G. S. H. Fox Strangways (ed.), *The Life and Letters of Lady Sarah Lennox*, 2. vols (London: J. Murray 1901), vol. 2, p. 115.

127 Shortly prior to George Anne's birth her mother married Captain Bellamy, master of a trading vessel in Lisbon, which accounts for her surname. For a general account of George Anne's life, see Cyril Hughes Hartmann, *Enchanting Bellamy* (London: Heinemann, 1956).

128 For an account of Mrs Bellamy's (George Anne's mother) theatrical life, see Philip H. Highfill, Kalman A. Burnim and Edward A. Langhans, *A Biographical Dictionary of Actors, Actresses, Musicians, Dancers, Managers & Other Stage Personnel in London, 1660–1800*, vol. 2: Belfort to Byzand (Carbondale and Edwardsville: Illinois University Press, 1973), pp. 3–6.

129 George Anne Bellamy, *An Apology for the Life of George Anne Bellamy, Late of Covent Garden Theatre, Written by Herself*, 6 vols, 3rd edn (London: printed for the author, 1785), vol. 1, p. 48.

130 Ibid., pp. 53–9.

131 For an account of George Anne's acting career, see Philip H. Highfill et al., A *Biographical Dictionary of Actors*, vol. 2, pp. 6–20.

132 Bellamy, *An Apology*, vol. 4, pp. 154–6.

133 Ibid., p. 156.

134 Ibid., vol. 1, pp. 70–6.

135 Ibid., pp. 11–13.

136 Ibid., vol. 2, p. 176.

137 Dorset Historic Centre, Dorchester D-RWR/L/6, Papers in Chancery cases concerning will of John Calcraft Esq. (1772) and right to dower of Bridget Calcraft, 1773–90.

138 Lancashire Archives, Preston DDK/1217/13, Conveyance of Holwood House between Mr Nicholas Linwood and Mr John Calcraft, 28 February 1754.

139 Bellamy, *An Apology*, vol. 1, p. 183.

140 Bellamy, *An Apology*, vol. 2, pp. 196–7.

141 Ibid., p. 197.

142 Ibid., pp. 197–8.

143 Ibid., p. 198.

144 Ibid., p. 199.

145 TNA, PROB 11/980/239, Will of John Calcraft of Ingress, Kent, 25 August 1772.

146 BL, India Office Private Papers, Mss Eur G37/94/1, ff. 50–5, George Anne Bellamy to Lord Clive, 27 July 1767; Mss Eur G37/94/1, ff. 59–60, George Anne Bellamy to Lord Clive, 1767; Mss Eur G37/94/2, ff. 24–5, George Anne Bellamy to Lord Clive, 1767.

Chapter 5

1 On women and the estate, see McDonagh, *Elite Women and the Agricultural Landscape*.

2 Duchess of Marlborough to Lady Russell, Scarborough, 21 July 1732, in Thomson (ed.), *Letters of a Grandmother*, p. 52.

3 BL, Blenheim Papers, Add. MS. 61357, ff. 34–35b,74–77b, Henry Wise, Superintendent of Royal Gardens: Bills for work at Marlborough House, 1710–11.

4 Two drawings survive for this scheme: Bodleian Library, Oxford, MS Gough Drawings a4 f. 44 and a3 f. 31, both attributed to Charles Bridgeman, undated; reproduced in, Peter Willis, *Charles Bridgeman and the English Landscape Garden* (Newcastle upon Tyne: Elysium Press Publishers, 2002), plates 44a & b. See also, Frances Harris, 'Charles Bridgeman at Blenheim?', *Garden History*, vol. 13, no. 1 (Spring, 1985), p. 1.

5 WYAS, Leeds, Pawson MSS, Letter Book 6, Acc. 1038, B6 B23/9, John Waple to Frances Ingram, Lady Irwin, 24 August 1758, as cited in James Lomax, 'Temple Newnham: a Woman's Domain', in Larsen (ed.), *Maids and Mistresses*, p. 100.

6 Diary entry of Ralph Thoresby, 14 February 1721, in Hunter (ed.), *The Diary of Ralph Thoresby*, vol. 2, p. 313.

7 Diary entry of Ralph Thoresby, 3 November 1721, in Hunter (ed.), *The Diary of Ralph Thoresby*, vol. 2, p. 327.

8 Diary entry of Ralph Thoresby, 10 November 1721, in Hunter (ed.), *The Diary of Ralph Thoresby,* vol. 2, p. 328.

9 BL, Althorp Papers, Add. MS 75598, Lady Spencer to Dowager Lady Spencer, Althorp, 2 October 1788.

10 Ibid.

11 Ibid.

12 Ibid.

13 BL, Althorp Papers, Add MS 75598, Lavinia Spencer to Dowager Countess Spencer, Althorp, 13 December 1788.

14 Horace Walpole to Horace Mann, Arlington Street, 12 January 1748, in Lewis (ed.), *Horace Walpole's Correspondence,* vol. 19, pp. 456–7.

15 For a discussion on their disastrous marriage, see A. M. W. Stirling, *Coke of Norfolk and His Friends*, 2 vols (London: John Lane, The Bodley Head: 1908), vol. 1, pp. 49–61.

16 Lord Leicester to Lord Hartington, Holkham Hall, 31 January 1748, as quoted in C. W. James, *Chief Justice Coke, His Family & Descendants at Holkham* (London: Country Life Ltd., 1929), pp. 237–8.

17 Stirling, *Coke of Norfolk*, vol. 1, p. 61.

18 Lord Leicester to Lord Hartington, 1753, as quoted in James, *Chief Justice Coke*, p. 248.

19 HHA, Uncatalogued Box labelled 'Almshouses', Settlement dated 5 April 1755.

20 Plaque on the end of the Almshouses states that 'Endowed by her for the Benefit of Three Poor Men and Three Poor Women THOMAS Earl of THANET Her Father was a Benefactor By a Legacy he left her of Eight Hundred Pounds For Charitable Uses'.

21 HHA, 'Almshouses', Settlement dated 5 April 1755.

22 Ibid.

23 HHA, 'Almshouses', Settlement dated 16 March 1765.

24 Robert Potter, *Holkham A Poem to the Right Honourable the Earl of Leicester* (London: R. Manby, 1758), p. 7; Sarah Biller, *Holkham, the Scenes of My Childhood: And Other Poems* (London: Foxter and Hextall, 1839), p. 31.

25 John Chambers, *A General History of the County of Norfolk, Intended to Convey All the Information of a Norfolk Tour*, vol. 2 (Norwich: John Stacy, 1829), p. 598.

26 John Hutchins, *The History and Antiquities of the County of Dorset* (3rd edn, with additions by W. Shipp and J. W. Hodson, London, 1863), vol. 4, p. 440.

27 Martin, *Wives and Daughters,* p. 341.

28 Dorset Record Office, D/FSI, Box 188, Household Accounts (Melbury), 1747–51, as quoted in Martin, *Wives and Daughters,* p. 342.

29 Jonathan Betts and Tessa Murdoch, 'A Royal Gift? Mrs Strangways Horner's Small Silver Clock, 1740', *Science Museum Group Journal*, no. 11 (Spring 2009), online.

30 Martin, *Wives and Daughters,* pp. 17–24.

31 Ibid., p. 24.

32 Ibid.

33 Penrice Papers, Charlotte Traherne, 'Family Recollections', as quoted in Martin, *Wives and Daughters,* p. 341.

34 SM, Journal No. 2, 2 March 1789–21 December 1789, p. 55; SM, volume 68/5, John Soane, Presentation drawing of entrance gate, 18 September 1789; SM, Journal No. 1, 27 January 1791, p. 33.

35 SM, 47/1/81, Henry Hake Seward or Thomas Sword, Perspective of the church with the new chapel from the south-east, 21 May 1801; 47/1/82, Henry Hake Seward or Thomas Sword, 'Plan Shewing the Proposed Alteration', 21 May 1781; 47/1/83, Henry Hake Seward, Designs for the chapel, 14 April 1802; 47/1/84, Soane office, Designs for the chapel, 14 April 1802; 47/1/85, Soane Office, Design for the chapel, 9 June 1803.

36 Karen Bentall, 'Historic Bramley', *The Bramley Magazine* (2016), p. 24.

37 This double portrait was sold at Bonhams on 4 July 2018 and is now in a private collection.

38 Derby City Art Gallery and Museum, Joseph Wright, *D'Ewes Coke, His Wife Hannah and Daniel Parker Coke, MP*, 1780–2, oil on canvas, 152.4 × 177.8 cm.

39 Horace Walpole, *The History of Modern Taste in Gardening*, ed. John Dixon Hunt (New York: Ursus Press, 1995), p. 41.

40 Ibid., p. 42.

41 Ibid.

42 Peter Willis, 'From Desert to Eden: Charles Bridgeman's "Capital Stroke"', *The Burlington Magazine*, vol. 115, no. 840 (1973), p. 153.

43 Joanna Marschner, *Queen Caroline: Cultural Politics at the Early Eighteenth-Century Court* (New Haven and London: Yale University Press, 2014), p. 33.

44 Diary entry of Ralph Thoresby, 17 May 1722, in Hunter (ed.), *The Diary of Ralph Thoresby,* vol. 2, p. 339.

45 Diary entry of Ralph Thoresby, 16 May 1722, in Hunter (ed.), *The Diary of Ralph Thoresby*, vol. 2, p. 337.

46 National Library of Ireland, Dublin, Family Papers of Smythe and Barbavilla, MS 41,580/36–39, C. Fox to Mrs Jane Bonnell, Ledston, 6 June, undated [*c.* 1720].

47 Willis, *Charles Bridgeman*, p. 61 and pp. 180–1.

48 Ibid., Plate 48b [*c.* 1731].

49 Ibid., p. 180, the references for which are: Bodleian Library, M.S. Gough Drawings a.3 f. 19, Plan of Ledston Hall and Park; M.S. Gough Drawings a.4. f. 85, Plan of Ledston Hall and Park, Yorkshire.

50 Reproduced in John Harris, *The Artist and the Country House: A History of Country House and Garden View Painting in Britain 1540–1870* (London: Sotheby Park Bernet, 1979), pp. 192–3.

51 Colin Briden, 'Ledston Hall, Ledston, Yorkshire – Conservation Plan', 2007, p. 11 and 63.

52 BL, Add MS 4809, f.141v, Charles Bridgeman to Alexander Pope, Broadstreet, 28 September 1724.

53 Norfolk Record Office, Norwich, MC 184/10/3, Alexander Pope (att.), design for the pleasure grounds at Marble Hill, *c.* 1724.

54 Norfolk Record Office, MC184/10/1, 'The Plan of the House Garden & Inclosures of Marblehill 10 Miles West from London Belonging to the Right Honourable The Countess of Suffolk', *c.* 1749.

55 Duchess of Queensbury to George II, 27 February 1728, as quoted in John Hervey, *Memoirs of the Reign of George the Second*, ed. John Wilson Croker (Philadelphia: Lea and Blancard, 1848), vol. 1, p. 142.

56 Duchess of Queensbury and John Gay to Henrietta Howard, 20 August 1730, in *Letters to and from Henrietta, Countess of Suffolk, and Her Second Husband, the Hon. George Berkeley: from 1712 to 1767*, 2 vols (London: John Murray, 1824), vol. 1, p. 382.

57 Henrietta Howard to John Gay, Kensington, 5 September 1731, in *Letters to and from Henrietta*, vol. 2, pp. 20–1.

58 For discussions about the 1st Dukes garden at Wrest, see Linda Cabe Halpern, 'The Duke of Kent's Garden at Wrest Park', *Journal of Garden History*, vol. 15, no. 3 (1995), pp. 149–78.

59 For an account of the garden's development, see Linda Cabe Halpern, 'Wrest Park 1686–1730s: Exploring Dutch Influence', *Garden History*, vol. 30, no. 2 (2002), pp. 131–52.

60 BLARS, L30/9a/5/118, Lady Grey to Catherine Talbot, Wrest Park, 13 October 1748.

61 See, Andrew Hann, 'A Tale of Two Advisors: Jemima, Marchioness Grey and the Improvement of the Gardens at Wrest Park in the Mid-18th Century', *Journal of the Women's History Network*, vol. 2, no. 13 (Summer 2019), pp. 4–14.

62 BLARS, L30/9a/3/20, Lady Grey to Lady Mary Gregory, Wrest Park, 3 October 1758.

63 BLARS, L30/9a/9/124, Lady Grey to Catherine Talbot, Wimpole, 19 September 1769.

64 BLARS, L30/9/97/20, Agneta Yorke to Lady Grey, Tittenhanger, 13 October 1771.

65 For accounts of Elizabeth's improvements to Sandleford see, Baird, *Mistress of the House*, pp. 213–17; Stephen Bending, *Green Retreats: Women, Gardens and Eighteenth-Century Culture* (Cambridge: Cambridge University Press, 2013), pp. 159–72.

66 HL, MO3530, Elizabeth Montagu to Elizabeth Carter, Sandleford, 11 July 1782, as quoted in Bending, *Green Retreats*, p. 158.

67 Elizabeth Montagu to unknown, December 1782, in John Doran, *A Lady of the Last Century (Mrs. Elizabeth Montagu)* (London: R. Bentley and Son, 1873), p. 303.

68 Lady Holland to Lady Kildare, 9 October 1759, in Fitzgerald (ed.), *Correspondence*, vol. 1, p. 259.

69 For a biography, see Jane Brown, *My Darling Heriott: Henrietta Luxborough, Poetic Gardener and Irrepressible Exile* (London: HarperPress, 2006).

70 ODNB online, 'Henrietta Knight, Lady Luxborough (1699–1756)'.

71 BL, Knight Papers, Add. MS 45889 ff. 9–10, Henrietta Knight to Robert Knight Jr., n.d.

72 Ibid.

73 Bending, *Green Retreats*, p. 212.

74 Ibid., p. 219.

75 Helen Sard Hughes, *The Gentle Hertford: Her Life and Letters* (New York: Macmillan, 1940), p. 145.

76 Bending, *Green Retreats*, p. 220.

77 John Hannett, *The Forest of Arden, Its Towns, Villages, and Hamlets: A Topographical and Historical Account of the District between and around Henley-in-Arden and Hampton-in-Arden in the County of Warwick* (London: Simkin, Marshall, and J. Russell Smith, 1863), p. 102.

78 Lady Luxborough to William Shenstone, Barrells, 8 September 1749, in Lady Luxborough, *Letters Written by the Late Right Honourable Lady Luxborough, to William Shenstone, Esq* (Dublin: Printed for Caler Jenkins, 1776), p. 121.

79 Lady Luxborough to William Shenstone, Barrells, 25 February 1750, in Luxborough, *Letters*, p. 191.

80 Lady Luxborough to William Shenstone, Barrells, 4 January 1749, in Luxborough, *Letters*, p. 79.

81 Lady Luxborough to William Shenstone, Barrells, 4 June 1749, in Luxborough, *Letters*, pp. 97–8.

82 Lady Luxborough to William Shenstone, Barrells, 27 May 1751, in Luxborough, *Letters*, p. 264.

83 Lady Luxborough to William Shenstone, Barrells, 4 June 1749, in Luxborough, *Letters*, pp. 97–8.

84 Lady Luxborough to William Shenstone, Barrells, 8 November 1749, in Luxborough, *Letters*, p. 140.

85 Ibid.

86 Lady Luxborough to William Shenstone, Barrells, Easter Sunday 1748, in Luxborough, *Letters*, p. 15.

87 Ibid.

88 Bending, *Green Retreats*, p. 229.

89 Karen Lipsedge, *Domestic Space in Eighteenth-Century British Novels* (Basingstoke: Palgrave Macmillan, 2012), p. 135.

90 For discussions on women and the ornamental dairy, see Meredith Martin, *Dairy Queens: The Politics of Pastoral Architecture from Catherine de' Medici to Marie-Antoinette* (Cambridge, MA: Harvard University Press, 2011); *idem*, 'Interiors and Interiority in the Ornamental Dairy Tradition', *Eighteenth Century Fiction*, vol. 20, no. 3 (2008), pp. 357–84; Pierre de la Ruffinière du Prey, 'Eight Maids-a-Milking: Ornamental Dairies and Their Owners', *Country Life*, 181 (5 March 1987), pp. 120–2.

91 4 August 1828, Prince Pückler-Muskau, *Tour in England Ireland and France in the Years 1828 and 1829*, vol. 1 (London: Effingham Wilson, 1832), p. 143.

92 Daniel Defoe, *A Tour thro' the Whole Island of Great Britain* (1724–6) ed. P. N. Furbank and W. R. Owens (New Haven and London: Yale University Press, 1991), p. 72.

93 For discussions of Queen Caroline's dairy see, Meredith, 'Interiors and Interiority', pp. 363–4. For Princess Amelia's see, du Prey, 'Eight Maids-a-Milking', p. 120. For Queen Charlotte's, see Christopher Christie, *The British Country House in the Eighteenth Century* (Manchester: Manchester University Press, 2000), p. 159.

94 Anon., *A Description of the Royal Gardens at Richmond in Surry, the Village, and Places Adjacent* (London, 1736), p. 9.

95 Martin, 'Interiors and Interiority', p. 364.

96 BL, Althorp Papers, Add MS 75927, Lady Spencer to Earl Spencer, Althorp, 20 October 1787.

97 George Alexander Cooke, *Topographical and Statistical Description of the County of Surrey* (London: C. Cooke, 1802), p. 158.

98 SM, Adam volume 23/52, Adam Office hand, possibly Joseph Bonomi, 'Design of a Chimney Piece for Lady Derby's room in the Dairy Building at Knowsley', 24 February 1777, pen, pencil and wash on laid paper (406 x 293).

99 V&A, 3306:161, John Soane, 'Dairy Design for Lady Craven', 1781, pen and ink with grey, green, brown and pink. For a discussion of Dance's involvement in this design, see Jill Lever, 'The Soane-Dance Collaboration, 1771–1799', *Architectural History*, vol. 53 (2010), p. 169.

100 Martin, 'Dairy Queens: Sexuality, Space, and Subjectivity', pp. 231–2; Whitaker, 'Dairy Culture', pp. 42–3.

101 Elizabeth Montagu to unknown, 23 August 1747, in Climenson (ed.), *Elizabeth Montagu*, vol. 1, p. 245.

102 Jeremy Musson, 'Her Grace's Grotto Comes Out of Its Shell', *Country Life*, vol. 191, no. 39 (25 September 1997), pp. 86–7.

103 Banham, *Encyclopaedia*, p. 536.

104 Stella Tillyard, *Aristocrats: Caroline, Emily, Louisa and Sarah Lennox, 1740–1832* (London: Chatto & Windus, 1994), p. 16.

105 James Howley, *The Follies and Garden Buildings of Ireland* (New Haven and London: Yale University Press, 1993), pp. 35–6.

106 For discussions on A La Ronde, see, for example, Freya Gowrley, 'Craft(ing) Narratives: Specimens, Souvenirs, and "Morsels" in A la Ronde's Specimen Table', *Eighteenth-Century Fiction*, vol. 31, no. 1 (2018), pp. 77–97; M. L. R. Tudor, *A La Ronde (The Round House) Exmouth and the Parminter Collection* (Exeter: W.V.Cole and Sons Ltd., *c.* 1970).

107 Duchess of Portland to Mrs Ann Granville, Whitehall, 21 June 1737, in Llanover (ed.), *Autobiography*, 1st ser., vol. 1, p. 608.

108 Mary Delany to Mary Port *née* Dewes, 19 November 1771, Bulstrode, in Llanover (ed.), *Autobiography*, 2nd ser., vol. 1, p. 374.

109 Madeline Pelling, 'Female Friendship and Domestic Craft at Bulstrode Park', *Journal for Eighteenth-Century Studies*, vol. 41, no. 1 (2018), p. 101.

110 Lady Mary Wortley Montagu to Lady Pomfret [March 1739] in Lord Wharncliffe (ed.), *The Letters and Works of Lady Mary Wortley Montagu* (London: Richard Bentley, 1837), vol. 2, p. 223.

111 Ibid.

112 For discussions on Soubise, see Monica L. Miller, *Slaves to Fashion: Black Dandyism and the Styling of Black Diasporic Identity* (Durham: Duke University Press, 2009), pp. 57–72; Peter McNeil, *Pretty Gentlemen: Macaroni Men and the Eighteenth-century Fashion World* (New Haven: Yale University Press, 2018), pp. 118–20.

113 BL, Add. MS 41134, ff. 13–14, Sir William Chambers letter books Vol II, Duchess of Queensbury to William Chambers, Amesbury, 25 November 1772.

114 Ibid.

115 Ibid.

116 Ibid.

Chapter 6

1 Duchess of Marlborough to the Duchess of Bedford, 21 July 1732, Thomson (ed.), *Letters of a Grandmother*, p. 52.

2 See, for example, A. T. Friedman, 'Architecture, Authority, and the Female Gaze: Planning and Representation in the Early Modern Country House', *Assemblage*, vol. 18 (1992), pp. 40–61; Laurence, 'Women Using Building in Seventeenth-Century England'; French; 'A Widow Building in Elizabethan England'; Elizabeth V. Chew, 'Repaired by Me to My Exceeding Great Cost

and Charges': Anne Clifford and the Uses of Architecture', in Helen Hills (ed.), *Architecture and the Politics of Gender in Early Modern Europe* (Ashgate: Aldershot, 2003), pp. 99–114.

3 For discussions on female architectural patronage in the nineteenth and twentieth centuries, see Megan Leyland, 'Patronage and the Architectural Profession: The Country House in Nineteenth-Century Northamptonshire' (PhD thesis, University of Leicester, 2016); Susan Lewis, 'The Artistic and Architectural Patronage of Angela Burdett Coutts' (PhD thesis, Royal Holloway, University of London, 2012); Brenda Martin, Penny Sparke (eds), *Women's Places: Architecture and Design 1860–1960* (Ashgate: Aldershot, 2005); Lynne Walker, 'Women Patron Builders in Britain: Identity, Difference and Memory in Spatial and Material Culture', in D. Cherry and J. Holland (eds), *Local/Global: Women Artists in the Nineteenth Century* (Ashgate: Aldershot, 2006), pp. 121–36.

4 *Architectural Magazine*, vol. 3 (1836), p. 497.

5 Ibid.

6 See Lynne Walker, 'The Entry of Women into the Architectural Profession in Britain', *Woman's Art Journal*, vol. 7, no. 1 (1986), pp. 13–18; *idem*, *Drawing on Diversity Women: Architecture and Practice* (London, 1997), pp. 1–26; E. Darling and L. Whitworth (eds), *Women and the Making of Built Space in England, 1870–1950* (Ashgate: Aldershot, 2007).

7 Lynne Walker, 'Golden Age or False Dawn? Women Architects in the Early 20th Century', Report for Historic England, n.d., p. 2. https://historicengland.org.uk/content/docs/research/women-architects-early-20th-century-pdf/.

8 RIBA Archive, London. MS.SP 4/1, address delivered by Donaldson at the official opening meeting of the Royal Institute of British Architects, 15 June 1835.

9 Lynne Walker, 'Women and Architecture', in Iain Borden, Barbara Penner and Jane Rendell (eds), *Gender, Space Architecture: An Interdisciplinary Introduction* (London: Routledge, 1999), p. 252.

10 Ibid.

11 As quoted in Walker, 'Golden Age or False Dawn?', p. 5.

12 Iain Jackson and Jessica Holland, *The Architecture of Edwin Maxwell Fry and Jane Drew* (London: Routledge, 2016), p. 2.

13 Ibid.

14 Ibid., p. 101.

15 Frank Knight cited in Sile Flower, Jean McFarlane and Ruth Plant (eds), *Jane B. Drew Architect: A Tribute from Colleagues and Friends for Her 75th Birthday 24th March 1986* (Bristol: Bristol Centre for the Advancement of Architecture, 1986), p. 42.

BIBLIOGRAPHY

Manuscript sources

London Archives

British Library, London

Althorp Papers:

Add. MS 75622: Correspondence of Georgiana, Lady Spencer with Caroline Howe, wife of John Howe, and sister of Richard, 1st Earl Howe, March–April 1784.

Add. MS 75623: Correspondence of Georgiana, Lady Spencer with Caroline Howe, wife of John Howe, and sister of Richard, 1st Earl Howe, May–June 1784.

Add. MS 75627: Correspondence of Georgiana, Lady Spencer with Caroline Howe, wife of John Howe, and sister of Richard, 1st Earl Howe, May–December 1785.

Add. MS 75684: Letters from George Simon Harcourt, 2nd Earl Harcourt to Georgiana, Lady Spencer, 1756–1814.

Add. MS 75927: Correspondence of Lavinia, Lady Spencer to Earl Spencer, 1786–October 1788.

Blenheim Papers:

Add. MS 61353: Correspondence of the Duke and Duchess of Marlborough with Sir John Vanbrugh, Samuel Travers, Nicholas Hawksmoor, Henry Wise and others, concerning the building and gardens at Blenheim Palace, 1705–25.

Add MS 61354: Proposals, contracts, estimates, accounts, memoranda, etc., concerning the building, furnishings and gardens at Blenheim, including (ff. 126–63) a series of interior elevations, chiefly of rooms on the upper stories, 1705–35.

Add. MS. 61357: Correspondence, particularly with Sir Christopher Wren and his son, accounts, estimates and narratives of the Duchess, relating to the building and furnishing of Marlborough House, 1710–15.

Add. MS 61423, particularly ff. 110–79b: Narrative relating to the Duchess of Marlborough, compiled by Gilbert Burnet, Bishop of Salisbury, *c.* 1711.

Add. MS 61459: Correspondence with Arthur Maynwaring, M.P., 1707–12.

Add. MS 61477: Letters to the Duchess of Marlborough and her Secretary, James Stephens, 1728–41.

Add MS 61478, ff. 9–12b, 17, 31–4b, 39, 43–8b, 51: Letters relating to the payment of Charles Bridgeman for the gardens at Wimbledon House, 1739–41.

Coke Papers:

Add. MS 69965: Architectural papers of Thomas Coke (1675–1727) of Melbourne, Derbyshire, particularly ff. 45–54, of plans and estimates relating to Drayton House, Northamptonshire, home of Lady Elizabeth Germain, widow of Sir John Germain.

Evelyn Papers:

Add. MS 78530, f. 12, Duchess of Marlborough to Mrs Jael Boscawen, 20 September 1718.

Hamilton and Greville Papers:

Add. MS 40714, f. 116 r., 'Major General Clerk and the Right Hon'ble the Countess Dowager of Warwick in Acct with Robert & James Adam', n.d.

Hardwicke Papers:

Add. MS 35386: Letters of Agneta, widow of the Hon. Charles Yorke, to her stepson Philip, 3rd Earl of Hardwicke, relating to personal and family affairs, 1773–1810.

Add. MS 35693, f. 135: Rev. Hadley Cox to Philip Yorke, April 1769.

Holland House Papers:

Add. MS 51340, particularly ff. 1–62b: Letters to 1st Lord Ilchester and Lady Ilchester from his sister, Charlotte Digby, 1719–71.

Add. MS 61811, ff. 26–47: Plans and surveys relating to St Anne's Hill House and Estate, Chertsey, n.d., mid-19th century.

Knight Papers:

Add. MS 45889, particularly ff. 7–15, 30, 48, 56, 62: Correspondence and papers of Robert Knight, M.P., with his first wife, Henrietta Knight.

Letters of Robert Adam:

RP 3031/1: Five photocopied letters written to Robert Adam from his clients, including one from Elizabeth, Countess of Home, 24 February 1775.

Letters-Books of Sir William Chambers:

Add. MS 41134, Vol. II: Correspondence of Sir William Chambers, 1772–5.

Portland Papers:

Add. MS 70432, Misc 13: Draft letters from Henrietta, Countess of Oxford, to Lady Mary Wortley Montagu, 1743–54.

India Office Private Papers:

Mss Eur G37/94/2, ff. 24–5: George Anne Bellamy to Lord Clive, 1767.

Mss Eur G37/94/1, ff. 50–5: George Anne Bellamy to Lord Clive, 27 July 1767.

Mss Eur G37/94/1, ff. 59–60: George Anne Bellamy to Lord Clive, 1767.

Letters Written to Henrietta Howard, Countess of Suffolk:

Add. MS 22626, Vol. II. 9: 4th Earl of Chesterfield to Henrietta Howard, *c.* 1725–66.

Pope's Homer:
Vol. III, Add MS 4809, f. 141v: Charles Bridgeman to Alexander Pope, Broadstreet, 28 September 1724.

17th–18th Century Burney Collection Newspapers:
Gazetteer and London Daily Advertiser
General Evening Post
London Chronicle
London Evening Post
London Gazette
Morning Chronicle and London Advertiser
Public Advertiser

The National Archives, Kew

Records created, acquired and inherited by Chancery, and also of the Wardrobe, Royal Household, Exchequer and various commissions:
C 107/149, *Cornelys v Fermor* (1760–61).
C 12/1289/16, *Cornelys v Bodycoate* (1762).
C 12/1471/1, *Cornelys v Fermor* (1763, amended 1764).
C 12/1585/16, *Fermor v Cornelys* (1763).
C 12/1518/16, *Fermor v Chamberlain* (1772).
C 12/392/28, *Cornelys v Burger* (1772).
C 202/159/18: Charlotte Digby's enclosure of the highway in Thames Ditton, 11 January 1771.

Records of the Prerogative Court of Canterbury:
PROB, 11/761: Will of William Kent, made 13 October 1743, codicil 10 April 1748, proved 18 June 1748.
PROB 11/803/199: Will of the Right Honourable Thomas Earl of Pomfret and Baron of Lempster, 20 July 1753.
PROB, 11/862/216: Will of the Right Honourable, Lady Jane Coke, Widow of Longford, Derbyshire, 19 January 1761.
PROB 11/980/239: Will of John Calcraft of Ingress, Kent, 25 August 1772.
PROB, 11/1112/304: Will of the Right Honourable Elizabeth Countess of Home, Dowager, Widow of Portman Square, Middlesex, 24 January 1784.

Victoria and Albert Museum, London

Prints, Drawings and Paintings Collection:
E.3237-1934: Contract elevation of the north front of Peper Harrow House for the 3rd Viscount Midleton, signed by William Chambers, 11 March 1765.
E.3238-1934: Contract elevation of the south front, with a sketch plan of a window or door opening for Peper Harrow House for the 3rd Viscount Midleton, signed by William Chambers, 11 March 1765.
3306:161, John Soane, 'Dairy Design for Lady Craven', 1781.

The Sir John Soane's Museum, London

i) The Drawings of Robert Adam

Drawings relating to Hatchlands Park, Surrey:

Adam volume 35/80: Stiff Leadbetter with pencil annotations by Robert Adam, survey plan of the ground floor, Hatchlands, 1757.

Adam volume 11/6–11/15: Adam office hand, possibly Laurent-Benoit Dewez, various ceiling designs, 1759.

Adam volume 11/13 & 14: Adam office hand, possibly Laurent-Benoit Dewez, designs for a chimneypiece for the drawing room (now the library), as executed, 1759.

Adam volume 22/11 & 12: Adam office hand, possibly Robert Adam, designs for a chimneypiece for the great dining room (now the saloon and picture gallery), executed with minor alterations, 1759.

Adam volume 35/81–35/83: Adam office hand, possibly Agostino Brunias, finished drawings and a record drawing for the walls of the great dining room (now the saloon and picture gallery), 1759.

Drawings Relating to the Admiral Edward Boscawen Monument, Cornwall:

Adam volume 19/1: Finished drawing for the funerary monument of Admiral Boscawen, as executed, 1761.

Adam volume 54/2/20; 54/2/17; 54/2/25; 54/2/24; 54/2/28; 19/23; 54/2/32; 19/5; 54/2/31; 19/4; 19/3; 54/2/18; 54/2/29; 19/2: Preliminary and finished designs for the funerary monument of Admiral Boscawen, all unexecuted, 1761.

Drawings Relating to Home House, Portman Square, London:

There are seventy-three Robert Adam drawings relating to Home House, of which below are a selection relating to the drawing rooms, music room, staircase, Etruscan dressing room and the Cumberlands' picture frames:

Adam volume 3/106; 5/1–6, 8–9; 6/63, 67, 110; 8/41, 48; 12/160–8; 14/116–17, 119, 132, 134; 17/63, 129, 195–6; 18/67, 69, 80; 20/162–7; 23/63–9; 25/15, 26–7, 217; 50/33–8; 52/3, 68, 74; 53/7–8; 54/7/165.

Drawings Relating to Clerk House, Mansfield Street, London:

Adam volume 14/57–8: Adam office hand, designs for a drawing room ceiling, June 1779.

Adam volume 23/160: Adam office hand based on pencil drawing by Robert Adam, 'Chimney piece for the Drawing room at General Clerks', June 1779.

Adam volume 23/280–4: Adam office hand, designs for window shutter panels for Clerk House, June 1779.

Adam volume 44/1–9: Adam office hand, plans, sections and elevation plans of Clerk House, 1779.

Drawings Relating to Knowsley Park, Lancashire:

Adam volume 23/52: Adam office hand, possibly Joseph Bonomi, 'Design of a Chimney Piece for Lady Derby's Room in the Dairy Building at Knowsley', 24 February 1777.

ii) The Drawings of Sir John Soane

Drawings Relating to Pembroke Lodge, Richmond Park:
Drawings dating from 1785 to 1798: Volume 41/54; 41/79v; 29/3/1–12; 81/2/49.

Drawings Relating to No. 49 (Formally 44) Grosvenor Square, London:
Drawings dating from 1797 to 1800: Volume 39/1/45–54; 77/2/12; 77/3/17, 46; 81/1/43–4; 81/2/34, 48, 84.

Drawings Relating to Sydney Lodge, Hamble, Hampshire:
Drawings dating from 1793 to 1796: Volume 59/38–9; 46/3/16–20; 80/1/58–9; 81/2/8–10, 22, 45, 82.

Drawings Relating to Wokefield Park, Berkshire:
Volume 68/5: John Soane, presentation drawing of entrance gate, 18 September 1789.

Drawings Relating to the New Chapel at St James' Church, Bramley, Hampshire:
Drawings dating 1801–3: Volume 47/1/81–9.

Sir John Soane's Journals:
Journal No. 1, 1791.
Journal No. 2, 1789
Journal No. 5, 1809.
Journal No. 6, 1813.

iii) Drawings by other Architects

Drawings Relating to No. 18 Arlington Street, London:
43/5/5: Design for the courtyard front, inscribed on verso with 'Sketch of a Gothic Building February 1757'.
43/5/8: Richard Briggs, copy of a design for the park front, n.d.
43/5/9: Richard Briggs, copy of the Park Front design, slightly different, n.d.

The Royal Academy of Arts, London

Drawings Relating to Polwarth Villa:
09/440: John Yenn, floor plan and south elevation of Lady Polwarth's villa, *c.* 1780.

Royal Institute of British Architects (RIBA), Architectural Library, London

Drawing Relating to No. 44 Berkeley Square, London:
SC50/2: Designed by William Kent, drafted by Stephen Wright, design for the coffered ceiling of the saloon at 44 Berkeley Square, *c.* 1742–4.

SD92/7: Stephen Wright (att.), measured drawing, plan and two sections of the staircase at No. 44 Berkeley Square, with scale, *c.* 1743.

Drawings Relating to Montagu House, Portman Square, London:

DR127/2: Joseph Bonomi, interior perspective of the Great Drawing Room, 1790.

SA5/3(2, 4–9): Joseph Bonomi, various design for interior decoration, 1780–90.

Speeches/Addresses:

MS.SP 4/1: Address delivered by Donaldson at the official opening meeting of the Royal Institute of British Architects, 15 June 1835.

The London Metropolitan Archives, London

ACC/2552/001: Private Act of Parliament for vesting estate in manor of Kempton in trustees for sale to Lady Jane Coke, 1755.

Lambeth Archives, London

Drawings Relating to Polwarth Lodge, Putney Heath:

LP26/188/POL1-7: John Yenn, drawings and designs for Polwarth Lodge, *c.* 1792.

SP 26/188/LUC 1: Unknown artist, north elevation of Lady Polwarth's villa, n.d., *c.* 1810.

Drawings Relating to Grantham House, Putney Heath:

LP26/188/GRAM1-10: John Yenn, drawings and designs for Polwarth Lodge, *c.* 1792.

Irish Archives

Irish Architectural Archive, Dublin

Charleville Forest Drawings Collection:

86/24/17: Charles William Bury (att.), perspective sketch of proposed castle at Charleville, *c.* 1800.

Townley Hall Collection:

85/156/14: Blayney and Anna Maria Townley, proposed plan of the principal floor of Townley Hall, n.d.

National Library of Ireland, Dublin

Family Papers of Smythe and Barbavilla:

MS 41,580/36–39: C. Fox to Mrs Jane Bonnell, Ledston, 6 June, undated, *c.* 1720.

AD 2496–2499: Anna Maria Townley (att.), plans of each floor of Townley Hall, *c.* 1797.

Public Records Office of Northern Ireland, Belfast

Tighe Papers:

D/2685/14/1, typescript family history entitled 'The Tighe Story' by Rear-Admiral W.G.S. Tighe, p. 21.

Provincial Archives

Bedford and Luton Archives and Record Services, Bedford

Wrest Park [Lucas] Papers:

Marriage Settlements:

L22/127–8, Marriage settlement of Lord Grantham and Mary Jemima Grey, 15–16 August 1780.

L32/11–13, Will of Henry Grey, Duke of Kent (three official copies), 29 May 1740.

Correspondence:

L30/9a/1–2: Letters of Jemima, Marchioness Grey to Lady Mary Gregory, 1740–57.

L30/9a/3: Letters of Jemima, Marchioness Grey to Lady Mary Gregory and Catherine Talbot, 1737–60.

L30/9a/4–8: Letters of Jemima, Marchioness Grey to Catherine Talbot, 1744–67.

L30/9a/9: Letters of Jemima, Marchioness Grey to Catherine Talbot (until November 1769) and Mary Yorke, her youngest daughter, 1770–5.

L30/9/11: Letters from George Byfield, architect, to Jemima, Marchioness Grey, 1790.

L30/9/21: Letters to Jemima, Marchioness Grey, from Lady Charlotte Capell, 1748–50.

L30/9/60: Letters from Lady Polwarth to her mother, Jemima, Marchioness Grey, 1772–95.

L30/9/73: Letters from Joseph Pawsey, Steward at Wrest Park, to Jemima, Marchioness Grey, 1790–6.

L30/9/81: Letters from Lady Grantham, to her mother, Jemima, Marchioness Grey, *c*. 1780–96.

L30/9/97: Letters to Jemima, Marchioness Grey, from Agneta Yorke (née Johnson) (sister-in-law, wife of Charles Yorke), 1763–96.

L30/11/122: Letters to Lady Polwarth from her mother, Jemima, Marchioness Grey, 1761–94.

L30/11/240: Letters from Lady Grantham to her sister Lady Polwarth, 1780–1829.

L30/23: Correspondence between Lady Polwarth and her cousin, Jemima Mary Gregory, 1765–94.

Papers Relating to No. 4 St James's Square, London:

L21/94–5: Conveyance (lease & release) relating to No. 4 St James's Square, 31 January to 1 February 1677/8.

L21/124: Lease of No. 4 St James's Square, 21 June 1743.

L31/276: Estimate for alterations at St James' Square for Jemima, Marchioness Grey, n.d., *c.* 1790.

Papers Relating to Wrest Park, Bedfordshire:

L31/184/1: 'An Inventory of the Furniture, Linnen, Plate and Other Goods Belonging to the Most Noble Henry Duke of Kent Late Deceased at Rest House in the Parish of Silsoe in the County of Bedford Taken the 19th, 20th, 21st, 23rd of June 1740 by Whose Names Are Hereunder Written'.

L31/230–41: Building accounts at Wrest Park, *c.* 1676.

L31/260–5: Letter from John Smith (architect) to Philip Yorke, Earl of Hardwicke, with five variant plans for the drawing room alterations, 1763.

L31/266: 'Estimate for Building the Drawing Room &c at Wrest', John Smith, n.d., *c.* 1763.

L31/267: Letter from John Smith (architect) to Philip Yorke, Earl of Hardwicke, 1763.

L31/268–72: Five variant plans for the drawing room alterations, 1763.

L31/273: Bill for hanging Indian paper, in Marchioness Grey's hand, n.d., *c.* 1760s.

L31/274: Bill for various repairs to Wrest, in Marchioness Grey's hand, n.d., *c.* 1760s.

L31/277: Estimate for alterations at Wrest Park, 1791.

L31/278: Design for a 'New Dairy at Wrest', 22 May 1796.

L31/318: Bill for the new cold bath and bridge, Edward Stevens, 1770.

L33/146: Design for a new house, superimposed over the ground floor plan of the existing (old) Wrest Park house, 1818.

L33/149: Ground floor plan, entitled 'The House at Wrest Park, as Altered By the Grey', paper watermarked 1824.

L33/213: Pencil drawing of the interior of the Library of Wrest Park house, by J. C. Buckler, 1831.

Papers Relating to Newby Park, Yorkshire:

L31/191: Inventory of household goods and furniture at Newby Park, 1786 (or 1795?).

L33/275: Block plan of Newby Park, adjoining buildings and park and gardens, n.d.

L33/276: Three ink sketches of Newby Park, mounted on one sheet of paper, two dated 24 June 1784.

Papers Relating to Polwarth Lodge, Putney Heath:

L31/280: Particulars of a Villa &c. to be sold on the north side of Putney Common, *c.* 1800.

L31/281: Valuation of fixtures belonging to Charles Bembridge at his house on Putney Heath, 10 June 1791.

L31/282: Plan of the bedchamber wing to Lady Polwarth's house Putney Heath, *c.* 1791.
L31/283–4: Signed receipts from John Yenn, architect at Polwarth Lodge, 1791–3.
L33/261–4: John Yenn, plans and elevation of Polwarth Lodge, *c.* 1791.

Birmingham Central Library, Birmingham

Matthew Boulton and Family Papers:

MS 3782/12/93/17: Elizabeth Montagu to Matthew Boulton, Sandleford, 20 August 1780.

Gloucester Archives, Gloucester

Beaufort (of Badminton) and Berkeley Family (of Stoke Gifford) Papers:

D2700/PB2/8: Memorandum of agreement for sale of Beaufort House to the Duke of Cumberland, with plan, inventory and valuation of goods and furniture proposed to be sold [Linnell], 1761.
D2700/QJ3/14: Thomas Conway's accounts and vouchers (as auditor, and London steward; general payments for 5th Duke), 1766–76.
D2700/QP3/1/6: Stoke rentals, including disbursements made, 1787–98.
D2700/QB3/3/23: House and Park Account Book, 1776.
D2700/QP3/4/8: Stoke cash accounts, 1787–93.
D2700/QP3/6/6: Building account vouchers, bundles 1–13, 1760–3.
D2700/QP3/9/38: Estate vouchers, 1779.
D2700/QP4/6/1: 4th Duchess's papers, 1768–89.
D2700/QP4/6/4: Letters to the Duchess from Silas and Jonas Blandford enclosing accounts, and on general estate affairs; some copy letters from her with observations on the accounts and estate business, 1771–87.

Plymouth and West Devon Record Office, Plymouth

Parker of Saltram, Earls of Morley Papers:

1259/1/1-82: Letters from Anne Robinson to her brother, Frederick Robinson, 1778–91.
1259/1/200-35: Letters from Lady Grantham and her sons to Frederick Robinson, 1789–90.
1259/2/1-767: Letters of Hon. Katherine Gertrude Robinson (*née* Harris), particularly from her husband's family including, Anne Robinson (sister-in-law), Theresa Parker (niece), John, 2nd Lord Boringdon (nephew), Lady Grantham (sister-in-law), Thomas, 3rd Lord Grantham (nephew), Frederick J. Robinson (nephew), 1786–1813.
1259/5/20-22: Estate papers, 1784–93.

Lincolnshire Archives, Lincoln

2 ANC 12/D/D/36, p. 1: Lady Heathcote's Thomas Chippendale bill, 1800.

Surrey History Centre, Woking

Papers Relating to Boyle Farm, Thames Ditton:

188/4–5, 11–13: Deeds relating Boyle Farm 1763–83.

Papers Relating to Peper Harow, Surrey:

G145/92/44: Plan of design for ground floor, signed 'W Chambers', n.d., 1750s.

G145/Box44: Ledger of 'Accounts Branched from the Cash Accounts of the Rt Hon Lady Viscountess Midleton 1765–71', recording household and business accounts during her son's minority.

G145/Box64/8: Account book recording accounts of all English and Irish estates, entitled 'The Right Hon Lady Viscountess Midleton, in Account with Her Son Lord Viscount Midleton', covering the whole period of the minority, 1765–76.

Dorset History Centre, Dorchester

D-RWR/L/6: Papers in Chancery cases concerning will of John Calcraft Esq and the right to dower of Bridget Calcraft, 1773–90.

Lancashire Archives, Preston

DDK/1217/13: Conveyance of Holwood House between Mr Nicholas Linwood and Mr John Calcraft, 28 February 1754.

Norfolk Record Office, Norwich

MC184/10/1: 'The Plan of the House Garden & Inclosures of Marblehill 10 Miles West from London Belonging to the Right Honourable the Countess of Suffolk', *c.* 1750.

MC184/10/3: Alexander Pope (att.), design for the pleasure grounds at Marble Hill, *c.* 1724.

West Yorkshire Archive Service, Leeds

Now digitised and freely available from the West Yorkshire Archive Service. https://library.hud.ac.uk/calmview/TreeBrowse.aspx?src=CalmView.Catalog&field=RefNo&key=Yorke

WYL150/7/6: Manuscript diaries of Lady Amabel Yorke of Studley Royal, daughter of Philip 2nd Earl of Hardwicke and wife of Alexander Hume-Campbell, Lord Polwarth, collected from Fountains Hall, 37 vols, 1769–1831.

Wiltshire and Swindon Archives

Wilton House and Estate Papers:

2057/F6/15: Annotated plan of Wimbledon House, n.d., *c.* 1730s.

University of Manchester, the John Rylands Library

Mary Hamilton Papers:
GB 133 HAM/1/5/4/1: Architectural plan of Lady Warwick's house in Mansfield Street, London, 1775.

Country House Archives

Holkham Hall Archives, Norfolk

DD/FD 56B (1): Office copy of the will and Codicil of Thomas Earl of Leicester, 1759.
E/A/44: 'An account made by Ralph Cauldwell of all money paid by him for carrying on the buildings at Holkham as directed by the will of the late Right Honble Thomas Earl of Leicester', 1760–6.
H/Inv1: Lady Leicester's inventory which contains an accumulative total of £3096 05s 08d that she spent on furnishing Holkham from 1752 to 1771.
H/Inv 7: Lady Leicester's inventory annotated as 'an exact account of the furniture in Holkham House bought by Lady Leicester to compleat the apartments, and what she bought from Russell Street, and also the furniture she has removed to different rooms', May 1759 to November 1765.
Uncatalogued box labelled 'Almshouses': Settlements dated 5 April 1755; 16 March 1765.

Weston Park, Staffordshire

Library, acc. no. 118.0539, Godfrey Richards, *The First Book of Architecture by Andrea Palladio* (1663).

Saltram House, Devon

NT 871169, presentation drawing of a proposed elevation for a house, *c.* 1740s, pen and coloured wash.

Published Primary Material

'Beware the Ides of January, or Advice to the FAIR, on Their Return to London', *Gentleman's Magazine*, viii (January 1738).
A Description of the Royal Gardens at Richmond in Surry, the Village, and Places Adjacent (London, 1736).
Memoirs of the Celebrated Miss Fanny M[urray], 2nd edn (London, 1758; 1759).
The New British Jewel; or, Complete Housewife's Best Companion (London, [1770?]).
The Repertory of Arts, Manufactures, and Agriculture, vol. 17 (London: John Nichols & Son, 1810).

Trials for Adultery: Or the History of Divorces Being Select Trials at Doctor's Commons, for Adultery, Fornication, Cruelty, Impotence, Etc., 7 vols (London: Printed for S. Bladon, 1779–81).

Adam, R., *Ruins of the Palace of the Emperor Diocletian at Spaaltro in Dalmatia* (London, 1764).

Adam, R. and Adam, J., *The Works in Architecture of Robert and James Adam, Esquires*, 2 vols (London: Printed for the authors, 1778–9).

Anson (eds), E. and F., *Mary Hamilton: Letters and Diaries 1756–1816* (London: John Murray, 1925).

von Archenholz, J. W., *A Picture of England: Containing a Descriptions of the Laws, Customs, and Manners of England*, translated from French (Dublin: P. Byrne, 1790).

Aspinall-Oglander, C., (ed.), *Admiral's Wife, Being the Life and Times of the Hon. Mrs Edward Boscawen from 1719 to 1761* (London: Longmans, Green & Co., 1940).

Aspinall-Oglander, C., (ed.), *Admiral's Widow, Being the Life and Times of the Hon. Mrs Edward Boscawen from 1761 to 1805* (London: The Hogarth Press, 1942).

Barnard, T., *An Historical Character Relating to the Holy and Exemplary Life of the Right Honourable the Lady Elizabeth Hastings* (London, 1742).

Bellamy, G. A., *An Apology for the Life of George Anne Bellamy, Late of Covent Garden Theatre, Written by Herself*, 6 vols, 3rd edn (London: Printed for the author, 1785).

Biller, S., *Holkham, the Scenes of My Childhood: And Other Poems* (London: Foxter and Hextall, 1839).

Bitton, J. and Brayley, E. W., *Beauties of England and Wales, or, Delineations, Topographical, Historical, and Descriptive, of Each County*, 18 vols (London, 1801–15).

Blondel, J., *De la Distribution des Maisons de Plaisance, et de la Décoration des Edifices en General*, 2 vols (Paris: Charles-Antoine Jombert, 1737–8).

Blunt, R., (ed.), *Mrs. Montagu 'Queen of the Blues', Her Letters and Friendships from 1762 to 1800*, 2 vols (London: Constable and Company Ltd., 1923).

Bradley, R., *The Country Housewife and Lady's Director, in the Management of a House, and the Delights and Profits of a Farm*, 6th edn (1732).

Brettingham, M., [sr.], *The Plans, Elevations and Sections of Holkham in Norfolk* (London: Haberkorn, 1761).

Brettingham, M., [jr.], *The Plans, Elevations and Sections of Holkham in Norfolk, The Seat of the Late Earl of Leicester, to Which Are Added, The Ceilings and Chimney Pieces; and Also, a Descriptive Account of the Statues, Pictures, and Drawings; Not in the Former Edition* (London, 1773).

Burney, F., *Diary and Letters of Madame d'Arblay: As Edited by Her Niece*, 7 vols, ed. C. Barrett (London: Henry Colburn, 1842–6).

Campbell, C., *Vitruvius Britannicus*, 3 vols (London, 1715, 1717, 1725).

Castell, R., *Villas of the Ancients* (London, 1728).

Chambers, J., *A General History of the County of Norfolk, Intended to Convey All the Information of a Norfolk Tour*, 2 vols (Norwich: John Stacy, 1829).

Chambers, W., *Designs of Chinese Buildings, Furniture, Dresses, Machines, and Utensils* (London, 1757).

Chambers, W., *Plans, Elevations, Sections and Perspective Views of the Gardens and Buildings at Kew in Surrey* (London, 1763).

Chatterton, Lady G., *Home Sketches and Foreign Recollections*, 3 vols (London: Saunders and Otley, 1841).

Chippendale, T., *The Gentleman and Cabinet Maker's Director* (London, 1754).

Climenson, E. J., (ed.), *Elizabeth Montagu: The Queen of the Bluestockings, Her Correspondence from 1720 to 1761*, 2 vols (London, 1906).

Cooke, G. A., *Topographical and Statistical Description of the County of Surrey* (London: C. Cooke, 1802).

Coxe, W., *Travels in Switzerland and in the Country of the Grisons: In a Series of Letters to William* Melmoth, *esq. from William Coxe*, 1st edn, 3 vols (London: Printed for T. Cadell, 1789).

Coxe, W., *Memoirs of the Duke of Marlborough*, 6 vols (London, 1820).

Croker, J. W., *Letters to and from Henrietta, Countess of Suffolk, and Her Second Husband, the Hon. George Berkeley: From 1712 to 1767*, 2 vols (London: John Murray, 1824).

Defoe, D., *A Tour thro' the Whole Island of Great Britain* (1724–26) ed. P. N. Furbank and W. R. Owens (New Haven and London: Yale University Press, 1991).

Dethloff, D., Murdoch, T., Sloan, K. and Elam, C., (eds), *Burning Bright: Essays in Honour of David Bindman* (London: University College London Press, 2015).

Dickins, L. and Stanton, M., *An Eighteenth-Century Correspondence* (London: John Murray, 1910).

Dobrée, E. and Webb, G., (eds), *The Complete Works of Sir John Vanbrugh*, 4 vols (London: Nonsuch Press, 1927–8).

Doran, J., *A Lady of the Last Century (Mrs. Elizabeth Montagu)* (London: R. Bentley and Son, 1873).

Fitzgerald, B., (ed.), *Correspondence of Emily, Duchess of Leinster, 1731–1814*, 3 vols (Dublin: Stationery Office, 1949–57).

Fox Strangways, G. S. H., (ed.), *The Life and Letters of Lady Sarah Lennox*, 2 vols (London: J. Murray 1901).

Fraser, W., *Memorials of the Montgomeries, Earls of Eglinton*, 2 vols (Edinburgh, 1859).

Gibbs, J., *Book of Architecture, Containing Designs of Buildings and Ornaments* (London, 1728).

Gillet, T., (ed.), *Correspondence between Frances, Countess of Hartford, (Afterwards Duchess of Somerset), and Henrietta Louisa, Countess of Pomfret, Between the Years 1738 and 1741*, 3 vols (London: Richard Phillips, 1805–6).

Grieg, J., (ed.), *Diaries of a Duchess, Extracts from the Diaries of the First Duchess of Northumberland*, 1716–76 (London: Hodder and Stoughton, 1926).

Grundy, I., *Lady Mary Wortley Montagu, Comet of the Enlightenment* (Oxford: Oxford University Press, 1999).

Halsband, R., (ed.), *The Complete Letters of Lady Mary Wortley Montagu*, 3 vols (Oxford: Oxford University Press, 1965–7).

Hannett, J., *The Forest of Arden, Its Towns, Villages, and Hamlets: A Topographical and Historical Account of the District between and around Henley-in-Arden and Hampton-in-Arden in the County of Warwick* (London: Simkin, Marshall and J. Russell Smith, 1863).

Hare, F., *Frauds and Abuses at St. Paul's. In a Letter to a Member of Parliament* (London: 1712).

Herbert, Lord, (ed.), *The Pembroke Papers Letters and Diaries of Henry, Tenth Earl of Pembroke and His Circle* (1734–80) vol. 1 (1780–94) vol. 2 (London: 1942, 1950).

Hervey, Lady, *Letters of Mary Lepel, Lady Hervey: With a Memoir and Illustrative Notes* (London: John Murray, 1821).

Hervey, J., *Memoirs of the Reign of George the Second*, ed. John Wilson Croker, 2 vols (Philadelphia: Lea and Blancard, 1848).

Home, J. A., (ed.), *The Letters and Journals of Lady Mary Coke*, 4 vols (Edinburgh: David Douglas, 1889).

Home, J. A., (ed.), *Letters of Lady Louisa Stuart to Miss Louisa Clinton*, 2 vols (Edinburgh: David Douglas, 1901).

Hughes, H. S., *The Gentle Hertford: Her Life and Letters* (New York: Macmillan, 1940).

Hunter, Rev. J., (ed.), *The Diary of Ralph Thoresby, F. R. S., Author of the Topography of Leeds (1677–1724)*, 2 vols (London: Henry Colburn and Richard Bentley, 1830).

Hutchins, John, *The History and Antiquities of the County of Dorset*, 4 vols (3rd edn, with additions by W. Shipp and J. W. Hodson, London, 1861–73).

Ilchester, Countess of, and Stavordale, Lord, (eds), *The Life and Letters of Lady Sarah Lennox, 1745–1826*, 2 edns, 2 vols (London: John Murray, 1901, 1902).

Jesse, J. H., *George Selwyn and His Contemporaries: with Memoirs and Notes*, 4 vols (London: Richard Bentley, 1843).

Kent, W., *The Designs of Inigo Jones: Consisting of Plans and Elevations for Publick and Private Buildings* (London, 1727).

von Kielmansegge, Count F., *Diary of a Journey to England the Years 1761–1762*, trans by. Countess Kielmansegge (London: Longmans & mone: chk casing 1902).

King, R. J., *A Handbook for Travellers in Surrey, Hampshire, and the Isle of Wight* (London: John Murray, 1858).

King, W., (ed.), *Memoirs of Sarah, Duchess of Marlborough* (New York: Dutton, 1930).

Kirby, J., *Dr. Brook Taylor's Method of Perspective Made Easy; Both in Theory and Practice: In Two Books. Being an Attempt to Make the Art of Perspective Easy and Familiar; to Adapt It Entirely to the Arts of Design; and to Make It an Entertaining Study to Any Gentleman Who Shall Chuse So Polite an Amusement …* (London, 1768).

Langlois, N., *L'Architecture a La Mode ou sont les Nouveaux Dessins pour la Décoration des Bâtimens et Jardins* (Paris, 1700–16).

Leoni, G., *The Architecture of A. Palladio in Four Books Containing a Short Treatise on the Five Orders* (London: printed by John Watts, 1715).

Lewis, W. S., (ed.), *Notes by Lady Louisa Stuart on George Selwyn and His Contemporaries by John Heneage Jesse* (New York; London: Oxford University Press, H. Milford, 1928).

Lewis, W. S., (ed.), *The Yale Edition of Horace Walpole's Correspondence*, 48 vols (New Haven: Yale University Press, 1937–83).

Llanover, Lady, (ed.), *Autobiography and Correspondence of Mary Granville, Mrs Delany*, 1st ser., 3 vols (London, 1861), 2nd ser., 3 vols (London, 1862).

Lock, M., *A New Drawing Book of Ornaments* (London, 1740).

Luxborough, Lady, *Letters Written by the Late Right Honourable Lady Luxborough, to William Shenstone, Esq* (Dublin: Printed for Caler Jenkins, 1776).
Macky, J., *A Journey through England*, 2 vols (London: John Hooke, 1724).
Mariette, J., *L'Architecture Française*, 5 vols (Paris, 1727–38).
Mossner, E. C. and Ross, I. S., (eds), *The Glasgow Edition of the Works and Correspondence of Adam Smith*, vol. 6 (Oxford: Oxford University Press, 1987).
Mure, W., (ed.), *Selections from the Family Papers Preserved at Caldwell*, 3 vols. (Glasgow: Maitland Club, 1853–4).
Murray, J., (ed.), *The Autobiographies of Edward Gibbon: Printed Verbatim from Hitherto Unpublished Mss.*, 2 edns (London: John Murray, 1896–7).
O'Carroll, G., (ed.), *Robert Day: The Diaries and the Addresses to Grand Juries, 1793–1829* (Tralee: Polymath, 2004).
O'Day, R., (ed.), *Cassandra Brydges, Duchess of Chandos, 1670–1735: Life and Letters* (Woodbridge: Boydell Press, 2007).
Percy, R. and Percy, S., *The Percy Anecdotes: Women* (London: T. Boys, 1822).
Potter, R., *Holkham A Poem to the Right Honourable the Earl of Leicester* (London: R. Manby, 1758).
Prothero, R. E., (ed.), *Private Letters of Edward Gibbon, (1753–1794)*, 2 vols (London: John Murray, 1896).
Pückler-Muskau, H. F. H., *Tour in England Ireland and France in the Years 1828 and 1829*, vol. 1 (London: Effingham Wilson, 1832).
Rathborne, Mrs A., (ed.), *Letters from Lady Jane Coke to Her Friend, Mrs. Eyre at Derby, 1747–1758* (London: Swan Sonnenschein & Co., 1899).
Rees, A., *The Cyclopaedia; or, Universal Dictionary of Arts, Sciences, and Literature* (London: Longman et al.,1803).
Percy, R. and Percy, S., *The Percy Anecdotes: Women* (London: T. Boys, 1822).
Roberts, W., (ed.), *Memoirs of the Life and Correspondence of Mrs. Hannah More*, 2 vols (New York: Harper and Brothers, 1834).
Robinson, J. R., *'Old Q'; A Memoir of William Douglas, Fourth Duke of Queensberry, K.T., One of 'the Fathers of the Turf,' with a Full Account of His Celebrated Matches and Wagers, etc*, 2nd edn (London: S. Low, Marston and company Ltd., 1895).
Richardson, G., *The New Vitruvius Britannicus*, 2 vols (London: J. Taylor, 1802–8, 1808–10).
Rogers, S., *Poems*, 11 edns (London, 1812–60).
Rogers, S., *Recollections*, 2 edns (London, 1859).
Rubenhold, H., (ed.), *Harris's List of Covent Garden Ladies* (London: Transworld Publishers, 2012).
Russell, Lord J., (ed.), *Memorials and Correspondence of Charles James Fox*, 4 vols (London: Richard Bentley, 1853–7).
Savile, G., Marquis of Halifax, *The Lady's New Year's Gift: Or, Advice to a Daughter* (London, 1688).
Scott-Moncrieff, R., (ed.), *The Household Book of Lady Grisel Baille 1692–1733*, 2 ser., 2 vols (Edinburgh: Scottish History Society, 1911).
Sheldon, A., *The Authentic and Interesting Memoirs of Miss Ann Sheldon*, 4 vols (London, 1788).
Snyder, H. L., (ed.), *The Marlborough-Godolphin Correspondence*, 2 vols (Oxford: Oxford University Press, 1975).

Steele, E., *The Memoirs of Mrs. Sophia Baddeley, Late of Drury Lane Theatre*, 6 vols (London: Literary Press, 1787).
Stephens, F. G. et al., *Catalogue of Prints and Drawings in the British Museum: Division I. Political and Personal Satires (No. 2061 to No. 4838)*, vol. 3, part. 1 (London, 1877).
Stirling, A. M. W., *Coke of Norfolk and His Friends*, 2 vols (London, 1908).
Stuart, J. and Revett, N., *The Antiquities of Athens* (London: John Haberkorn, 1762).
Thomson, A. T., *Memoirs of Sarah Duchess of Marlborough and the Court of Queen Anne*, 2 vols (London: Henry Colburn, 1839).
Thomson, G. S., (ed.), *Letters of a Grandmother. 1732–1735. Being the Correspondence of Sarah Duchess of Marlborough with Her Granddaughter Diana Duchess of Bedford* (London: Jonathan Cape, 1943).
Troide, E. and Cooke, S. J., (eds), *The Early Journals and Letters of Fanny Burney: 1782–1783*, vol. 5 (Kingston, ON: McGill-Queen's Press, 1988).
Walker, Capt. G., *Authentick Memoirs of the Life Intrigues and Adventures of the Celebrated Sally Salisbury: With True Characters of Her Most Considerable Gallants*, 4 vols (London, 1723–4).
Walpole, H., *Anecdotes of Paintings in England [1760–1795]*, eds. F. W. Hilles and P. B. Daghlian, 5 vols (New Haven: Yale University Press and London, H. Milford: Oxford University Press, 1937).
Walpole, H., *Anecdotes of Painting in England*, 4 vols, 4 edns (Strawberry Hill, 1763–3, 1765).
Walpole, H., *The History of Modern Taste in Gardening*, ed. John Dixon Hunt (New York: Ursus Press, 1995).
Ward, G. A., (ed.), *Journal and Letters of the Late Samuel Curwen, Judge of Admiralty, etc., an American Refugee in England from 1775–1784* (New York: C. S. Francis, 1842).
Wharncliffe, L., (ed.), *The Letters and Works of Lady Mary Wortley Montagu*, 2 vols (London: Richard Bentley, 1837).
Wheler, G. H., (ed.), *Hastings Wheler Family Letters: 1693–1704. Lady Betty Hastings and Her Brother*, Part 1. (London: privately printed at the Chiswick Press, 1929).
Wilkes, J., *Encyclopaedia Londinensis, or, Universal Dictionary of Arts, Sciences, and Literature*, 24 vols (London, 1810–29).
Wood, A. C., (ed.) *The Continuation of the History of the Willoughby Family, by Cassandra, Duchess of Chandos* (Eton, Windsor: Shakespeare Head Press for University of Nottingham, 1958).
Woolfe, J. and Gandon, J., *Vitruvius Britannicus*, 2 vols (London: J. Woolfe and J. Gandon, 1767, 1771).
Yorke, P. C., *The Life and Correspondence of Philip Yorke, Earl of Hardwicke, Lord High Chancellor of Great Britain*, 3 vols (Cambridge: Cambridge University Press, 1913).

Historic Manuscripts Commission (HMC) Reports:

HMC, Russell-Astley, *Report on the Manuscripts of Mrs. Frankland-Russell-Astley, of Chequers Court, Bucks* (London, 1900).

Parliamentary Papers:

Reports from the Committee upon Expired and Expiring Laws, 16 vols (London: Ordered to be printed by the House of Commons, 1808–37).

Periodicals:

The Covent Garden Magazine or the Amorous Repository, Calculated Solely for the Entertainment of the Polite World, and the Finishing of a Young Man's Education, 4 vols (London: G. Allen, 1772–5).

The Town and Country Magazine, or, Universal Repository of Knowledge, Instruction, and Entertainment, 24 vols (London: printed for A. Hamilton, 1769–96).

Secondary Material

Books:

Adshead, D. and Taylor, A. H. B., (eds), *Hardwick Hall: A Great Old Castle of Romance* (New Haven: Yale University Press, 2016).

Arnold, D., (ed.), *The Georgian Country House: Architecture, Landscape and Society* (Stroud: Sutton Publishing, 1998).

Baird, R., *Mistress of the House: Great Ladies and Grand Houses 1670–1830* (London: Weidenfeld & Nicolson, 2003).

Banham, J., (ed.), *Encyclopaedia of Interior Design* (London and Chicago: Fitzroy Dearborn Publishers, 1997).

Bending, S., *Green Retreats: Women, Gardens and Eighteenth-Century Culture* (Cambridge: Cambridge University Press, 2013).

Bermingham, A., *Learning to Draw: Studies in the Cultural History of a Polite and Useful Art* (New Haven: Published for the Paul Mellon Centre for Studies in British Art by Yale University Press, 2000).

Berry, H., *The Castrato and His Wife* (Oxford: Oxford University Press, 2011).

Blanning, T. C. W., *The Culture of Power and the Power of Culture: Old Regime Europe 1660–1789* (Oxford: Oxford University Press, 2002).

Bolton, A. T., *The Architecture of Robert and James Adam, 1758–1794*, 2 vols (London: Country Life and Southampton: George Newnes, 1922).

Borden, I., Penner, B. and Rendell, J., *Gender, Space Architecture: An Interdisciplinary Introduction* (London: Routledge, 1999).

Borman, T., *King's Mistress, Queens Servant: The Life and Times of Henrietta Howard* (London: Vintage, 2010).

Brooks, A. and Pevsner, N., *Worcestershire* [rev. and expanded edn], (New Haven, Conn.; London: Yale University Press, 2007).

Brown, J., *My Darling Heriott: Henrietta Luxborough, Poetic Gardener and Irrepressible Exile* (London: HarperPress, 2006).

Chalus, E., *Elite Women in English Political Life c.1754–1790* (Oxford: Clarendon Press, 2005).

Chapman, C., *Eighteenth-Century Women Artists: Their Trials, Tribulations and Triumphs* (London: Unicorn Publishing Group LLP, 2017).

Cherry, D. and Holland, J., (eds), *Local/Global: Women Artists in the Nineteenth Century* (Ashgate: Aldershot, 2006).
Christie, C., *The British Country House in the Eighteenth Century* (Manchester: Manchester University Press, 2000).
Clark, A., *Scandal: The Sexual Politics of the British Constitution* (Princeton: Princeton University Press, 2004).
Colvin, H., *A Biographical Dictionary of British Architects 1600–1840*, 3rd edn (New Haven, CT and London: Yale University Press, 1995).
Colvin, H., (ed.), *The History of the King's Works*, vol. 5 (London: HMSO, 1976).
Coutu, J., *Persuasion and Propaganda: Monuments and the Eighteenth-Century British Empire* (Montreal: McGill-Queen's University Press, 2006).
Cruickshank, D., *The Secret History of Georgian London: How the Wages of Sin Shaped the Capital* (London: Random House, 2010).
Darley, G., *John Soane: An Accidental Romantic* (New Haven and London: Yale University Press, 1999).
Darling, E. and Whitworth, L., (eds), *Women and the Making of Built Space in England, 1870–1950* (Ashgate: Aldershot, 2007).
Dethloff, D., Murdoch, T., Sloan, K., and Elam, C., (eds), *Burning Bright: Essays in Honour of David Bindman* (London: University College London Press, 2015).
Desmond, R., *Kew: The History of the Royal Botanic Gardens* (London: Harvill with the Royal Botanic Gardens, Kew, 1998).
Dickinson, H. T., (ed.), *British Ideas and Issues, 1660–1820: 2*, (New York: AMS Press, 1723; 1998).
Donington, K., Hanley, R. and Moody, J., (eds), *Britain's History and Memory of Transatlantic Slavery: Local Nuances of a 'National Sin'* (Liverpool: Liverpool University Press, 2016).
Dooley, T., O'Riordan, M., and Ridgway, C., (eds), *Women and the Country House in Ireland and Britain* (Dublin: Four Courts Press, 2018.
Dresser, D. and Hann, A., (eds), *Slavery and the British Country House* (English Heritage, 2013).
Eger, E., (ed.), *Bluestockings Displayed: Portraiture, Performance and Patronage, 1730–1830* (Cambridge: Cambridge University Press, 2013).
Eger, E., (ed.), *Bluestockings: Women of Reason from Enlightenment to Romanticism* (Basingstoke: Palgrave Macmillan, 2010).
Eger, E. and Peltz, L., (eds), *Brilliant Women: 18th-Century Bluestockings* (New Haven: Yale University Press, 2008)
Erickson, A. L., *Women and Property in Early Modern England* (London: Routledge, 1995).
Farrant, S., *Georgian Brighton 1750–1820* (Brighton: University of Sussex, 1980).
Field, O., *The Favourite: Sarah, Duchess of Marlborough* (London: Hodder and Stoughton, 2002).
Flower, S., McFarlane, J. and Plant, R., (eds), *Jane B. Drew Architect: A Tribute from Colleagues and Friends for Her 75th Birthday 24th March 1986* (Bristol: Bristol Centre for the Advancement of Architecture, 1986).
Fowler, J. and Cornforth, J., *English Decoration in the 18th Century* (London: Barrie and Jenkins, 1974).
Franklin, G., Dermott, N. and Brodie, A., *Ramsgate: The Town and Its Seaside Heritage* (Swindon: Historic England, 2020).
Gerhold, D., *Villas and Mansions of Roehampton and Putney Heath* (London: Wandsworth Historical Society, 1997).

Girouard, M., *Life in the English Country House: A Social and Architectural History* (London and New Haven: Yale University Press, 1978).
Goodman, E., (ed.), *Art and Culture in the Eighteenth Century: New Dimensions and Multiple Perspectives* (Newark: University of Delaware Press, 2001).
Gowrley, F., *Domestic Space in Britain, 1750–1840: Materiality, Sociability and Emotion* (London: Bloomsbury, 2022).
Green, D., *Blenheim Palace* (London: Country Life, 1951).
Greeves, L., *Houses of the National Trust* (London: National Trust Books, 2008).
Hallett, M., Myrone, M. and Llewellyn, N., (eds), *Court, Country, City: British Art and Architecture, 1660–1735* (New Haven and London: Yale Center for British Art: The Paul Mellon Centre for Studies in British Art, 2016).
Halsband, R., *Lord Hervey: Eighteenth-Century Courtier* (Oxford: Clarendon Press, 1973).
Hamlett, L., *Mural Painting in Britain 1630–1730: Experiencing Histories* (London: Abingdon, 2020).
Harris, J., *Sir William Chambers: Knight of the Polar Star* (London: A. Zwemmer Ltd., 1970).
Harris, J. *The Artist and the Country House: A History of Country House and Garden View Painting in Britain 1540–1870* (London: Sotheby Park Bernet, 1979).
Harris, J., *A Passion for Building: The Amateur Architect in England 1650–1850* (London: Sir John Soane's Museum, 2007).
Harris, J. and Snodin, M., (eds), *Sir William Chambers: Architect to George III* (New Haven and London: Yale University Press, 1996).
Hartmann, C. H., *Enchanting Bellamy* (London: Heinemann, 1956).
Hayward, H. and Kirkham, P., *William and John Linnell: Eighteenth-Century London Furniture-Makers*, 2 vols (London, 1980).
Hicks, C., *Improper Pursuits: The Scandalous Life of Lady Di Beauclerk* (Basingstoke and Oxford: Macmillan, 2001).
Hickman, K., *Courtesans* (London: HarperCollins, 2004).
Highfill, P., Burnim, K. and Langhans, E., *A Biographical Dictionary of Actors, Actresses, Musicians, Dancers, Managers & Other Stage Personnel in London, 1660–1800*, 16 vols (Carbondale and Edwardsville: Illinois University Press, 1973–94).
Hills, H., (ed.), *Architecture and the Politics of Gender in Early Modern Europe* (Ashgate: Aldershot, 2003).
Hind, C., (ed.), *The Rococo in England: A Symposium* (London: Victoria and Albert Museum, 1986).
Howley, H., *The Follies and Garden Buildings of Ireland* (New Haven and London: Yale University Press, 1993).
Hubbard, K., *Devices and Desires: Bess of Hardwick and the Building of Elizabethan England* (London: Chatto & Windus, 2018).
Huxtable, S., Fowler, C., Kefalas, C. and Slocombe, E., (eds), 'Interim Report on the Connections between Colonialism and Properties Now in the Care of the National Trust, Including Links with Historic Slavery' (Swindon: National Trust, 2020).
Jackson, I. and Holland, J., *The Architecture of Edwin Maxwell Fry and Jane Drew* (London: Routledge, 2016).
James, C. W., *Chief Justice Coke, His Family & Descendants at Holkham* (London: Country Life Ltd., 1929).

Johnson, J., *Excellent Cassandra. The Life and Times of the Duchess of Chandos* (Gloucester: Sutton, 1981).
Jones, J., (ed.), *Women in the Eighteenth Century: Constructions of Femininity* (London and New York: Routledge, 1990).
Kelly, G., (ed.), *Bluestocking Feminism: Writings of the Bluestocking Circle, 1738–1785*, 6 vols (London: Pickering & Chatto, 1999).
Knight, C., *London's Country Houses* (Andover: Phillimore, 2010).
Knott, S. and Taylor, B., (eds) *Women, Gender and Enlightenment* (London: Palgrave Macmillan, 2005).
Larsen, R., (ed.), *Maids and Mistresses: Celebrating 300 Years of Women and the Country House* (York: Yorkshire Country House Partnership, 2004).
Lawrence, C., (ed.), *Women and Art in Early Modern Europe: Patrons, Collectors, and Connoisseurs* (Pennsylvania: State University Press, 1997).
Levy, A., (ed.), *Widowhood and Visual Culture in Early Modern Europe* (London: Routledge, 2003).
Lewis, J. S., *Sacred to Female Patriotism: Gender, Class, and Politics in Late Georgian Britain* (New York and London: Routledge, 2003).
Leyland, M. and Parker, E., *Marble Hill* (London: English Heritage, 2022).
Linnane, F., *Madams: Bawds & Brothel-Keepers of London* (Stroud: The History Press, 2011).
Linstrum, D., *West Yorkshire: Architects and Architecture* (London: Lund Humphries, 1978).
Lipsedge, K., *Domestic Space in Eighteenth-Century British Novels* (Basingstoke: Palgrave Macmillan, 2012).
Lloyd, C., (ed.), *The Naval Miscellany*, 4 vols (London: Navy Records Society, 1952).
Lummis, T. and Marsh, J., *The Woman's Domain: Women and the English Country House* (London: Penguin Books Ltd., 1993).
Malcomson, A. P. W., *The Pursuit of an Heiress: Aristocratic Marriage in Ireland 1740–1840* (Belfast: Ulster Historic Foundation, 2006).
Mandler, P., *The Fall and Rise of the Stately Home* (New Haven: Yale University Press, 1997).
Marschner, J., *Queen Caroline: Cultural Politics at the Early Eighteenth-Century Court* (New Haven and London: Yale University Press, 2014).
Marschner, J., Bindham, D. and Ford, L., (eds), *Enlightened Princesses: Caroline, Augusta, Charlotte, and the Shaping of the Modern World* (New Haven: Yale University Press: London: Historic Royal Palaces, 2017)
Martin, B. and Sparke, P., (eds), *Women's Places: Architecture and Design 1860–1960* (Ashgate: Aldershot, 2005).
Martin, J., *Wives and Daughters: Women and Children in the English Country House* (Hambledon and London: Continuum, 2004).
Martin, M., *Dairy Queens: The Politics of Pastoral Architecture from Catherine de' Medici to Marie-Antoinette* (Cambridge, MA: Harvard University Press, 2011).
McDonagh, B., *Elite Women and the Agricultural Landscape, 1700–1830* (Abingdon: Routledge, 2018).
McKellar, S., and Sparke, P., (eds), *Interior Design and Identity* (Manchester: Manchester University Press, 2004).
McNeil, P., *Pretty Gentlemen: Macaroni Men and the Eighteenth-Century Fashion World* (New Haven: Yale University Press, 2018).

Miller, C. and Thomas, S., (ed.), *Drawing from the Past: William Weddell and the Transformation of Newby Hall* (Leeds: Leeds Museums and Galleries, 2004).

Miller, M. L., *Slaves to Fashion: Black Dandyism and the Styling of Black Diasporic Identity* (Durham: Duke University Press, 2009).

Mingay, G. E., *English Landed Society in the Eighteenth Century* (London, 1963).

Moore, L., *Amphibious Thing: The Life of Lord Hervey* (London: Penguin Group, 2000).

Morley, J., *The Making of the Royal Pavilion, Brighton: Design and Drawings* (London: Philip Wilson for Sotheby Publications, 1984).

Musson, J. and Cannadine, D., (eds), *The Country House: Past, Present, Future: Great Houses of the British Isles* (New York: Rizzoli, 2018).

Myers, S. H., *The Bluestocking Circle: Women, Friendship, and the Life of the Mind in Eighteenth-Century England* (Oxford: Clarendon Press, 1990).

O'Brien, K., *Women and Enlightenment in Eighteenth-Century Britain* (Cambridge: Cambridge University Press, 2009).

Oliver, J. W., *The Life of William Beckford* (London: Oxford University Press, 1932).

Peakman, J., *Peg Plunkett: Memoirs of a Whore* (London: Quercus Publishing Ltd., 2015).

Pearson, J., *Women's Reading in Britain, 1750–1835: A Dangerous Recreation* (Cambridge: Cambridge University Press, 1999).

Phillippy, P., (ed.), *A History of Early Modern Women's Writing* (Cambridge: Cambridge University Press, 2018).

Pointon, M., *Strategies for Showing: Women, Possession, and Representation in English Visual Culture, 1665–1800* (Oxford: Oxford University Press, 1997).

Porter, D., *The Chinese Taste in Eighteenth-Century England* (Cambridge: Cambridge University Press, 2010).

Postle, M., (ed.), *Art and the Country House* (Online Publication: Paul Mellon Centre, 2020).

Rendell, M., *In Bed with the Georgians: Sex, Scandal and Satire in the 18th Century* (Barnsley: Pen & Sword History, 2016).

Retford, K. and Avery-Quash, S., (eds), *The Georgian London Town House Building: Collecting and Display* (London and New York: Bloomsbury Visual Arts, 2019).

Rictor, N., *My Dear Boy: Gay Love Letters through the Centuries* (San Francisco: Leyland Publications, 1998).

Rowan, A., *Designs for Castles and Country Villas by Robert & James Adam* (Oxford: Rizzoli Publishing, 1985).

Roworth, W. W., (ed.), *Angelica Kauffman: A Continental Artist in Georgian England* (London: Reaktion Books, 1992).

Rykwert, J. and Rykwert, A., *Robert and James Adam: The Men and the Style* (Architectural Documents) (New York: Electa/Rizzoli, 1985).

Sloboda, S., *Chinoiserie: Commerce and Critical Ornament in Eighteenth-Century Britain* (Manchester: Manchester University Press, 2014).

Smylitopoulos, C., (ed.), *Agents of Space: Eighteenth-Century Art, Architecture, and Visual Culture* (Newcastle: Cambridge Scholars, 2016).

Snodin, M., (ed.), *Sir William Chambers* (London: V&A Publications, 1996).

Spies-Gans, P., *A Revolution on Canvas: The Rise of Women Artists in Britain and France, 1760–1830* (London: Paul Mellon Centre, 2022).

Stewart, R., *The Town House in Georgian London* (London: Yale University Press, 2009).

Stuart, D. M., *Molly Lepell, Lady Hervey* (London: George G. Harrap & Co. Ltd., 1936).

Styles, J. and Vickery, A., (eds), *Gender, Taste, and Material Culture in Britain and North America, 1700–1830* (New Haven: Yale Centre for British Art, 2006).

Sumeray, D. and Sheppard, J., *London Plaques* (Bloomsbury: Shire Publications, 2011).

Summers, J., *Empress of Pleasure* (London: Penguin Book Group, 2004).

Tague, I., *Women of Quality: Accepting and Contesting Ideals of Femininity in England, 1690–1760* (Woodbridge: The Boydell Press, 2002).

Thorpe, R., *Women, Architecture and the Building in the East of Ireland, c. 1790–1840* (Dublin: Four Courts Press, 2013).

Tillyard, S., *Aristocrats: Caroline, Emily, Louisa and Sarah Lennox, 1740–1832* (London: Chatto & Windus, 1994).

Vickery, A., *The Gentleman's Daughter: Women's Lives in Georgian England* (New Haven and London: Yale University Press, 1998).

Vickery, A., (ed.), *Women, Privilege, and Power: British Politics, 1750 to the Present* (Stanford: Stanford University Press, 2001).

Vickery, A., *Behind Closed Doors: At Home in Georgian England* (New Haven and London: Yale University Press, 2009).

Walker, L., *Drawing on Diversity Women: Architecture and Practice* (London, 1997), pp. 1–26.

Walton, J., *The English Seaside Resort: A Social History 1750–1914* (Leicester: Leicester University Press, 1983).

Weber, S., (ed.), *William Kent: Designing Georgian Britain* (New Haven and London: Yale University Press, 2013).

Whinney, M., *Home House: No. 20 Portman Square* (London: Country Life Publications, 1969).

White, B., *Queen of the Courtesans: Fanny Murray* (Stroud: The History Press, 2014).

Williams, G., *Weston Park: The House, the Families and the Influence* (Woodbridge: Boydell & Brewer, 2002).

Williams, K., *The Villas of Palladio* (New York: Princeton Architectural Press, 2003).

Willis, P., *Charles Bridgeman and the English Landscape Garden* (Newcastle upon Tyne: Elysium Press Publishers, 2002).

Wilson, R. and Mackley, A., *Creating Paradise: the Building of the English Country House* (London: Hambledon, 2000).

Winn, J. A., *Queen Anne: Patroness of Arts* (Oxford: Oxford University Press, 2014).

Zarmakoupi, M., *Designing for Luxury on the Bay of Naples: Villas and Landscapes (c. 100 BCE–79 CE)* (Oxford: Oxford University Press, 2014).

Articles and Essays:

Adshead, D., 'Wedgwood, Wimpole and Wrest: The Landscape Drawings of Lady Amabel Polwarth', *Apollo* (April 1996), pp. 31–7.

Aymonino, A. and Guerci, M., 'The Architectural Transformation of Northumberland House under the 7th Duke of Somerset and the 1st Duke and Duchess of Northumberland, 1748–86', *The Antiquaries Journal*, vol. 96 (2016), pp. 315–61.

Baird, R., '"The Queen of the Bluestockings": Elizabeth Montagu's House at 23 Hill Street Rediscovered', *Apollo*, vol. 157 (2003), pp. 43–9.

Beckett, J. V., 'Elizabeth Montagu: Bluestocking Turned Landlady', *Huntington Library Quarterly*, vol. 49, no. 2 (Spring 1986), pp. 149–64.

Betts, J. and Murdoch, T., 'A Royal Gift? Mrs Strangways Horner's Small Silver Clock, 1740', *Science Museum Group Journal*, no. 11 (2009), online.

Bonomi, P., 'Lord Cornbury Redressed: The Governor and the Problem Portrait', *The William and Mary Quarterly*, vol. 51, no. 1 (January 1994), pp. 106–18.

Boyington, A., 'The Countess of Leicester and Her Contribution to Holkham Hall', *The Georgian Group Journal*, vol. 22 (2014), pp. 53–66.

Bristol, K. 'The Painted Rooms of Athenian Stuart', *The Georgian Group Journal*, vol. 10 (2000), pp. 167–79.

Bristol, K., '22 Portman Square: Mrs Montagu and Her "Palais De La Vieillesse"', *British Art Journal*, vol. 2, no. 3 (2001), pp. 72–85.

Chalus, E., 'Elite Women, Social Politics, and the Political World of Late Eighteenth-Century England', *The Historical Journal*, vol. 43, no. 3 (September 2000), pp. 669–97.

Child, E., 'Elizabeth Montagu, Bluestocking Businesswoman', *Huntington Library Quarterly*, vol. 65, no. 1/2 (2002), pp. 153–73.

Collett-White, J., 'The Old House at Wrest – Part I', *The Bedfordshire Magazine*, vol. 22, no. 176 (1991), pp. 322–6.

Collett-White, J., 'The Old House at Wrest – Part II', *The Bedfordshire Magazine* 23, no. 177 (1991), pp. 4–12.

Collett-White, J., 'Inventories of Bedfordshire Country Houses, 1714–1830', *Bedfordshire Historical Record Society*, vol. 74 (1995), pp. 243–51.

Connolly, S. J., 'A Woman's Life in Mid Eighteenth-Century Ireland: The Case of Letitia Bushe', *The Historical* Journal, vol. 43, no. 2 (June 2000), pp. 433–51.

Cousins, M., 'Hagley Park, Worcestershire', *Garden History*, vol. 35 (2007), pp. iii–iv, vi–xii, and 1–152.

Culley, A., 'The Sentimental Satire of Sophia Baddeley', *Studies in English Literature, 1500–1900*, vol. 48, no. 3 (2008), pp. 677–92.

Evans, W., 'Paradise on a Limited Budget: How Norborne Berkeley Funded His Improvements at Stoke Park', *Trans. Bristol & Gloucestershire Archaeological Society*, vol. 12, no. 6 (2008), pp. 157–65.

Erickson, A. L., 'Common Law vs. Common Practice: The Use of Marriage Settlements in Early Modern England', *Economic History Review*, 2nd ser., vol. 43, no. 1 (1990), pp. 21–39.

Freeman, S., 'An Englishwoman's Home Is Her Castle: Lady Pomfret's House at 18 Arlington Street', *The Georgian Group Journal*, vol. 20 (2012), pp. 87–102.

Friedman, A. T., 'Architecture, Authority, and the Female Gaze: Planning and Representation in the Early Modern Country House', *Assemblage*, vol. 18 (1992), pp. 40–61.

Godber, J., 'Marchioness Grey of Wrest Park', *Bedfordshire Historical Society*, vol. 47 (1968), entire volume.

Goodison, J., 'A Puzzle Solved: Furniture at Newby Hall, Yorkshire', *The Burlington Magazine*, vol. 151, no. 1270 (2009), pp. 28–31.

Hagglund, E., 'Cassandra Willoughby's Visits to Country Houses', *The Georgian Group Journal*, vol. 11 (2001), pp. 185–202.

Halpern, L. C., 'The Duke of Kent's Garden at Wrest Park', *Journal of Garden History*, vol. 15, no. 3 (1995), pp. 149–78.
Halpern, L. C., 'Wrest Park 1686–1730s: Exploring Dutch Influence', *Garden History*, vol. 30, no. 2 (2002), pp. 131–52.
Hann, A., 'A Tale of Two Advisors: Jemima, Marchioness Grey and the Improvement of the Gardens at Wrest Park in the Mid-18th Century', *Journal of the Women's History Network*, vol. 2, no. 13 (2019), pp. 4–14.
Harris, E., 'Holywell House, St Albans: An Early Work by William Talman?', *Architectural History*, vol. 28 (1985), pp. 32–9.
Harris, E., 'Home House: Adam versus Wyatt', *The Burlington Magazine*, vol. 139, no. 1130 (1997), pp. 308–21.
Harris, F., 'Charles Bridgeman at Blenheim?', *Garden History*, vol. 13, no. 1 (1985), pp. 1–3.
Harris, F., 'Holywell House: A Gothic Villa at St Albans', *British Library Journal*, vol. 12, no. 2 (1986), pp. 176–83.
Harris, F., '"The Best Workmen of All Sorts" The Building of Wimbledon House, 1730–1742', *The Georgian Group Journal*, vol. 2 (1992), pp. 87–90.
Harris, J., 'William Kent's 44 Berkeley Square', *Apollo*, vol. 126, no. 306 (1987), pp. 100–4.
Hawkes, W., 'Walpole Right or Wrong? More on No. 18 Arlington Street', *The Georgian Group Journal*, vol. 21 (2013), pp. 204–11.
Haynes, C., 'Of Her Making: The Cultural Practice of Mary, 9th Duchess of Norfolk', *Tulsa Studies in Women's Literature*, vol. 31, no. 1/2 (2012), pp. 77–98.
Hewlings, R., 'The Architect of Weston Park, Staffordshire', *Georgian Group Journal*, vol. 20 (2012), pp. 22–32.
Jay, E., 'Queen Caroline's Library and Its European Contexts', *Book History*, vol. 9 (2006), pp. 31–55.
Jeffares, N., 'Two English Portraits by Liotard: Lady Anne Somerset and Catherine, Lady Hawke', *British Art Journal*, vol. 15, no. 3 (Spring 2015), pp. 3–10.
Jones, A., 'Letters from Mary Yorke, the Wife of the Bishop of Ely 1781–1808', *PCAS*, vol. 94 (2005), pp. 147–84.
Lambert, D. and Harding, S., 'Thomas Wright at Stoke Park', *Garden History*, vol. 17, no. 1 (1989), pp. 68–82.
Laurence, A., 'Women Using Building in Seventeenth-Century England: A Question of Sources?', *Transactions of the Royal Historical Society*, vol. 13 (2003), pp. 293–303.
Laurence, A., 'Lady Betty Hastings, Her Half-Sisters and the South Sea Bubble: Family Fortunes and Strategies', *Women's History Review*, vol. 15, no. 4 (2006), pp. 533–40.
Laurence, A., 'Women Investors, "That Nasty South Sea Affair" and the Rage to Speculate in Early Eighteenth-Century England', *Accounting, Business and Financial History*, vol. 16, no. 2 (2006), pp. 245–64.
Laurence, A., 'Lady Betty Hastings (1682–1739): Godly Patron', *Women's History Review*, vol. 19, no. 2 (2010), pp. 201–13.
Learmouth, J., 'The London Town House of Lady Isabella Finch', *The Georgian Group Journal*, vol. 25 (2017), pp. 73–94.
Lever, J., 'The Soane-Dance Collaboration, 1771–1799', *Architectural History*, vol. 53 (2010), pp. 163–90.

Lewis, J. S., 'When a House Is Not a Home: Elite English Women and the Eighteenth-Century Country House', *Journal of British Studies*, vol. 48, no. 2 (2009), pp. 336–63.

Lewis, L., 'Elizabeth, Countess of Home, and Her House in Portman Square', *The Burlington Magazine*, vol. 109, no. 773 (1967), pp. 443–53

Lindfield, P., 'The Countess of Pomfret's Gothic Revival Furniture', *The Georgian Group Journal*, vol. 22 (2014), pp. 77–94.

Malcomson, A., 'A Woman Scorned? Theodosia, Countess of Clanwilliam (1743–1817)', *Familia: Ulster Genealogical Review*, vol. 2, no. 15 (1999), pp. 1–25.

Martin, M., 'Interiors and Interiority in the Ornamental Dairy Tradition', *Eighteenth Century Fiction*, vol. 20, no. 3 (2008), pp. 357–84.

McCarthy, M., 'The Building of Hagley Hall, Worcestershire', *The Burlington Magazine*, vol. 118, no. 877 (1976), pp. 214–25.

Musgrave, C., 'A London Palazzo: 44 Berkeley Square', *Connoisseur* (1964), pp. 74–80.

O'Kane, F., '"Obliges me to dip my hands in mortar": Catherine O'Brien's Influence at Dromoland', *Irish Architectural and Decorative Studies*, vol. 7 (2007), pp. 80–105.

Pelling, M., 'Female Friendship and Domestic Craft at Bulstrode Park', *Journal for Eighteenth-Century Studies*, vol. 41, no. 1 (2018), pp. 101–20.

Phillips, G. L., 'Mrs. Montagu and the Climbing-Boys', *The Review of English Studies*, vol. 25, no. 99 (1949), pp. 237–44.

Pullins, D., 'Reassessing Elizabeth Montagu's Architectural Patronage at 23 Hill Street, London', *The Burlington Magazine*, vol. 150, no. 1263 (2008), pp. 400–4.

Pullins, D., 'Robert Adam's Neoclassical Chinoiserie', *West 86th: A Journal of Decorative Arts, Design History, and Material Culture*, vol. 24, no. 2 (Sep., 2017), pp. 177–200.

Reeve, M. M., 'Gothic Architecture, Sexuality, and License at Horace Walpole's Strawberry Hill', *Art Bulletin*, vol. 95, no. 3 (2013b), pp. 411–39.

Retford, K., 'Reynolds's Portrait of Mrs Theresa Parker: A Case Study in Context', *British Art Journal*, vol. 4, no. 3 (2003), pp. 80–6.

Rodwell, K., 'The Dower House, Stoke Park, Bristol: A Study in Structural Archaeology', *Post-Medieval Archaeology*, vol. 42, no. 1 (2008), pp. 1–48.

Rogal, S. J., 'John Vanbrugh and the Blenheim Palace Controversy', *Journal of the Society of Architectural Historians*, vol. 33, no. 4 (1974), pp. 293–303.

Schlarman, J., 'The Social Geography of Grosvenor Square: Mapping Gender and Politics, 1720–1760', *The London Journal*, vol. 28, no. 1 (2003), pp. 8–28.

Scott, B., 'Lady Elizabeth Hastings', *The Yorkshire Archaeological Journal*, vol. 55 (1983), pp. 109–12.

Sloan, K., 'Alexander Cozens and Amateurs Drawn to Etch', *Print Quarterly*, vol. 28, no. 4 (December 2011), pp. 405–9.

Smith, P., 'Lady Oxford's Alterations at Welbeck Abbey 1741–55', *The Georgian Group Journal*, vol. 11 (2001), pp. 133–68.

Standen, E. A., 'Country Children: Some Enfants De Boucher in Gobelins Tapestry', *Metropolitan Museum Journal*, vol. 29 (1994), pp. 111–33.

Stanford, C., 'Revisiting the Origins of Coade Stone', *The Georgian Group Journal*, vol. 14 (2016), pp. 95–116.

Stewart, R., 'Choice and Reasoning in the Eighteenth-Century London House', *Revue belge de Philologie et d'Histoire*, vol. 94, no. 2 (2016), pp. 363–78.

Sturtz, L. L., 'The "Dimduke" and the Duchess of Chandos: Gender and Power in Jamaican Plantation Management – a Case Study or, a Different Story of "A Man [and his wife] from a Place Called Hope"', *Revista/Review Interamericana*, vol. 29 (1999), pp. 1–15.
Thom, C., 'Robert Adam's First Marylebone House: The Story of General Robert Clerk, the Countess of Warwick and Their Mansion in Mansfield Street', *The Georgian Group Journal*, vol. 23 (2015), pp. 125–46.
Turnbull, L., 'Elizabeth Montagu: "A Critick, a Coal Owner, a Land Steward, a Sociable Creature"', *Huntington Library Quarterly*, vol. 81, no. 4 (2018), pp. 657–86.
Vickery, A., 'Hidden from History: The Royal Academy's Female Founders', *RA Magazine* (June 2016). https://www.royalacademy.org.uk/article/ra-magazine-summer-2016-hidden-from-history#related-articles
Walker, L., 'The Entry of Women into the Architectural Profession in Britain', *Woman's Art Journal*, vol. 7, no. 1 (1986), pp. 13–18.
Willis, P., 'From Desert to Eden: Charles Bridgeman's "Capital Stroke"', *The Burlington Magazine*, vol. 115, no. 840 (1973), pp. 150–7.
Willson, A. B., 'Alexander Pope's Grotto in Twickenham', *Garden History*, vol. 26, no. 1 (1998), pp. 31–59.
Worsley, L., 'Female Architectural Patronage in the Eighteenth Century and the Case of Henrietta Cavendish Holles Harley', *Architectural History*, vol. 48 (2005), pp. 139–62.
Young, H., 'Negotiating Female Property- and Slave-Ownership in the Aristocratic World', *The Historical Journal*, vol. 63, no. 3 (2020), pp. 581–602.

Country Life Magazine:

Draper, M. P. G., 'When Marlborough's Duchess Built', *Country Life*, 132 (July–December 1962), pp. 248–50.
du Prey, P., 'Eight Maids-a-Milking: Ornamental Dairies and Their Owners', *Country Life*, 181 (5 March 1987), pp. 120–2.
Girourad, M., '44, Berkeley Square, London', *Country Life*, 132 (27 December 1962), pp. 1648–51.
Houfe, S., 'A Taste for the Gothick: Diaries of the Countess of Pomfret I', *Country Life*, 161 (24 March 1977), pp. 728–30.
Houfe, S., 'Antiquarian Inclinations: Diaries of the Countess of Pomfret II', *Country Life*, 161 (31 March 1977), pp. 800–2.
Musson, J., 'Her Grace's Grotto Comes Out of Its Shell', *Country Life*, vol. 191, 39 (25 September 1997), pp. 86–7.

Oxford Dictionary of National Biography:

Chalus, E. H., 'Finch, Lady (Cecilia) Isabella (1700–1771)', *ODNB*. http://www.oxforddnb.com/view/article/68377, accessed 12 April 2017.
Hagglund, E., 'Willoughby, Cassandra [married name Cassandra Brydges, duchess of Chandos] (1670–1735)', *OBNB*. http://www.oxforddnb.com/view/article/72388, accessed 2 June 2017.

Henderson, T. F., revised by Stuart Handley, 'Home, William, Eighth Earl of Home, (d. 1761)', *ODNB*. https://doi.org/10.1093/ref:odnb/13649, accessed 12 May 2022.

Survey of London, via British History Online:

Sheppard, F. H. W., (ed.), 'The Pantheon', in *Survey of London: Volumes 31 and 32, St James Westminster, Part 2* (London, 1963), pp. 268–83. *BHO*. http://www.british-history.ac.uk/survey-london/vols31-2/pt2/pp268-283, accessed 20 March 2022.

Sheppard, F. H. W., (ed.), 'Soho Square Area: Portland Estate, Carlisle House, Soho Square', in *Survey of London: Volumes 33 and 34, St Anne Soho* (London, 1966), pp. 73–9. *BHO*. http://www.british-history.ac.uk/survey-london/vols33-4/pp73-79, accessed 17 March 2022.

Sheppard, F. H. W., (ed.), 'Soho Square Area: Portland Estate, Introduction', in *Survey of London: Volumes 33 and 34, St Anne Soho* (London, 1966), pp. 42–51, *BHO*. http://www.british-history.ac.uk/survey-london/vols33-4/pp42-51, accessed 1 May 2022.

Sheppard, F. H. W., (ed.), 'Grosvenor Square: Introduction' in *Survey of London: Volume 40, the Grosvenor Estate in Mayfair, Part 2 (The Buildings)* (London, 1980), pp. 112–17. *BHO*. http://www.british-history.ac.uk/survey-london/vol40/pt2/pp112-117, accessed 20 April 2021.

Sheppard, F. H. W., (ed.), 'Grosvenor Square: Individual Houses Built before 1926', in *Survey of London: Volume 40, the Grosvenor Estate in Mayfair, Part 2 (The Buildings)*, pp. 117–66. *BHO*. http://www.british-history.ac.uk/survey-london/vol40/pt2/pp117-166, accessed 23 April 2022.

Unpublished Dissertations and Theses:

Boyington, A., 'Maids, Wives and Widows: Female Architectural Patronage in Eighteenth-Century Britain' (PhD thesis, University of Cambridge, 2017).

Boyington, A., 'Margaret Coke, Countess of Leicester: A Re-Evaluation of Her Contributions to Holkham' (Master's dissertation, University of Cambridge, 2013).

Byrne, G., 'The Redecoration and Alteration of Castletown House by Lady Louisa Conolly 1759–76' (PhD thesis, Maynooth University, 1997).

Dudley, D. L., 'Henrietta Louisa Jeffreys, Oxford University and the Pomfret Benefaction of 1755: Vertu Made Visible' (PhD thesis, University of Victoria, 2004).

Learmouth, J., 'Elite Women and the West End Town House: Creating, Maintaining and Inhabiting a Residence in London, c.1710–c.1750' (PhD thesis, Birkbeck, University of London, 2021).

Legard, J., 'Vanbrugh, Blenheim Palace, and the Meanings of Baroque Architecture' (PhD thesis, University of York, 2013).

Lewis, S., 'The Artistic and Architectural Patronage of Angela Burdett Coutts' (PhD thesis, Royal Holloway, University of London, 2012).

Purcell, E., 'Women's Agency within the Montagu Property Network, c.1709–1827' (PhD thesis, University of Leicester, 2018).

Smith, R., 'Sarah, Duchess of Marlborough: An Analysis of Her Relationship with Architecture' (MA dissertation, Courtauld Institute of Art, University of London, 1998).

Szpila, K., 'Sarah Jenyns Churchill at Blenheim Palace – Setting the Record Straight: A Re-Evaluation of the Activity of the First Duchess of Marlborough as Patron of the Arts' (PhD thesis, Temple University USA, 1997).

Warleigh-Lack, C., 'John Carr of York and Hidden Architectural Histories' (PhD thesis, Middlesex University, 2013).

Webb, H. S., 'The Architectural Activity of Sarah Churchill, Duchess of Marlborough' (MA dissertation Courtauld Institute of Art, University of London, 2011).

Young, H., 'Gender and Absentee Slave-Ownership in Late Eighteenth and Early Nineteenth-Century Britain' (PhD thesis, University College London, forthcoming).

INDEX